Advancing Suicide Research

Kairi Kõlves, Merike Sisask, Peeter Värnik, Airi Värnik,
and Diego De Leo (Eds.)

Advancing Suicide Research

hogrefe

Library of Congress Cataloging in Publication information for the print version of this book is available via the Library of Congress Marc Database under the LC Control Number 2020945109

Library and Archives Canada Cataloguing in Publication
Title: Advancing suicide research / Kairi Kõlves, Merike Sisask, Peeter Värnik, Airi Värnik, and Diego De Leo (Eds.).
Names: Kõlves, Kairi, editor. | Sisask, Merike, editor. | Värnik, Peeter, editor. | Värnik, Airi, editor. | De Leo, Diego, 1951- editor.
Description: Includes bibliographical references and index.
Identifiers: Canadiana (print) 20200328220 | Canadiana (ebook) 20200328301 | ISBN 9780889375598 (hardcover) | ISBN 9781616765590 (PDF) | ISBN 9781613345597 (EPUB)
Subjects: LCSH: Suicide—Research. | LCSH: Suicide—Prevention.
Classification: LCC HV6545 .A38 2020 | DDC 362.28—dc23

www.hogrefe.com

PUBLISHING OFFICES

USA:	Hogrefe Publishing Corporation, 361 Newbury Street, 5th Floor, Boston, MA 02115 Phone (857) 880-2002; E-mail customerservice@hogrefe.com
EUROPE:	Hogrefe Publishing GmbH, Merkelstr. 3, 37085 Göttingen, Germany Phone +49 551 99950-0, Fax +49 551 99950-111; E-mail publishing@hogrefe.com

SALES & DISTRIBUTION

USA:	Hogrefe Publishing, Customer Services Department, 30 Amberwood Parkway, Ashland, OH 44805 Phone (800) 228-3749, Fax (419) 281-6883; E-mail customerservice@hogrefe.com
UK:	Hogrefe Publishing, c/o Marston Book Services Ltd., 160 Eastern Ave., Milton Park, Abingdon, OX14 4SB Phone +44 1235 465577, Fax +44 1235 465556; E-mail direct.orders@marston.co.uk
EUROPE:	Hogrefe Publishing, Merkelstr. 3, 37085 Göttingen, Germany Phone +49 551 99950-0, Fax +49 551 99950-111; E-mail publishing@hogrefe.com

OTHER OFFICES

CANADA:	Hogrefe Publishing, 82 Laird Drive, East York, Ontario, M4G 3V1
SWITZERLAND:	Hogrefe Publishing, Länggass-Strasse 76, 3012 Bern

Printed and bound in the Czech Republic

ISBN 978-0-88937-559-8 (print) • ISBN 978-0-61676-559-0 (PDF) • ISBN 978-0-61334-559-7 (EPUB)
https://doi.org/10.1027/00559-000

Dedication

Allison Milner (1983–2019)

This book is dedicated to the memory of Associate Professor Allison Milner. She was a passionate and gifted academic who was an inspiration to us all. She devoted her academic career to helping those most in need through her research in mental health and suicide prevention. Her untimely death in an accident is a tragic loss. We are grateful for her contribution to the book.

Allison Joy Milner (May 1, 1983 – Aug 12, 2019) was a social epidemiologist focusing on workplace mental health and suicide prevention. Her research career started at the Australian Institute for Suicide Research and Prevention at Griffith University working on the Queensland Suicide Register and the World Health Organization's project Suicide in At Risk Territories (the WHO/START study). She continued her doctoral studies on suicide and globalization and was awarded a PhD by Griffith University in 2010. Her postdoctoral studies brought her to the University of Melbourne in 2012, where she finished a master's degree in epidemiology. In 2015, she was appointed as the Deputy Director of the Work, Health and Wellbeing Unit at Deakin University. She became Associate Professor and Deputy Head of the Disability and Health Unit at the Centre for Health Equity, Melbourne School of Population and Global Health at the University of Melbourne in 2018.

Despite her tragically short life, Allison was a very productive academic, publishing over 170 peer-reviewed papers (Scopus), numerous book chapters and reports. Allison was the National Academic Director of Mates in Construction, Co-Chair of the IASP Special Interest Group on Suicide in the Workplace, and a member of different boards and committees. Allison was a recipient of a number of awards including, the National Emerging New Researcher Award from Suicide Prevention Australia in 2011; a Tall Poppy Science Award in 2014; the Vice Chancellor's Award for Excellence in Research (Deakin University) in 2015; the Griffith University Outstanding Higher Degree Research Health Alumnus award in 2017.

She was a devoted wife to Rohan and mother to Byron and Theo, and a dear friend and colleague to many of us, and she is greatly missed.

Acknowledgments

We are grateful to Dr. Victoria Ross and Dr. Damian Shaw-Williams for their help with language editing.

Kairi Kõlves' editing and writing contribution to this book was supported by the Academic Studies Program of Griffith University, Brisbane, Australia. Merike Sisask was supported by the Estonian Research Council (Grant PRG71 "Contemporary Demographic Developments in Estonia: In Search of Pathways Towards a More Sustainable Society").

Contents

Foreword

Suicide is a serious public health issue causing about 800,000 deaths globally, every year. Most suicides can be prevented with some evidence-based interventions, both at the single health care practitioner level and at the level of national policy.

High-quality data on suicide and suicidal behavior is lacking. According to the World Health Organization (WHO), only 80 countries have good-quality registered data on suicides that can be used to estimate suicide rates. More countries should invest in starting to register suicidal behavior and share their data.

Suicide is an enigmatic behavior. Most living creatures carry a genetic instinct for survival even in highly unfavorable circumstances. For most nonsuicidal people, it is hard to understand the extreme mental pain that causes a person to take their own life. The data we have today seem to indicate that suicidal behavior is a multifactorial trait, and death by suicide is an acute event that occurs in psychologically and biologically vulnerable people, usually suffering from chronic mental pain. In the fight with this global epidemic, we need a considerable international effort, good science, and an evidence-based approach by multidisciplinary teams. Only an evidence-based approach can lead to effective and safe interventions.

Advancing Suicide Research is the most comprehensive text in the field of suicide research methods. A group of leading researchers in suicidology, Kairi Kõlves, Merike Sisask, Peeter Värnik, Airi Värnik, and Diego De Leo, have joined together to present us with a reference book that describes every method used for suicide research. Focusing on quantitative, qualitative, and mixed methods approaches, the book covers everything a researcher in suicidology may need.

An important aspect of this book is the consolidation of definitions so that all of us are on the same page, as well as providing a complete list of ethical aspects for this sensitive area of research. The book covers most of the known measures of suicidal behavior, offering a reliable and valid tool that allows for data pooling from different locations and populations. It then goes on to cover observational studies, interventional studies, and linkage studies. Of great importance is its coverage of qualitative and mixed approaches. Sometimes the story of a single suicide victim can teach us a great deal and lead to new hypotheses. The book covers the whole spectrum of studies from case reports to meta-analyses. It ends with some strong chapters on prevention and postmortem studies and on technological advances.

This book will be of great interest for a wide range of readers, from students and junior PhD scientists, to experienced researchers who are familiar with and use only a single method and want to learn other methods. Also, policy makers, clinicians, and other practitioners interested in suicide research will find the text easy to read and understandable.

Prof. Gil Zalsman, MD, MHA, BSc
President of the International Academy for Suicide Research (IASR)
Director, Geha Mental Health Center and Adolescent Day Unit
Professor of Child Psychiatry, Tel Aviv University, Israel

Preface

Suicidal behavior has a significant global human toll. Despite differing levels of suicidality and circumstances among nations, in 2014 the World Health Organization led the global call for suicide prevention using a public health approach. Research is the underlying feature of the public health model in suicide prevention. It plays a vital role in improving our knowledge about suicidal behavior, and developing and evaluating suicide prevention interventions. To advance the quality of suicide research and prevention, this book focuses on conducting suicide research by presenting key concepts from the public health perspective. We are grateful that a wide range of experts working in suicide research have contributed their wisdom and knowledge it.

Before formulating research questions and considering the most suitable research designs and methods, it is important to contemplate the work in the field that has been completed to date. Chapter 1 does this, giving a brief summary of the historical contributions to modern suicide research. Considering different terminologies, Chapter 2 focuses on definitions and nomenclatures of suicidal behavior. Chapter 3 sets the scene for the use of a public health approach to suicide research to identify the patterns of suicidal behavior and explore risk and protective factors, as well as develop and evaluate interventions. Ethics is an important concern in conducting research, and ethical challenges in suicide research are addressed in detail in Chapter 4.

Epidemiology is the cornerstone of public health; the proper use of epidemiological measures and study designs is also central to the success of suicide research and prevention. Chapter 5 focuses on measures in suicide research, and that focus is continued in Chapters 6 and 7, which present the use of observational and intervention studies and discuss their strengths and weaknesses. Chapter 8 explores the potential use of data linkages as an alternative to conducting observation and intervention studies.

While epidemiology is positivistic by nature, utilizing quantitative methods, there is a growing need for qualitative methods in public health and health research more widely. This need has also grown in suicide research, as presented in Chapter 9. In addition, mixed methods designs incorporating both quantitative and qualitative methods have been welcomed in suicide research in the last decade and are discussed in Chapter 10.

Further, a number of other essential topics in suicide research are covered. Chapter 11 explores the use of a psychological autopsy as an important research tool since the 1950s. Chapter 12 addresses the need to test one's methodology in the form of a feasibility or pilot study before conducting a large-scale study. Chapter 13 considers the need for systematic literature reviews and meta-analyses, with methodological issues being addressed in detail. Chapter 14 presents different approaches to designing evaluations in suicide prevention; Chapter 15 adds considerations from an economic perspective. The final chapter addresses new technologies and their application to the future of suicide research.

We hope that students, practitioners, and policy makers may find some valuable elements here to improve their knowledge, but also that academics working in the field may benefit from insights into methodology or concepts they have not utilized before.

Kairi Kõlves, Merike Sisask, Peeter Värnik, Airi Värnik, and Diego De Leo

Chapter 1

The Roots of Suicide Research

From Historical Underpinnings to Frameworks for Modern Suicide Research

Morton M. Silverman

Summary

This chapter will briefly summarize the historical contributions to our understanding of suicide and suicidal behaviors, with a focus on the last 3 centuries. Political, legal, and theological contributions have shaped our approaches to the investigation of suicidal behaviors, as have the contributions of emerging scientific methods and theories. Key themes, findings, and lines of research over the centuries will be compared, emphasizing their influences on the foundations and development of modern suicide research. Various lines of research and scientific paradigms have contributed to many aspects of the understanding and prevention of suicidal behaviors, including epidemiology, risk detection, concepts of clinical course, and approaches to treatment, evaluation, and follow-up.

Suicide and self-destructive behaviors have been chronicled as far back as the Old Testament. However, scientific approaches to understanding suicide and its many vicissitudes are a much later development. The history of suicide and suicide-related behaviors, as well as the early investigations into their etiology, pathogenesis, and expression, are briefly summarized below. The scientific study of suicide began at the end of the 19th century, but has only increased exponentially in the last 60 years. Furthermore, there has been an explosion of meta-analyses of studies that focus on all forms of suicide-related thoughts and behaviors, including the components used for identification and assessment, the efficacy of interventions, and the methodologies to study different aspects of suicide-related behaviors.

No one risk factor or set of risk factors can explain why a particular individual will die by suicide (Franklin et al., 2017). No one theory can explain the full range of self-injurious or suicidal behaviors. No one individual approach will be sufficient in preventing death by suicide. Understanding its development, expression, and resolution cannot be reduced to a small set of variables. No single scientific discipline can address the complex challenge of understanding the risk for suicidal behaviors, as suicide is the end product of a complex interplay of neurobiological, psychological, and social processes (O'Connor & Portzky, 2018b). As a behavior, suicide-related phenomena have precursors, but just as suicide-related behaviors have different manifestations and expressions, so do the precursors (Robinson & Pirkis, 2014).

Foundations of Suicide Research

Suicide research owes its foundation and approaches to many related research disciplines and associated investigations, including psychology, psychiatry, medicine, sociology, theology, social work, public health, epidemiology, traditional statistics, and implementation science. The range of research areas includes, but is not limited to, risk assessment studies (assessment and classification of suicide risk); epidemiological studies (rates, risk factors, and protective factors); intervention studies (general intervention issues and methods, practice guidelines, efficacy of universal interventions, efficacy of selective interventions, and efficacy of indicated interventions); evaluation of policies, programs, and services; biological research (neurobiology and genetics); social science (social forces and economic determinants); media studies; nomenclature and classification studies; implementation science; etc.

This brief overview of the history of suicide owes a great deal to the published works of scholars who have extensively studied and critiqued available treatises and historical documents (Anderson, 1987; Berrios & Mohanna, 1990; Goldney & Schioldann, 2002; MacDonald & Murphy, 1990; Minois, 1995/1999; Murray, 1998; Tondo, 2014; van Hooff, 2000). The interested reader is encouraged to access these texts and chapters for a much more detailed and richer understanding of the history of investigations and writings about suicide, especially in Western cultures. In this brief overview of the historical underpinnings for modern suicide research, the main focus is on the publications and philosophical perspectives that specifically relate to death by suicide before 1900 (Minois, 1995/1999).

A Brief History of Suicide in Antiquity and Western Cultures up to 1800

References to suicide are found in the Old Testament of the Bible and appear in almost every cultures' oral and written histories. However, the purpose of this brief review is to highlight some key events that have served as the impetus for the later development of the field of suicidology, and, in particular, the development and evolution of suicide research. Hence, the selection of time periods and countries is rather eclectic.

From as far back as ancient Greece, suicide was not considered acceptable. From the 4th century BC, suicidal decedents were usually denied burial or traditional preburial preparation or cremation, and were considered to have committed a grievously antisocial act. Only those deaths by suicides in which it was possible to find a sufficient reason for self-destruction were deemed comprehensible (e.g., heroism, love-rejection, or serious or painful illness). The standard of *being understandable* was considered the key to assessing suicide to be a justified action (Tondo, 2014). Judgments concerning suicide changed when ancient Greek philosophers became interested in the primacy of reason over the emotions. They based their prohibition of suicide primarily based on its incomprehensibility or irrationality, and it was viewed as an aberration against the natural order to survive. Emotion-driven behaviors became a focus of attention and resulted in laws and customs imposing limits on the expression of such behaviors. To this day, the quest to remains understand and explain self-destructive behaviors from a rational and/or emotional perspective.

Of note is the fact that Plato (424–347 BC) was opposed to suicide, because he claimed that men are social individuals with a responsibility to others. Aristotle (384–322 BC) disapproved of suicide because he saw it as a transgression against a civic duty and as an act of cowardice. Here we see the beginnings of a sociological perspective to explain suicide.

The two prominent philosophical schools of ancient Rome, Epicureanism and Stoicism, approved of suicide, but for different reasons. The Epicureans believed that the goal of man was the pursuit of happiness, and when this could not be achieved, life lost its purpose. The Stoics placed reason, virtue, and morality above pleasure and common interests, sometimes to the point of reaching a state of detachment and a lack of interest in life (Tondo, 2014).

In medieval England, laws against suicide were promulgated in AD 967, including the distinction maintained over the centuries between those who died by suicide when of sound mind and those who were *insane*. Suicide was not considered a sinful or criminal act in cases of insanity.

In Italy, Thomas Aquinas (1225–1274) condemned suicide because it was an act against nature and against the benevolence we should have toward ourselves, and he therefore considered it to be a mortal sin. It was also seen as an insult against the community to which we belong and to which we have duties. Finally, it represents an act of defiance and rejection of the laws of God who gave us life and is the only one who may decide to take it back (Tondo, 2014).

During the Renaissance (14th–17th centuries), the growing interest in humanism resulted in frank admiration for suicide in which intellectuals found an implicit message of freedom. The Protestant Reformation stimulated growth of individual thinking and efforts to set aside the rules and rigidity of the Catholic Church, leading to a more liberal and questioning attitude toward suicide. Of note is that the Anglican clergyman John Donne (1572–1631), in his essay on the topic of violent death (published after his death, in 1647), wrote about the *paradox* that self-murder is not a sin against nature, and he justified the act of suicide. His perspective was that human nature was guided by rationality, and it could be considered appropriate to die by suicide and not contrary to reason. Furthermore, Donne argued that the Bible did not condemn suicide.

The French writer Michel Eyquem de Montaigne (1533–1592) wrote in his essays (1580) quite favorably about understanding the wish to die as a reasonable option. However, he did not encourage anyone to die by suicide. The English political philosopher Thomas Hobbes (1588–1679) saw suicide as a destructive act against natural law, which therefore should not be allowed. However, starting around 1600, attitudes in European legal systems toward suicide generally became less punitive.

The French philosopher Rene Descartes (1596–1650) argued against suicide from a pragmatic stance. For example, life is not always happy but often does offer consolations, and that good things may be even more frequent than the bad ones. He rejected the idea of sin and punishment with regard to the act of suicide. He also expressed doubts about the mental health of people who died by suicide (Minois, 1995/1999; Tondo, 2014). Another important French philosopher Voltaire (nom de plume for Francoise-Marie Arouet) (1694–1778) defended suicide in cases of extreme necessity.

The Scottish Enlightenment philosopher David Hume (1711–1776), in his *Essays on Suicide and the Immortality of the Soul* (1755) expressed a tolerant view of suicide, stating that suicide could not be seen as an offense against God, and that the commandant "Thou shalt not kill" only applied to homicidal acts.

The philosopher Immanuel Kant (1724–1804), in his *Metaphysics of Ethics* (1786), reasoned that suicide is contrary to the love we owe to ourselves, and that suicide could not be considered an act of free choice.

The German philosopher Arthur Schopenhauer (1788–1860) wrote in his book *On Suicide, in The World as Will and Representation* (1818) that suicide did not offer a plausible escape from difficulties intrinsic to an essentially irrational world. Those who died by suicide indeed wanted to live, but not on the terms that were offered; they needed to give up life because they were unable to give up the will to live better (Tondo, 2014).

Foundational Publications of Suicide Research Since the 1600s

The following is a summary of some of the foundational publications of suicide research. However, it is difficult, at best, to ascertain with any degree of certainty how influential any of these texts were on the manner in which suicide and suicidal behaviors were viewed by the general populations at the time, or the extent to which they influenced the thinking and actions of contemporaneous scientists, philosophers, and theologians.

The Englishman Robert Burton (1577–1640), in his *Anatomy of Melancholy* (1621), suggested that melancholy, a mental illness, was associated with suicide. He placed suicide in a nonreligious, more contemporary perspective and described conditions contributing to suicide, including agitation, hopelessness, and impulsivity. Of note, these very conditions are still being investigated today as they relate to suicide.

Goldney and Schioldann (2002) report that 18th- and 19th-century research specifically devoted to suicide is in fact "voluminous" (p. 13), with the identification of works published as early as 1744, 1767, and 1786. They note that much of the pre-Durkheim suicide research does not predominantly focus on a medical model, but gives due regard to identifying sociological factors, thus elevating sociological factors to an important role in effecting suicide.

A number of English clergymen published important works on suicide, including John Sym (1637), John Donne (1647), and John Adams (1700). By 1700, the term *suicide* had replaced *self-murder* and the subject began to interest the emerging scientific disciplines. By the 1700s, the majority of suicides were judged to be based on mental illness (Minois, 1995/1999). The English clergyman Charles Moore's (1771–1826) two volumes titled *A Full Inquiry into the Subject of Suicide* (Moore, 1790) included observations about the association between gambling and suicide, genetic and hereditary factors, the role of stigma in distorting the counting of true cases, and the association between alcohol and suicide.

In 1788, the English physician William Rowley (1742–1806) wrote a medical treatise that incorporated religious, sociological, epidemiological, and psychological perspectives. He argued that suicide was an act against religion and so a crime against civility, because it deprived others of expected physical and mental services, and was immoral for being contrary to the individual's duties to maintain relational ties. Although he seems to espouse a rather sociological perspective, he also introduced ideas concerning remote causes of suicide, which might include mental illness or bodily pain. In addition, he described proximate causes, including not being sufficiently brave or balanced as to endure misfortunes, or not being of sound mind. He concluded that when an individual contemplates suicide, his mental status must necessarily be compromised (Tondo, 2014).

Early medical views of suicide were attributed primarily to early 19th-century French authors, particularly Jean-Etienne Dominique Esquirol (1821; a student of Phillippe Pinel), although he incorporated both illness and social factors in his postulated causes of suicide (Berrios & Mohanna, 1990). In 1828, George Man Burrows, in his *Commentaries on the Causes, Forms, Symptoms, and Treatment, Moral and Medical, of Insanity* (Burrows, 1828), referred to suicide as a feature of melancholia, and provided comparative data among a number of European cities.

In 1835, the Belgian mathematician and statistician-sociologist Adolphe Quetelet (1796–1874) published his book, translated as *About Man and the Development of His faculties, or an Essay on Social Statistics* (Quetelet, 1835/1968). This text ushered in the statistical study of suicide.

In 1840, the Englishman Forbes Winslow published *The Anatomy of Suicide*, which was based on statistical data. Pierre-Egiste Lisle (1856), another Frenchman, provided evidence that factors other than mental illness caused suicide, including debt, gambling, and marital discord.

In 1858, John Charles Bucknill and Daniel Hack Tuke published their famous textbook of English psychiatry, *A Manual of Psychological Medicine containing the History, Nosology, Description, Statistics, Diagnosis, Pathology, and Treatment of Insanity* (Bucknill & Tuke, 1858). References to suicide included a classification of psychiatric illnesses; a discussion of modes of death; and the influence on suicide of age, sex, marriage, and the seasons; as well as the possibility of hereditary transmission.

In Australia, George Stephen (1874) published a review of suicide in the state of Victoria. Although legalistic and moralistic, he also incorporated sociological and mental illness factors in his comments. The Italian psychiatrist Enrico Morselli (1852–1929) published his seminal work translated as *Suicide. Essay of Moral Comparative Statistics* (Morselli, 1879) (translated into English in 1881), considered by many at the time as the most important work of 19th-century suicidology. Although heavily reliant on statistics, it covered such topics as social influences, biological influences, psychological influences, and methods and places of suicide. In addition, it included analyses of age and suicide in different countries, education and suicide rates, and the relationship between mental illness and suicide.

In 1885, William Wynn Westcott, in England, published his book *A Social Science Treatise. Suicide: Its History, Literature, Jurisprudence, Causation and Prevention* (Westcott, 1885). As the title suggests, it covers a wide range of topics, including rates and means of suicide, its causes, the effect of urban and rural life, the influence of mental illnesses, and the effects of physical illness and hereditary factors. He noted that most suicide studies were dependent on statistics, to the neglect of research into mental states and emotions. Nevertheless, he regarded suicide as a social problem.

Two separate reviews published in 1892 by Daniel Hack Tuke and George H. Savage, represent a rather sophisticated analysis of factors contributing to suicide at the time, prior to the publication of Emile Durkheim's famous *Le Suicide* in 1897 (Goldney & Schioldann, 2002). These two reviews appeared in Tuke's *Dictionary of Psychological Medicine*, published in 1892 (Tuke, 1892). Tuke and Savage were psychiatrists, and their perspective was medical (psychiatric). Tuke's treatise focuses on the history, epidemiology, and etiology of suicide. Savage's treatise is psychiatric in perspective.

Emile Durkheim (1858–1917) is often considered to be the founder of scientific suicide research, following the English translation in 1951 of his sociological treatise, *Le Suicide: Etude de Sociologie,* originally published in 1897 (Durkheim, 1897/1951). Durkheim's focus was on sociology, not psychology. He believed that the individual's relationship to society was the core dynamic in understanding deaths by suicides. As stated by Berman (2002), "He did not deny that psychological conditions played a role as determinants of individual suicides, but, as they were not readily generalizable, he did not believe they affected suicide rates" (p. 9).

Scientific suicide research in the second half of the 20th century, and well into the 21st, is notable for its references to Durkheim's methodology and the almost obligatory comparisons of any new findings to his original typology. Furthermore, since the publication of *Le Suicide*, there have been many articles and books written about Durkheim and his theories – both positive and negative. Durkheim lived in 19th- and early 20th-century France, where the meaning or importance of risk factors he studied (e.g., divorce and religious affiliation) differed from that of secularized, modern, Western societies as we experience them today. Nevertheless, his sociological and epidemiological approach to understanding suicide provided the foundation for further research in the 20th & 21st centuries.

As discussed by Bille-Brahe (2000), Durkheim concluded that

> while the individual suicide seems to be the result of individual factors and circumstances, the *frequency of suicide* is nevertheless determined by the moral and psychological climate in the society in question. This means that the *variations* in the frequency of suicide can only be explained by the fact that certain societal conditions enhance or discourage the propensity to react to problems and pain, not by trying to remove the problems and the pain, but by removing oneself.... In the opinion of Durkheim, man is first and foremost *a social being*, who has survived through history by living and collaborating with his fellow human beings. (Bille-Brahe, 2000, p. 195)

The feelings of belongingness and social integration are contrasted with the need for autonomy and the attainment of individual wishes and goals (i.e., integration vs. disintegration). As is evident from a 21st-century perspective, such themes have remained grist for the mill in suicide research.

Although there do not appear to be any books devoted solely to suicide published in the US in the 19th century, Motto (1993) published a comprehensive review of 19th-century reports of suicide that appeared in the *American Journal of Insanity*, beginning in 1845. Amariah Brigham, the editor of the journal, commented in his first editorial, on the probable underreporting of suicides, as well as making reference to possible biological factors contributing to suicide. In 1849, Brigham commented in the journal, on familial and genetic factors in suicide. In 1877, John E. Tyler reported that members of the New England Psychological Society emphasized the importance of melancholia as contributing to suicide.

As summarized by van Hooff (2000), “Suicide became the mortal sin of self-murder in [early] Christian doctrine. This paradigm was challenged by Renaissance thinking and refined by Christian reformers, to be fundamentally rejected by the Enlightenment” (p. 122). During the 19th century, the prevailing attitude in Western culture shifted from the old ideas of suicide being a sin or a crime (and therefore punishable by law), to seeing suicide as an understandable behavior associated with an illness or with an extreme life condition. As van Hooff (2000) states,

> No longer was a suicide regarded by the public as a sinner but as a sufferer.... No longer was suicide regarded as a heroic act of free will or as a mortal sin, but as a disease. The interest in soul and society was the result of the anxious awareness that modern man lived in an unnatural habitat. No longer had he his place in a close network formed by family, village, and church, but he got lost in huge cities. (van Hooff, 2000, p. 120)

It is important to remember that at approximately the same time, both the fields of psychology and sociology were developing as valid scientific specialties.

In the 20th century, these two *understandings* (i.e., illness vs. extreme life condition) evolved into distinct research approaches, one focusing on *social determinants of suicide* (e.g., environmental factors) and the other on *psychological-medical determinants* (e.g., mental illnesses). In the 21st century, new technologies, methodologies, statistical tools, theories, and approaches to understanding the etiology and pathogenesis of what makes people suicidal, have all led to a virtual explosion of suicide research and their applications for the treatment and prevention of those at-risk for suicide and suicide-related behaviors.

Brief Overview of Modern Suicide Research Since the 1950s

It is a challenging task to present a comprehensive overview of modern suicide research in a single chapter. In the attempt to place some limits on this survey of relevant suicide research as it informs our current efforts, it has been decided to look exclusively at the major English-language research studies beginning in the 1950s up to the present. Needless to say, any topical list would be somewhat arbitrary and idiosyncratic to one reading of the suicide research in the last 70 years. Inasmuch as suicide and suicide-related behaviors are multidetermined and multifactorial, the research study of these behaviors has taken many shapes and forms. Suicide research, by its very nature, is interdisciplinary and multifaceted. In attempting to provide a broad-brush landscape of suicide research by topics or themes, it is inevitable that there is some redundancy and overlap.

The worldwide increased attention to suicide and suicide-related behaviors since the 1950s has resulted in an impressive expansion in suicide-related research, which has occurred on all fronts, including psychiatry, psychology, social sciences, biology, and genetics, to name but a few major research endeavors. There has been a greater focus on risk in specific subgroups, defined according to demographic and diagnostic categories. With the recognition that risk factors for suicide and suicide-related behaviors are often multidimensional, multidetermined, and multifactorial, research studies have expanded their scope in order to describe more precisely the characteristics of individuals at increased risk. There has been more attention to the development and evaluation of the effectiveness of psychological and pharmacological treatments for individuals who self-injure and to the complex and difficult challenges inherent in developing, implementing, and evaluating the effectiveness of preventive strategies at the national and local levels. The majority of the more recent suicide research has still been mainly conducted in Western countries, including European, North American, and Scandinavian countries, as well as Australia and New Zealand. Other regions of the world (e.g., Asian countries such as India, China, and Japan) have also added a great deal to the knowledge base of suicidology. Most of these studies have been quantitative (e.g., identifying risk factors, epidemiology, surveillance, and demographics), rather than qualitative (e.g., in-depth analysis of personal stories) or even clinical (e.g., intervention studies).

Even though there has been a virtual revolution in the quantity and quality of suicide research since the 1950s, the major question remains of why has there has not been a significant and sustained reduction in suicide rates worldwide. Part of the answer is that both suicide research and suicide prevention are difficult to conduct and evaluate. The incidence of suicide is low compared that of other illnesses, making it difficult to enroll sufficient numbers of at-risk subjects in research studies. Furthermore, from a clinical perspective, there is no accurate method to determine if any individual is going to die by suicide in the next day(s), week(s), month(s), or year(s). The potential risk for death by suicide has been shown to be correlated with a number of risk factors, which include signs and symptoms, distorted cognitive states, and other high-risk behaviors. Yet there are distinct risk factor characteristics that differentiate between nonsuicidal self-injury, suicide ideations, suicide intent, suicide planning, suicide attempts, and death by suicide, making it difficult to develop algorithms for predicting suicide and/or suicide-related behaviors across populations. This is especially true when individuals present with clinically different expressions of suicidal thoughts and behaviors.

Although not always clearly stated, one of the overarching goals of all suicide research, if not the main goal, is to prevent suicide. To do so, the traditional approach has been to first understand and be able to identify the components of the suicidal process (either the chain of events that lead to suicidal behaviors, or the individual thoughts and behaviors that are often associated with suicidal behaviors), who is most likely to engage in these behaviors, and under what conditions (e.g., when, where, why). Once identified, these events and behaviors (i.e., precursors or causative agents) are targeted to be ameliorated, decreased, alleviated, amended, transformed, or eliminated in the at-risk population(s). This requires the development and implementation of interventions that are targeted to the identified factors in the targeted populations, based on an understanding of the etiologies and factors that lead to the expression of these events and behaviors. Once implemented, the interventions need to be evaluated for, at least, their validity, efficacy, reliability, fidelity, generalizability, and strength over time. If we are able to get to the point of declaring an intervention to be successful in the short-run (and, hopefully, in the long-run as well), we then have the challenge of disseminating the interventions in an efficient and effective manner, recognizing that translating and implementing interventions are affected by cultural, religious, and geopolitical differences.

Whether based on conventional research methodologies (e.g., randomized controlled trials) or on innovative methodologies, all approaches to the treatment of suicidal individuals and to the prevention of suicidal behaviors should be based on a thorough knowledge of causes and risk factors. A major contribution to our knowledge base comes from epidemiological studies in which the distribution of the occurrence of suicidal behaviors across the general population and the factors that influence this distribution are investigated. However, substantial methodological controversies and disparities have emerged when comparing epidemiological studies from different countries and regions of the world. There are differences in procedures of ascertainment of suicide and suicidal behaviors between and among countries – in no small part due to different national religious and cultural values placed on self-injurious behaviors, differences in terminologies and definitions, and differences in methods of collecting the data. Stigma regarding the reporting and documentation of suicidal behaviors and deaths remains a major challenge worldwide. Methods of investigating these injuries and deaths differ widely, as does the range of official ascertainment procedures and protocols.

Suicide research in the last 60–70 years has focused on its causes, precipitants, and potential methods of prevention and treatment, although much of the focus has been on risk factors (Franklin et al., 2017; Ribeiro et al., 2016). Different research traditions have approached this quest from their own unique perspectives. For example, biological studies have explored the neurobiological, biochemical, cognitive, behavioral, genetic, and epigenetic correlates of suicide in an effort to identify suicide-specific biomarkers. Such markers could help clinicians predict suicide risk, move the field toward evidence-based diagnosis, and provide concrete biological treatment targets (Sudol & Oquendo, 2016). A major goal of biological studies is to map the neural circuitry and the biological mechanisms involved in the etiology and expression of suicide and suicide-related behaviors.

Relatively little is known about which interventions may be effective in reducing risk for suicide and suicide-related behaviors (Robinson et al., 2008), in particular among youths (Burns et al., 2005; Robinson et al., 2011). Previous research suggests that although youths receive a reasonable amount of research attention, the majority of studies have focused on epidemiological as opposed to intervention research. For example, although young people are a highly researched group in terms of published articles, most studies have been epidemiological in nature, reporting on rates of, and risk factors for, suicide, as opposed to reporting on the effectiveness of individual interventions (Robinson et al., 2008). This lack of emphasis on applied clinical research means that relatively little is known about what does and does not work in reducing suicide risk, which hampers both policy initiatives and preventive efforts more generally (Robinson & Pirkis, 2014).

Suicide research has slowly been moving from the identification and characterization of risk (risk factor research) at the micro and macro levels, to prediction of risk (screening, risk assessment), to tailored interventions (population and individual based), to prevention at the micro and macro levels (public education and media). In fact, the suicide research field really started at the macro level with the work of Durkheim (1897/1951) who attempted to answer the questions of who is at risk, when, and why. In the US, a statistical approach to identifying those at risk for suicide was undertaken by Louis I. Dublin & Bessie Bunzel in 1933 (Dublin & Bunzel, 1933). The micro level has advanced to include measuring variables at the interpersonal, intrapersonal, and intrapsychic domains. Clinical research has tended to focus on high-risk inpatient and outpatient clinical populations. One overriding goal of all of these research approaches is to answer the question, what is the pathogenesis of suicide? If causal relationships can be established, then there is the hope that tailored interventions can be developed, implemented, and evaluated that directly address these causal pathways.

However, the underpinnings of this approach are based on the medical model of identifying a pathogen for a specific illness, developing a way to measure its presence in humans, and then developing treatments to eradicate or diminish the virulence of the pathogen. The search has been for a single anatomical, physiological, biological and/or genetic, environmental, cultural, psychological, psychiatric, etc., *pathogen* that leads to the development and expression of suicide-related behaviors. If not a single pathogen, what combination or interchange of pathogens will lead to suicidal behaviors? What is the time course for such development? What triggers the expression of suicidal behaviors? Of course, adopting the medical model to the study of suicide suggests that we understand suicide as a disease, illness, or disorder that manifests itself in self-destructive behaviors. At this point in time, we best understand suicide-related behaviors as a comorbid condition, symptom, or expression of some other disorder, disease, or dysfunction (e.g., mental disorder, substance disorder) – not as a stand-alone illness. What complicates this scenario is that we have yet to clearly delineate the pathogenesis of many mental disorders that are often associated with suicidal behaviors, and our treatment of these associated disorders is often directed to addressing symptoms, not underlying pathogens.

In a critical analysis of the recent suicide research literature, Hjelmeland and Knizek (2016b) conclude that current mainstream suicide research almost unilaterally focuses on *explanations* of suicidal behaviors, very often using the linear cause-and-effect framework in the search for underlying causes of suicidal behaviors. The main framework for such studies relies on the biomedical model. "The field is dominated by repetitive risk factor studies, reductionist biological studies, and, to a lesser extent, intervention studies (e.g., randomized control studies, RCTs), with inherent limitations" (Hjelmeland & Knizek, 2016b, p. 696). They observe that studies focusing on explanations of suicidal behaviors most often use "hypothetico-deductive or experimental methodologies," usually employing quantitative approaches. From their perspective, the consequence is reductionism.

> The problem with risk factor studies is that they do not tell us *how* the common risk factors are related to suicidal behavior, if indeed they are, or *why* it is that the vast majority of people suffering from one or some of them do *not* kill themselves. (Hjelmeland & Knizek, 2016b, p. 697)

They argue that to move the field forward, there needs to be an increase in studies focusing on *understanding* suicidal behaviors in different cultural contexts, necessitating a shift from quantitative to qualitative research studies. Such studies focus on how individuals interpret themselves, their actions, and their surroundings (Hjelmeland & Knizek, 2010).

There may be cultural differences in how important different factors are for people's lives and hence for suicide and also individual differences both across and within cultural groups in terms of how a risk factor *is perceived* or *experienced*. It is not the risk factors per se, but the *significance* or *meaning* the individual assigns to them in their particular context that is decisive (Hjelmeland & Knizek, 2016a, p. 697).

There has been a growth in theories of suicidal ideation and behavior since the mid-1980s (O'Connor et al., 2016), beginning with Shneidman's cubic model of suicide (Shneidman, 1985). Three recent research-based theories (i.e., the interpersonal psychological theory, the integrated motivational-volitional model, and the three-step theory) fit within the *ideation-to-action framework* (Joiner, 2005; Klonsky & May, 2015; O'Connor, 2011; O'Connor et al., 2016; O'Connor & Kirtley, 2018; O'Connor & Portzky, 2018a; Van Orden et al., 2010). This framework describes those theories which posit that the factors associated with suicidal ideation are distinct from those that govern behavioral reactions – that is, a suicide attempt and/or death by suicide (Klonsky et al., 2016; Klonsky et al., 2017; O'Connor & Nock, 2014). These new research-based theoretical developments have not only been important to enhance understanding of the complexities of the suicidal processes, but they are also forming the basis for the development of psychological and psychosocial interventions to reduce risk of suicide and self-harm.

Trends in Suicide Research Publications

It is instructive to look at the only three bibliometric studies of journals that exclusively publish suicide research. There are at least four key international journals that are devoted exclusively to the topic of suicide: *Crisis: The Journal of Crisis Intervention and Suicide Prevention*, *Suicide and Life-Threatening Behavior* (SLTB), *Archives of Suicide Research* (ASR), and *Suicidology Online*. Cardinal (2008) examined articles published in SLTB over a 30-year time frame, in three 5-year periods, namely, 1971–1975, 1984–1988, and 1997–2001, and proposed explanations for the trends and characteristics identified. Of particular note was that the percentage of the journal devoted to publication of research studies did not change over this time period (approximately 60 % of the journal's pages), although the number of pages per issue increased. However, the proportion of research articles covering adolescents more than doubled, from 27.9 % in 1971–1975 to 60.8 % in 1997–2001 – but represented only 18.3 % of all research articles published between 1997–2001. The distribution in terms of the ages of participants does not mirror the distribution of suicide rates in the US or in many parts of the world. Cardinal (2008) suggests that the inordinate number of articles focusing on the adolescents perhaps had to do with a concern for potential years of life lost. Also, it could have been a methodological issue, given that it was easier to access adolescents as a research group. Yet another reason may be purely emotional. Adolescents may be seen as the next generation, the heirs apparent, and their suicides may be perceived as being more tragic or more important than suicides in other age groups.

In contrast was the finding that the percentage of research articles in SLTB focusing on the *old* and *very old* dropped markedly between the periods of 1971–1974 and 1997–2001. With the demographic changes occurring over time in industrialized countries, especially the aging of the population, it is imperative that more future studies are focused on the *old* and *very old* age groups.

The gender distribution among SLTB articles is another interesting enigma. Men accounted for approximately 80 % of all deaths by suicide during this time period, but the proportion of research articles did not represent this fact. Research studies focusing solely on males dropped from 10.8 % in 1971–1975 to 7.7 % in 1997–2001, whereas research studies focusing solely on females remained fairly constant, at 5.4 % and 4.6 %, respectively.

In addition, this study found that the number of authors per article in SLTB increased dramatically over the years. This might be explained by the fact that suicide research had become increasingly complex, that a higher degree of specialization by researchers necessitated the establishment of multidisciplinary teams to pursue this research, and that cooperation among researchers was facilitated by new technologies.

Goldblatt et al. (2012) examined the abstracts of every paper published in *Crisis,* ASR, and SLTB, for the 5 years between 2006 and 2010, and they categorized each paper by subject. They found that the journals were similar with respect to subject allocation. Most papers dealt with epidemiological issues (32.7–40.1 % of abstracts), prevention (5.8–15.3 %), and research (8.3–10.6 %). Clinical papers made up from 2.8 % to 8.2 % of the studies published. They concluded that English-language suicide journals publish a preponderance of epidemiological studies, and that clinical studies are relatively underrepresented.

Hjelmeland (2016) scrutinized the type of studies and findings of all publications in the same printed journals in the period 2011–2012, and found that approximately 60 % of the studies in ASR and SLTB, and almost 30 % in *Crisis,* focused on risk factors for suicidal behaviors. The proportion of qualitative studies (or studies containing a qualitative component) was 5.6 % compared with barely 3 % in the period 2005–2008 (Hjelmeland & Knizek, 2011).

Recent Developments in Suicide Research

What has fueled the rapid increase in suicide research is the advancement, refinement, and sophistication of statistical methods; surveillance techniques and approaches; biological and genetic research; and research methodologies for the study of low-base rate behaviors at the individual and population level. As each research area makes dramatic strides, there have been pendulum swings in the foci and thrust of suicide research. Such pendulum swings are reflected in the ever-expanding long lists of risk factors and protective factors associated with suicide and suicide-related behaviors. Franklin et al. (2017) called for a paradigm shift in how we study suicide and suicide-related behaviors. One of the key messages for future research from Glenn and colleagues' recent meta-analysis is that we need to move beyond the *usual suspects* of suicide risk factors (e.g., mental disorders and sociodemographic factors) to understand the processes that combine to lead to this deadly outcome (Glenn et al., 2018).

The use of new technologies (including social media and naturalistic real-time monitoring via smartphones) to increase understanding of suicidal behavior and to better identify suicide risk is an exciting development. With the proliferation of smartphone ownership globally, in low- and middle-income countries (James, 2014) as well as in high-income countries, there has been much interest in using it as a tool for real-time monitoring and intervention (de Beurs et al., 2015; Chapter 16 in the present work). Given the field's continued inability to predict suicidal behavior with sufficient sensitivity and specificity (de Beurs et al., 2015; Franklin et al., 2017; O'Connor & Nock, 2014), the use of smartphone technologies affords the opportunity to assess risk factors repeatedly, in real time and in naturalistic settings (de Beurs et al., 2015; Michaels et al., 2015).

It is hoped that the use of such technologies will better capture the waxing and waning nature of suicidal ideation (Joiner & Rudd, 2000; Zisook et al., 2009) and account for the complex interaction between the risk factors which predict the transition to suicide attempts (de Beurs et al., 2015; O'Connor & Kirtley, 2018). If the promise of new technologies is realized, individuals or clinicians may be able to better identify windows of acute risk in real time (based, in part, on social media and moment-to-moment monitoring), alert others, and hopefully complete interventions to alleviate that risk. Needless to say, there are many practical and ethical barriers that have yet to be overcome, but they are not insurmountable.

The use of *ecological momentary assessment* (via mobile phones) has already been shown to be feasible (Husky et al., 2014; Palmier-Claus et al., 2011), and it offers considerable promise in enhancing our prediction of the suicidal ideation–suicide attempts gap (Myin-Germeys et al., 2009). Also in Asia, text mining and machine learning approaches have been applied to Chinese social media to identify language markers of suicide risk and emotional distress (Cheng et al., 2017). Social media are also being used frequently by young people as a means of communicating distress (Marchant et al., 2017). Although these developments are exciting, best practice guidelines need to be developed to ensure these technologies are implemented safely and ethically (Michaels et al., 2015).

The use of innovative study designs and new techniques are important developments. The statistical and computing power of big data and machine learning is now being applied to suicide risk assessment. Such approaches have the advantage of being able to combine large numbers of risk factors in the prediction of suicide risk, and they have already been shown to be moderately successful (Franklin et al., 2017; Hettige et al., 2017; Kessler et al., 2017). Another technique is the retrospective *timeline follow-back* (TLFB) methodology (Sobell & Sobell, 1992) which systematically assesses behaviors and events in the days and weeks preceding an index event. Its application within a case-crossover design to understand suicide risk in the days and hours preceding a suicide attempt is novel. Implicit cognitions toward death assess one's automatic associations with life or death, and may serve to predict suicidal behavior (Nock et al., 2010). Finally, *network analysis* is a new statistical technique that has been applied to psychopathology in general and suicidal behavior specifically in recent years (de Beurs, 2017; de Beurs et al., 2017; Fried et al., 2017). Network analysis allows the investigation of complex associations between risk factors or symptoms. It also determines which symptoms are central within a network, thereby highlighting specific treatment targets with the potential to be most powerful in reducing risk of suicidal behavior.

As noted above, a recent meta-analytic review of longitudinal studies assessing suicidal thoughts and behaviors (Franklin et al., 2017) concluded that traditional statistical approaches may not be ideal in accurately predicting the occurrence of suicidal behaviors. Rather, several studies have applied machine learning techniques to electronic health records within large medical databases. For instance, Walsh, Ribeiro, and Franklin (2017) found that machine learning algorithms, applied to a large sample of adult patients with a claim code for self-injury, were relatively accurate (i.e., area under the curve = 0.84) predictors of future suicide attempts.

Another new development has been the recognition of the importance of postvention and involvement of those with *lived experience* (including suicide attempt survivors and suicide bereavement survivors) as key to suicide research and prevention activities (O'Connor & Portzky, 2018b). Lezine (2016) recently described the vital work of suicide prevention through personal experience. Involving those with lived experience in conducting suicide research allows the person with lived experience (peer specialist) to provide crucial insights into how to have conversations around suicide and how best to ask the questions about thoughts of suicide directly (Huisman & van Bergen, 2019).

Conclusions

Although the recent epidemiological data suggest that we have made very little headway in significantly reducing the overall worldwide suicide rate in the last 50 years, the research findings have been accumulating. The building blocks have been put in place: The critical factors have been identified and methodologies to study the problems have been evolving (Silverman et al., 2014).

We are on the brink of new breakthroughs in many areas and lines of research. As suicide prevention research has advanced to address risk detection, clinical course, treatment development, comparative effectiveness, implementation, evaluation, and follow-up parameters, the contexts for research have also become more diverse. There is continual reinforcement and innovative engagement across many lines of inquiry. Progress will require interdisciplinary, collaborative science; likewise, coordinated, collaborative approaches to supporting research, involving both public and private partners, can effectively advance the prevention of suicide through cross-cutting and interactive research (Silverman et al., 2014).

References

Anderson, O. (1987). *Suicide in Victorian and Edwardian England*. Oxford, UK: Oxford University Press.

Berman, A.L. (2002). Forward. In R. Goldney & J.A. Schioldann (Eds.), *Pre-Durkheim suicidology: The 1892 reviews of Tuke and Savage*. Burnside, Australia: Adelaide Academic Press.

Berrios, G.E., & Mohanna, M. (1990). Durkheim and French psychiatric views on suicide during the 19th century: A conceptual history. *British Journal of Psychiatry, 156*(1), 1–9. https://doi.org/10.1192/bjp.156.1.1

Bille-Brahe, U. (2000). Sociology and suicidal behaviour. In K. Hawton & K. van Heeringen (Eds.), *The international handbook of suicide and attempted suicide* (pp. 193–207). Chichester, UK: Wiley.

Bucknill, J.C., & Tuke, D.H. (1858). *A manual of psychological medicine*. London, UK: John Churchill.

Burns, J., Dudley, M., Hazell, P., & Patton, G. (2005). Clinical management of deliberate self-harm in young people: the need for evidence-based approaches to reduce repetition. *Australian and New Zealand Journal of Psychiatry, 39*(3), 121–128. https://doi.org/10.1080/j.1440-1614.2005.01532.x

Burrows, G.M. (1828). *Commentaries on the causes, forms, symptoms, and treatment, moral and medical, of insanity*. London, UK: Thomas and George Underwood.

Burton, R. (1989–94). *The anatomy of melancholy*. Oxford, UK: Clarendon Press.

Cardinal, C. (2008). Three decades of Suicide and Life-Threatening Behavior: A bibliometric study. *Suicide and Life-Threatening Behavior, 38*(3), 260–273. https://doi.org/10.1521/suli.2008.38.3.260

Cheng, Q., Li, T.M., Kwok, C.-L., Zhu, T., & Yip, P.S. (2017). Assessing suicide risk and emotional distress in Chinese social media: A text mining and machine learning study. *Journal of Medical Internet Research, 19*(7), e243. https://doi.org/10.2196/jmir.7276

de Beurs, D. (2017). Network analysis: A novel approach to understand suicidal behaviour. *International Journal of Environmental Research and Public Health, 14*(3), 219. https://doi.org/10.3390/ijerph14030219

de Beurs, D., Kirtley, O., Kerkhof, A., Portzky, G., & O'Connor, R.C. (2015). The role of mobile phone technology in understanding and preventing suicidal behavior. *Crisis, 36*, 79–82. https://doi.org/10.1027/0227-5910/a000316

de Beurs, D., van Borkulo, C.D., & O'Connor, R.C. (2017). Association between suicidal symptoms and repeat suicidal behaviour within a sample of hospital-treated suicide attempters. *BJPsych Open, 3*(3), 120–126. https://doi.org/10.1192/bjpo.bp.116.004275

Dublin, L., & Bunzel, B. (1933). *To be or not to be: A study of suicide*. New York, NY: Harrison Smith and Robert Haas. https://doi.org/10.1037/11221-000

Durkheim, E. (1951). *Suicide: A study in sociology*. Glencoe, IL: Routledge & K. Paul. (Original work published in 1897)

Esquirol, J. (1821). Suicide. In *Dictionaire des sciences médicales: par une société de médecins et de chirurgiens*. Paris, France: Panckouche.

Franklin, J.C., Ribeiro, J.D., Fox, K.R., Bentley, K.H., Kleiman, E.M., Huang, X., ... Nock, M.K. (2017). Risk factors for suicidal thoughts and behaviors: a meta-analysis of 50 years of research. *Psychological Bulletin, 143*(2), 187. https://doi.org/10.1037/bul0000084

Fried, E.I., van Borkulo, C.D., Cramer, A.O., Boschloo, L., Schoevers, R.A., & Borsboom, D. (2017). Mental disorders as networks of problems: a review of recent insights. *Social Psychiatry and Psychiatric Epidemiology, 52*(1), 1–10. https://doi.org/10.1007/s00127-016-1319-z

Glenn, C.R., Kleiman, E.M., Cha, C.B., Deming, C.A., Franklin, J.C., & Nock, M.K. (2018). Understanding suicide risk within the Research Domain Criteria (RDoC) framework: A meta-analytic review. *Depression and Anxiety, 35*(1), 65–88. https://doi.org/10.1002/da.22686

Goldblatt, M.J., Schechter, M., Maltsberger, J.T., & Ronningstam, E. (2012). Comparison of journals of suicidology. *Crisis, 33*(5), 301–305. https://doi.org/10.1027/0227-5910/a000146

Goldney, R., & Schioldann, J.A. (2002). *Pre-Durkheim suicidology: The 1892 reviews of Tuke and Savage*. Burnside, Australia: Adelaide Academic Press.

Hettige, N.C., Nguyen, T.B., Yuan, C., Rajakulendran, T., Baddour, J., Bhagwat, N., ... De Luca, V. (2017). Classification of suicide attempters in schizophrenia using sociocultural and clinical features: A machine learning approach. *General Hospital Psychiatry, 47*, 20–28. https://doi.org/10.1016/j.genhosppsych.2017.03.001

Hjelmeland, H. (2016). A critical look at current suicide research. In J. White, I. Marsh, M. Kral, & J. Morris (Eds.), *Critical suicidology: Transforming suicide research and prevention for the 21st century* (pp. 31–55). Vancouver, Canada: UBC Press.

Hjelmeland, H., & Knizek, B.L. (2010). Why we need qualitative research in suicidology. *Suicide and Life-Threatening Behavior, 40*(1), 74–80. https://doi.org/10.1521/suli.2010.40.1.74

Hjelmeland, H., & Knizek, B.L. (2011). What kind of research do we need in suicidology today? In R.C. O'Connor, S. Platt, & J. Gordon (Eds.), *International handbook of suicide prevention: Research, policy and practice* (pp. 591–608). Chichester, UK: Wiley-Blackwell. https://doi.org/10.1002/9781119998556.ch34

Hjelmeland, H., & Knizek, B.L. (2016a). Qualitative evidence in suicide: Findings from qualitative psychological autopsy studies. In K. Olson, R. Young, & I.Z. Schultz (Eds.), *Handbook of qualitative health research for evidence-based practice* (pp. 355–371). New York, NY: Springer. https://doi.org/10.1007/978-1-4939-2920-7_21

Hjelmeland, H., & Knizek, B.L. (2016b). Time to change direction in suicide research. In R.C. O'Connor & J. Pirkis (Eds.), *The international handbook of suicide prevention* (2nd ed., Vol. 2, pp. 696–709). Chichester, UK: Wiley. https://doi.org/10.1002/9781118903223.ch39

Huisman, A., & van Bergen, D.D. (2019). Peer specialists in suicide prevention: Possibilities and pitfalls. *Psychological Services, 16*(3), 372–380. https://doi.org/10.1037/ser0000255

Husky, M., Olié, E., Guillaume, S., Genty, C., Swendsen, J., & Courtet, P. (2014). Feasibility and validity of ecological momentary assessment in the investigation of suicide risk. *Psychiatry Research, 220*(1), 564–570. https://doi.org/10.1016/j.psychres.2014.08.019

James, J. (2014). Relative and absolute components of leapfrogging in mobile phones by developing countries. *Telematics and Informatics, 31*(1), 52–61. https://doi.org/10.1016/j.tele.2013.03.001

Joiner, T. (2005). *Why people die by suicide*. Cambridge, MA: Harvard University Press.

Joiner, T., & Rudd, M. D. (2000). Intensity and duration of suicidal crises vary as a function of previous suicide attempts and negative life events. *Journal of Consulting and Clinical Psychology, 68*(5), 909–916. https://doi.org/10.1037/0022-006X.68.5.909

Kessler, R. C., Hwang, I., Hoffmire, C. A., McCarthy, J. F., Petukhova, M. V., Rosellini, A. J., ... Katz, I. R. (2017). Developing a practical suicide risk prediction model for targeting high-risk patients in the Veterans Health Administration. *International Journal of Methods in Psychiatric Research, 26*(3), e1575. https://doi.org/10.1002/mpr.1575

Klonsky, E. D., & May, A. M. (2015). The three-step theory (3ST): A new theory of suicide rooted in the "ideation-to-action" framework. *International Journal of Cognitive Therapy, 8*(2), 114–129. https://doi.org/10.1521/ijct.2015.8.2.114

Klonsky, E. D., May, A. M., & Saffer, B. Y. (2016). Suicide, suicide attempts, and suicidal ideation. In D. Cannon & T. Widiger (Eds.), *Annual review of clinical psychology* (Vol. 12, pp. 307–330). Palo Alto, CA: Annual Reviews.

Klonsky, E. D., Qiu, T., & Saffer, B. Y. (2017). Recent advances in differentiating suicide attempters from suicide ideators. *Current opinion in psychiatry, 30*(1), 15–20. https://doi.org/10.1097/YCO.0000000000000294

Lezine, D. A. (2016). Suicide prevention through personal experience. In R. C. O'Connor & J. Pirkis (Eds.), *International handbook of suicide prevention* (2nd ed., pp. 681–695). Chichester, UK: Wiley Blackwell.

Lisle, É. (1856). *Du suicide: Statistique, médecine, histoire et législation*. Paris, France: J. B. Baillière.

MacDonald, M. M., & Murphy, T. R. (1990). *Sleepless souls: Suicide in early modern England*. Oxford, UK: Oxford University Press.

Marchant, A., Hawton, K., Stewart, A., Montgomery, P., Singaravelu, V., Lloyd, K., ... John, A. (2017). A systematic review of the relationship between internet use, self-harm and suicidal behaviour in young people: The good, the bad and the unknown. *PLoS One, 12*(8), e0181722. https://doi.org/10.1371/journal.pone.0181722

Michaels, M. S., Chu, C., Silva, C., Schulman, B. E., & Joiner, T. (2015). Considerations regarding online methods for suicide-related research and suicide risk assessment. *Suicide and Life-Threatening Behavior, 45*(1), 10–17. https://doi.org/10.1111/sltb.12105

Minois, G. (1995/1999). *Histoire du suicide: la société occidentale face à la mort volontaire*. Paris, France: Libraire Artheme Fayard.

Moore, C. (1790). *A full inquiry into the subject of suicide: To which are added (as being closely connected with the subject) two treatises on duelling and gaming*. London, UK: J. F. & C. Rivington.

Morselli, E. (1879). *Il suicidio: Saggio di statistica morale comparata* (Vol. 21). Milano, Italy: Fratelli Dumolard.

Motto, J. A. (1993). Looking back. In A. Leenaars (Ed.), *Suicidology*. Northvale, NJ: Jason Aronson.

Murray, A. (1998). *Suicide in the Middle Ages*. Oxford, UK: Oxford University Press.

Myin-Germeys, I., Oorschot, M., Collip, D., Lataster, J., Delespaul, P., & Van Os, J. (2009). Experience sampling research in psychopathology: Opening the black box of daily life. *Psychological Medicine, 39*(9), 1533–1547. https://doi.org/10.1017/S0033291708004947

Nock, M. K., Park, J. M., Finn, C. T., Deliberto, T. L., Dour, H. J., & Banaji, M. R. (2010). Measuring the suicidal mind: Implicit cognition predicts suicidal behavior. *Psychological Science, 21*(4), 511–517. https://doi.org/10.1177/0956797610364762

O'Connor, R. C. (2011). Towards an integrated motivational–volitional model of suicidal behaviour. In R. C. O'Connor, S. Platt, & J. Gordon (Eds.), *International handbook of suicide prevention: Research, policy and practice* (pp. 181–198). Chichester, UK: Wiley-Blackwell. https://doi.org/10.1002/9781119998556.ch11

O'Connor, R. C., Cleare, S., Eschle, S., Wetherall, K., & Kirtley, O. (2016). The Integrated motivational-volitional model of suicidal behavior: An update. In R. C. O'Connor & J. Pirkis (Eds.), *The international handbook of suicide prevention* (2nd ed., pp. 220–240). London, UK: Wiley. https://doi.org/10.1002/9781118903223.ch13

O'Connor, R. C., & Kirtley, O. (2018). The integrated motivational-volitional model of suicidal behaviour. *Philosophical Transactions of the Royal Society B: Biological Sciences, 373*(1754), 20170268. https://doi.org/10.1098/rstb.2017.0268

O'Connor, R.C., & Nock, M.K. (2014). The psychology of suicidal behaviour. *Lancet Psychiatry, 1*(1), 73–85. https://doi.org/10.1016/S2215-0366(14)70222-6

O'Connor, R.C., & Portzky, G. (2018a). The relationship between entrapment and suicidal behavior through the lens of the integrated motivational–volitional model of suicidal behavior. *Current Opinion in Psychology, 22,* 12–17. https://doi.org/10.1016/j.copsyc.2017.07.021

O'Connor, R.C., & Portzky, G. (2018b). Looking to the future: A synthesis of new developments and challenges in suicide research and prevention. *Frontiers in Psychology, 9,* 9:2139. https://doi.org/10.3389/fpsyg.2018.02139

Palmier-Claus, J.E., Myin-Germeys, I., Barkus, E., Bentley, L., Udachina, A., Delespaul, P.A.E.G., ... Dunn, G. (2011). Experience sampling research in individuals with mental illness: reflections and guidance. *Acta Psychiatrica Scandinavica, 123*(1), 12–20. https://doi.org/10.1111/j.1600-0447.2010.01596.x

Quetelet, A. (1835). *Sur l'homme et le development de ses faculties, ou Essai de psysique sociale* (Vol. 2). (Reprinted in 1968 by Burt Franklin, New York).

Ribeiro, J., Franklin, J., Fox, K.R., Bentley, K., Kleiman, E.M., Chang, B., & Nock, M.K. (2016). Self-injurious thoughts and behaviors as risk factors for future suicide ideation, attempts, and death: A meta-analysis of longitudinal studies. *Psychological Medicine, 46*(2), 225–236. https://doi.org/10.1017/S0033291715001804

Robinson, J., Hetrick, S.E., & Martin, C. (2011). Preventing suicide in young people: Systematic review. *Australian and New Zealand Journal of Psychiatry, 45*(1), 3–26. https://doi.org/10.3109/00048674.2010.511147

Robinson, J., & Pirkis, J. (2014). Research priorities in suicide prevention: An examination of Australian-based research 2007–11. *Australian Health Review, 38*(1), 18–24. https://doi.org/10.1071/AH13058

Robinson, J., Pirkis, J., Krysinska, K., Niner, S., Jorm, A.F., Dudley, M., ... Harrigan, S. (2008). Research priorities in suicide prevention in Australia a comparison of current research efforts and stakeholder-identified priorities. *Crisis, 29*(4), 180–190. https://doi.org/10.1027/0227-5910.29.4.180

Shneidman, E.S. (1985). *Definition of suicide*. Chichester, UK: Wiley.

Silverman, M.M., Pirkis, J.E. P., Pearson, J.L. P., & Sherrill, J.T. P. (2014). Reflections on Expert Recommendations for U.S. Research Priorities in Suicide Prevention. *American Journal of Preventive Medicine, 47*(3), S97–S101.

Sobell, L.C., & Sobell, M.B. (1992). Timeline followback: A technique for assessing self-reported alcohol consumption. In R. Litten & J. Allen (Eds.), *Measuring alcohol consumption: Psychosocial and biological methods.* Totowa, NJ: Humana Press.

Stephen, G. (1874). *Suicide in Victoria*. Melbourne, Australia: Samuel Mullen.

Sudol, K., & Oquendo, M.A. (2016). Visualizing the suicidal brain: Neuroimaging and suicide prevention. In R.C. O'Connor & J. Pirkis (Eds.), *The international handbook of suicide prevention* (2nd ed., pp. 189–205). Chichester, UK: Wiley.

Tondo, L. (2014). Brief history of suicide in Western cultures. In S.H. Koslow, P. Ruiz, & C.B. Nemeroff (Eds.), *A concise guide to understanding suicide: Epidemiology, pathophysiology, and prevention* (pp. 3–12). Cambridge, UK: Cambridge University Press. https://doi.org/10.1017/CBO9781139519502.003

Tuke, D.H. (1892). *A dictionary of psychological medicine*. London, UK: Churchill.

van Hooff, A.J. L. (2000). A historical perspective on suicide. In R.W. Maris, A.L. Berman, & M.M. Silverman (Eds.), *Comprehensive textbook of suicidology* (pp. 96–123). New York, NY: Guilford Press.

Van Orden, K.A., Witte, T.K., Cukrowicz, K.C., Braithwaite, S.R., Selby, E.A., & Joiner, T. (2010). The interpersonal theory of suicide. *Psychological Review, 117*(2), 575. https://doi.org/10.1037/a0018697

Walsh, C.G., Ribeiro, J.D., & Franklin, J.C. (2017). Predicting risk of suicide attempts over time through machine learning. *Clinical Psychological Science, 5*(3), 457–469. https://doi.org/10.1177/2167702617691560

Westcott, W.W. (1885). *A social science treatise. Suicide. Its history, literature, jurisprudence, causation, and prevention*. London, UK: H.K. Lewis.

Zisook, S., Trivedi, M.H., Warden, D., Lebowitz, B., Thase, M.E., Stewart, J.W., ... Rush, A.J. (2009). Clinical correlates of the worsening or emergence of suicidal ideation during SSRI treatment of depression: An examination of citalopram in the STAR*D study. *Journal of Affective Disorders, 117*(1), 63–73. https://doi.org/10.1016/j.jad.2009.01.002

Chapter 2
Definitions in Suicide Research

Benjamin Goodfellow

Summary

The definitions of suicide and other suicidal behaviors are central to research and everyday practice. Common definitions and terms are important in order to compare results of studies conducted by different research teams and advance toward a better understanding and prevention of suicidal behaviors. This chapter aims to present a range of challenges related to terminology and definitions in suicide research. A brief overview of the history of the sterm *suicide* and description of modern English language definitions in suicide research will be presented. A non-Western perspective will be illustrated with an example from the Pacific island of New Caledonia. Some considerations of nomenclature and classification, and a review of terms to be avoided in suicide research are discussed.

Each death by suicide is a dramatic result of a complex interplay of factors, with each story being unique. Yet, despite this complexity, suicide death can be qualified in a universal way as an act by which a person is the cause of his or her own death. Despite numerous attempts, however, there is still no universally agreed definition of suicide. Different definitions of suicide complicate the determination of cause of death and lead us to question the reliability of suicide mortality data worldwide (De Leo, 2015). Lack of a universal definition impacts the work of coroners, police investigators, clinicians, and researchers. Furthermore, it hinders epidemiological studies, including identification of risk and protective factors and evaluating the effectiveness of suicide prevention interventions and developing public health strategies.

This chapter will explore this complex topic by providing some historical context and reviewing contemporary definitions of fatal and nonfatal suicidal behavior. Further challenges from a cultural perspective will be presented in a brief overview of terms used in New Caledonia, as an example of a non-Western environment. Finally, considerations of nomenclature, classification, and terms to be avoided in suicide research will be presented.

Origins of the Word *Suicide* in Europe

The term *suicide* was coined in England during the 17th century and first appeared in a text by Sir Thomas Browne, *Religio Medici*, written in 1636 and published in 1642 (Minois, 1995). According to Minois (1995), the appearance of this word was related to Browne's urge to distinguish suicide from the murder of another person. Browne also wanted to distinguish the Christian and totally condemnable *self-killing* from Cato's heathen *suicidium*. The term was built from the Latin words *sui* (self) and *caedes* (murder). The English term then passed into French, Spanish, Italian, and Portuguese languages during the 18th century. Minois highlights that from the Middle Ages up to the Renaissance, the act of killing oneself was always tightly bound with moral values and constantly dealt with in ambivalent ways. The history of suicide in Europe throughout that period was characterized by the struggle between those who wanted to condemn it entirely and those who considered there was some noble form of suicide that was acceptable and sometimes even admirable. This noble form of suicide had nothing to do with the self-killing of the commoners, viewed by the Church as a form of despair and thus the worst form of sin. The word *suicide* according to Minois (1995), is thus bound up with the moral values of the 17th-century Western world.

Barbagli (2015) attributes the same origin to the word *suicide*. He details its progressive use in England and its slow progress throughout Europe during the 18th century. Similarly to Minois (1995), he highlights the fact that suicide was a neologism created to name an already existing behavior that until then was only referred to using the word *murder*. Suicide was just as condemnable as murder and was considered the worst sin. In certain parts of Europe during some periods, killing oneself was actually considered to be even worse than killing someone else (Barbagli, 2015). According to Barbagli (2015), the appearance of the new word *suicide* in the 17th century corresponded to an important shift in moral values in Europe during that time. Suicide was progressively less condemned in Europe during the 18th and 19th centuries (Minois, 1995; Barbagli, 2015). According to Minois (1995), this led to the progressive medicalization of suicide. Barbagli (2015) states that the shift in attitudes is one of the determining causes of the supposed rise in suicide rates in Europe during the 18th and 19th centuries.

Two Founding Definitions of Suicide

One would suppose that what Minois (1995) described as the "progressive medicalization of suicide" during the 18th and 19th century, would logically have resulted in a vast wealth of scientific literature at the beginning of the 20th century. However, in 1938, Menninger (1938) notes that this was surprisingly not the case. He contrasts this to the fact that suicide rates were high in America at the time and suggested this was related to the taboo surrounding the topic of suicide. It appears that the scientific study of suicide took some time to finally develop into an academic discipline in the 1960s (Maris, 1993). To give a context before presenting a review of contemporary suicide definitions, two definitions from influential theories about suicide by Durkheim (1897) and Menninger (1938) will be briefly presented.

In 1897, the French sociologist Emile Durkheim published *Le suicide. Étude de sociologie* (*Suicide: A Study in Sociology;* Durkheim, 1897), in which he applied suicide as a subject to introduce a scientific (empirical) methodology in sociology. His book has been considered as the starting point of empirical sociology, and also of suicide research. Throughout this work, he details a fourfold etiological typology of suicide (i.e., egoistic vs. altruistic and anomic vs. fatalistic suicide). In his Introduction, Durkheim augments his definition of suicide: "All cases of death resulting directly or indirectly from a positive or negative act of the victim himself, which he knows will produce this result" (Durkheim, 1897, p. 5; translated from the French). The major components of this definition – that is, death resulting from self-inflicted action (or inaction) and knowledge of the (direct or indirect) consequences of the action, can be found in later definitions. Durkheim deliberately excludes intent from his definition, and his argument for doing so is that intent is not observable. He also states that intent cannot be observed by oneself introspectively either. Indeed, the main point of his book is to detail the external causes of suicide, while considering that psychiatric disorders could only modestly, if at all, explain the varying rates of suicide across the countries in Europe at that time.

In his book *Man Against Himself,* the American psychiatrist Karl Menninger (1938) gives a definition of suicide which could appear to be in contradiction with that of Durkheim. Menninger's definition is in line with Freud's theory of the death instinct and its etiological relation to suicide, although he states that none of Freud's writings were ever entirely focused on the issue of suicide:

> Suicide must be regarded as a peculiar kind of death which entails three internal elements: the element of dying, the element of killing, and the element of being killed. Each of these requires separate analysis. Each is an act for which there exists motives, unconscious and conscious. The latter are usually evident enough; the unconscious motives are now to be our chief consideration. (Menninger, 1938, p. 24)

Menninger further details these *unconscious motives* – that is, the wish to kill, the wish to be killed, and the wish to die. According to the author the wish to kill is related to the primary aggressiveness that every human being experiences during their development. The wish to be killed is related to the turning back onto the self of this aggressiveness resulting from the impossibility of maintaining normal external emotional investments. The wish to die is related to a direct emanation of the death instinct. All of these motives or instincts are more or less tempered and sometimes neutralized by the presence of erotic, constructive, or life instincts, and this explains the various degrees of self-destruction that can be encountered in clinical practice. Indeed, according to Menninger, suicide is one of various forms that self-destruction can take in human behavior. Whether self-destruction's outcome is death, automutilation, addiction, or psychosis, is mainly a question of degree of self-destruction.

These two classic definitions are provided here to illustrate how context and theoretical framework have a determining influence on the meaning of terms. In these two examples, the same term, *suicide*, has two radically different and even opposing meanings, despite the fact that they are both products of Western society four decades apart (Goodfellow, 2018). This opposition illustrates a debate that took place among Western scholars at the beginning of the 20th century regarding the causes of suicide. These two scholars, however, seemed to share a common conception of *intent* that is not immediately accessible to observation. Durkheim decided to set it aside, as it is not accessible to empirical science, and to focus on "external" causes, and Menninger suggested diving into the unconscious "depths" of the human mind to access it, in line with the dominant psychoanalytic conception of the human mind during the first half of the last century.

Contemporary English Language Terms and Definitions for Suicidal Behaviors

The contemporary period in suicide research can be considered to have begun in the 1960s (Maris, 1993). It was possibly under the main influence of Edwin Shneidman, director of the Los Angeles Suicide Prevention Center and author of many works on suicide prevention, that suicidology started to become an autonomous academic discipline. Subsequently, the topic of definitions of suicidal behaviors was increasingly discussed in the literature, and from these discussions, a more structured approach emerged.

Four characteristics have been identified as the most common features of the definition of suicide (De Leo, Burgis, Bertolote, Kerkhof, & Bille-Brahe, 2004; De Leo, Burgis, Bertolote, Kerkhof, & Bille-Brahe, 2006; Farberow, 1980; Maris, Berman, & Silverman, 2000; Silverman, 2006).

- An *outcome* is what results from a suicidal behavior; the first visible consequence of the behavior. The person can die, get injured, or not sustain any injury as a consequence of harming or attempting to harm themselves. An outcome is a way to characterize a behavior. For instance, one can distinguish between fatal and nonfatal suicidal behavior based on the fact that the person dies or survives as a result of the behavior.
- *Intent* is the purpose of a person's behavior. This should be distinguished from the motive of a behavior (i.e., the reason the person wants to die) – for instance, the loss of a partner, the loss of a job, or financial difficulties. Intent points to what the person wished to achieve by harming themselves. Intent also points to what the person harming themselves *expects* the result of the behavior will be – that is, dying, injuring or poisoning oneself without dying, calling for help, or influencing someone else. In the case of accidental death, a person may take some risky behavior such as driving fast on a dangerous road, and die in a high-speed car crash, without actually expecting to die, because they are overconfident in their own driving skills. On the other hand, a person may drive recklessly while *intentionally* taking the risk of dying. The intent of the driver would not be an *explicit* intent to die in this case, although it would be considered a particular form of *suicidal* intent (i.e., a suicide-*related* intent).
- *Knowledge of a potentially fatal outcome* points to the person's *understanding* of the consequences of their behavior. It first refers to the person's inherent *ability* to understand the consequences of a particular behavior. For instance, a young child sitting on the edge of a high wall may not understand that they could die as a consequence of falling or jumping from such a height. They may not even understand the irreversibility of death. Knowledge also points to the *information* required to understand the consequence of a particular behavior. For instance, a person may overdose on a medication but have no idea of the toxic effects of this medication or no clear idea of what dose is actually toxic. Knowledge is connected to intent in terms of the fact that what a person *expects* to result from a behavior depends on what a person *understands* of the consequence of that behavior.
- The *agency* in a behavior refers to who is the *agent* of the behavior – that is, who takes the actions necessary to implement the behavior. For instance, the agent of a suicide by hanging is a person who ties a noose, puts it around their neck, and takes the step or pushes aside the stool or ladder they are standing on. The agent of a suicide can also be the person who goes to the roof of a high building and jumps, takes a lethal dose of drugs, shoots themselves with a gun, etc. In a case of homicide, on the other hand, the agent is not the person who dies, but an *outside* agent (e.g., a person who shot a gun at the victim). The agent of a suicide can be *active*, as in the case of hanging above, or *passive*, as when a person remains intentionally in front of a moving train.

Those four features were used to analyze and compare the various definitions identified in a systematic literature review of contemporary definitions of fatal and nonfatal suicidal behavior (Goodfellow, Kõlves, & De Leo, 2019a). After screening approximately 5,000 records published between 1960 and 2017, the reviewers found 19 definitions of suicide and 7 definitions of nonfatal suicidal behaviors in 29 publications. Definitions were selected if they presented an original definition of the authors' own conception or a modification of a previous definition that changed its logical nature. The vast majority of definitions of suicide (17 out of 19) mentioned death or an equivalent as the *outcome*, whereas for nonfatal behavior, outcomes were variable as expected. An *intent to die* was included in the majority of definitions of suicide (15 out of 19), whereas only one out of seven definitions of nonfatal suicidal behavior listed *intent to die*. Twelve out of 19 definitions of suicide explicitly stated *knowledge* of the consequences of the act, and for nonfatal suicidal behavior, only the definition of *suicide attempt* by Stengel (1964) explicitly stated the *knowledge of a potentially fatal outcome*. Self-infliction was noted in only 10 out of 19 definitions of suicide; the other definitions included the possibility of an outside *agent* at various stages of the act. In contrast, six out of seven definitions of nonfatal suicidal behaviors specifically mentioned self-infliction (Goodfellow et al., 2019a). A selection of the most often cited definitions of suicide are presented in Table 2.1.

Table 2.1 A selection of contemporary definitions of suicide in chronological order of publication

Authors (year, page)	Definition	Outcome	Intent	Knowledge of potential fatal outcome	Agency (self)
Beck et al. (1973, p. 7)	"A Completed Suicide refers to a willful, self-inflicted, life threatening act which has resulted in death."	Death	"Willful"	Not specified	Yes
Shneidman (1985, p. 203)	"Currently in the western world, suicide is a conscious act of self-induced annihilation, best understood as a multidimensional malaise in a needful individual who defines an issue for which the suicide is perceived as the best solution."	Annihilation or cessation, (i.e., end of life as individual experiences it)	Yes: annihilation. Can be ordered (e.g., by an emperor)	Yes	By self or others
O'Carroll et al. (1996, pp. 246–247)	"Death from injury, poisoning, or suffocation where there is evidence (either explicit or implicit) that the injury was self-inflicted and the decedent intended to kill himself/herself."	Death	Yes: to die	Not specified	Yes
De Leo et al. (2006, p. 12)	"Suicide is an act with a fatal outcome, which the deceased, knowing or expecting a potentially fatal outcome, has initiated and carried out with the purpose of bringing about wanted changes."	Death	Yes: some intent to die	Yes	Yes
Silverman et al. (2007, p. 273)	"Suicide ... a self-inflicted death with evidence (either explicit or implicit) of intent to die."	Death	Yes: to die	Yes	Yes
Crosby et al. (2011, p. 23)	"Suicide: Death caused by self-directed injurious behavior with any intent to die as a result of the behavior."	Death	Yes: to die	Not specified	Yes

Based on "Contemporary Definitions of Suicidal Behavior: A Systematic Literature Review," by B. Goodfellow, K. Kõlves, & D. De Leo, 2019, *Suicide & Life-Threatening Behavior, 49*(2), 488–504.

To summarize, there is a high level of consensus in published English language definitions of suicide, especially for *outcome* and *intent*. In contrast, self-infliction (as an *agent*) was less present in definitions of suicide, whereas it was the most characteristic feature of definitions of nonfatal suicidal behaviors. One of the findings of this review was that the four characteristics of the definition of suicide enabled one to grasp the content of practically all published definitions and to track their variability (Goodfellow et al., 2019a).

Regarding suicide, other European languages use words with a slightly different etymological meaning (i.e., *murder* of oneself), such as for instance, the German *selbstmord*, the Estonian *enesetapp*, or the Finnish *itsemurha*. This reflects back to the historical and moral underpinnings of the concept of suicide mentioned earlier. Moving further away from the English language and Western culture, the issues related to translation become more challenging. The experience of the author of this present chapter, as a practicing psychiatrist and researcher in New Caledonia, can give some complementary perspective to the topic of definitions in suicidology. A brief historical insight into suicide in New Caledonia in Box 2.1 illustrates a different culture's concepts of suicide in a small population evolving over time.

Box 2.1. Definition of suicide in New Caledonia

New Caledonia is a Melanesian archipelago and French overseas territory situated in the southwestern Pacific. Its population is approximately 260,000 inhabitants and comprises many ethnic groups, the main being indigenous Kanak. The Kanak people are descendants of the first Austronesian settlers in approximately 1,000 BC (Irwin, 1994; Kirch, 2000) and speak 28 different vernacular languages.

The first reference to suicide in New Caledonia in the published literature was by Leenhardt (1947). He describes examples of suicide in the Hoauïlou region (*ajië* linguistic area) as an illustration of the way the Kanak perceive life and death to be on a continuum, with blurred limits, in comparison with European perceptions. Leenhardt states that suicide has an important social role in the Kanak community and equates it to the search for a transcendent existence. Further, Barbagli (2015) criticized Durkheim's argument (1897) that altruistic suicide is endemic among "lower societies," as Durkheim considered populations in the Pacific to be – on the contrary, claimed Barbagli, suicide is often used as a means to gain power over an oppressor. Death and thus *intent to die* in the definition of suicide probably have very different meanings compared with a Western understanding.

Over 20 terms describing suicidal behaviors have been identified in local Kanak languages. The vast majority of these terms refer to a particular method used to die by suicide, with hanging being the most common suicide method in New Caledonia (Goodfellow et al., 2020). The method sometimes has a cultural function and meaning. For instance, according to Lercari (2002), the *ajië* word *yiwé* means to make a noose, as in *yöi dèxâ wêê yiwé rö wêwa*, she or he ties a noose to the ceiling (to the joist). According to Drilë Sam (1995), the Drehu term for suicide is hnöjua (p. 65), a term composed of *hnö* meaning a trap made of a noose, and *jua* meaning a peninsula. There is a myth from Lifou that mentions a boy intentionally diving from the peninsula into the ocean with his horse. The myth describes how the young boy changes life and does not actually go to his own end, but rather carries on in another form of life, beyond the end of the *jua*. Only three of the terms recorded have not been found to be etymologically related to a particular method. Out of these, the expression *kèè-pè mûgé rè muru rèè* (to take one's own life again) could have a similar etymological construction to suicide – that is, one part implying death (i.e., *taking life*) and another reflective part (i.e., one's own).

Suicide came to be named, defined, and moralized by indigenous populations according to Western Christian standards like many other behaviors since the French colonization from 1853. Today, suicide is morally condemned by the Kanak authorities, which are strongly influenced by Christian morals. However, local church and cultural representatives often seek assistance in preventing suicide. This could be paralleled with the change in official attitude of the Catholic

Church toward suicide that took place, according to Barbagli (2015), from the 19th century. French is the only official shared language in New Caledonia, hence the definitions of suicide and nonfatal suicidal behavior today rely on medical appreciation and police investigation rules in a French-speaking environment.

Nomenclatures and Classifications: A Few Important Considerations

Returning to definitions from the contemporary Western research perspective, it is important to explain further that definitions of suicidal behaviors should be organized into a set of mutually exclusive logically defined terms – that is, a *nomenclature*. Nomenclature lays the groundwork for the development of a classification of suicidal behaviors. Papers by O'Carroll et al. (1996) and Silverman (2006) note that a distinction has to be made between a nomenclature and a classification. This distinction relies mainly on the purpose of each: a nomenclature is used to communicate concepts, whereas a classification is used to describe what is interpreted as reality. To move from a definition (e.g., of suicide) in a nomenclature toward a definition in a classification, a process called *operationalization* is necessary. An *operational definition* in a classification usually aims to be precise and has a set of modifiers to make that definition conform to observed phenomena. For instance, modifiers of suicide can be the lethality of method, the level of intent, or the environment in which the behavior took place (home, street, etc.).

A systematic review of contemporary nomenclatures of suicidal behaviors highlighted the similarities and differences between 13 nomenclatures published in 1960–2017 (Goodfellow, Kõlves, & De Leo, 2018). The main similarity was that these nomenclatures were developed based on taxonomical rules related to *outcome* for the vast majority, and for all nomenclatures these rules were related to *intent*. The latter was frequently a distinguishing characteristic. For instance, in the nomenclature of O'Carroll et al. (1996), the broad category of *suicide-related behavior* was divided between *instrumental suicide-related behavior* and *suicidal act*, based on the absence or presence of intent to die, respectively. However, the 13 nomenclatures were different in the way intent or outcome had priority over each other in the logic of taxonomy. For instance, in the nomenclature of Posner et al. (2007), the main categories were *suicidal, non-suicidal*, or *undetermined events*, based on the presence of intent to die, whereas in the nomenclature of Silverman et al. (2007), the main categories were *concept* categories (i.e., *ideations, communications,* and *behaviors*). In the last nomenclature, intent was still the main distinguishing feature for behaviors.

Whether *outcome* or *intent* had priority, intent to die was central in all nomenclatures (Goodfellow et al., 2018). It should be noted that nomenclatures are usually based on a particular definition of suicide, and as mentioned earlier (see the beginning of this section), the vast majority of existing published definitions of suicide include intent to die as a central characteristic (Goodfellow et al., 2019a). Thus, this has a direct impact in terms of taxonomy – that is, the organization of terms into different categories and subcategories. Classifications are based on nomenclatures, which implies they will have the same overall taxonomy. Therefore, centering or not centering a definition of suicide on intent to die will have implications all along the way from nomenclature and its underlying taxonomy, to the resulting classification.

A review of contemporary classifications revealed a lack of consensus among the 19 published classifications (Goodfellow, Kõlves, & De Leo, 2019b). Indeed, very few classifications have reached widespread international use, and the existing classifications were very different from each other. Overall classifications have tended to become more and more precise and operational over time. Indeed, the more recent classifications included very structured, precise, and practical classification schemes which enabled their use in clinical or death registration contexts. Most of these classification schemes suggested a method to evidence intent, such as the Operational Criteria for the Determination of Suicide of Rosenberg et al. (1988). Furthermore, Shah and Ganesvaran (1999) suggested a detailed classification of levels of intent. Most classifications were comprehensive, encompassing the whole spectrum of suicidal behaviors (e.g., O'Carroll et al, 1996; Posner et al., 2007; Silverman et al, 2007). However, some do not detail different types of behavior or ideation – for example, the World Health Organization (WHO) *International Classification of Diseases,* 10th revision (ICD-10; WHO, 2016).

Stigmatizing and Misleading Terms

It is important that the terms used in suicide research should be as neutral as much as possible and avoid distorting the object under study. Furthermore, dissemination of research results should not be harmful to those with a *lived experience*. Indeed, some authors deem some regularly used English language terms to be unacceptable and argue against their morally laden, stigmatizing, and misleading character. A selection of documents published since 1989 is presented in Table 2.2 outlining stigmatizing or misleading terminology and proposed alternatives (Goodfellow, 2018).

Most authors have questioned the term *completed suicide*. For example, Lester (1989) questioned the term *completed* in the *completed suicide* formulation, and consequently also the *attempted suicide* formulation. He stated that an attempted suicide may be more rational and adaptive than the former and may thus be the successful form of the behavior. Again, Canetto and Lester (1995) argumented against *completed suicide*, stating that the final goal of suicidal behaviors may not be death but rather communication of distress. Canetto (1997) linked these arguments to a gendered approach to suicidal behavior in American patterns of language. Her main argument was that the terms *attempted* and *completed suicide* confounded intent and outcome and implied intention. Attempted suicide was equivalent to an unfinished act and a failure, whereas completed suicide was equated with a completed act and a success. She went on to state that failure was related to female gender and success to male gender, and that this could encourage nonfatal suicidal behavior in women and discourage it in men. These patterns of language were congruent with patterns of epidemiology. She proposed using a terminology based on outcome rather than intent and thus distinguish between *fatal* and *nonfatal* suicidal behavior.

Similarly, the Alberta Mental Health Board in (2009) Canada and Olson (2011) considered terms *committed suicide*, *completed suicide*, *successful suicide*, and *failed suicide attempt* as unacceptable because they had criminal connotations or they were misleading. Olson (2011) emphasized that reducing the stigma of suicide implied encouraging dialogue by using neutral and compassionate language. The Alberta Mental Health Board (2009) recommended the use of *suicide*, *death by suicide*, or *died by suicide*. Beaton et al. (2013) further argued that the terms *commit*, *committed*, or *committing* were problematic and stigmatizing, although still

Table 2.2 Stigmatizing or misleading terminology and proposed alternatives in a selection of documents

Authors	Unacceptable terms	Proposed alternatives
Lester, 1989	• Completed suicide	• None proposed
Canetto & Lester, 1995	• Completed suicide	• None proposed
Canetto, 1997	• Attempted suicide • Completed suicide	• Nonfatal suicidal behavior • Fatal suicidal behavior • Suicidal behavior
Alberta Mental Health Board, 2009	• Committed suicide • Completed suicide • Successful • Failure	• Suicide • Death by suicide • Died by suicide
Olson, 2011	• Commit suicide • Successful suicide • Failed suicide attempt • Completed suicide	• None proposed
Crosby et al., 2011 (CDC)	• Completed suicide • Failed attempt • Nonfatal suicide • Parasuicide • Successful suicide • Suicidality • Suicide gesture • Manipulative act • Suicide threat	• Suicide • Suicide attempt • Suicidal self-directed violence • Nonsuicidal self-directed violence • Suicidal thoughts • Suicidal behavior
Beaton, Forster, & Maple, 2013	• Commit • Committed • Committing	• None proposed
Mindframe (n.d.)	• Successful suicide • Unsuccessful suicide • Committed suicide • Failed suicide • Suicide bid	• Died by suicide • Took their own life • Suicide death • Suicide attempt • Nonfatal attempt

Notes. CDC = Centers for Disease Control and Prevention.

in use in the specialized literature. They stressed that language could have negative effects and lead people bereaved by suicide to be silent.

Some organizations have proposed recommended terminology for specific purposes. The American Centers for Disease Control and Prevention published recommendations for Self-Directed Violence Surveillance (Crosby, Ortega, & Melanson, 2011) and the Self-Directed Violence Classification System. In the recommendations, a list of unacceptable terms was published, with the reasons for their unacceptability, and proposed alternate terms (Table 2.2). In Australia, Mindframe (n.d.) has provided recommended terminology for the media. Nevertheless, languages are developing, and they reflect changing cultural norms and morals; thus terminology is in continuous change.

Conclusions

This chapter has examined the historical and cultural context in which the term *suicide* appeared in Europe during the 17th century, followed by terms and definitions used by contemporary authors in the English language. To contrast this, some examples were provided of terms and expressions for suicide used by indigenous populations living in the Pacific island of New Caledonia. The historical and cultural context of the process by which this terminology was progressively abandoned in favor of the word *suicide* was then outlined. After a few considerations of the topics of nomenclature and classification, the chapter ended with a nonexhaustive review of stigmatizing and misleading English-language terms. This chapter has highlighted the complexity underlying the topic of definitions in suicide research and the many challenges in building a universal nomenclature and a universal classification of suicidal behaviors.

References

Alberta Mental Health Board. (2009). *What's in a word? The language of suicide.* Retrieved from http://www.plelearningexchange.ca/wp-content/uploads/2016/05/Language-of-Suicide-Alberta-Health-Services.pdf

Barbagli, M. (2015). *Farewell to the world: A history of suicide.* Cambridge, UK: Polity Press.

Beaton, S., Forster, P., & Maple, M. (2013). Letter to the editor: Suicide bereavement and the media. *Advances in Mental Health, 11*(2), 204–206. https://doi.org/10.5172/jamh.2013.11.2.204

Beck, A.T., Davis, J.H., Frederick, C.J., Perklin, S., Pokorny, A.D., Schulman, R.E., ... Wittlin, B. (1973). Classification and nomenclature. In H.L.P. Resnik & B.C. Hathorne (Eds.), *Suicide prevention in the 70's* (pp. 7–12). Rockville, MD: Center for Studies of Suicide Prevention, National Institute of Mental Health.

Canetto, S.S. (1997). Gender and suicidal behavior: Theories and evidence. In R.W. Maris, M.M. Silverman, & S.S. Canetto (Eds.), *Review of suicidology, 1997.* New York, NY: Guilford Press.

Canetto, S.S., & Lester, D. (1995). Women and suicidal behavior: Issues and dilemmas. In S.S. Canetto & D. Lester (Eds.), *Women and suicidal behavior* (pp. 3–8). New York, NY: Springer.

Crosby, A.E., Ortega, L., & Melanson, C. (2011). *Self-directed violence surveillance: uniform definitions and recommended data elements* (Version 1.0.). Atlanta, GA: Centers for Disease Control and Prevention, National Center for Injury Prevention and Control.

De Leo, D. (2015). Can we rely on suicide mortality data? *Crisis, 36*(1), 1–3. https://doi.org/10.1027/0227-5910/a000315

De Leo, D., Burgis, S., Bertolote, J.M., Kerkhof, A.J., & Bille-Brahe, U. (2004). Definitions of suicidal behavior. In D. De Leo (Ed.), *Suicidal behavior: Theories and research findings* (pp. 17–39). Boston, MA: Hogrefe & Huber.

De Leo, D., Burgis, S., Bertolote, J.M., Kerkhof, A.J., & Bille-Brahe, U. (2006). Definitions of suicidal behavior: lessons learned from the WHO/EURO multicentre Study. *Crisis, 27*(1), 4–15. https://doi.org/10.1027/0227-5910.27.1.4

Drilë Sam, L. (1995). *Dictionnaire drehu-français.* Nouméa, New Caledonia: Académie des Langues Kanak & Centre de documentation pédagogique de Nouvelle-Calédonie.

Durkheim, E. (1897). *Le suicide. Étude de sociologie.* Paris, France: Presses Universitaires de France.

Farberow, N.L. (1980). Indirect self-destructive behavior: Classification and characteristics. In N.L. Farberow (Ed.), *The many faces of suicide: Indirect self-destructive behavior* (pp. 15–27). New York, NY: McGraw-Hill.

Goodfellow, B. (2018). *Terms and definitions for suicide: Steps towards the elaboration of an international and intercultural nomenclature for suicidal behaviors* (Unpublished doctoral dissertation). Griffith University, Brisbane, Australia.

Goodfellow, B., Kõlves, K., & De Leo, D. (2018). Contemporary nomenclatures of suicidal behaviors: A systematic literature review. *Suicide & Life-Threatening Behavior, 48*(3), 353–366. https://doi.org/10.1111/sltb.12354

Goodfellow, B., Kõlves, K., & De Leo, D. (2019a). Contemporary definitions of suicidal behavior: A systematic literature review. *Suicide & Life-Threatening Behavior, 49*(2), 488–504. https://doi.org/10.1111/sltb.12457

Goodfellow, B., Kõlves, K., & De Leo, D. (2019b). Contemporary classifications of suicidal behavior: A systematic literature review. *Crisis, 41*(3), 179–186. https://doi.org/10.1027/0227-5910/a000622

Goodfellow, B., Kõlves, K., Selefen, A.-C., Massain, T., Amadéo, S., & De Leo, D. (2020). The WHO-START Study in New Caledonia: A psychological autopsy case series. *Journal of Affective Disorders, 262*, 366–372. https://doi.org/10.1016/j.jad.2019.11.020

Irwin, G. (1994). *The prehistoric exploration and colonisation of the Pacific*. Cambridge, UK: Cambridge University Press.

Kirch, P.V. (2000). *On the road of the winds: An archaeological history of the Pacific Islands before European contact*. Berkeley, CA: University of California Press.

Leenhardt, M. (1947). *Do kamo: la personne et le mythe dans le monde Melanesien* [Do Kamo: Person and myth in the Melanesian world]. Paris, France: Gallimard.

Lercari, C. (2002). *Dictionnaire ajië-français à l'usage des étudiants* [Ajië-French dictionary for student use]. Nouméa, New Caledonia: Centre de documentation pédagogique de Nouvelle-Calédonie.

Lester, D. (1989). The study of suicide from a feminist perspective. *Crisis, 11*(1), 38–43.

Maris, R.W. (1993). The evolution of suicidology. In A.A. Leenaars, A.L. Berman, P. Cantor, & R.E. Litman, (Eds.), *Suicidology: essays in honor of Edwin S. Shneidman*. Northvale, NJ: Jason Aronson.

Maris, R.W., Berman, A.L., & Silverman, M.M. (2000). The theoretical component in suicidology. In R.W. Maris, A.L. Berman, & M.M. Silverman (Eds.), *Comprehensive textbook of suicidology* (pp. 26–61). New York, NY: Guilford Press.

Menninger, K.A. (1938). *Man against himself*. New York, NY: Harcourt, Brace.

Mindframe. (n.d.). *Language*. Retrieved from https://mindframe.org.au/suicide/communicating-about-suicide/language.

Minois, G. (1995). *Histoire du suicide*. Paris, France: Fayard.

O'Carroll, P.W., Berman, A.L., Maris, R.W., Moscicki, E.K., Tanney, B.L., & Silverman, M.M. (1996). Beyond the Tower of Babel: a nomenclature for suicidology. *Suicide & Life-Threatening Behavior, 26*(3), 237–252.

Olson, R. (2011). *Suicide and language*. Retrieved from https://www.suicideinfo.ca/resource/suicideandlanguage/

Posner, K., Oquendo, M.A., Gould, M., Stanley, B., & Davies, M. (2007). Columbia Classification Algorithm of Suicide Assessment (C-CASA): Classification of suicidal events in the FDA's pediatric suicidal risk analysis of antidepressants. *American Journal of Psychiatry, 164*(7), 1035–1043. https://doi.org/10.1176/ajp.2007.164.7.1035

Rosenberg, M. L., Davidson, L. E., Smith, J. C., Berman, A. L., Buzbee, H., Gantner, G., ... Murray, D. (1988). Operational criteria for the determination of suicide. *Journal of Forensic Science, 33*(6), 1445–1456. https://doi.org/10.1520/JFS12589J

Shah, A., & Ganesvaran, T. (1999). A possible clinical classification for the psychopathology of suicidal intent among psychiatric inpatients committing suicide. *International Journal of Psychiatry in Clinical Practice, 3*(3), 199–204. https://doi.org/10.3109/13651509909022734

Shneidman, E. (1985). *Definition of suicide*. Lanham, MD: Rowman and Littlefield Publishers, Inc.

Silverman, M.M. (2006). The language of suicidology. *Suicide & Life-Threatening Behavior, 36*(5), 519–532. https://doi.org/10.1521/suli.2006.36.5.519

Silverman, M.M., Berman, A.L., Sanddal, N.D., O'Carroll P, W., & Joiner, T.E. (2007). Rebuilding the tower of Babel: A revised nomenclature for the study of suicide and suicidal behaviors. Part 2: Suicide-related ideations, communications, and behaviors. *Suicide & Life-Threatening Behavior, 37*(3), 264–277. https://doi.org/10.1521/suli.2007.37.3.264

Stengel, E. (1964). The suicidal attempt as a behavior pattern, and its definition. In E. Stengel (Ed.), *Suicide and attempted suicide* (pp. 67–73). London, UK: Penguin Books.

World Health Organization. (2016). *International classification of diseases* (10th ed.). Retrieved from https://icd.who.int/browse10/2016/en

Chapter 3
Public Health Approach to Suicide Research

Paul S. F. Yip and Lynn Tang

Summary

Reducing suicide rates requires concerted efforts from multiple sectors in the community. A public health approach to suicide prevention entails strategies targeted for the general public and measures specifically developed for at-risk populations. This chapter elaborates on the World Health Organization's recommendation for a public health approach to identify the patterns of suicide, and explore risk and protective factors against suicide, as well as develop and evaluate interventions. It then illustrates how research informed by a public health approach has been realized to develop localized and community-wide suicide prevention strategies in Hong Kong. These studies have included the use of innovative data collection methods to monitor suicide trends and evaluation studies on lethal means restriction measures, responsible media reportage, school-based preventive programs for youths, and community intervention programs for districts where suicide clusters occur

Suicide is a worldwide public health concern. It is a public health issue not only because nearly 800,000 people lose their life to suicide each year (World Health Organization [WHO], 2018) or because the years of life lost result in economic losses to society (Yip, Liu, & Law, 2008), but most importantly, because one life lost to suicide is too many. The ripple effect of suicide does not just have an impact on friends and families who are bereaved by the suicide or suicide attempts of their loved ones. It can trigger further suicides within the community and lead to the formation of *suicide clusters* where suicide rates increase within a certain time frame, within a defined geographical area (Joiner, 1999).

While suicide cuts across all demographic levels and all corners of the world, observational studies show different patterns of suicide rates. For example, suicide is the second leading cause of death in 15- to 29-year-olds, and 79 % of suicides take place in low- and middle-income countries (WHO, 2018). Hence suicide prevention requires concerted efforts from all sectors of the community to develop strategies for the general public and targeted measures for at-risk populations. This warrants a public health approach supported by systematic research to inform and develop evidence-based and cost-effective suicide prevention strategies that resonate across the whole population (WHO, 2018; Yip, 2005, 2011).

The causes of suicide are multifactorial and complex, covering biopsychosocial and environmental factors. The work of suicide prevention is a continuous process, encompassing challenges in the journey as well as demanding responsive and proactive measures, which at the same time ought to have a sustaining impact in the community.

This chapter will first elaborate the importance of a public health approach to suicide research and prevention. Then it will discuss the recommendations put forth by WHO and their implications in suicide research. Examples from suicide prevention research in Hong Kong will demonstrate how some of the WHO's recommendations can be put into practice in a local context. Subsequently, these suicide prevention strategies or programs have brought about changes in suicide rate.

Why Do We Need a Public Health Approach to Suicide Prevention?

A public health approach entails three levels of preventive strategies – namely, universal (interventions for the general public), selective (interventions for the at-risk groups), and indicated (interventions for people at high risk), as shown in Figure 3.1 (Gordon, 1987). This classification allows the development of tailor-made prevention measures for different groups with a balance of benefits against risk and cost.

For suicide prevention, the strength of a public health approach is reflected in the following characteristics. First, it is population based. Research evidence supports the strength of population-based suicide prevention strategies over clinical strategies targeting only high-risk groups. A UK study showed that a strategy that was effective for high-risk groups, had only a modest effect on population suicide rates. In the contrast, measures that aimed at actively reducing risk among the whole population were more likely to result in suicide reduction (Lewis, Hawton, & Jones, 1997). Figure 3.2 illustrates this phenomenon (Yip, 2005). Considering the mental health of a population drawn as a normally distributed curve, reducing the suicidal risk of the population at large with a universal program (i.e., shifting the whole curve to the left) would in turn reduce the number of people in the high-risk zone. This is supported by the *Rose theorem,* which states that a large number of people exposed to a low risk may precipitate more cases than a small number exposed to a high risk (Rose, 1992).

Second, a public health approach that aims to protect people against suicide risks should target changing the environment. The metaphor of flooding can illustrate the importance of addressing environmental factors (Yip, 2005). While a rescue team would work hard to save the lives of victims being swept downstream when a flood occurs, upstream factors – that is, the causes of the flood, such as deforestation – need to be dealt with to effectively reduce the number of victims being put at risk in the long run. Nevertheless, we still need to save those

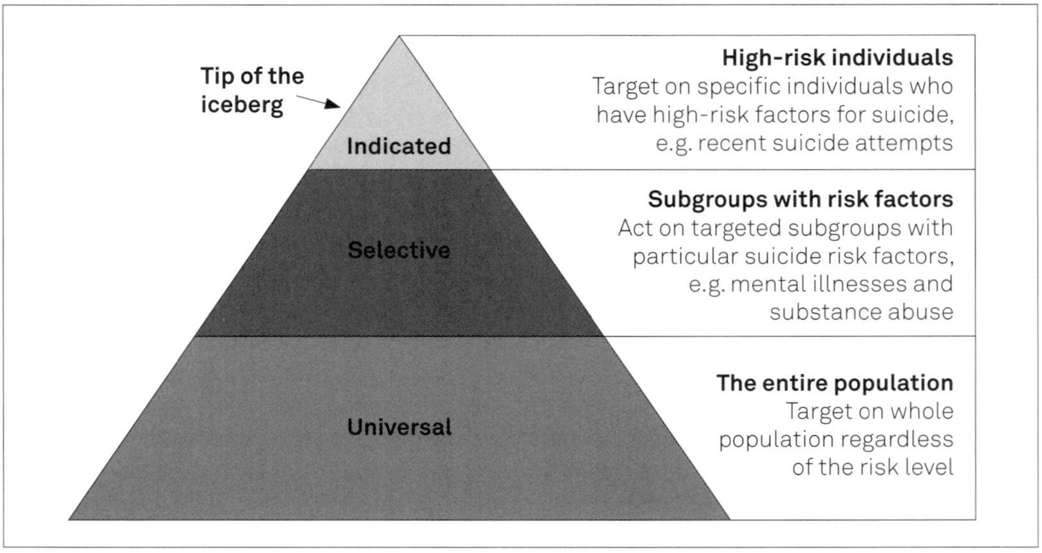

Figure 3.1 The three levels of suicide preventive strategies. Based on "Towards Evidence-Based Suicide Prevention Programs," by the World Health Organization, Regional Office for the Western Pacific. © 2010 by the WHO.

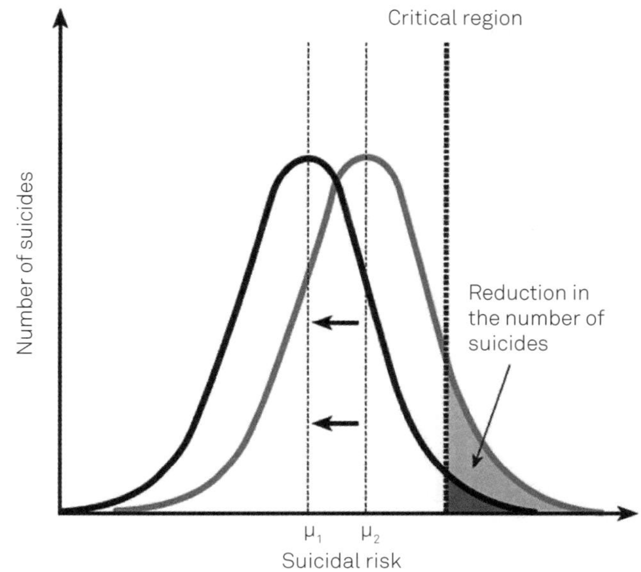

Figure 3.2 Effect of a shift in mean suicidal risk of a population. μ_1 = new population mean; μ_0 = original population mean. Reprinted with permission from "A Public Health Approach to Suicide Prevention" by P. S. F. Yip, 2005, *Hong Kong Journal of Psychiatry, 15*, p. 29–31. © The Hong Kong College of Psychiatrists Ltd.

people who are drowning during the flood. It is not much good to ask them to learn to swim during the occurrence of the flood. For suicide, upstream factors resulting in an increase of suicide rates are signals of a malfunctioning society that requires policy intervention at all levels – for example, to address divorced families, unemployment, and poverty. Suicide intervention is crucial to stopping tragedies from happening, but suicide *prevention* and tackling the causes contributing to the changing patterns and epidemics of suicide are paramount. Concerted efforts among different sectors of the societies should target the wider populations to reduce upstream environmental risk factors before the symptoms appear. An example of such a policy measure would be the increasing of minimum wages in some states in US, which was found to curb the rise of suicide rates (Gertner, Rotter, & Shafer, 2019).

Third, a public health approach would involve multiple avenues. At an individual level, suicide behavior can be understood as a complex process ranging from suicidal ideation, to suicide planning, to suicide attempt, to death resulting from suicide. Multiple interacting factors covering biological, genetic, psychological, social, environmental, and circumstantial factors are at play to contribute to a range of low to high suicide risk levels (Wasserman, 2001). While improving access to clinical interventions in mental health services for people at risk of suicidal behavior should be a public health policy goal, this should be combined with creative use of multiple avenues for suicide prevention so that different risk factors can be addressed, and protective factors can be strengthened. This especially applies to countries with high demands from a large population but with limited resources and high prevalence of stigma that make improving access to mental health services difficult (Yip, 2005).

The WHO promotes a public health approach and calls for countries to employ a multisectoral approach involving different stakeholders to address suicide (WHO, 2014). Around 40 countries have adopted a national suicide prevention strategy to tackle suicide comprehensively and systematically (WHO, 2018). To identify effective suicide prevention strategies, comprehensive research on the universal, selective, and indicated level tactics are required to inform evidence-based practice based on the local resources and contexts (Law et al., 2019).

WHO Recommendations and Their Implications for Research

The WHO recommends four steps in a public health approach, with each step supported by different types of research (WHO, 2014, p. 13):

1. Surveillance to define the problem of suicidal behavior. This entails systematic data collection to identify patterns of suicide and the different rates of suicide.
2. Identify risk and protective factors. This requires research to understand the causes of suicidal behavior and who is affected by it.
3. Develop and evaluate interventions. Research would seek to evaluate interventions to see what works and who benefits.
4. Implementation to scale up effective policies and programs. This prompts further evaluation research to measure the impact of the programs.

As shown in Figure 3.3, the public health approach in suicide research can be understood as a cycle to develop suicide prevention programs strategically (WHO, 2014). It involves a chain of different research agenda utilizing different data sources and multiple methods as well as mobilizing stakeholders in different sectors to inform the next step of the cycle.

On top of these steps, recently the WHO (2018) has started using LIVE LIFE to embody the key ingredients of a national suicide prevention strategy. LIVE represents leadership, intervention, vision, and evaluation: *leadership* to mobilize stakeholders; *intervention* to

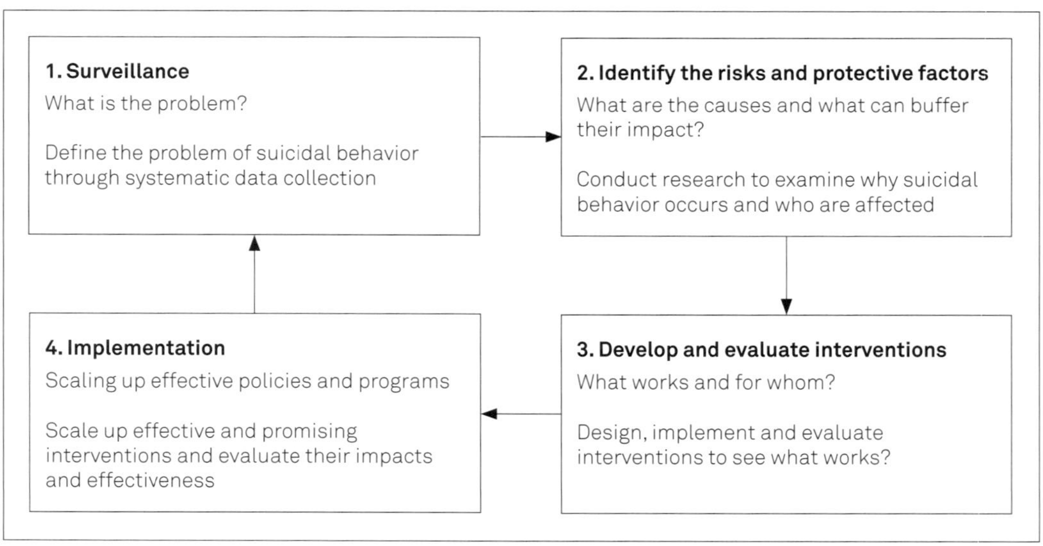

Figure 3.3 Steps in a public health model. Reprinted with permission from "Preventing Suicide: A Global Imperative," by the World Health Organization, p. 13. © 2014 by the WHO.

implement effective preventive measures and provide services for people in need, such as suicide attempters; *vision* to keep steering toward the goal of suicide reduction and identify resource and funding opportunities to achieve this; and *evaluation* to measure if the interventions have achieved the desired impact. LIFE refers to less, interaction, form, and early: *less* refers to restricting access to suicide means; *interaction* with media to ensure responsible reporting; *form* means giving the young problem-solving, coping, and life skills; and *early* refers to early identification to provide support and care to people at risk of suicide. All these are required to reduce suicide rates successfully.

In the following, we select work done by the Centre of Suicide Research and Prevention (CSRP) at the University of Hong Kong to illustrate the different research studies and methods used under a public health approach to suicide prevention. The CSRP adopts a public health approach as an overarching framework to inform and develop suicide prevention programs and research. It acts as a multidisciplinary research hub to coordinate community stakeholders to tackle suicide at all levels. The following research examples illustrate the universal, selective, and indicated preventions; the four steps in a public health model; and the ingredients in LIVE LIFE as described above.

Research Examples from Hong Kong

Background

Hong Kong has a population of 7 million and has experienced one of the most rapid increases in suicide rate since 1997. That rate has increased from 12.0 per 100,000 in 1997 to a historical high of 18.8/100,000 in 2003. It then started to fall and leveled off at about 11.5/100,000 in 2018 (CSRP, 2019). The increase of more than 60 % in the 6-year period took everyone by surprise, and the community as a whole was not well prepared for it. Thus, the continual reduction of the suicide rate since 2003 has been encouraging. The CSRP has been promoting a public health approach to suicide prevention in Hong Kong and the region since 2002. It works closely with community partners and the government. Below are some examples of how the CSRP has utilized suicide research methods within a public health framework.

Improving the Monitoring and Surveillance System

CSRP has constructed a monitoring system to track suicide trends, using suicide data from the Coroner's Court, the Hong Kong Police Force, the Hospital Authority, and from media reports (Law et al., 2019). Any unnatural death has to be investigated by the Coroner's Court in Hong Kong, as is true in the UK. The Coroner's Court has provided the support to allow us to access the information in these investigations. We have also developed a number of methods to improve the estimation of suicide rate in a timely manner (Cui et al., 2004; Lin, Yip, & Huggins, 2008). Also a new method has been proposed based on newspaper reporting (Zeng, Chau, & Yip, 2019). Further, *geographic information system* analysis has been used to understand social determinants relating to suicide (Hsu, Chang, Lee, & Yip, 2015; Hsu, Chang, & Yip, 2017) and any suicide clusters (Lai et al., 2020). A robust monitoring and surveillance system using big data analytics enables us to have a better understanding of the trend of suicide risk and thus develop more effective interventions (Lai et al., 2020; Chai et al., 2020) (see Chapter 5 for further details regarding suicide and suicide attempt surveillance).

Restricting Access to Suicide Means

Restricting access to suicide means is a key suicide prevention strategy (WHO, 2018; Sinyor et al., 2019). Charcoal burning has become one of the major suicide methods in Hong Kong, with cases rising from 2 % of all suicides in 1998, to over 26 % in 2003. In 2006–2007, the CSRP conducted a 12-month exploratory controlled trial in Tuen Mun (intervention region) and Yuen Long (the control region) (Yip et al., 2010). Researchers enlisted the help of supermarkets to lock charcoal packs away from open shelves, so customers had to make purchase requests to the shop assistants. In this double-blind trial, the program was not publicly announced, and frontline staff members did not know about the experiment. The observed changes in the suicide rate between preintervention and postintervention in Tuen Mun (from 17.9 to 12.2 per 100,000) and Yuen Long (from 12.7 to 12.5 per 100,000) were minus 31.8 % and minus 1.6 %, respectively. The difference can be mainly attributed to the reduction in suicides by charcoal burning in Tuen Mun by 53.5 %. This gives evidential support to the key WHO suicide prevention strategy that reducing access to suicide means can reduce suicide (see Chapter 7 for more on intervention studies, Chapter 14 for evaluating suicide prevention approaches).

Using insights from research into charcoal burning suicides, in the face of the outbreak of helium suicides in Hong Kong in 2014, the CSRP proactively engaged stakeholders from multiple sectors, such as the fire services department, the police force, the hospital authority, and compressed gas sellers to restrict access to helium tanks by the public (Yip et al., 2017). Subsequently, the rate of helium suicide did not escalate to the high levels seen with charcoal-burning suicide. This suggests that it was worthwhile to scale up the intervention strategy to prevent new lethal means from spreading in the community. It is important to be able to do that at an early stage before it has become a home-grown method in the community. For the prevention of helium suicides, a concerted effort with the relevant authorities was important to implement the restriction of this lethal means effectively (Chang et al., 2016).

Advocating Responsible Media Coverage

Promoting responsible media coverage has been shown to be another useful method for suicide prevention. Using data from a case-control psychological autopsy (PA) study of 150 suicides, a study by CSRP showed a contagious and copycat effect of media reporting of suicide (Cheng & Yip, 2012). The reports of the PA cases from five major Hong Kong newspapers were reviewed to identify if there was a mismatch in terms of the cases' profile and risk factors. Using this method, it was found that accounts of risk factors were seldom accurate (< 46 %). It was also found that the local press in Hong Kong often oversimplified the suicide causes, with stereotypes. For example, in media reports, male suicides were said to be significantly associated with unemployment and unmanageable debt, but this was not identified in the coroner's reports for those suicide cases. (For more on case-control studies, see Chapter 6, and for the PA method, see Chapter 11.)

Another analysis showed that prominent reporting of celebrity suicide was found to significantly increase suicide rates in the short-term (Fu & Yip, 2009; Niederkrotenthaler et al., 2020). Fu and Yip (2009) employed an ecological retrospective time series analysis and a meta-analysis of suicide deaths in three Asian regions (Hong Kong, Taiwan, and South Korea). Elevated risks for suicide associated with excessive media coverage of celebrity suicide were found. The same-gender- and same-method-specific increases suggested that for people who identify more with the celebrity, their risk of suicide may increase. This suggests the need for targeted intervention toward preventing same-gender and same-method suicides following a celebrity suicide, and calls for media to understand the potential risk of reporting celebrity suicide and the need to comply with the WHO guidelines for suicide news reporting. (For more on ecological studies, see Chapter 6, and for meta-analysis, Chapter 13.)

With the evidence from this research, the CSRP actively engages with the media to promote responsible reporting. Research shows that such engagement strategies work (Cheng, Chen, Lee, & Yip, 2018). In response to a spate of student suicides in 2016, after the CSRP's engagement with the media, acute descriptive reporting with graphic and sensationalized descriptions in news reports of student suicides dropped sharply and has remained low since then. Preventive reporting, publishing preventive information such as on where to seek help or stories about people with similar experiences who found a way to cope, increased sharply in March and April 2016, and the higher intensity of preventive reporting was found to have a protective effect on student suicide.

Raising Mental Health Awareness Among Youths

The increase of suicide among young people is of rising concern both locally and globally, despite the reduction of overall suicide numbers. Equipping young people with coping and life skills is an important universal prevention strategy. The CSRP developed and implemented a universal, school-based pilot program for preventing depression among adolescents (Wong et al., 2012). Based on the cognitive behavior model, it aims to reduce depressive symptoms and increase students' knowledge of life skills such as goal setting, conflict resolution, and anger management. Using a quasiexperimental design, a study was carried out to examine the effectiveness of the program. The results indicated that students in the intervention group showed an improvement in help-seeking attitudes and self-esteem. Those who had more depressive symptoms showed heightened cognitive-restructuring skills and support-seeking behaviors. This research demonstrates the effectiveness of school-based prevention programs among youths.

These promising results prompted the CSRP to further expand and upscale the school-based program. A new digital game and school-based program that integrates a cognitive behavior approach and positive psychology was developed. An evaluation study based on a quasiexperimental design was carried out, with primary school student participants being assessed preintervention and postintervention, with a 6-month follow-up (Lai et al., 2016; Shum et al., 2019). Students' mental health knowledge, levels of anxiety symptoms, positive and negative thinking, perspective taking, and self-esteem were measured. The program was found to elevate the knowledge of mental health and promote perspective taking. The results did not indicate a reduction in anxiety symptoms or negative automatic thoughts. This suggests that while the program can have a helpful effect for student mental health, further intervention is needed to promote the translation of improved understanding to behavioral change. Thus, this sort of evaluation can help us understand whether a program can effect changes, as well as identifying room for improvements in designing and delivering the programs. The CSRP has been working closely with the Education Bureau of the Hong Kong SAR to monitor the suicidal risk in the school population.

Mobilizing Community Stakeholders to Prevent Suicide

Mobilizing different stakeholders is considered vital to prevent suicide. An evaluation study of a community-based suicide prevention program on Cheung Chau Island, once a visitor suicide hotspot, was carried out to evaluate the effectiveness of the program (Wong et al., 2009; Yip et al., 2010). A local multidisciplinary suicide prevention taskforce was formed in 2002, led by a member of the Cheung Chau Rural Committee who is an authoritative figure in the local community. Local mental health professionals, police officers, and managers and owners of holiday flats, as well as social workers were also part of the taskforce. An integrative program with activities designed as universal intervention (e.g., organizing psycho-educational workshops and developing communication networks among representatives of different sectors in the community), selective intervention (e.g., raising awareness of storekeepers and holiday flat owners to approach tenants proactively, especially those who behaved strangely), and indicated intervention (e.g., providing face-to-face and 24-hr hotline services for at-risk individuals). Examining the rates of both visitor and resident suicides and suicide attempts on Cheung Chau Island between the preimplementation period and the postimplementation period, it was found that the program was effective in reducing the number of visitor suicides from 37 deaths to 6. The program has proven to be a good practice model for a multidisciplinary taskforce and the application of a public health approach to provide interventions at the universal, selective, and indicated levels.

The evaluation of the effectiveness of this program has informed the development of a comprehensive suicide prevention strategy in the North District, another region in Hong Kong, with an aim to reduce the suicide cluster in the district. The program has also mobilized the collective strengths and resources of stakeholders, for community consensus building; facilitated a referral system for individuals at-risk; and raised mental health awareness in the district. To study this, trend analysis and Geographic Information System analysis were used to compare the suicide rates of the housing estate with six reported suicides within four months (study site) and three other housing estates (control sites) in the North District, both sites with similar socio-demographic profiles. A significant decreasing trend of suicide was found (from 8 cases in 2011 to 0 cases in 2015), and the suicide cluster has been reduced.

Evaluation using focus group interviews also helps identify stigmatization and attitudes of indifference as barriers to intervention. Six elements contributing to the positive results in the community-based intervention were identified in the evaluation: leadership, hierarchical support with clear lines of reporting, temporal and spatial monitoring system, multidisciplinary collaboration with a sense of ownership, structured and multilayered interventions, engagement of the stakeholders throughout the study period, and feedback as quality control and assurance (Lai et al., 2020).

Thus, evaluation research of community-based suicide prevention can provide evidence for the effectiveness of the program as well as identifying pointers for good practice. Lessons learned can inform future suicide prevention strategies in the community.

In sum, the research and intervention of the CSRP along with community stakeholders illustrate the importance of implementing suicide prevention activities at different levels and through multiple avenues. Research highlights areas in need of intervention. In particular, evaluation of suicide prevention programs using a myriad of research methods helps us understand what works and why, as well as to identity barriers to suicide prevention.

Conclusions

Suicide prevention requires a collective effort from all members of the community. A public health approach can help us conceptualize and design programs targeting universal, selective, and indicated interventions for the general public and to at-risk groups. It also helps to change the environment to enhance the protective factors against distress and suicide. Suicide research within a public health framework thus informs what needs to be done in suicide prevention with different target groups. This requires monitoring systems to identify the changing trends of suicide rates and patterns. Evaluation research is essential to evaluate the effectiveness of the programs so that preventive measures can have a more precise and effective impact. This helps us to jettison strategies that may not be useful and upscale those that are beneficial. Thus, research informed by a public health framework can help us envision and develop an overarching national strategy on suicide prevention, as recommended by WHO (2018).

The examples in Hong Kong are encouraging, and suicide prevention programs have been implemented effectively in the community there. Suicide prevention is possible, but there is no silver bullet. We need to understand the problem locally and work with stakeholders, making creative use of multiple methods to identify areas for prevention and to evaluate the impact of the intervention and sustain its effect.

References

Centre for Suicide Research and Prevention. (2019). *Suicide rate statistics.* Retrieved from https://csrp.hku.hk/statistics/

Chai, Y., Luo, H., Wong, G.H.Y., Tang, J.Y.S., Lam, T.-C., Wong, I., & Yip, P.S.F. (2020). Risk of self-harm after the diagnosis of psychiatric disorders: A nested case-control study in Hong Kong, 2000–2010. *Lancet Psychiatry*, *7*(2), 135–147. https://doi.org/10.1016/S2215-0366(20)30004-3

Chang, S.S., Cheng, Q., Lee, E.S., & Yip, P.S.F. (2016). Suicide by gassing in Hong Kong 2005–2013: Emerging trends and characteristics of suicide by helium inhalation. *Journal of Affective Disorders*, *192*, 162–166. https://doi.org/10.1016/j.jad.2015.12.026

Cheng, Q., Chen, F., Lee, E.S.T., & Yip, P.S.F. (2018). The role of media in preventing student suicides: A Hong Kong experience. *Journal of Affective Disorders, 227,* 643–648. https://doi.org/10.1016/j.jad.2017.11.007

Cheng, Q., & Yip, P.S.F. (2012). Suicide news reporting accuracy and stereotyping in Hong Kong. *Journal of Affective Disorders, 141*(2–3), 270–275. https://doi.org/10.1016/j.jad.2012.03.036

Cui, J.S., Yip, P.S., & Chau, P. (2004). Estimation of reporting delay and suicide incidence in Hong Kong. *Statistics in Medicine, 23*(3), 467–476. https://doi.org/10.1002/sim.1604

Fu, K.-W., & Yip, P.S.F. (2009). Estimating the risk of suicide following the suicide deaths of 3 Asian entertainment celebrities: A meta-analytic approach. *Journal of Clinical Psychiatry, 70*(6), 869. https://doi.org/10.4088/JCP.08m04240

Gertner, A.K., Rotter, J.S., & Shafer, P.R. (2019). Association between state minimum wages and suicide rates in the U.S. *American Journal of Preventive Medicine, 56*(5), 648–654. https://doi.org/10.1016/j.amepre.2018.12.008

Gordon, R. (1987). An operational classification of disease prevention. In J.A. Steinberg & M.M. Silverman (Eds.), *Preventing mental disorders: A research perspective* (pp. 20–26). Rockville, MD: Department of Health and Human Services.

Hsu, C.Y., Chang, S.S., Lee, E.S.T., & Yip, P.S.F. (2015). Geography of suicide in Hong Kong: Spatial patterning, and socioeconomic correlates and inequalities. *Social Science & Medicine, 130,* 190–203. https://doi.org/10.1016/j.socscimed.2015.02.019

Hsu, C., Chang, S., & Yip, P. (2017). Individual-, household- and neighbourhood-level characteristics associated with life satisfaction: A multilevel analysis of a population-based sample from Hong Kong. *Urban Studies*, *54*(16), 3700–3717.

Joiner, T. (1999). The clustering and contagion of suicide. *Current Directions in Psychological Science, 8*(3), 89–92. https://doi.org/10.1111/1467-8721.00021

Lai, C.C.S., Law, Y.W., Shum, A., Ip, F.W.L., & Yip, P.S.F. (2020). A community-based response to a suicide cluster: A Hong Kong experience. *Crisis, 41*(3), 163–171. https://doi.org/10.1027/0227-5910/a000616

Lai, E.S., Kwok, C.L., Wong, P.W., Fu, K.W., Law, Y.W., & Yip, P.S.F. (2016). The effectiveness and sustainability of a universal school-based programme for preventing depression in Chinese Adolescents: A follow-up study using quasi-experimental design. *PLOS One, 11*(2), e0149854. https://doi.org/10.1371/journal.pone.0149854

Law, Y.W., Yeung, T.L., Ip, F.W.L., & Yip, P.S.F. (2019). Evidence-based suicide prevention: Collective impact of engagement with community stakeholders. *Journal of Evidence-Informed Social Work, 16*(2), 1–17.

Lewis, G., Hawton, K., & Jones, P. (1997). Strategies for preventing suicide. *British Journal of Psychiatry, 171*, 351–354. https://doi.org/10.1192/bjp.171.4.351

Lin, H., Yip, P.S., & Huggins, R.M. (2008). A double-nonparametric procedure for estimating the number of delay-reported cases. *Statistics in Medicine, 27*(17), 3325–3339. https://doi.org/10.1002/sim.3183

Niederkrotenthaler, T., Braun, M., Pirkis, J., Till, B., Stack, S., Sinyor, M., ... Spittal, M.J. (2020). Association between suicide reporting and suicide: Systematic review and meta-analysis. *BMJ, 368*, m575.

Rose, G. (1992). *The strategy of preventive medicine.* Oxford, UK: Oxford University Press.

Shum, A.K.Y., Lai, E.S.Y., Leung, W.G., Cheng, M.N.S., Wong, H.K., So, S.W.K., ... Yip, P.S.F. (2019). A digital game and school-based intervention for students in Hong Kong: Quasi-experimental design. *Journal of Medical Internet Research, 21*(4), e12003. https://doi.org/10.2196/12003

Sinyor, M., Williams, M., Vincent, M., Schaffer, A., Yip, P.S.F., & Gunnell, D. (2019). Suicide deaths by gas inhalation in Toronto: An observational study of emerging methods of suicide. *Journal of Affective Disorders, 243*, 226–231. https://doi.org/10.1016/j.jad.2018.09.017

Wasserman, D. (2001). A stress-vulnerability model and the development of the suicidal process. In D. Wasserman (Ed.), *Suicide: An unnecessary death* (pp. 13–27). London, UK: Martin Dunitz.

Wong, P.W.C., Fu, K.W., Chan, K.Y.K., Chan, W.S.C., Liu, P.M.Y., Law, Y.W., & Yip, P.S.F. (2012). Effectiveness of a universal school-based programme for preventing depression in Chinese adolescents: A quasi-experimental pilot study. *Journal of Affective Disorders, 142*(1–3), 106–114 https://doi.org/10.1016/j.jad.2012.03.050

Wong, P.W.C., Liu, P.M.Y., Chan, W.S.C., Law, Y.W., Law, S.C.K., Fu, K.W., ... Yip, P.S.F. (2009). An integrative suicide prevention program for visitor charcoal burning suicide and suicide pact. *Suicide and Life-Threatening Behavior, 39*(1), 82–90. https://doi.org/10.1521/suli.2009.39.1.82

World Health Organization. (2014). *Preventing suicide: A global imperative.* Retrieved from https://apps.who.int/iris/handle/10665/131056

World Health Organization. (2018). *National suicide prevention strategies: Progress, examples and indicators.* Retrieved from https://apps.who.int/iris/handle/10665/279765

Yip, P.S.F. (2005). A public health approach to suicide prevention. *Hong Kong Journal of Psychiatry, 15*, 29–31.

Yip, P.S.F. (2011). Towards evidence-based suicide prevention programs. *Crisis, 32*(3), 117–120. https://doi.org/10.1027/0227-5910/a000100

Yip, P.S.F., Cheng, Q., Chang, S.-S., Lee, E.S.T., Lai, C.-S.C., Chen, F., ... Beh, P. (2017). A public health approach in responding to the spread of helium suicide in Hong Kong: A case report. *Crisis, 38*(4), 269–277. https://doi.org/10.1027/0227-5910/a000449

Yip, P.S.F., Law, C.K., Fu, K.W., Law, Y.W., Wong, P.W.C., & Xu, Y. (2010). Restricting the means of suicide by charcoal-burning. *British Journal of Psychiatry, 196*(3), 241–242. https://doi.org/10.1192/bjp.bp.109.065185

Yip, P.S.F., Liu, K.Y., & Law, C.K. (2008). Years of life lost from suicide in China, 1990–2000. *Crisis, 29*(3), 131–136. https://doi.org/10.1027/0227-5910.29.3.131

Zeng, X.Y., Chau, P.H., & Yip, P.S.F. (2019). Improving the monitoring of suicide incidence by estimating the probability of news reporting. *Statistics in Medicine, 38*(26), 5103–5112. https://doi.org/10.1002/sim.8353

Chapter 4

Ethical Aspects of Suicide Research

Karl Andriessen, Georgia Dempster, Karolina Krysinska, Eleanor Bailey, and Jo Robinson

Summary

Research is essential for advancing our understanding of suicidal behavior and its prevention, and to offer effective help to those at-risk. However, suicide research entails a range of ethical challenges, which have started to receive some attention. This chapter discusses challenges regarding conducting studies with suicidal people and those bereaved by suicide, and specific ethical concerns regarding suicide research in the context of online and social media environments. It reports on the experiences of researchers and research ethics committees regarding obtaining ethics approval for suicide studies, and provides practical recommendations regarding preparing and conducting suicide-related studies.

> *Because the privacy of my nightmare had been of my own designing, no one close to me had any real idea of the psychological company I had been keeping. The gap between private experience and its public expression was absolute; my persuasiveness to others was unimaginably frightening.*
>
> Kay Redfield Jamison, 1999

Suicide research is essential for advancing our understanding of suicidal behavior and its prevention, and to offer effective help to those at-risk. However, research in this field entails ethical challenges. For example, including potentially suicidal people in a study to investigate the efficacy of an intervention may seem essential from the point of view of researchers, who wish to find out if the intervention works for the population in need. Yet, anticipating that that research participation could cause undue distress and increase the risk of suicidal behavior in the participants, the research ethics committee may disagree (Hom, Podlogar, Stanley, & Joiner, 2017). Acknowledging that ethics committees and institutional review boards play the same role in reviewing ethics applications for research studies across countries, this chapter uses *research ethics committee* as a generic term. The chapter is organized into four sections dedicated to ethical issues in research with suicidal people, research with people bereaved by suicide, suicide research using the Internet and social media, and the experiences of researchers and research ethics committees regarding obtaining ethics approval for suicide studies.

Ethical Issues When Conducting Research With Potentially Suicidal People

International human research ethics guidelines emphasize the importance of the protection of human subjects. For example, the World Medical Association (2013) Declaration of Helsinki (in brief: the Declaration) states that "medical research is subject to ethical standards that promote and ensure respect for all human subjects and protect their health and rights" (principle no. 7; World Medical Association, 2013). Additionally, the Declaration states that "it is the duty of physicians who are involved in medical research to protect the life, health, dignity, integrity, right to self-determination, privacy, and confidentiality of personal information of research subjects" (principle no. 9; World Medical Association, 2013). Hence, it is recommended that practitioners, researchers, and research ethics committees carefully consider the risks versus benefits of research design and participation. A positive risk-benefit balance must exist with benefit to individual participants and to society outweighing the overall risks of undertaking the research (Emanuel, Wendler, & Grady, 2000).

There are, however, several ambiguities and dilemmas in the process of balancing the potential risks versus benefits of asking study participants about suicidal ideation or behavior. One ambiguity concerns the concepts of suicidal ideation and behavior. There is no internationally agreed upon set of terms or categories covering the variety of communications, thoughts, or behaviors that are associated with self-injury, ranging from nonsuicidal self-injury to fatal suicidal behavior with intent to die (Silverman & De Leo, 2016). Still, the Declaration states that research with a vulnerable group is only justified when the research is responsive to needs of that group, the research cannot be carried out with a nonvulnerable group, and the group will benefit from the research findings (principle no. 20; World Medical Association, 2013). Hence, without a consensus on the concepts of suicidal ideation and behavior, researchers and research ethics committees may hold different views on, or assessments of, suicide risk. Moreover, having a globally consistent set of terms and definitions would enable the aggregation of data across different studies around the world (see also Chapter 2 about definitions in suicide research). This is considered imperative for our understanding of suicidal behavior, because at a population level, suicide is a relatively rare event (Silverman & De Leo, 2016).

Further, there is a lack of knowledge about how to actually ask study participants about suicidal ideation or behavior (Berman & Silverman, 2017). Research has shown that if questions are framed in different ways, they will yield different answers. For example, Valtonen et al. (2009) examined the prevalence of suicidal ideation in 191 patients with bipolar disorder. The study applied three reliable instruments: the Scale for Suicide Ideation (Beck, Kovacs, & Weissman, 1979), the Beck Depression Inventory (Beck, Steer, & Garbin, 1988), and the Hamilton Rating Scale for Depression (Hamilton, 1986). Suicidal ideation was found in more than two thirds of participants (74 %) on at least one scale, but in less than one third (29 %) on all three scales (Valtonen et al., 2009). The study showed that the determination of suicide risk might vary according to the definition and measures used (Valtonen et al., 2009).

Whether to ask participants about suicidal ideation is an important ethical consideration in the research design. A recent meta-analysis of 18 studies from the peer-reviewed and unpublished literature from 2000 to 2017 concluded that asking study participants suicide-related questions led to small, yet significant reductions in suicidal ideation and a decreased probability of engaging in suicidal behavior, compared with study participants who had not received such questions (Blades, Stritzke, Page, & Brown, 2018). Crawford et al. (2011) conducted a trial with depressed patients to assess whether being screened for suicidal ideation had a short-term impact on participants' thoughts about suicide. The study concluded that screening for suicidal ideation in primary care among participants with depressive symptoms did not induce suicidal feelings (Crawford et al., 2011). Still, despite this evidence, not all clinicians or patients support such assessment of suicidal behavior. A study of general practitioners and their patients in the UK showed that while most primary care doctors and patients supported the assessment of suicidal behavior, a minority felt uncomfortable with it

(Bajaj et al., 2008). However, given that many suicidal patients have contact with a primary care physician in the period before their suicide, primary care constitutes an important setting for research of assessment of suicidal behavior (Luoma, Martin, & Pearson, 2002). Hence, overly cautious research based on an assumption that suicide assessment will make participants more likely to experience suicidal thoughts or behavior might obstruct necessary research in this field (Blades et al., 2018).

Outside the sphere of mental health research, population-level clinical research provides an opportunity for participant suicide screening and referral to support services. Given the large populations in some epidemiological studies, such screening can provide the opportunity for suicide prevention interventions (Hom et al., 2017). Additionally, from an ethical perspective, not being able to manage the answers from study participants, indicating that they might be at-risk of suicide, is an insufficient reason to avoid asking the important questions. Not asking a participant does not remove the risk that they might engage in suicidal behavior and does not dismiss the researchers from their duty of care for participants (Michaels, Chu, Silva, Schulman, & Joiner, 2015). In a study investigating the opinions of patients about screening for suicide risk in an adult medical inpatient unit, most participants (81%) supported screening. The study also highlighted that patient opinions are a useful method to inform considered implementation of suicide risk screening in hospital settings (Snyder et al., 2017).

Ethical Issues When Conducting Research With People Bereaved by Suicide

Experiencing a death by suicide can have a devastating and lasting impact on the bereaved individuals, increasing their risk of mental health problems and suicidal behavior. Some of the bereaved may feel that the suicide loss has changed their lives (Grad & Andriessen, 2016). Still, many bereaved people go through a grief process, with varying levels of intrapsychic work and social and/or professional support, which enables them to cope, make sense, and create new meanings after the loss (Neimeyer & Sands, 2017). In addition, a need to vent and to share grief experiences, a desire to gain insight to better understand the suicide, and willingness to help others may motivate people bereaved by suicide to participate in research studies (Dyregrov et al., 2011b).

Despite the accumulating evidence regarding the positive experience of participation in postvention studies, and the lack of short-term and long-term negative effects (Dyregrov et al., 2011a; Hawton, Houston, Malmbergand, & Simkin, 2003; Henry & Greenfield, 2009; Wong et al., 2010), research ethics committees have raised concerns regarding potential harm to bereaved research participants (Moore, Maple, Mitchell, & Cerel, 2013; Omerov, Steineck, Dyregrov, Runeson, & Nyberg, 2014; Omerov, Titelman, & Nyberg, 2018). These concerns include an assumption that talking about the grief experience will traumatize and increase the suicide risk of the bereaved, and uncertainty that research participants will receive sufficient support. Research ethics committees have also raised issues regarding the recruitment process, ensuring confidentiality and data security, and a potential for coercion related to self-identification as a suicide survivor (Moore et al., 2013). Several studies have explored experiences of people bereaved by suicide, who participate in research studies (Andriessen, Krysinska, Draper, Dudley, & Mitchell, 2018), and their findings, summarized in the following paragraphs, can inform researchers, members of research ethics committees, and people bereaved by suicide who wish to participate in such studies.

Most bereaved participants reported a positive or a neutral experience of research participation, did not regret their decision to take part, and/or would recommend involvement in studies to other bereaved people (Dyregrov, 2004; Omerov et al., 2014; Wong et al., 2010). Moreover, the positive evaluation of research participation can be maintained for up to 10 years after the study (Saarinen et al., 2000). A sense of altruism, social support, and personal growth contributed to these positive experiences (Dyregrov et al., 2011a; Henry & Greenfield, 2009; Kizza et al., 2011). Research participation can also provide an opportunity to obtain professional help (Beskow et al., 1991; Cooper, 1999; Omerov et al., 2014; Saarinen et al., 2000) or resources (Hawton et al., 2003; Kizza et al., 2011).

Although most bereaved individuals have either a positive or a neutral reaction to being approached to participate in a study, some may have a negative reaction or object to contact (Cooper, 1999; Hawton et al., 2003; Runeson & Beskow, 1991; Wong et al., 2010). Also, a minority reported having a negative or distressing experience as a research participant, due to feelings of guilt, sadness, depression, self-reproach, and anger, as well as reactivation of painful or negative memories (Hawton et al., 2003; Henry & Greenfield, 2009; Kizza et al., 2011; Wong et al., 2010). Some participants regretted having exposed themselves and/or the deceased, or they had complaints about the study methodology (Åsgård & Carlsson-Bergström, 1991; Dyregrov, 2004; Omerov et al., 2014). Nonetheless, a distressing or painful experience does not necessarily preclude an overall positive evaluation of research participation. Remembering the past may be upsetting, but it may also help to achieve insight and support the meaning-making process (Cooper, 1999; Dyregrov et al., 2011a; Newman & Kaloupek, 2004).

Studies have yielded inconclusive results regarding the factors that mediate how the bereaved experience research participation. Nonetheless, sociodemographic factors, such as gender, age of the deceased and the research participant, type of relationship to the deceased, the method of suicide, time between the death and the interview, and having received counseling in the past, can affect the experience (Dyregrov et al., 2011a; Hawton et al., 2003). Other participant-related features, such as psychiatric problems, history of trauma and adverse life events, personality traits (such as neuroticism), and low social support, may affect the vulnerability of some research participants (Jorm et al., 2007). No studies to date have explored the impact of interviewer-related variables, such as age, gender, education, and professional biases (Pouliot & De Leo, 2006).

Further research would help to clarify factors and mechanisms related to participation versus nonparticipation in suicide bereavement research, and the likelihood of a positive or a negative research experience. Although the risk of lasting negative effects appears to be low, it is essential to provide optimum care to all participants, including providing alternatives to participation, and ensuring the availability of support information and resources during and after a study. Box 4.1 provides an overview of recommendations for researchers when conducting research with people bereaved by suicide.

Box 4.1. Practical recommendations for researchers

- Researchers must provide accurate information about the content and the methodology of the study, its potential risks and benefits, and the voluntary nature of participation. Alternatives to research participation, such as information and support resources, should be provided.
- Researchers should establish a relationship based on trust and understanding, and they should conduct interviews with empathy, care, and respect for the emotional boundaries of

the interviewee. Researchers may not force the participant to explore areas that are painful or troublesome.

- It is crucial to respect the balance between what the interviewees gain (e.g., an opportunity to share painful experiences with a professional) and what they give (e.g., helping the researchers).
- Involvement of the target group in designing research and piloting the study methods (e.g., an interview), may contribute to the acceptability of the study method and content.
- Focusing the interviews on selected topics rather than conducting broad-scale interviews, may limit the practical and emotional burden on participants.
- Participants in acute distress should not be recruited. Those most vulnerable and with higher psychological morbidity might decline participation to avoid additional stress. This underlines the importance of providing accurate information to potential participants.
- Researchers need to consider differences in the psychosocial costs and impact of different methods of data collection. For example, an interview or a writing task may be more psychologically demanding than a paper-and-pencil or a Web-based instrument.

Ethical Issues Regarding Suicide Research Using the Internet and Social Media

In recent years there has been a proliferation of use of the Internet and social media for the detection, prevention, and treatment of mental health problems and suicidal behavior. The Internet may offer advantages over face-to-face methods of research and clinical practice, including wide reach, cost-effectiveness, and ability to combat stigma-related issues (i.e., through enabling anonymous participation; Marchant et al., 2017; Robinson et al., 2015). However, the use of the Internet and social media introduces unique ethical issues regarding the usage of publicly available data posted on social networking sites, and trialing Internet-based interventions for people who are, or have been, suicidal.

Data publicly available on social networking sites, such as Twitter, have in recent years been analyzed using techniques such as *natural language processing* and *machine learning* to assess the prevalence of mental health problems and suicidal ideation, and attempt to predict who might be at-risk (Coppersmith, Leary, Crutchley, & Fine, 2018). Similarly, studies have used qualitative techniques, such as thematic or content analysis, to examine posts published in online environments, for example, to better understand suicide-related discourse (e.g., Niederkrotenthaler et al., 2016). Key ethical issues in such research concern consent (i.e., does the posting of information to a social media site imply consent for that information to be used in research?), users' expectations of their privacy and use of their data, and adequacy of strategies applied by researchers to anonymize data prior to publication (Conway & O'Connor, 2016; Coppersmith et al., 2018; Moreno, Goniu, Moreno, & Diekema, 2013; Zimmer 2010).

Where such data may be used to predict suicide risk at an individual level and allow for intervention with users who are believed to be at immediate risk, there exists a "trade-off between privacy and prevention" – that is, a need to balance protection of users' privacy against the potentially life-saving benefits of such technology (Coppersmith et al., 2018, p. 7). Further, on a broader level, a dilemma exists between maintaining high ethical standards – for example, regarding obtaining informed consent for any use of an individual's data – while still being able to capitalize on the availability of rich, large (publicly available) datasets for research purposes; in particular, when is hoped that the research will ultimately lead to improved outcomes in mental health and suicidal behavior.

Research suggests that social media users are, for the most part, aware of the public and permanent nature of content posted online, and they believe that consumers are responsible for protecting their own data – for example, via privacy settings or self-censorship (Mikal, Hurst & Conway, 2016). Some social media users, however, may be less likely to protect their data and may unknowingly imply consent to research, perhaps due to a lack awareness of the implications of this (e.g., due to sociodemographic factors, such as age or education level; Mikal et al., 2016). This may also be true for other subgroups of the population who at times have a limited capacity to provide informed consent, such as people with severe mental health problems (Van Staden & Krüger, 2003) or children and adolescents (Kuther & Posada, 2004). It is therefore imperative that researchers be aware of the potential personal implications of publishing data collected via social media, and exercise sensitivity in drawing conclusions about mental health and suicide risk which have the capacity to have an impact at both an individual and population level (Conway & O'Connor, 2016).

Use of publicly available social media data for research is not exempt from the requirement for ethical review – at least, not in Australia (National Health and Medical Research Council, 2018) – although in most cases, it would be considered low-risk research. Researchers planning to use such data must therefore submit applications to their governing research ethics committee before proceeding. Finally, some authors (e.g., Flick 2016) have argued for social media sites themselves to introduce informed consent processes, which users must agree to before their data are used in any research affiliated with the social media company.

In addition to the concerns regarding using publicly available social media data, there are also unique ethical issues concerning the delivery and evaluation of Internet-based interventions for suicidal people. Arguably the most significant of these relate to (a) risk management, given the difficulty associated with assessing and responding to suicide risk from a distance; and (b) duty of care, particularly where online interventions allow participants to communicate with the research team outside of normal working hours. These issues have long been documented to occur in the provision of online therapy in clinical settings (e.g., Fitzgerald et al., 2010), and an emerging evidence base suggests they are also true, if not more complex, for research settings (e.g., Cosgrove et al., 2017).

The ethical concerns, such as the risk of normalization or contagion of suicidal behavior, may be heightened when online interventions are based on social media, rather than static websites (Robinson et al., 2015; Bailey et al., 2018). Ethical issues may also arise if researchers, during their studies, either deliberately or accidentally access the social media profiles of participants. This has been documented to occur in clinical practice (Lehavot, Ben-Zeev, & Neville, 2012) in research projects unrelated to suicide prevention (Young & Garett, 2018), and has been known anecdotally to occur in research by members of the author group of a study specifically related to suicide prevention (Robinson et al., 2017). It is therefore recommended that researchers, in designing study protocols, specify restrictions regarding accessing participants' social media profiles. Where this may be unavoidable, protocols should clearly stipulate if and how any risk will be responded to.

Bailey and colleagues (2020) surveyed international researchers in the field of Internet-based interventions for suicide prevention. Although there were similar ethical and practical concerns in the studies of online and offline interventions for people at-risk of suicide, some key differences were apparent. In particular, respondents highlighted the difficulty to adequately assess and manage suicide risk in an online environment. These difficulties were addressed by the implementation of comprehensive safety protocols which required participants and/or their treating medical or mental health professional to be contacted in case of an emergency. Some respondents had also excluded acutely suicidal participants or those with severe mental health problems, such as psychosis. In discussing the impact of these measures on their research, respondents reported that the requirement for contact information to be provided as part of the safety procedures precluded some individuals, who would have been prepared to participate anonymously, from taking part. Given anonymity is one of the established benefits of online treatment, researchers felt their samples did not represent those who would typically use online interventions. Additionally, where high-risk participants were excluded from studies, respondents noted that this presented the ethical challenge of potentially precluding those who are arguably most vulnerable from receiving much-needed support. This could lead to key gaps in knowledge regarding what works for those at the higher end of the suicidality spectrum, a concern shared with research involving face-to-face interventions (Hom et al., 2017).

Experiences of Researchers and Research Ethics Committees in Obtaining Ethics Approval for Suicide Studies

Two recent studies surveyed Australian and international researchers regarding their experiences with obtaining ethical approval for suicide studies (Andriessen et al., 2019a, 2019b). Most respondents in both surveys had received requests from their research ethics committee to make minor revisions to their original study application prior to approval, and many had also received requests for major revisions. The Australian sample was less likely than the international sample to have submitted applications that returned no revisions (12 % vs. 50 %), and about 10 % of the Australian sample had been denied ethical approval, while no respondents in the international sample reported this. Researchers in both studies reported that the ethics committees raised similar concerns, with the key concerns relating to potential harm to participants (i.e., in terms of increasing distress or suicidality via participation in research) and appropriate management of any distress or suicide risk. Other concerns raised by the committees included issues regarding sensitively accessing the study population, the capacity of participants to consent to research, clarification of the study design and/or outcome measures, and safe storage of data. These findings were in line with those of similar previous research (Lakeman & Fitzgerald, 2009a).

To address concerns raised by the research ethics committees, most researchers made modifications to the study design and/or ethics application (Andriessen et al., 2019a, 2019b). Modifications included clarifying procedures, amending materials, increasing the amount of support provided to participants, and changing the recruitment strategy or inclusion criteria. Many respondents in both studies reported that they consulted with their research ethics committee to better understand the issues raised and reach a consensus on how to proceed, although some noted that this was time-consuming. Some researchers reported that they provided evidence from the literature – for example, to show that asking about suicide does not induce suicidal ideation (Blades et al., 2018).

Half or more of the respondents in both studies reported that responding to the concerns of the research ethics committee ultimately had a positive impact on their research, whereas one-in-five and one-in-four researchers in the Australian and international studies, respectively, reported a negative impact (Andriessen et al., 2019a, 2019b). Positive impacts were related to clarification of study procedures, increasing the confidence of the study team (e.g., regarding monitoring and managing risk), and gaining experience to help with future ethics applications. Negative impacts were mostly attributed to delays to the study and limitations on study design. Finally, respondents in both studies formulated recommendations to other researchers which included anticipating potential concerns ahead of time and establishing a collaborative relationship with research ethics committees.

To our knowledge, only one study consulted directly with research ethics committee members regarding their views on research with participants who are (or have been) suicidal. Lakeman and Fitzgerald (2009b) surveyed 125 members of research ethics committees from five countries (Australia, Canada, the UK, New Zealand, and Ireland). Ethical concerns raised included weighing the benefits of research participation against the potential risks posed to a vulnerable population (as discussed in previous paragraphs), the ability of researchers to access the population of suicidal participants in an appropriate and sensitive manner, the potential for harm to participants (particularly whether research participation might induce or trigger suicidal ideation), ensuring adequate supports are available to participants, duty of care of the research team, and whether participants are competent to consent to research. Other issues raised, albeit less commonly, included researchers' competency to manage sensitive situations, maintaining participant confidentiality, and dealing with the families of participants. Research ethics committee members were also asked to formulate advice to researchers. They recommended consultations with multiple parties (including research ethics committees, other experienced researchers, and potential participants) in designing research, justifying all methodology and procedures, and ensuring that adequate support is available to participants and researchers alike (Lakeman & Fitzgerald, 2009b). Box 4.2 summarizes the main recommendations to researchers submitting suicide-related ethics applications.

Box 4.2. Recommendations for researchers preparing suicide-related ethics applications

- Anticipate possible concerns by being clear in the descriptions of the study aims and design, the potential risks to participants, and the procedures to manage those risks.
- Provide evidence, such as from the literature, that suicide research can be conducted in a safe way.
- Provide justifications from research ethics guidelines.
- Learn how your research ethics committee works, establish a collaborative relationship, and consult with other researchers.
- Include enough time in the study design to go through the ethics approval procedure.

Notably, while ethics committee members in the study by Lakeman and Fitzgerald (2009b) were concerned with the impact on the well-being of the researchers, this was not raised by the researchers who participated in the parallel study (Lakeman & Fitzgerald 2009a). In addition, impact on researchers was not a major concern reported in more recent studies (Andriessen et al., 2019a, 2019b). Little research has examined if and how suicide prevention researchers are emotionally impacted by their research, and the subsequent impact of this, if any, on their work. Mckenzie et al. (2017) conducted qualitative interviews with non-clinically trained research assistants who worked with emergency department data as part of a suicide prevention trial. The study concluded that these research assistants were at risk of secondary trauma, and should be provided with adequate training, supervision, and support.

In another study, Boden and colleagues (2016) discussed their own experiences of conducting qualitative research into the experience of suicide. They considered attendance to the emotional reactions of researchers vital in protecting their own well-being, managing ethical issues that arose, and in ensuring objective data collection and interpretation (Boden et al., 2016). Overall, suicide prevention researchers can be affected and at-risk of poor mental health outcomes because of their work, and further research in this field might be needed.

Conclusions

Major ethical challenges are inherent in suicide prevention research, especially regarding the inclusion of suicidal people or people considered at-risk of suicidal behavior, such as bereaved individuals, as research participants. Still, researchers and research ethics committees share a common goal of conducting ethically sound and safe research to the benefit of humankind. Research findings suggest that a collaborative relationship between researchers and research ethics committees should ensure that suicide prevention research is conducted to the highest standards. This also holds true for new ethical challenges that appear in the context of online and social media research, especially regarding the usage of publicly available data harvested from social networking sites, and trialing Internet-based interventions for people at-risk of suicidal behavior.

References

Andriessen, K., Krysinska, K., Draper, B., Dudley, M., & Mitchell, P. B. (2018). Harmful or helpful? A systematic review of how those bereaved through suicide experience research participation. *Crisis, 39*(5), 364–376. https://doi.org/10.1027/0227-5910/a000515

Andriessen, K., Reifels, L., Krysinska, K., Robinson, J., Dempster, G., & Pirkis, J. (2019a). Ethical concerns in suicide research: Results of an international researcher survey. *Journal of Empirical Research on Human Research Ethics, 14*(4), 383–394. https://doi.org/10.1177/1556264619859734

Andriessen, K., Reifels, L., Krysinska, K., Robinson, J., Dempster, G., & Pirkis, J. (2019b). Dealing with ethical concerns in suicide research: A survey of Australian researchers. *International Journal of Environmental Research and Public Health, 16*(7), 1094. https://doi.org/10.3390/ijerph16071094

Åsgård, U., & Carlsson-Bergström, M. (1991). Interviews with survivors of suicides: Procedures and follow-up of interview subjects. *Crisis, 12*(1), 21–33.

Bailey, E., Rice, S., Robinson, J., Nedeljkovic, M., & Alvarez-Jimenez, M. (2018). Theoretical and empirical foundations of a novel online social networking intervention for youth suicide prevention: A conceptual review. *Journal of Affective Disorders, 238,* 499–505. https://doi.org/10.1016/j.jad.2018.06.028

Bailey, E., Mühlmann, C., Rice, S., Nedeljkovic, M., Alvarez-Jimenez, M., Sander, L., ... Robinson, J. (2020). Ethical issues and practical barriers in internet-based suicide prevention research: A review and investigator survey. *BMC Medical Ethics, 21,* 1–16. https://doi.org/10.1186/s12910-020-00479-1

Bajaj, P., Borreani, E., Ghosh, P., Methuen, C., Patel, M., & Joseph, M. (2008). Screening for suicidal thoughts in primary care: The views of patients and general practitioners. *Mental Health in Family Medicine, 5*(4), 229–235.

Beck, A. T., Kovacs, M., & Weissman, A. (1979). Assessment of suicidal intention: The Scale for Suicide Ideation. *Journal of Consulting and Clinical Psychology, 47*(2), 343–352. https://doi.org/10.1037/0022-006X.47.2.343

Beck, A. T., Steer, R. A., & Garbin, M. G. (1988). Psychometric properties of the Beck Depression Inventory: Twenty-five years of evaluation. *Clinical Psychology Review, 8*(1), 77–100. https://doi.org/10.1016/0272-7358(88)90050-5

Berman, A. L., & Silverman, M. M. (2017). How to ask about suicide? A question in need of an empirical answer. *Crisis, 38*(4), 213–216. https://doi.org/10.1027/0227-5910/a000501

Beskow, J., Runeson, B., & Åsgård, U. (1991). Ethical aspects of psychological autopsy. *Acta Psychiatrica Scandinavica, 84*(5), 482–487. https://doi.org/10.1111/j.1600-0447.1991.tb03181.x

Blades, C. A., Stritzke, W. G. K., Page, A. C., & Brown, J. D. (2018). The benefits and risks of asking research participants about suicide: A meta-analysis of the impact of exposure to suicide-related content. *Clinical Psychology Review, 64,* 1–12. https://doi.org/10.1016/j.cpr.2018.07.001

Boden, Z. V., Gibson, S., Owen, G. J., & Benson, O. (2016). Feelings and intersubjectivity in qualitative suicide research. *Qualitative Health Research, 26*(8), 1078–1090. https://doi.org/10.1177/1049732315576709

Conway, M., & O'Connor, D. (2016). Social media, big data, and mental health: Current advances and ethical implications. *Current Opinion in Psychology, 9,* 77–82. https://doi.org/10.1016/j.copsyc.2016.01.004

Cooper, J. (1999). Ethical issues and their practical application in a psychological autopsy study of suicide. *Journal of Clinical Nursing, 8*(4), 467–475. https://doi.org/10.1046/j.1365-2702.1999.00276.x

Coppersmith, G., Leary, R., Crutchley, P., & Fine, A. (2018). Natural language processing of social media as screening for suicide risk. *Biomedical Informatics Insights, 10.* https://doi.org/10.1177/1178222618792860

Cosgrove, V., Gliddon, E., Berk, L., Grimm, D., Lauder, S., Dodd, S., ... Suppes, T. (2017). Online ethics: Where will the interface of mental health and the internet lead us? *International Journal of Bipolar Disorders, 5*(1), 26. https://doi.org/10.1186/s40345-017-0095-3

Crawford, M. J., Thana, L., Methuen, C., Ghosh, P., Stanley, S. V., Ross, J., ... Bajaj, P. (2011). Impact of screening for risk of suicide: Randomised controlled trial. *British Journal of Psychiatry, 198*(5), 379–384. https://doi.org/10.1192/bjp.bp.110.083592

Dyregrov, K. (2004). Bereaved parents' experience of research participation. *Social Science and Medicine, 58*(2), 391–400. https://doi.org/10.1016/S0277-9536(03)00205-3

Dyregrov, K. M., Dieserud, G., Hjelmeland, H. M., Straiton, M., Rasmussen, M. L., Knizek, B. L., & Leenaars, A. A. (2011a). Meaning-making through psychological autopsy interviews: The value of participating in qualitative research for those bereaved by suicide. *Death Studies, 35*(8), 685–710. https://doi.org/10.1080/07481187.2011.553310

Dyregrov, K., Dieserud, G., Straiton, M., Rasmussen, M. L., Hjelmeland, H., Knizek, B. L., & Leenaars, A. A. (2011b). Motivation for research participation among people bereaved by suicide. *Omega: Journal of Death and Dying, 62*(2), 149–168. https://doi.org/10.2190/OM.62.2.d

Emanuel, E. J., Wendler, D., & Grady, C. (2000). What makes clinical research ethical? *Journal of the American Medical Association, 283*(20), 2701–2711. https://doi.org/10.1001/jama.283.20.2701

Fitzgerald, T. D., Hunter, P. V., Hadjistavropoulos, T., & Koocher, G. P. (2010). Ethical and legal considerations for internet-based psychotherapy. *Cognitive Behavior Therapy, 39*(3), 173–187. https://doi.org/10.1080/16506071003636046

Flick, C. (2016). Informed consent and the Facebook emotional manipulation study. *Research Ethics, 12*(1), 14–28. https://doi.org/10.1177/1747016115599568

Grad, O., & Andriessen, K. (2016). Surviving the legacy of suicide. In R. O'Connor & J. Pirkis (Eds.), *International handbook of suicide prevention* (2nd ed., pp. 663–680). Chichester, UK: Wiley-Blackwell. https://doi.org/10.1002/9781118903223.ch37

Hamilton, M. (1986). The Hamilton Rating Scale for Depression. In N. Sartorius & T. A. Ban (Eds.), *Assessment of depression.* Berlin, Heidelberg: Springer. https://doi.org/10.1007/978-3-642-70486-4_14

Hawton, K., Houston, K., Malmbergand, A., & Simkin, S. (2003). Psychological autopsy interviews in suicide research: The reactions of informants. *Archives of Suicide Research, 7*(1), 73–82. https://doi.org/10.1080/13811110301566

Henry, M., & Greenfield, B. J. (2009). Therapeutic effects of psychological autopsies: The impact of investigating suicides on interviewees. *Crisis, 30*(1), 20–24. https://doi.org/10.1027/0227-5910.30.1.20

Hom, M. A., Podlogar, M. C., Stanley, I. H., & Joiner, T. E., Jr. (2017). Ethical issues and practical challenges in suicide research. *Crisis, 38*(2), 107–114. https://doi.org/10.1027/0227-5910/a000415

Jorm, A. F., Kelly, C. M., & Morgan, A. J. (2007). Participant distress in psychiatric research: A systematic review. *Psychological Medicine, 37*(7), 917–926. https://doi.org/10.1017/S0033291706009779

Kizza, D., Hjelmeland, H., Kinyanda, E., & Knizek, B. L. (2011). Qualitative psychological autopsy interviews on suicide in post-conflict Northern Uganda: The participants' perceptions. *Omega: Journal of Death and Dying, 63*(3), 235–254. https://doi.org/10.2190/OM.63.3.c

Kuther, T.L., & Posada, M. (2004). Children and adolescents' capacity to provide informed consent for participation in research. *Advances in Psychology Research, 32,* 163–173.

Lakeman, R., & Fitzgerald, M. (2009a). Ethical suicide research: A survey of researchers. *International Journal of Mental Health Nursing, 18*(1), 10–17. https://doi.org/10.1111/j.1447-0349.2008.00569.x

Lakeman, R., & Fitzgerald, M. (2009b). The ethics of suicide research: The views of ethics committee members. *Crisis, 30*(1), 13–19. https://doi.org/10.1027/0227-5910.30.1.13

Lehavot, K., Ben-Zeev, D., & Neville, R.E. (2012). Ethical considerations and social media: A case of suicidal postings on Facebook. *Journal of Dual Diagnosis, 8,* 341–346. https://doi.org/10.1080/15504263.2012.718928

Luoma, J.B., Martin, C.E., & Pearson, J.L. (2002). Contact with mental health and primary care providers before suicide: A review of the evidence. *American Journal of Psychiatry, 159,* 909–916. https://doi.org/10.1176/appi.ajp.159.6.909

Marchant, A., Hawton, K., Stewart, A., Montgomery, P., Singaravelu, V., Lloyd, K., ... John, A. (2017). A systematic review of the relationship between internet use, self-harm and suicidal behavior in young people: The good, the bad and the unknown. *PLoS One, 12*(8), e0181722. https://doi.org/10.1371/journal.pone.0181722

Mckenzie, S.K., Li, C., Jenkin, G., & Collings, S. (2017). Ethical considerations in sensitive suicide research reliant on non-clinical researchers. *Research Ethics, 13*(3–4), 173–183. https://doi.org/10.1177/1747016116649996

Michaels, M.S., Chu, C., Silva, C., Schulman, B.E., & Joiner, T. (2015). Considerations regarding online methods for suicide-related research and suicide risk assessment. *Suicide and Life-Threatening Behavior, 45*(1), 10–17. https://doi.org/10.1111/sltb.12105

Mikal, J., Hurst, S., & Conway, M. (2016). Ethical issues in using Twitter for population-level depression monitoring: A qualitative study. *BMC Medical Ethics, 17*(1), 22. https://doi.org/10.1186/s12910-016-0105-5

Moore, M., Maple, M., Mitchell, A.M., & Cerel, J. (2013). Challenges and opportunities for suicide bereavement research. *Crisis, 34*(5), 297–304. https://doi.org/10.1027/0227-5910/a000191

Moreno, M.A., Goniu, N., Moreno, P.S., & Diekema, D. (2013). Ethics of social media research: Common concerns and practical considerations. *Cyberpsychology, Behavior, and Social Networking, 16*(9), 708–713. https://doi.org/10.1089/cyber.2012.0334

National Health and Medical Research Council. (2018). *The National Statement on Ethical Conduct in Human Research 2007, updated 2018.* Retrieved from https://www.nhmrc.gov.au/about-us/publications/national-statement-ethical-conduct-human-research-2007-updated-2018.

Neimeyer, R., & Sands, D. (2017). Suicide loss and the quest for meaning. In K. Andriessen, K. Krysinska & O. Grad (Eds.), *Postvention in action: The international handbook of suicide bereavement support* (pp. 71–84). Göttingen, Germany: Hogrefe Publishing.

Newman, E., & Kaloupek, D.G. (2004). The risks and benefits of participating in trauma-focused research studies. *Journal of Traumatic Stress, 17*(5), 383–394. https://doi.org/10.1023/B:JOTS.0000048951.02568.3a

Niederkrotenthaler, T., Gould, M., Sonneck, G., Stack, S., & Till, B. (2016). Predictors of psychological improvement on non-professional suicide message boards: Content analysis. *Psychological Medicine, 45*(16), 3429–3442. https://doi.org/10.1017/S003329171600221X

Omerov, P., Steineck, G., Dyregrov, K., Runeson, B., & Nyberg, U. (2014). The ethics of doing nothing. Suicide-bereavement and research: Ethical and methodological considerations. *Psychological Medicine, 44*(16), 3409–3420. https://doi.org/10.1017/S0033291713001670

Omerov, P., Titelman, D., & Nyberg, U. (2018). *Population-based surveys that include suicide-bereaved family members: Ethical and methodological considerations.* Thousand Oaks, CA: SAGE. https://doi.org/10.4135/9781526455918

Pouliot, L., & De Leo, D. (2006). Critical issues in psychological autopsy studies. *Suicide and Life-Threatening Behavior, 36,* 491–510. https://doi.org/10.1521/suli.2006.36.5.491

Redfield Jamison, K. (1999). *Night falls fast: Understanding suicide.* New York, NY: Alfred A. Knopf/Random House.

Robinson, J., Bailey, E., Hetrick, S., Paix, S., O'Donnell, M., Cox, G., ... Skehan, J. (2017). Developing social media-based suicide prevention messages in partnership with young people: Exploratory study. *JMIR Mental Health, 4*(4), e40. https://doi.org/10.2196/mental.7847

Robinson, J., Cox, G., Bailey, E., Hetrick, S., Rodrigues, M., Fisher, S., & Herrman, H. (2015). Social media and suicide prevention: A systematic review. *Early Intervention in Psychiatry, 10*(2), 103–121. https://doi.org/10.1111/eip.12229

Runeson, B., & Beskow, J. (1991). Reactions of survivors of suicide victims to interviews. *Acta Psychiatrica Scandinavica, 83*(3), 169–173. https://doi.org/10.1111/j.1600-0447.1991.tb05518.x

Saarinen, P.I., Hintikka, J., Vnamäki, H., Lehtonen, J., & Lönqvist, J. (2000). Is it possible to adapt to the suicide of a close individual? Results of a 10-year prospective follow-up study. *International Journal of Social Psychiatry, 46*(3), 182–190. https://doi.org/10.1177/002076400004600304

Silverman, M.M., & De Leo, D. (2016). Why there is a need for an international nomenclature and classification system for suicide. *Crisis, 37*(2), 83–87. https://doi.org/10.1027/0227-5910/a000419

Snyder, D.J., Ballard, E.D., Stanley, I.H., Ludi, E., Kohn-Godbout, J., & Horowitz, L.M. (2017). Patient opinions about screening for suicide risk in the adult medical inpatient unit. *Journal of Behavioral Health Services & Research, 44*(3), 364–372. https://doi.org/10.1007/s11414-016-9498-7

Valtonen, H.M., Suominen, K., Sokero, P., Mantere, O., Arvilommi, P., Leppamaki, S., & Isometsa, E.T. (2009). How suicidal bipolar patients are depends on how suicidal ideation is defined. *Journal of Affective Disorders, 118*(1–3), 48–54. https://doi.org/10.1016/j.jad.2009.02.008

Van Staden, C.W., & Krüger, C. (2003). Incapacity to give informed consent owing to mental disorder. *Journal of Medical Ethics, 29*(1), 41–43. https://doi.org/10.1136/jme.29.1.41

Wong, P.W., Chan, W.S., Beh, P.S., Yau, F.W., Yip, P.S., & Hawton, K. (2010). Research participation experiences of informants of suicide and control cases. *Crisis, 31*(5), 238–246. https://doi.org/10.1027/0227-5910/a000025

World Medical Association. (2013). *WMA Declaration of Helsinki – Ethical principles for medical research involving human subjects.* Retrieved from https://www.wma.net/policies-post/wma-declaration-of-helsinki-ethical-principles-for-medical-research-involving-human-subjects/

Young, S.D., & Garett, R. (2018). Ethical issues in addressing social media posts about suicidal intentions during an online study among youth: Case study. *JMIR Mental Health, 5*(2), e33. https://doi.org/10.2196/mental.8971

Zimmer, M. (2010). "But the data is already public": On the ethics of research in Facebook. *Ethics and Information Technology, 12*(4), 313–325. https://doi.org/10.1007/s10676-010-9227-5

Chapter 5
Measures in Suicide Research

Peeter Värnik and Ella Arensman

Summary

Suicide has a major impact on society, in terms of both its high social and economic implications. Therefore, it is essential to have reliable measures and indicators for evaluation and decision making. The current chapter introduces and explains selected measures, which are important in suicide research in order to measure changes over time, as well as the impact of suicide prevention activities. References are made to several World Health Organization (WHO) databases and other notable publications. Topics regarding data quality are discussed in connection with death registration and the International Classification of Diseases. Measures related to suicide attempts and self-harm surveillance systems are discussed, as there is a strong association between suicide attempts or self-harm, and suicide.

The decision to kill oneself is made on a personal level, but it has been acknowledged for more than a century to be a social act that can be investigated at societal levels (Durkheim, 1897/2002). Suicide is an important indicator of mental health, reflecting the general well-being of society and therefore is often prioritized as a separate prevention target or as part of a wider mental health promotion strategy.

The negative impacts of suicide manifest in various ways. On average, people die by suicide at a much younger age than from other causes of death. Suicide is one of the main causes of premature mortality in industrialized countries (Gunnell & Middleton, 2003; Norheim et al., 2015). Hence, the proportion of potential years of life lost due to suicide is several times higher than the proportion of suicide deaths. On a personal level, suicide deprives individuals of the opportunity to experience what the whole life cycle can offer. It impacts negatively on an established network of ties between people and leaves a void among family members, friends, and acquaintances, sometimes affecting them for many years or for their whole lifetime. The number of suicide attempts is several times higher than the number of actual suicides, especially as, in addition to known attempts, which have been reported and treated in a hospital or emergency department, there are many more people at the community level not reaching out for medical help (WHO, 2018). There are indications that for each adult who has died by suicide, there may have been more than 20 others attempting suicide. The estimated annual global prevalence of self-reported suicide attempts is approximately 4 per 1,000 adults (WHO, 2014). In the US, in 2016, for example, there were almost 45,000 suicide deaths, and suicide attempts accounted for almost 500,000 emergency department visits (Simon et al., 2018). Suicide attempts may cause serious injury and long-term disability reducing healthy life expectancy. Therefore, in addition to human suffering, direct and indirect economic costs are involved (discussed in more detail in Chapter 15).

"Preventing suicide is a global imperative," stated the WHO in 2014, publishing a comprehensive overview of the most important aspects of suicidal behavior (WHO, 2014). That overview includes contributions from more than a hundred scholars and is excellent in its relative brevity and easiness to read, yet thorough enough to take positions on key questions, while providing answers and instructions for practical application. One such instruction was to approach suicide prevention according to a public health model, which is presented in detail in Chapter 3. In the current chapter, we take a thorough look at different options for measurement and the use of public health indicators, including mortality and burden of disease, as well as some other indicators specific to suicide research.

Main Measures and Indicators of Suicide

The most obvious indicator is the *number of suicides*, which helps us to understand the magnitude of the issue. While data about deaths are gathered continuously, and sometimes other time periods are used, the time frame most frequently set for presentation and analysis is the calendar year. The number of suicides worldwide was estimated to be 804,000 in 2012, according to the WHO report (WHO, 2014), and similarly, the more recent general WHO health report states that "there were nearly 800,000 deaths from suicide in 2018" (WHO, 2019, p. 31). Several scholars have quoted 1 million cases per year (Khan & Syed, 2011; Pompili et al., 2013) or more (Rockett, 2010), and depending on the perspective, this may be correct, as we shall examine later in the chapter. The overall situation, certainly, seems to have improved from what it was 20 years ago, but globally there are only 60 countries with reliable suicide figures (WHO, 2018). A prediction, made at the turn of the century by the WHO, looks pessimistic in hindsight: "In the year 2020, approximately 1.53 million people will die from suicide based on current trends and according to WHO estimates" (Bertolote & Fleischmann, 2002, p. 181). This was based on an increasing trend at the end of the 20th century, which has now reversed in many parts of the world.

Suicide mortality can be compared with all-cause mortality by calculating the *proportion of suicides* and all deaths. However, this measure is not frequently used. On a regular basis, the WHO provides estimates in their report *Global Health Estimates* (WHO, 2018), where, for example, the underlying data tables show that there were 793,307 suicides and 56,873,804 deaths globally in 2016. The proportion of suicides therefore was 1.4%. While that is a period indicator and requires more complex calculations to arrive at birth cohort indicators, it is a close enough approximation to illustrate this proportion in the following way: Imagine a small school, where 72 pupils are admitted per year (e.g., 3 classes with 24 pupils each); on average, one pupil will die by suicide at some point in their life.

Suicide as a cause of death is often compared with other deaths by injury. According to the *Global Health Estimates* for 2016, fatal road traffic injuries amounted to 1,402,302 (2.5% of total), and 476,898 (0.8% of total) deaths were due to interpersonal violence (i.e. homicide). All injury deaths amounted to 4,883,194 (8.6% of total) (WHO, 2018).

The most common and quoted measure, of course, is the *suicide rate*, which contrasts suicides with living people. Ideally, these mortality rates are calculated by dividing cases by person-years. But because these are rarely available, mid-year counts of the population or the beginning-of-year population are used. In an annual time frame, suicide is a rare event in a population, which means that the calculated rate is very small. To make it easier to understand and use, the result is usually multiplied by 100,000 (i.e., shown in the form of cases per 100,000 of population). Rates per 10,000 or 1 million can also be and have been used. Notably, in older texts of British origin (Barraclough, 1972) or from countries that share a history with Britain, authors tended to use rates per million.

In addition to crude death rates described in the previous paragraph, it is possible to calculate *age-standardized suicide rates*, if the number of deaths is available by age group. This eliminates the effects of population age structure, thereby facilitating an improved comparison between regions and over time. There are two main techniques for age standardization – direct and indirect methods. *Direct standardization* requires that we know the age-specific rates of mortality of the population studied. Standardized rates are calculated by applying these rates to a standard population age distribution. *Indirect standardization* does not require age-specific rates of mortality, it only requires the total number of deaths and the age structure of the population studied. Standardized rates are obtained by applying the age-specific mortality rates of the whole population to the population studied. Without age-specific rates of the studied population, indirect standardization may be the only feasible method. However, with the increasing availability of age-specific rates, the use of direct age standardization has become the predominant technique in most applications of demography and epidemiology (Ahmad et al., 2001). While direct standardization is generally preferred, indirect standardization is used to compare mortality in subpopulations (observed vs. expected rates), and it is preferable when there are small numbers in particular age groups.

There are several versions of standard populations used for calculating rates and the choice of method for standardization slightly affects the numerical outcome (Värnik & Wasserman, 2016). World, European, WHO, and US standard populations are most often used. While a few decades ago, presenting age-standardized rates was the norm, it seems that lately the WHO has taken a half-step back and uses standardized and nonstandardized rates equally. The explanation for this seems to be an acknowledgment that, while most of the suicide-related research has been conducted in high-income countries with fairly similar population age structures and somewhat similar suicide age dependency, the bulk of suicides – 75.5%, according to the WHO in 2012 (WHO, 2014) – occur in low- and middle-income countries with entirely different population age structures and suicide age dependency.

The previously described measures can be applied to any group, geographical unit, or time period. The WHO has divided the world into six regions, which is the first level of global analysis, followed by country-level analysis. Countries are further divided and subdivided into smaller areas. At some level of subdivision, the population becomes too small to provide meaningful analytical data, which means that the chance of a rare event starts to play a more important role than any statistical trend. The same principle applies to groups and subgroups (e.g., divided by age and sex as described in the following paragraphs). Governments and people are generally most interested in data at the country level. The current top 25 countries according to their crude suicide rates by the WHO estimates are shown in Table 5.1 (WHO, 2018). It is important to note that differences within countries (i.e., between different areas) can be large and possibly even larger than between countries, where suicide rates can differ more than a hundred times.

According to the WHO data tables (WHO, 2018), crude suicide rates have been declining from 2000 to 2016 in two out of three countries.

Time trends provide very valuable analytical information on the aggregate level – change over a longer period of time might simultaneously reflect the potential development of underlying causes and prevention efforts in the geographical setting or in a specific group. Nevertheless, it is not easy to separate these two.

Several problems hinder the analysis of long-term trends. The most obvious is that data from the previous century does not exist for many countries, notably from the low- and middle-income group. Data from 2000 onwards are easily available, although a fair proportion of it is based on estimates, not measurements. Data from 1980 onwards are accessible, but one must consider issues related to cause of death determination and classification and the change in coding of deaths, which will be discussed later in the chapter (see the section Quality of Measurements).

Table 5.1 Crude suicide rates in 2016, per 100,000 population in top 25 countries, change in rates from 2000 to 2016, and male to female rate ratio for 2016

Rank	Country	Total	Male	Female	Change from 2000 to 2016	M/F ratio
1	Lithuania	31.9	58.1	9.5	−37%	6.1
2	Russian Federation	31.0	55.9	9.4	−41%	5.9
3	Guyana	29.2	43.7	14.4	25%	3.0
4	Republic of Korea	26.9	38.4	15.4	82%	2.5
5	Belarus	26.2	46.9	8.2	−39%	5.7
6	Suriname	22.8	34.7	10.9	−3%	3.2
7	Kazakhstan	22.5	38.3	7.6	−34%	5.0
8	Ukraine	22.4	41.1	6.3	−39%	6.5
9	Latvia	21.2	37.6	7.3	−39%	5.2
10	Lesotho	21.2	17.8	24.4	18%	0.7
11	Belgium	20.7	27.8	13.8	−9%	2.0
12	Hungary	19.1	29.7	9.6	−41%	3.1
13	Slovenia	18.6	30.4	6.9	−43%	4.4
14	Japan	18.5	26.0	11.4	−25%	2.3
15	Uruguay	18.4	29.2	8.3	6%	3.5
16	Estonia	17.8	30.6	6.6	−40%	4.6
17	France	17.7	23.9	11.7	−21%	2.0
18	Switzerland	17.2	22.0	12.4	−21%	1.8
19	Croatia	16.5	25.6	7.9	−23%	3.2
20	Equatorial Guinea	16.4	23.5	7.7	6%	3.1
21	India	16.3	17.8	14.7	−6%	1.2
22	Poland	16.2	28.9	4.3	−4%	6.7
23	Finland	15.9	23.9	8.1	−35%	3.0
24	Republic of Moldova	15.9	27.9	4.7	−3%	5.9
25	Austria	15.6	23.9	7.7	−22%	3.1

Based on "World Health Statistics 2019: Monitoring Health for the SDGs," by the World Health Organization. © 2019 by the WHO.

Data from 1950 are available from the WHO but cover only a few dozen countries with noticeable blanks and incur further complications of recoding. Data before World War II are available for a very few countries, mostly due to the initiatives of individual researchers. The earliest statistical reports on suicide rates date back to the mid-19th century (Värnik &

Wasserman, 2016). There is great variation in suicide rate trends starting so far back in time. Description and analysis can be found for the US (Shields, Hunsaker, & Hunsaker, 2005), Russia (Jukkala, Mäkinen, & Stickley, 2015), England and Wales (Thomas & Gunnell, 2010), Switzerland (Ajdacic-Gross et al., 2006), Italy (Condorelli, 2013), Denmark (Paerregaard, 1980), and some other countries. In addition, analysis of time trends and other uses of suicide rates in ecological studies suffer from other biases, including confounding and the ecological fallacy (ecological studies are discussed in Chapter 6).

Age and Gender Patterns

Gender differences have been observed throughout the world in relation to suicidal behavior. The latest data (WHO, 2019) estimate that globally, for every female suicide death, there are nearly two male deaths (13.5 and 7.7 deaths per 100,000 population, in men and women in 2016, respectively), while the annual global crude suicide mortality rate is 10.6 per 100,000 total population. The male-to-female suicide rate ratio was the highest (3.7) in the WHO European Region, with Poland and Ukraine in leading positions with rate ratios of 6.7 and 6.5, respectively (Table 5.1). The rate ratio was 2.7 in high-income countries. This general pattern has persisted for a long period, with several authors from the 19th century stating that the earliest statistics showed that approximately three out of every four completed suicides in both Europe and North America were found among males (Kushner, 1993). The highest female suicide mortality rates were seen in the WHO South-East Asia Region (11.6 per 100,000) and in lower- and middle-income countries (8.8 per 100,000) (WHO, 2019). According to the *Global Health Estimates* latest data there were eight countries in 2016 where the female suicide rate was higher than the male rate, and four of those were large Asian countries – China, Pakistan, Bangladesh, and Myanmar, with male-to-female suicide rate ratios of 0.9, 0.9, 0.7, and 0.6, respectively. In China this pattern has persisted for at least several decades (He & Lester, 1997; Phillips, Li, & Zhang, 2002; Pritchard, 1996).

Suicide has been found to have a strong *age dependency*. There are some notable differences globally though. In high-income countries, where suicidality has been studied in far more detail, it is predominantly the elderly who die by suicide. In lower- and middle-income countries, however, depending on the part of the world, it may be quite the opposite. Girard described four different age patterns and showed how each of these curves is typical of a certain level of societal development, starting from the lowest: with a peak in adolescents and young adults; a bimodal pattern with peaks among middle-aged adults and the elderly; with a peak in the elderly; and finally, a convex pattern, with a decline in older ages (Girard, 1993). This very clear framework was developed at a time when there was not much knowledge about suicides in lower- and middle-income countries. Therefore, it does not always apply – notably for the WHO estimates for Africa.

Potential Years of Life Lost

Suicide research aims to reduce premature death by suicide, which is a clear example of a context where the use of *potential years of life lost* (PYLL; sometimes also abbreviated YPLL or YLL) gives an improved understanding of the issue. The introduction of the concept of PYLL comes from Mary Dempsey, who observed a substantial decline in the tuberculosis mortality rate in the US but argued that it failed to tell the entire story. Public health problems cannot be adequately judged on the basis only of comparative death rates, without some consideration of the PYLL, since from the standpoint of society, the death of a person in the prime of life constitutes a greater loss than the death of one of advanced years (Dempsey, 1947). She calculated PYLL by simply subtracting the age at death from a fixed number – the expectation of life at birth. Greville immediately improved the calculation method suggesting the use of life expectancy at the age of death from demographic life tables. He noted that Dempsey's method results in substantial understatement of PYLL, and that this understatement is greater in the case of deaths from cancer and heart disease, the majority of which occur at relatively older ages compared with death by tuberculosis (Greville, 1948).

A few years later, Haenszel proposed the calculation of the standardized rate for mortality defined in units of lost years of life and compared five different methods, including life table and fixed maximum value (65 and 75 years). He concluded that the results obtained from any of the five suggested the schemes are roughly comparable and that all accentuate differences in time and between diagnoses in a more pronounced manner than the standardized death rate (Haenszel, 1950). However, the fact that many acceptable approaches to perform calculations give similar but not identical results, hinders this very useful approach somewhat. The method of calculating PYLL varies from author to author, each producing different rankings of leading causes of death. One can choose between heart disease, cancer, or accidents as the leading cause of premature death, depending on which method is used (Gardner & Sanborn, 1990). In their latest work, the WHO has, after carefully considering many approaches with different gender and age combinations, settled on 28 preventable causes using a standard life table for calculation of years of life lost for a death at a given age, based on the projected frontier life expectancy for 2050, with a life expectancy at birth of 92 years (WHO, 2018).

National suicide reduction targets should focus on PYLL and overall suicide rates (Gunnell & Middleton, 2003), and many researchers have made use of the PYLL methodology to estimate the social and economic burden of premature mortality from suicide (Doessel, Williams, & Whiteford, 2009; Etzersdorfer, Klein, Baus, Sonneck, & Kapusta, 2015; Law, Yip, & Chen, 2011; Vienonen et al., 2019; Zhang et al., 2010). Many countries freely present their statistical data, but unfortunately, many of those are not methodologically compatible. Table 5.2 illustrates one possible approach with PYLL-80.

The WHO offers PYLL estimates for 183 countries and all causes of mortality, in 2000, 2010, 2015, and 2016, using their methodology.

Quality of Measurements

The WHO has made a great effort to estimate suicide mortality globally, including country-specific rates. Yet, differences in data quality are substantial – in high-income countries close to 100 % of estimates are based on vital registration data, while at the other end of spectrum are countries with no vital registration (WHO, 2014). The bulk of suicide research still concerns high-income countries, where currently available data are used for all purposes, from individual-level studies to international strategy building. There are, however, many aspects to consider.

The source of official suicide mortality data is the focal point of interest. It concerns death registration in general and the quality of injury death diagnostics in particular. The process of suicide registration starts after the fact of death has been established by a medical doctor, and suspicion of injury death has been raised. It ends with registration of the death in the national mortality statistics (Värnik et al., 2010). Organizations responsible for death registra-

Table 5.2 Potential years of life lost (PYLL) at ages 0–80 per 100,000 inhabitants in Finland

	Total PYLL			PYLL for females			PYLL for males		
Year	All deaths	Suicides	%	All deaths	Suicides	%	All deaths	Suicides	%
2002	8,141	731	9.0%	5,055	326	6.4%	11,389	1126	9.9%
2003	8,124	697	8.6%	5,055	325	6.4%	11,343	1062	9.4%
2004	8,180	666	8.1%	5,115	329	6.4%	11,378	997	8.8%
2005	8,117	656	8.1%	5,068	323	6.4%	11,291	982	8.7%
2006	8,038	631	7.9%	4,995	312	6.2%	11,197	943	8.4%
2007	7,870	643	8.2%	4,832	297	6.1%	11,014	983	8.9%
2008	7,798	636	8.2%	4,833	310	6.4%	10,863	955	8.8%
2009	7,644	632	8.3%	4,774	308	6.5%	10,609	948	8.9%
2010	7,453	602	8.1%	4,694	293	6.2%	10,302	903	8.8%
2011	7,262	564	7.8%	4,640	269	5.8%	9,967	852	8.5%
2012	7,036	541	7.7%	4,535	263	5.8%	9,616	811	8.4%
2013	6,831	513	7.5%	4,444	258	5.8%	9,293	762	8.2%
2014	6,584	479	7.3%	4,261	233	5.5%	8,980	718	8.0%
2015	6,443	456	7.1%	4,182	216	5.2%	8,774	689	7.9%
2016	6,354	463	7.3%	4,166	223	5.4%	8,610	696	8.1%

Based on data from the Finnish Institute for Health and Welfare, Helsinki, Finland. Retrieved from https://sotkanet.fi/sotkanet/en/taulukko/?indicator=s44KBQA=&region=s07MBAA=&year=sy5ztC7V0zUEAA==&gender=m;f;t&abs=f&color=f&buildVersion=3.0-SNAPSHOT&buildTimestamp=201911131146

tion are encouraged to use uniform reporting standards. Since 1893, the *International Classification of Diseases* (ICD) has undergone 10 revisions, occasioning serious discontinuities in the statistical series (Meslé & Vallin, 1996). The ICD-10 was adopted by the WHO in 1990 (WHO, 2004), and is currently in use in most high-income countries. The 11th Revision of the ICD (ICD-11) was presented at the 72nd World Health Assembly, having been launched in 2018. Over a decade in the making, ICD-11 has now been updated for the 21st century. In this iteration of the ICD, special attention has been given to mental health (Lancet, 2019).

Ideally, all suicide deaths would be diagnosed as suicides, and nonsuicide deaths as nonsuicides. Information that is available to investigators, however, is sometimes imperfect and, therefore, does not facilitate that distinction. The crucial element is the *intent* to die. According to the diagnostic tool the ICD-10, deaths from external causes are diagnosed in Chapter XX under codes V1–Y98, with suicide as a separate subcategory under codes X60–X84 using the term *intentional self-harm*. It includes 25 codes for different types of poisoning, hanging, drowning, firearm use, jumping, and others, which can be used for calculating method-specific mortality. Often Y87.0 *Sequelae of intentional self-harm* is also included in suicide research. Notably, the list of diagnoses is exactly the same for deaths of undetermined intent (Y10–Y34 in ICD-10), the only difference being whether the intent to die was uncertain

(Värnik & Wasserman, 2016). In the ICD-11, suicide is diagnosed in Chapter 23 under codes PB80–PD3Z still using the term *intentional self-harm*, with more than 100 different diagnoses.

The required degree of certainty is the key to diagnostic differentiation. Two distinct approaches are identifiable in different countries: the *legal approach*, which is applied mainly in *coronial systems*, and the *medical approach*, applied mainly in *medicolegal systems* and their variation, *forensic systems*. When legal criteria are used, the decision to classify a death as suicide is expected to be *beyond reasonable doubt*. In the medical approach, decisions about causes of death are reached in the same way as for any other diagnosis – that is, on the basis of the *balance of probabilities* (Värnik et al., 2010).

Suicide is a socially delicate subject, and its diagnostics are further complicated by sociocultural factors, such as criminalization, stigmatization, religiousness, etc., which vary from country to country (Mishara & Weisstub, 2016).

In summary, evidentiary standards for classifying a death as suicidal are high (Rockett, 2017). Many researchers have found that the number of suicides is often underestimated due to cultural, political, legal, and economic circumstances. It may be reported under other subcategories of external causes of death, the most likely being death by injury of undetermined intent. Underestimations differ by method of suicide; for example, suicide by hanging or firearm has better validity than suicide by poisoning or drowning, because it is much harder to determine intent for the latter.

Validity and Reliability

Suicide research often uses epidemiological tools for analysis, and the same approach that is common to evaluate diagnostics of diseases or conditions is applicable to suicide certification. In epidemiology the *validity* is defined as the ability to distinguish between who has a disease and who does not. Validity has two components: sensitivity and specificity. *Sensitivity* is defined as the ability to correctly identify those who have the disease. *Specificity* is defined as the ability to correctly identify those who do not have the disease (Celentano & Szklo, 2018). The validity of suicide certification, similarly, involves sensitivity or true positivity (correctly diagnosed as suicides; *true positives* in Figure 5.1) and specificity or true negativity (correctly diagnosed as nonsuicides; *true negatives* in Figure 5.1). Only sensitivity appears to be problematic for suicide research and prevention (Rockett, 2017).

Regardless of the sensitivity and specificity of a test, if the test results cannot be reproduced, the value and usefulness of the test are minimal (Celentano & Szklo, 2018). Therefore, in suicide research, to evaluate the diagnostic quality, reliability (repeatability or reproducibility) must be assessed in addition to validity. Reliability of suicide death certification is of particular interest across regions and over time. To check for reliability, it is possible to rediagnose the cases and compare results versus the original diagnoses. If individual level data are not available, it is possible to quantify the temporal reliability by using the Spearman rank-order correlation coefficient to calculate the association between suicide rates and potential suicide reservoirs over time (Höfer, Rockett, Värnik, Etzersdorfer, & Kapusta, 2012).

		Actual cause of death	
		Suicide	Not suicide
Diagnosed cause of death	Suicide	True positives *(TP)*	False positives *(FP)*
	Not suicide	False Negatives *(FN)*	True Negatives (TN)
		Sensitivity	**Specificity**
		$\frac{TP}{TP + FN}$	$\frac{TN}{TN + FP}$

Figure 5.1 Sensitivity and specificity in suicide diagnostics.

Prevalence and Incidence in Suicide Research

Two key concepts in epidemiology are prevalence and incidence of a disease or a condition. The *prevalence* of disease tells us what proportion of a population has the disease at a specific point in time (*point prevalence*) or during a specified time (*period prevalence*). Prevalence is traditionally calculated in cross-sectional studies (see Chapter 6 for details).

The *incidence* of disease measures how quickly people are catching the disease, and it differs from prevalence because it considers only new cases that have occurred in a specific time period (Webb & Bain, 2011). Incidence and prevalence are morbidity measures, which should not be used in the context of suicide mortality, although suicide deaths can be considered as incident cases, and we can see that in some studies. Incidence can be used when analyzing suicide attempts, but it should only be applied to new cases. Prevalence is often used when describing suicidal ideation and suicide attempts in population-based studies.

Measuring Suicide Attempts and Self-Harm

Researchers and practitioners do their best to prevent suicidal behavior. However, it is very difficult to predict such a relatively rare event and hard to determine who would gain the most from preventive measures, to avoid death by suicide. Efforts have been made to find a combination of determinants that would form a *suicide prediction formula,* but this has remained elusive. Statistical models, which seem to have predictive value in one societal setting, may be much less relevant in another. Nevertheless, some universal truths about associations with indicators have been established.

Attitudes toward both suicide and suicide attempts have changed a great deal over time. Erwin Stengel conducted pioneering work on the nature of attempted suicide (Stengel, Cook, & Kreeger, 1958). He explained the importance of suicide attempts being taken seriously and treating these patients appropriately (Stengel, 1964). Suicidal ideation and behavior are obvious warning signs, and a prior suicide attempt is the single most important risk factor for suicide in the general population (WHO, 2014). In their meta-analysis based on all applicable studies, Harris and Barraclough (1997) calculated standardized suicide mortality ratios for populations with mental disorders and other risk factors compared with the general population. Previous suicide attempt by self-poisoning increased suicide risk by 40 times, and attempted suicide by any method elevated suicide risk by 38 times (Harris & Barraclough, 1997). A number of studies at different times and in different settings have confirmed the outcome of elevated risk of suicide after a suicide attempt, including cohort studies (Christiansen & Jensen, 2007; Hawton, Zahl, & Weatherall, 2003; Suominen et al., 2004; Tidemalm, Långström, Lichtenstein, & Runeson, 2008). The majority of these studies have the hospitalization of a suicide attempter as index attempt as their starting point. # suicide attempt repetition rates can be used as an indicator to assess the impact of assessment and intervention programs implemented at hospital level (Platt, Arensman, & Rezaeian, 2019).

Suicide attempts impact significantly on social and economic aspects of communities due to the utilization of health services to treat the injury, the psychological and social impact of the behavior on the individual and their associates, and occasionally, long-term disability due to injury (WHO, 2014). Therefore, suicide attempts have become recognized as a separate prevention target, although closely connected with suicide prevention. The main sources of information are hospital medical records, which are complemented by personal reporting (e.g., during surveys). Unlike the recording of deaths, there are no internationally accepted methods for standardizing the collection of information about suicide attempts, and the WHO does not routinely collect such data (WHO, 2014). Therefore, there are some practical measurement issues to be overcome, such as distinguishing between suicidal and nonsuicidal self-injury, number of episodes and individual patients, and ascertaining any loss of information during admitting and discharging procedures. The operational criteria of suicide attempts and self-harm are similar in most studies.

Surveillance of Self-Harm

With regard to terminology, the term *self-harm* offers common ground internationally. The concept of self-harm covers a spectrum that ranges in intent and motivation (WHO, 2016). However, it is recognized that this cannot always be translated with the same meaning in other languages and the term *suicide attempt* might be preferred in such instances (see Chapter 2 for further details regarding definitions). Research among young people engaging in self-harm has revealed that the majority reported multiple and often contradictory motives underlying their behavior. The majority also reported both death-oriented and nondeath motives at the time of their self-harm act, which reflects ambivalence rather than a static condition (Scoliers et al., 2009). What this means in practice is that the priority at the assessment stage is to determine the degree of suicidal intent in those who self-harm, rather than to distinguish between those with and without suicidal intent.

Public health surveillance provides the scientific and factual database essential to informed decision making and appropriate public health action. The key objective of surveillance is to provide information to guide interventions (Nsubuga et al., 2006). Surveillance systems for self-harm can play an important role in suicide prevention by providing important epidemiological data on rates of, and risk factors for, self-harm presentations (Witt & Robinson, 2019). Surveillance systems are a step forward from traditional data collection – that is, they concentrate on measuring aspects of suicide deaths. Electronic data systems make information available in close to real time.

Worldwide, only a few countries have reliable data on self-harm. A National Self-Harm Registry has been operating in Ireland since 2002 (Arensman, 2017; Perry et al., 2012). As of 2006, the Registry has obtained full coverage of all general and pediatric hospital emergency departments in the Republic of Ireland. The Registry collects data based on persons presenting to hospital emergency departments as a result of an episode of self-harm, as defined by the Registry. The National Self-Harm Registry Ireland provided the basis for the WHO's *Practice Manual for Establishing and Maintaining Surveillance Systems for Suicide Attempts and Self-Harm* (WHO, 2016).

An important incidence indicator is the *rate of self-harm* per 100,000 population. The annual incidence rate per 100,000 population should be calculated for the total population, for the male and female populations separately, and for subgroups by age and sex, based on the number of persons who have presented to a hospital following a suicide attempt or self-harm, in each calendar year. It is suggested that crude and age-standardized self-harm rates (including suicide attempts) should be calculated by dividing the number of persons who engaged in self-harm by the relevant population figure and multiplying the result by 100,000 (WHO, 2016).

It is advisable to adjust for the age composition of the population under study, because this ensures that differences observed by sex or by area are due to differences in the incidence of self-harm rather than differences in the composition of the populations. For instance, European age-standardized rates are the incidence rates that would be observed if the population under study had the same age composition as a theoretical European population. They can be calculated as follows: for each 5-year age group, the number of persons who engaged in self-harm is divided by the population at risk and then multiplied by the number in the European standard population.

The following points should be taken into account: Calculated rates that are based on fewer than 20 events may be unreliable measures of the underlying rate. If the same individual presents to the hospital more than once on the same calendar day, it should be clarified whether a second suicide attempt or act of self-harm has been made or whether the representation is due to absconding and returning, or being transferred to another hospital. If no second suicide attempt or act of self-harm has been made, this should be recorded as a single suicide attempt or self-harm event.

Repeat event analysis recording a unique person identification number allows for the analysis of *repeated suicide attempts and self-harm acts*. A repeated suicide attempt or act of self-harm should be defined as a representation to any hospital due to a further suicide attempt or self-harm act undertaken after leaving the hospital following presentation for a previous suicide attempt or self-harm act. An example of repeat event analysis is *conditional risk set analysis*, where analysis is stratified by event order (WHO, 2016).

Conclusions

Suicide as a worldwide public health issue reflects the general well-being of the society. It is essential to have measures for evaluation and decision making. Counting suicides and viewing them in the context of total mortality or other injury deaths is an important starting point. The most quoted measure is the suicide rate, which contrasts suicides with living people. In addition to crude death rates, age-standardized rates are calculated to eliminate the effects of population age structure, thereby facilitating an improved comparison between regions and over time. These measures can be applied to any group, geographical unit, or time period. Suicide research aims to reduce premature death, and therefore, potential years of life lost is an important indicator to assess the true magnitude and meaning of suicide among other death causes.

The source of official suicide mortality data is the focal point of interest regarding data quality. It concerns death registration and injury death diagnostics. The ICD-10 diagnostic tool is in use in most high-income countries, and the ICD-11 has been launched. The crucial element in suicide diagnostics is the intent to die, because this differentiates suicides from deaths of undetermined intent. Reliability and validity of suicide registration are questioned by some authors even for high-income countries, leading to estimations of serious undercounting. A prior suicide attempt is a powerful predictor of death by suicide. Establishing self-harm registries, and developing systems for real-time surveillance of suicide or suspected suicide, are the newest initiatives, which are designed to improve decision making and prevention.

References

Ahmad, O.B., Boschi-Pinto, C., Lopez, A.D., Murray, C.J., Lozano, R., & Inoue, M. (2001). *Age standardization of rates: A new WHO standard. 14.* Retrieved from https://www.who.int/healthinfo/paper31.pdf?ua=1

Ajdacic-Gross, V., Bopp, M., Gostynski, M., Lauber, C., Gutzwiller, F., & Rössler, W. (2006). *Age-period-cohort analysis of Swiss suicide data*, 1881–2000. *European Archives of Psychiatry and Clinical Neuroscience, 256*(4), 207–214. https://doi.org/10.1007/s00406-005-0627-1

Arensman, E. (2017). Suicide prevention in an international context. *Crisis, 38*(1), 1–6. https://doi.org/10.1027/0227-5910/a000461

Barraclough, B.M. (1972). Are the Scottish and English suicide rates really different? *British Journal of Psychiatry, 120*(556), 267–273. https://doi.org/10.1192/bjp.120.556.267

Bertolote, J.M., & Fleischmann, A. (2002). Suicide and psychiatric diagnosis: A worldwide perspective. *World Psychiatry, 1*(3), 181–185.

Celentano, D.D., & Szklo, M. (2018). *Gordis epidemiology* (6th ed.). Philadelphia, PA: Elsevier.

Christiansen, E., & Jensen, B.F. (2007). Risk of repetition of suicide attempt, suicide or all deaths after an episode of attempted suicide: A register-based survival analysis. *Australian and New Zealand Journal of Psychiatry, 41*(3), 257–265. https://doi.org/10.1080/00048670601172749

Condorelli, R. (2013). A Bayesian analysis of suicide data. *Quality & Quantity, 47*(2), 1143–1161. https://doi.org/10.1007/s11135-011-9608-9

Dempsey, M. (1947). Decline in tuberculosis: The death rate fails to tell the entire story. *American Review of Tuberculosis, 56*(2), 157–164. https://doi.org/10.1164/art.1947.56.2.157

Doessel, D.P., Williams, R.F.G., & Whiteford, H. (2009). Policy-appropriate measurement of suicide: Headcount vs. potential years of life lost, Australia, 1907–2005. *Archives of Suicide Research, 13*(1), 87–99. https://doi.org/10.1080/13811110802572197

Durkheim, É. (2002). *Suicide: A study in sociology.* London: Routledge Classics. (Original work published 1897)

Etzersdorfer, E., Klein, J., Baus, N., Sonneck, G., & Kapusta, N.D. (2015). Epidemiology of suicide in Austria during 2000–2010: Potential years of life lost: Time for the national suicide prevention program. *Wiener Klinische Wochenschrift, 127*(7), 308–313. https://doi.org/10.1007/s00508-015-0729-3

Gardner, J.W., & Sanborn, J.S. (1990). Years of potential life lost (YPLL) – What does it measure? *Epidemiology, 1*(4), 322–329. https://doi.org/10.1097/00001648-199007000-00012

Girard, C. (1993). Age, gender, and suicide: A cross-national analysis. *American Sociological Review, 58*(4), 553–574. https://doi.org/10.2307/2096076

Greville, T.N.E. (1948). Comments on Mary Dempsey's article on "Decline in tuberculosis: The death rate fails to tell the entire story." *American Review of Tuberculosis, 57*(4), 417–419. https://doi.org/10.1164/art.1948.57.4.417

Gunnell, D., & Middleton, N. (2003). National suicide rates as an indicator of the effect of suicide on premature mortality. *Lancet, 362*(9388), 961–962. https://doi.org/10.1016/S0140-6736(03)14367-X

Haenszel, W. (1950). A standardized rate for mortality defined in units of lost years of life. *American Journal of Public Health and the Nation's Health, 40*(1), 17–26. https://doi.org/10.2105/AJPH.40.1.17

Harris, E.C., & Barraclough, B. (1997). Suicide as an outcome for mental disorders: A meta-analysis. *British Journal of Psychiatry, 170*(3), 205–228. https://doi.org/10.1192/bjp.170.3.205

Hawton, K., Zahl, D., & Weatherall, R. (2003). Suicide following deliberate self-harm: Long-term follow-up of patients who presented to a general hospital. *British Journal of Psychiatry, 182,* 537–542. https://doi.org/10.1192/bjp.182.6.537

He, Z.X., & Lester, D. (1997). The gender difference in Chinese suicide rates. *Archives of Suicide Research, 3*(2), 81–89. https://doi.org/10.1023/A:1009649332566

Höfer, P., Rockett, I.R.H., Värnik, P., Etzersdorfer, E., & Kapusta, N.D. (2012). Forty years of increasing suicide mortality in Poland: Undercounting amidst a hanging epidemic? *BMC Public Health, 12*(1), 644. https://doi.org/10.1186/1471-2458-12-644

Jukkala, T., Mäkinen, I.H., & Stickley, A. (2015). The historical development of suicide mortality in Russia, 1870–2007. *Archives of Suicide Research, 19*(1), 117–130. https://doi.org/10.1080/13811118.2014.915774

Khan, M.M., & Syed, E.U. (2011). Suicide in Asia: Epidemiology, risk factors, and prevention. In R.C. O'Connor, S. Platt, & J. Gordon (Eds.), *International handbook of suicide prevention: Research, policy and practice* (pp. 487–506). https://doi.org/10.1002/9781119998556.ch28

Kushner, H.I. (1993). Suicide, gender, and the fear of modernity in nineteenth-century medical and social thought. *Journal of Social History, 26*(3), 461–490. https://doi.org/10.1353/jsh/26.3.461

Lancet. (2019). ICD-11 [Editorial]. *Lancet, 393*(10188), 2275. https://doi.org/10.1016/S0140-6736(19)31205-X

Law, C.-K., Yip, P.S.F., & Chen, Y.-Y. (2011). *The economic and potential years of life lost from suicide in Taiwan,* 1997–2007. *Crisis, 32*(3), 152–159. https://doi.org/10.1027/0227-5910/a000070

Meslé, F., & Vallin, J. (1996). Reconstructing long-term series of causes of death. *Historical Methods, 29*(2), 72–87. https://doi.org/10.1080/01615440.1996.10112731

Mishara, B.L., & Weisstub, D.N. (2016). The legal status of suicide: A global review. *International Journal of Law and Psychiatry, 44,* 54–74. https://doi.org/10.1016/j.ijlp.2015.08.032

Norheim, O.F., Jha, P., Admasu, K., Godal, T., Hum, R.J., Kruk, M.E., ... Peto, R. (2015). Avoiding 40% of the premature deaths in each country, 2010–30: Review of national mortality trends to help quantify the UN Sustainable Development Goal for health. *Lancet, 385*(9964), 239–252. https://doi.org/10.1016/S0140-6736(14)61591-9

Nsubuga, P., White, M.E., Thacker, S.B., Anderson, M.A., Blount, S.B., Broome, C.V., ... Trostle, M. (2006). Public Health Surveillance: A tool for targeting and monitoring interventions. In D.T. Jamison, J.G. Breman, A.R. Measham, G. Alleyne, M. Claeson, D.B. Evans, ... P. Musgrove (Eds.), *Disease control priorities in developing countries* (2nd ed.). New York, NY: Oxford Uni Press. Retrieved from http://www.ncbi.nlm.nih.gov/books/NBK11770/

Paerregaard, G. (1980). Suicide in Denmark: A statistical review for the past 150 years. *Suicide & Life-Threatening Behavior, 10*(3), 150–156. https://doi.org/10.1111/j.1943-278X.1980.tb00774.x

Perry, I.J., Corcoran, P., Fitzgerald, A.P., Keeley, H.S., Reulbach, U., & Arensman, E. (2012). The incidence and repetition of hospital-treated deliberate self harm: Findings from the world's first national registry. *PLoS One, 7*(2). https://doi.org/10.1371/journal.pone.0031663

Phillips, M.R., Li, X., & Zhang, Y. (2002). Suicide rates in China, 1995–99. *Lancet, 359*(9309), 835–840. https://doi.org/10.1016/S0140-6736(02)07954-0

Platt, S., Arensman, E., & Rezaeian, M. (2019). National suicide prevention strategies – Progress and challenges. *Crisis, 40*(2), 75–82. https://doi.org/10.1027/0227-5910/a000587

Pompili, M., Gonda, X., Serafini, G., Innamorati, M., Sher, L., Amore, M., ... Girardi, P. (2013). Epidemiology of suicide in bipolar disorders: A systematic review of the literature. *Bipolar Disorders, 15,* 457–490. https://doi.org/10.1111/bdi.12087

Pritchard, C. (1996). Suicide in the People's Republic of China categorized by age and gender: Evidence of the influence of culture on suicide. *Acta Psychiatrica Scandinavica, 93*(5), 362–367. https://doi.org/10.1111/j.1600-0447.1996.tb10661.x

Rockett, I.R.H. (2010). Counting suicides and making suicide count as a public health problem. *Crisis, 31*(5), 227–230. https://doi.org/10.1027/0227-5910/a000071

Rockett, I.R.H. (2017). The gender suicide gap and differential misclassification: A research autobiography. *International Review of Modern Sociology, 29*, 5–32.

Scoliers, G., Portzky, G., Madge, N., Hewitt, A., Hawton, K., de Wilde, E.J., ... van Heeringen, K. (2009). Reasons for adolescent deliberate self-harm: A cry of pain and/or a cry for help? *Social Psychiatry and Psychiatric Epidemiology, 44*(8), 601–607. https://doi.org/10.1007/s00127-008-0469-z

Shields, L.B.E., Hunsaker, D.M., & Hunsaker, J.C. (2005). Trends of suicide in the United States during the 20th century. In M. Tsokos (Ed.), *Forensic pathology reviews* (pp. 305–335). New York, NY: Humana Press. https://doi.org/10.1007/978-1-59259-910-3_10

Simon, G.E., Johnson, E., Lawrence, J.M., Rossom, R.C., Ahmedani, B., Lynch, F.L., ... Shortreed, S.M. (2018). Predicting suicide attempts and suicide deaths following outpatient visits using electronic health records. *American Journal of Psychiatry, 175*, 951–960. https://doi.org/10.1176/appi.ajp.2018.17101167

Stengel, E. (1964). *Suicide and attempted suicide*. London, UK: Penguin Books.

Stengel, E., Cook, N.G., & Kreeger, R.I. (1958). *Attempted suicide* (Maudsley Monograph No. 4). London, UK: Chapmann and Hall.

Suominen, K., Isometsä, E., Suokas, J., Haukka, J., Achte, K., & Lönnqvist, J. (2004). Completed suicide after a suicide attempt: A 37-year follow-up study. *American Journal of Psychiatry, 161*, 562–563. https://doi.org/10.1176/appi.ajp.161.3.562

Thomas, K., & Gunnell, D. (2010). Suicide in England and Wales 1861–2007: A time-trends analysis. *International Journal of Epidemiology, 39*(6), 1464–1475. https://doi.org/10.1093/ije/dyq094

Tidemalm, D., Långström, N., Lichtenstein, P., & Runeson, B. (2008). Risk of suicide after suicide attempt according to coexisting psychiatric disorder: Swedish cohort study with long term follow-up. *BMJ, 337*, a2205. https://doi.org/10.1136/bmj.a2205

Värnik, P., Sisask, M., Värnik, A., Laido, Z., Meise, U., Ibelshäuser, A., ... Hegerl, U. (2010). Suicide registration in eight European countries: A qualitative analysis of procedures and practices. *Forensic Science International, 202*(1–3), 86–92. https://doi.org/10.1016/j.forsciint.2010.04.032

Värnik, P., & Wasserman, D. (2016). Global suicide. *Biological Aspects of Suicidal Behavior, 30,* 1–10. https://doi.org/10.1159/000435765

Vienonen, M.A., Jousilahti, P.J., Mackiewicz, K., Oganov, R.G., Pisaryk, V.M., Denissov, G.R., ... Vohlonen, I.J. (2019). Preventable premature deaths (PYLL) in Northern Dimension partnership countries 2003–13. *European Journal of Public Health, 29*(4), 626–630. https://doi.org/10.1093/eurpub/cky278

Webb, P., & Bain, C. (2011). *Essential epidemiology: An introduction for students and health professionals* (2nd ed.). Cambridge, UK: Cambridge University Press.

Witt, K., & Robinson, J. (2019). Sentinel surveillance for self-harm. *Crisis, 40*(1), 1–6. https://doi.org/10.1027/0227-5910/a000583

World Health Organization. (2004). *ICD-10: International statistical classification of diseases and related health problems: tenth revision.* Retrieved from https://apps.who.int/iris/handle/10665/42980

World Health Organization. (2014). *Preventing suicide: A global imperative.* Geneva, Switzerland: Author. Retrieved from https://www.who.int/mental_health/suicide-prevention/world_report_2014/en/

World Health Organization. (2016). *Practice manual for establishing and maintaining surveillance systems for suicide attempts and self-harm.* Geneva, Switzerland: Author. Retrieved from https://apps.who.int/iris/bitstream/handle/10665/208895/9789241549578_eng.pdf?sequence=1

World Health Organization. (2018). *Global health estimates 2016: Disease burden by cause, age, sex, by country and by region, 2000–2016.* Retrieved from http://www.who.int/healthinfo/global_burden_disease/estimates/en/

World Health Organization. (2019). *World health statistics 2019: Monitoring health for the SDGs.* Retrieved from http://www.who.int/gho/publications/world_health_statistics/2019/en/

Zhang, J., Ma, J., Jia, C., Sun, J., Guo, X., Xu, A., & Li, W. (2010). Economic growth and suicide rate changes: A case in China from 1982 to 2005. *European Psychiatry, 25*(3), 159–163. https://doi.org/10.1016/j.eurpsy.2009.07.013

Chapter 6

Observational Studies in Suicide Research

Kairi Kõlves, Merike Sisask, and Ian R. H. Rockett

Summary

Observational study designs are extensively used in epidemiology. The appropriate study design to respond to the research question is crucial to the success of a study. The current chapter examines different types of observational study designs and their application in suicide research. Considerations about their suitability with regard to their nature, including strengths and limitations, time to implement, budget, and other practicalities for a researcher, study team, and stakeholders are of utmost importance and are discussed with examples from suicide research. Also discussed are causation and internal and external validity.

Once we have identified our research questions and established the aims of our study, we need to consider which study designs would be suitable in responding to these questions. The focus of the current chapter is the different types of study designs that are applicable to observational research. An observational study is one in which the exposure of interest is not manipulated by the investigator. Therefore, by definition, such studies are nonexperimental (Porta, 2008). Consideration of the appropriate study design is crucial to the success of a study. To choose the best possible design for our research question, we need to examine the nature of those designs including their strengths and limitations, time to implement, budget, and other practicalities for a researcher, study team, and stakeholders (e.g., the organization that requests a given study).

Descriptive and Analytical Studies

There are two main types of observational studies: descriptive (exploratory) and analytical. The usual criterion for differentiating the two is that an *analytical study* has a comparison or a control group (Centers for Disease Control and Prevention [CDC], 2012; Grimes & Schulz, 2002d). Nevertheless, this is not necessarily clear-cut. Some study designs might be descriptive under some circumstances and analytical under others (e.g., cross-sectional, see Figure 6.1), and epidemiologists can vary in how they categorize them.

Descriptive studies are the first step in an epidemiological enquiry about a specific condition or behavior (e.g., suicidal behavior). In sound epidemiological research, we need to answer five basic *W* questions – what, who, where, when, and why (CDC, 2012; Grimes & Schulz, 2002c; Webb, Bain, & Page, 2020). These questions correspond to case definition, person, place, time, and causes or risk factors. Descriptive studies are expected to cover the first four:

- Case definition – *what* condition (or behavior) are we studying? A case definition is a vital step in epidemiology to establish in detail how we measure the condition we are studying. This could also be referred to as an *operational definition* in suicide research. For example, we can define suicides as all deaths by intentional self-harm, according to *the International*

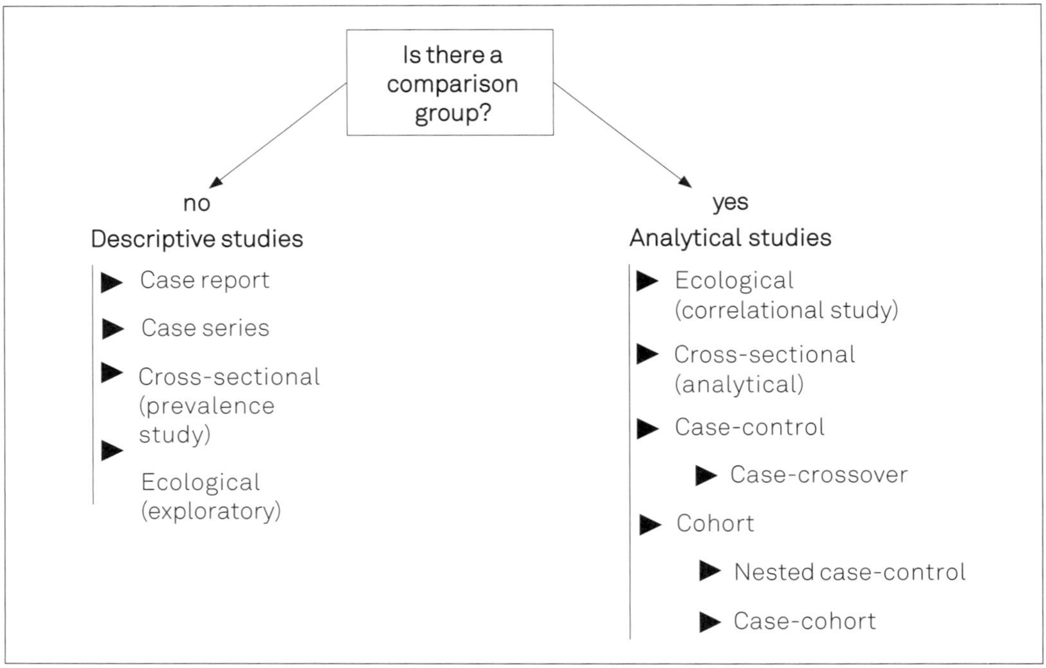

Figure 6.1 Descriptive and analytical study designs.

Statistical Classification of Diseases and Related Health Problems, 10th revision (codes X60–X84; World Health Organization [WHO], 2004).

- Person – *who* is at risk for the condition or event of interest? For example, who is more likely to die by suicide? What is the sociodemographic profile of these persons? Age and sex are the most commonly used personal characteristics. However, other characteristics are also important (e.g., marital status, occupation, ethnicity, and lifestyle factors) (CDC, 2012; Grimes & Schulz, 2002c).
- Place – *where* did the condition or event of interest occur? Where is the suicide rate lower or higher? We need to clarify the geographical location under study, such as a country, or urban versus rural location.
- Time – *when* did it occur? We have to specify the duration of our observation period as, for example, in weeks, months, or years.

Descriptive studies are useful for identifying the magnitude of the problem, which helps guide health policy and planning. They also provide first clues about potential determinants of the condition or event, although we cannot draw inferences about associations or causality. They can assist with hypothesis formulation (Rockett, 1999), which can be tested using analytical study designs (CDC, 2012; Grimes & Schulz, 2002c, 2002d; Webb et al., 2020). Traditionally, analytical studies have a control or comparison group, which helps us analyze *why* a behavior or condition occurred. We can then identify risk factors and possible causes (CDC, 2012; Grimes & Schulz, 2002c; Webb et al., 2020).

Prior to describing specific study designs, we need to explain two key terms in epidemiology – exposure and outcome. The *outcome* is the condition or event under study, while an *exposure* is the risk factor we are investigating that might be a cause of the outcome. In suicide research, our outcomes are suicides, suicide attempts, nonsuicidal self-injury, and suicidal ideation. We may have numerous kinds of exposures we would like to study.

Case Reports and Case Series

The starting point in identifying a new or recurrent condition is a *case report*, which contains a description of a specific case by a clinician or other expert (e.g., a pathologist) (Grimes & Schulz, 2002c; Webb et al., 2020). The majority of case reports in suicide research present unusual or new suicide methods to bring to the attention of researchers and clinicians the lethality of particular methods or potential new trends (Centini, Fiore, Riezzo, Rossi, & Fineschi, 2007; Madentzoglou, Kastanaki, Nathena, Kranioti, & Michalodimitrakis, 2013); trends that might warrant further research using more advanced designs. For example, the first case report where a female used an unusual suicide method sourced from the Internet, was recounted in a letter to the editor of the *Psychiatric Bulletin* in 1998 (Haut & Morrison, 1998). The authors highlighted their concerns about suicide methods being discussed on the Internet.

In addition to reporting about specific suicide methods, there are case reports focusing more intensively on different aspects of a person's life and potential factors leading to suicide using the *psychological autopsy* (PA) format (for more details on PAs, see Chapter 11). The PA was first developed to study deaths of equivocal intent. It is one of the main methods for enlightening decedent characteristics and circumstances of known or registered suicides. Information sources may include police and hospital reports, and interviews with close family members, other relatives, friends, and work acquaintances of the decedent, and also pertinent health care professionals. Some psychological case studies focus on famous people (e.g., Ernest Hemingway, by Martin, 2006) or unusual methods (e.g., suicide by an air force pilot using an aircraft, by Jones, 1977, or by a young artist using fire, by Värnik, Maris, & Maltsberger, 2003).

Case reports can be extended to a *case series* involving a more detailed description of the characteristics of cases sharing the same outcome (event, e.g., suicide). The main purpose is to identify emerging trends or examine common exposures, which would enable the formulation of hypotheses to be tested using more advanced study designs (Celentano & Moyses, 2018; Manja & Lakshminrusimha, 2014). Cases can be identified from surveillance systems, death registers, hospital records, or other sources. There are a few options for choosing cases for our study. One series might involve a series of (consecutive) cases or a sample with a specific exposure and the same outcome. For example, Saarinen, Lehtonen, and Lönnqvist (1999) analyzed 17 consecutive cases of suicide (outcome) in 1987–1988, where the individuals had all been diagnosed with schizophrenia (exposure), using a PA to collect information from relatives and mental health professionals. The authors described common problems in their treatment practices, with a focus on the ability of clinicians to recognize suicidality in patients.

A more common option for a case series is to choose cases on the basis of a specific outcome (e.g., suicide) – for example, a case series of suicides was reported for the small Pacific Island of New Caledonia for the period 2014–2015 (Box 6.1; Goodfellow et al., 2020).

Box 6.1. Example of a psychological autopsy case series from New Caledonia

Considering the lack of studies on suicides in New Caledonia, and in the Pacific Islands more generally, and given limited resources, a case series was used as the first step to profile suicides there. The psychological autopsy method was utilized to collect information from different sources, including face-to-face interviews with family members and relatives. The study received ethical clearance from the relevant human subjects committees in France and New Caledonia. All interviews were conducted by a clinical psychologist of local Kanak origin who was trained for the study. All informants signed consent forms, and the duration of the interviews was 2 to 4 hours. The interview was a French version of the WHO/START Study psychological autopsy study questionnaire, and incorporated a number of scales.

Information was collected about 52 (33 males and 19 females) of the 75 people who died by suicide during the study period – 69 % of all suicides in 2014–2015. Seventy-five percent of informants were women, and 44 % were first-degree family members. One third included multiple informants. Conflicting information between informants was resolved through a phone call. The family members of the remaining suicides either could not be contacted, or an interview could not be arranged, or they refused to participate. Sociodemographic characteristics of suicides not included in the analysis did not differ significantly from those of the inclusions.

People who died by suicide were compared by gender, age (below 30 vs. 30 years and older), and ethnicity (indigenous Kanak vs. other ethnicity). Results showed that Kanak were overrepresented in suicides (58 %), and they were significantly younger than non-Kanak people who died by suicide (26 vs. 41 years). A mental disorder was substantiated in 62 % of cases, with no significant differences between groups. Nevertheless, there were some differences by specific disorders, for example the Kanak had significantly more psychotic and associated conditions. Over a third had previously made a suicide attempt, and nearly a third had been exposed to a death by suicide. Overall the Kanak who died by suicide displayed fewer indicators of suicidality. Life events preceding suicide most often were arguments with a partner or spouse (60 %), and 44 % of suicides involved domestic violence. A quarter involved financial difficulties, which were significantly more frequent in the non-Kanak group. Also a quarter of decedents had experienced the death of a close family member or friend, but this was more common in Kanaks.

The main study limitations were a small number of cases and the absence of a control group – precluding determination of risk factors.

Vulnerability of young Kanaks to suicide reflects a situation apparent in some other Pacific Islands, and calls for a culturally appropriate means of suicide prevention.

Based on Goodfellow, B., Kõlves, K., Selefen, A.-C., Massain, T., Amadéo, S., & De Leo, D. (2020). The WHO/START study in New Caledonia: A psychological autopsy case series. *Journal of Affective Disorders, 262*, 366–372.

Case reports and cases series are common in medical research, as they are simple, fast, and inexpensive to generate (Celentano & Moyses, 2018). Although case series have lost some of their popularity (Dekkers, Egger, Altman, & Vandenbroucke, 2012) due to their limited generalizability and lack of a control (comparison) group, they can be incorporated in case-control studies and case-crossover studies, since they all share outcome-based sampling (Celentano & Moyses, 2018). Case reports and case series are also frequently used in qualitative research (see Chapter 9 for more on qualitative studies).

Cross-Sectional Studies

Cross-sectional studies are mostly based on surveys and can be descriptive or analytical. The main aim of descriptive cross-sectional studies is to measure the prevalence (percentage) of a specific outcome(s) (e.g., depression, suicidal behavior) in a defined population (population of interest) at a specific time point or period. Thus, they are also called *prevalence studies* (Bonita, Beaglehole, & Kjellström, 2006; Celentano & Moyses, 2018; Merrill, 2013). Prevalence is a proportion and not a rate. Measuring the prevalence of different conditions in a population of interest, across various demographic groups (e.g., sex and age) and for different regions (e.g., urban or rural) or other geographic units is helpful for health service planning. Cross-sectional studies are expected to represent the population of interest in order for the results to be generalizable. Hence, random samples are necessary. Information from repeat health surveys (also called serial cross-sectional studies, or panel studies if the initial respondents or participants are being resurveyed) using valid methods provides useful indications of trends (Bonita et al., 2006; Celentano & Moyses, 2018). Several countries run regular health surveys. Some are coordinated across different countries. For example, European Union member states run the European Health Interview Survey (EHIS) every 5 years (https://ec.europa.eu/eurostat/web/microdata/european-health-interview-survey). The EHIS comprises four blocks of questions: (1) demographic and socioeconomic variables; (2) health status, including such information as self-perceived health, chronic conditions, and comorbidities; (3) health care use, such as hospitalization, unmet needs, and preventive actions; and (4) health determinants, such as dietary habits, smoking, and alcohol consumption.

Some surveys also include suicidal behavior as an outcome. There are further studies specifically dedicated to measuring the prevalence of suicidal ideation and behavior in a specific population. Box 6.2 presents an example of a World Health Organization (WHO) SUPRE-MISS study community survey, which aimed to estimate the prevalence of these phenomena in a selection of primarily low- and middle-income countries (Bertolote et al., 2005).

Box 6.2. Example of a descriptive cross-sectional study to measure suicidal ideation and behavior in different locations

With the aim to identify prevalence of suicide ideation, plans, and attempts, between 2002 and 2004, the World Health Organization (WHO) conducted, within the frames of the Multisite Intervention Study of Suicidal Behaviors (WHO/SUPRE-MISS), a community survey in eight communities in different countries (Campinas in Brazil, Yuncheng in China, Tallinn in Estonia, South Chennai in India, Karaj in Iran, Durban in South Africa, Colombo in Sri Lanka, and Dong Da district of Hanoi in Vietnam), two additional sites in Brisbane in Australia and Stockholm in Sweden using similar surveys were included to the analyses. A common survey instrument was developed that included scales or questions about sociodemographic background, history of suicidal behavior, family context, mental and physical health, use of health services, substance use, and community stress and problems. The questionnaire was translated into local languages and pilot tested. The study protocols were approved by the relevant ethics committees in all surveyed countries. Each site used the most suitable random sampling source (e.g., from the list of residents of the census tracts, the street index). Response rates tended to be high in the majority of sites (except Brisbane, Durban, and Stockholm). Interviews were conducted by trained professionals mainly face-to-face, with the exception of Colombo and Stockholm where respondents completed the questionnaires themselves, and in Brisbane where phone interviews were conducted.

In cross-cultural studies, it is important to understand and consider the cultural context in order to preclude misinterpretation. A separate background instrument to describe the socio-cultural context of the sites was developed for the community description component of WHO/SUPRE-MISS and completed in local experts.

The highest prevalence of lifetime suicide ideation and plans was recorded in Durban (25.4% and 15.6%), and Karaj and Brisbane had the highest prevalence of lifetime suicide attempts (4.2% in both cases). A very low prevalence of suicide attempts was found in Hanoi (0.4%). The ratio between suicide thoughts, plans, and attempts differed notably between the sites. For example, suicidal ideation was 22 times more prevalent than suicide attempts in Hanoi. While the ratio did not differ that much in some sites. In Chennai, suicide plans were almost as prevalent as attempts. The need of medical attention for the suicide attempt (first if multiple) was identified for 22.2% in Hanoi up to 87.5% in Chennai.

The project faced a number of difficulties and, as described, there were a number of differences in the sampling and data collection methods. Furthermore, cultural differences between the sites made the comparisons challenging. Nevertheless, for a number of communities, it was the first study to identify the burden of lifetime suicidal ideation, plans, and suicide attempts, and contributed towards further suicide research and prevention efforts.

Based on Bertolote, J.M., Fleischmann, A., De Leo, D., Bolhari, J., Botega, N., De Silva, D., ... Värnik, A. (2005). Suicide attempts, plans, and ideation in culturally diverse sites: the WHO SUPRE-MISS community survey. *Psychological Medicine, 35*, 1457–1465.

Cross-sectional studies enable us to measure different exposure(s) at the same time as the outcome(s). The association between the exposure(s) and outcome is estimated in the frameworks of *analytical* cross-sectional studies. Considering that we can measure several exposures in a cross-sectional study, it is a suitable study design to begin investigating potential causes. Analytical cross-sectional studies are common in suicide research that evaluates risk factors for suicidal ideation and suicide attempts in a total population or in specific groups (e.g., in school children in a study by Kaess et al., 2014; in older adults by Almeida et al., 2012).

As well as prevalence, an important measure in cross-sectional studies is the prevalence ratio (see Box 6.3). Alternative statistical methods might be used in cross-sectional studies, depending on the nature of the data collected.

Although cross-sectional studies can be conducted relatively quickly, easily, and inexpensively, we need to consider their potential flaws. As the exposure and outcome are measured at the same time, or at similar times, we are often unable to identify temporality. This means that we cannot identify whether the exposure precedes or follows the outcome (causality). For example, measuring patterns of alcohol consumption (exposure) and suicidal ideation (outcome) at the same time does not allow us to identify when these behaviors first occurred, and whether a person was abusing alcohol before becoming suicidal; or if their suicidality precipitated the alcohol abuse, which could be *reverse causality* (Celentano & Moyses, 2018).

Furthermore, we need to consider *confounding factors* – namely, the possibility that both behaviors are associated with another exposure, which is the true cause (explained further below in the section Internal Validity). One option to establish a temporal sequence is to ask subjects about their timelines. Nevertheless, we need to consider potential *recall bias*, especially if the potential exposure and outcome occurred proximally. *Bias* occurs when results differ systematically from the true value of the association between the exposure and outcome

Box 6.3. Measures of association

The principal measures of the strength of association are ratio or relative measures (relative risk).

Risk ratio (RR) shows how likely it is that an exposed person (e.g., with alcohol abuse) develops an outcome – incidence (e.g., first suicide attempt) relative to those without the exposure. It is calculated by dividing the risk or proportion of the outcome in the exposed group, with the risk of the outcome in the nonexposed group.

$$\text{Risk ratio} = \frac{\text{Risk in exposed}}{\text{Risk in unexposed}}$$

We can also calculate **rate ratio** by dividing the incidence rate in the exposed group by the incidence rate in the unexposed group.

Cross-sectional studies measure prevalence. The **prevalence ratio** is the ratio of the prevalence of the outcome in the exposed group (e.g., prevalence of suicidal ideation in those who are binge drinking) relative to the prevalence in the unexposed group (e.g., prevalence of suicidal ideation in those who are not binge drinking).

$$\text{Prevalence ratio} = \frac{\text{Prevalence in exposed}}{\text{Prevalence in unexposed}}$$

Odds Ratio

In case-control studies, we cannot calculate the RR, since we only have a limited selection of the population as controls. Therefore, the odds ratio (OR) serves as the measure of the strength of association. In case-control studies, the OR shows the odds of an exposure (e.g., alcohol dependency) in cases (e.g., suicide) compared with controls.

$$\text{Odds ratio} = \frac{\text{Odds of exposure in cases}}{\text{Odds of exposure in controls}}$$

The magnitude of the odds ratio is very similar to that of the risk ratio, particularly if the outcome is a rare one like suicide.

How to interpret?

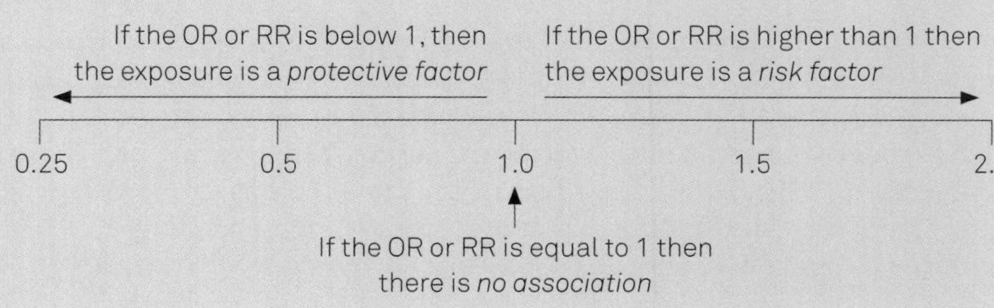

(Bonita et al., 2006). As previously noted, national cross-sectional studies aim to estimate prevalence. Therefore, the researchers usually limit their questions about suicidal ideation and behavior to lifetime and past year (e.g., the National Mental Health Survey in Australia; Slade, Teesson, & Burgess, 2009). This limits the use of these studies for analytical purposes in terms of etiology and for establishing causality. In addition, cross-sectional studies traditionally use self-report questions or scales (Fadnes, Taube, & Tylleskär, 2009). Thus, our results are subject to potential underreporting or overreporting. There is the possibility that people are reluctant to disclose their suicidal behavior, or they underestimate their risky behavior (e.g., alcohol use), while they are more likely to overestimate healthy behaviors (social desirability). Another source of bias is a low response rate, which is unlikely to be random across the characteristics of the respondents or participants (Webb et al., 2020).

Cross-sectional studies are required to measure the prevalence of different conditions. Nevertheless, to conduct a reliable survey we need a well-designed questionnaire, an appropriate sample of sufficient size, and a high response rate (Bonita et al., 2006).

Ecological Studies

An *ecological study* (also called a *correlational study*) is the only epidemiological research design where the unit of analysis is a group (e.g., country, state, community) rather than an individual (Bonita et al., 2006; Celentano & Moyses, 2018). This type of study measures the relationship between the exposure(s) and outcome(s) at the population rather than the individual level. Data in ecological studies are generally collected routinely for other purposes (e.g., national vital statistics such as births and deaths or censuses). In his sociological analysis of suicide, Durkheim (1897/2002) mainly used group level data (e.g., suicide rates in different countries by religious affiliation in the second half of the 19th century), and numerous studies testing his hypotheses have been conducted using ecological study designs. Thus ecological studies are often considered sociological studies in suicide research (Wray, Colen, & Pescosolido, 2011).

Morgenstern (1995, 2008) distinguished three types of measures:

1. *aggregate measures* are summary characteristics of observations of groups (e.g., the prevalence of suicidal ideation or alcohol consumption, or suicide rates);
2. *environmental measures* are physical characteristics of each group's locality (e.g., annual rainfall or hours of daylight); and
3. *global measures* are those that can only apply to whole populations (e.g., a suicide prevention strategy or a Gini index as a measure of inequality).

There are inconsistencies across epidemiology textbooks as to whether ecological studies are descriptive or analytical. This might be due to different types of ecological study designs, which are rarely described systematically. Nevertheless, they can be categorized as etiological (analytical) or exploratory (descriptive) depending on whether we measure the exposure or not (Morgenstern, 1995, 2008). In addition, they can be further grouped depending on whether they focus on place (multi-group design), time (time-trend design), or both place and time (mixed design) (Morgenstern, 1995, 2008; Stevenson & McClure, 2005).

Multigroup Study (Focus Is Place)

In a *descriptive multigroup study*, we compare different countries or regions by the same outcome during the same time, describe spatial patterns, and generate hypotheses about potential causes. An example would be comparing age-standardized suicide rates around the world in a specific year (e.g., 2016). From such a comparison, we can note that suicide rates in males are particularly high in Eastern Europe compared with in other countries, or that suicide rates in females are high in Asian countries. From these observations, we can formulate hypotheses about potential causes, which can then be tested using analytical study designs.

An *analytical multigroup study* examines the association between the level of an exposure and the rate of an outcome using many groups at the same time. Figure 6.2 presents a histogram that tests a simple association between age-standardized suicide rates per 100,000 and pure alcohol consumption in liters per capita (age ≥ 15 years) in 41 European countries in 2014. There is a moderate correlation between the two variables ($r = .59, p < .001, n = 41$). Nevertheless, we cannot conclude this association is causal. Further assessment of causality between alcohol consumption and suicide must be made through analytical studies using individual-level data.

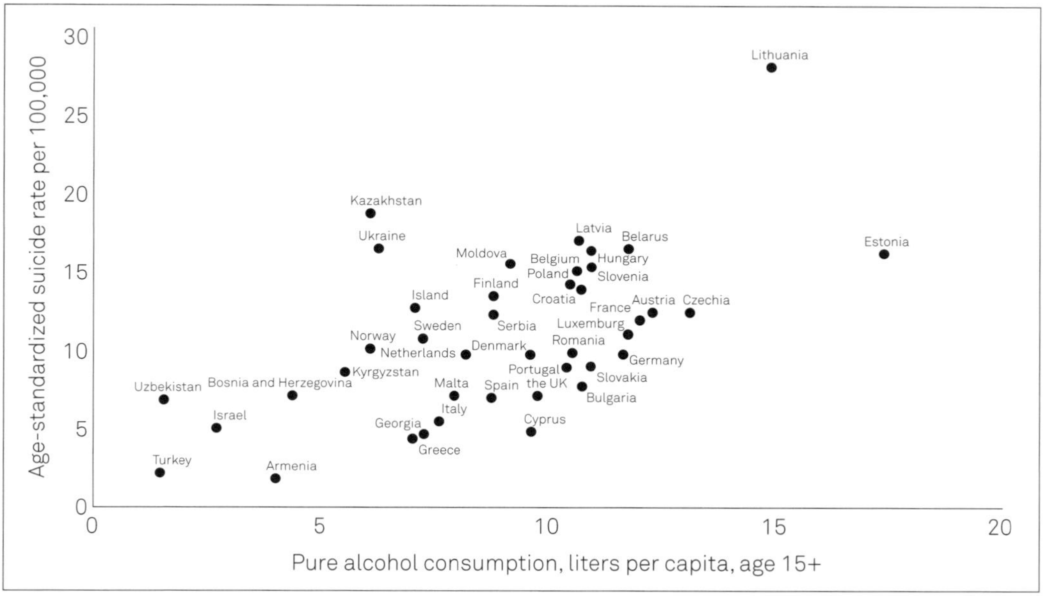

Figure 6.2 Age-standardized suicide rates per 100,000 and pure alcohol consumption in liters per capita (age 15+) in 41 European countries in 2014. $r = .59, p < .001, n = 41$. Based on data from the WHO European Health for All database (HFA-DB). Available at https://gateway.euro.who.int/en/datasets/european-health-for-all-database/

Time-Trend Study (Focus Is Time)

In a *descriptive time-trend study*, we compare the rates of an outcome in a population (e.g., by sex or age) in a specific geographical location over time. We explore temporal patterns and generate hypotheses about potential reasons behind the changes; a special type of study is an age-period-cohort analysis, whereby *age* is usually represented in years, *period* refers to a particular time (cross-sectional), and *cohort* usually refers to a group of people born in the same year or during another shared time interval.

In *analytical time-trend studies*, we can examine the association between the level of the exposure and the rate of outcome over time (Morgenstern, 1995). A relevant example, including both a descriptive and an analytical time-trend study, is reported in an article by Page and colleagues (2013). They analyzed the cohort effect in Australia between 1907 and 2010, and also the role of unemployment (people currently seeking employment) and underemployment (people in part-time employment but seeking additional work) for the period 1978–2010. A statistically significant increasing birth cohort effect was identified for males, especially those born after 1970–1974, indicating that the cohort experiencing high rates of suicides in 1990s had continuously higher rates compared with earlier cohorts. The authors suggest it is possible this cohort had been impacted by the experience of underemployment and casual employment, and that the rising suicide rates in this cohort were consistent with the frustration-aggression hypothesis, where frustration is triggered by unmet expectations about work and about the establishment of a career (Page, Milner, Morrell, & Taylor, 2013).

Mixed Study (Focus on Combination of Place and Time)

A *descriptive mixed study* combines the characteristics of the multigroup and time-trend designs. Figure 6.3 presents a simple time-trend analysis of age-standardized suicide rates in males in selected European countries in the period 1990–2014. We can describe these trends by country groups. We see relatively similar suicide trends for males in the Baltic States and Russia (all part of the former Soviet Union), with the Scandinavian and Western European countries (France, Germany) lying in the middle of the spectrum, and South European countries (Italy and Spain) registering the lowest rates. A number of potential hypotheses can then be formulated (e.g., suicidal behavior in males is related to sociopolitical and/or economic background) and tested.

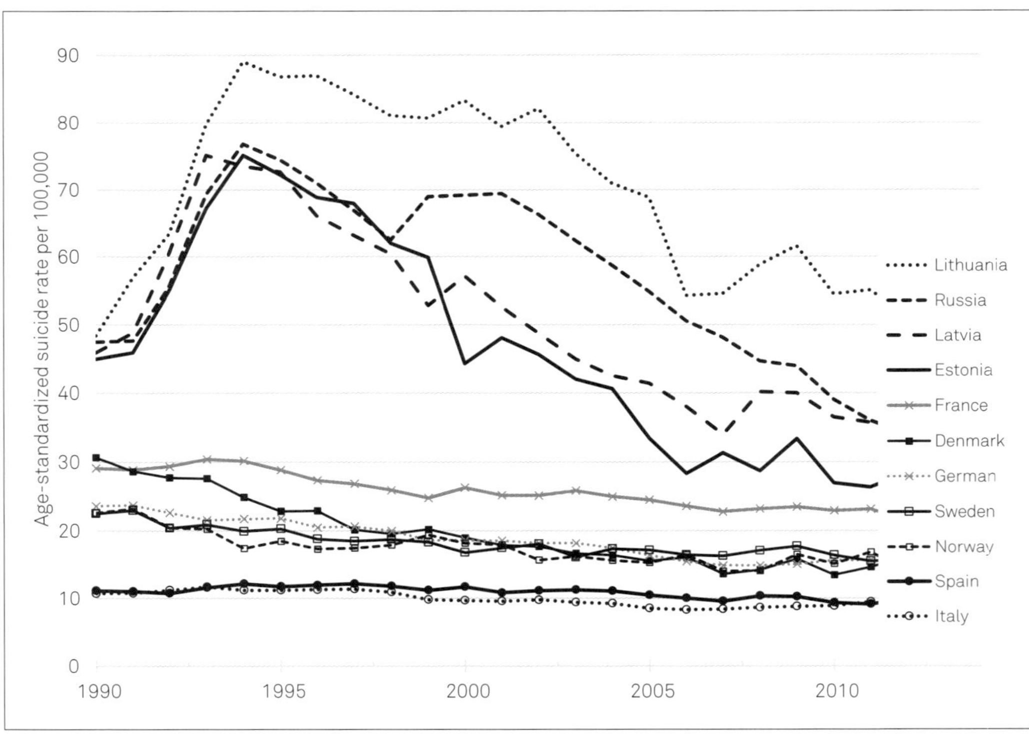

Figure 6.3 Age-standardized suicide rates in males in selected countries in 1990–2014. Based on data from the WHO European Health for All database (HFA-DB). Available at https://gateway.euro.who.int/en/datasets/european-health-for-all-database/

An *analytical mixed study* estimates the association between a change in the exposure and outcome across time for multiple groups (Morgenstern, 1995, 2008). Stuckler, Basu, Suhrcke, Coutts, and McKee (2009) analyzed mortality in 26 European countries during economic change between 1970 and 2007 in a mixed ecological study. They found that suicide mortality was particularly affected; a 1 % increase in the unemployment rate was associated with a 0.79 % rise in the suicide rate in the working-age population (below age 65 years). The authors suggested that active labor market programs might mitigate the adverse effects of unemployment on suicide in economic downturns; more specifically, there was no adverse effect of unemployment on suicide when active labor market investments exceeded US $190 per capita annually.

Statistical analyses utilized in ecological studies might vary from simple correlations to complex multilevel modeling, adjusting for confounding factors and autocorrelation. The main advantages of ecological studies are their capacity for hypothesis formulation or to test simple hypotheses at the aggregate level with limited time and resources (Stevenson & McClure, 2005; Webb et al., 2020). They are considered suitable for policy evaluation. Given that data are preexisting and at the group level, we do not need ethical approval of a research protocol from an institutional review board or research integrity committee to conduct ecological studies. However, there are a number of disadvantages of these studies. The main one is *ecological bias* (or the *ecological fallacy*), which refers to the inability of this kind of study to show an association at an individual level – for example, we may not necessarily find an association between alcohol drinking level and suicide at the individual level. Some ecological researchers argue ecological bias is not problematic if the aim was simply to measure an ecological effect. In the previous example, Stuckler and colleagues (2009) aimed to analyze economic change and labor market investments at the aggregate level. In addition, we need to exercise caution regarding potential misclassification emanating from differences in measuring outcomes and exposures between countries (or other groups) and changes over time. There is also the possibility that relevant data are not measurable or available at the aggregate level, and that studies may use *proxy measures* of the exposure of interest – for example, the prevalence of GPs or psychiatrists as a proxy for health care availability. Nevertheless, well-designed ecological studies facilitate our understanding of the wider social context of suicidal behavior.

Case-Control Studies

A *case-control study* is an analytical study design, which can be considered an extension of the case series design (described in the section Case Reports and Case Series) by adding a control (reference) group who do not have an outcome – a condition or behavior under investigation. The outcome (e.g., suicide) is always identified first, and we then look backwards to detect the presence of exposure(s) of interest – potential risk factors (e.g., mental illness; see Figure 6.4) (Bonita et al., 2006; Celentano & Moyses, 2018). Frequency of exposure(s) in cases and controls are compared in case-control studies (Celentano & Moyses, 2018). Case-control studies offer a good opportunity to analyze rare outcomes (such as suicide) and multiple exposures, which makes them well-suited for suicide research. They are used more frequently than other analytical study designs in epidemiology (Schulz & Grimes, 2002), which applies also to suicide research (Glenn, Franklin, Kearns, Lanzillo, & Nock, 2016; Pirkis, Nicholas, & Gunnell, 2020).

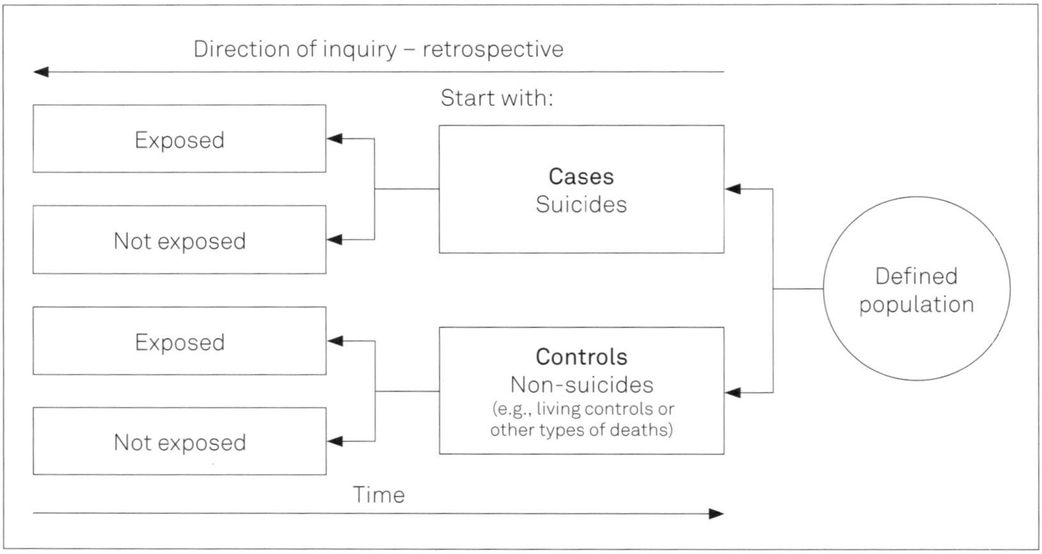

Figure 6.4 The case-control study design. Adapted with permission from "Basic Epidemiology," by R. Bonita, R. Beaglehole, & T. Kjellström, 2006, p. 45. © 2006 by the World Health Organization.

Selecting Cases and Controls

As previously noted, cases may be identified from different sources – for example, suicides are frequently identified from death registers, police records, or coronial information systems (Kõlves, Värnik, Tooding, & Wasserman, 2006; Milner et al., 2017), and suicide attempters from emergency departments or hospitals (Sisask et al., 2010). We need to consider whether to include people who made a suicide attempt for the first time (incidence cases) or all (a sample of) suicide attempters (prevalence cases). When choosing cases, we might include all cases who had the outcome in a specific time period (consecutive cases), or a selection of a representative sample of cases, depending on the frequency of the outcome of interest (Webb et al., 2020). However, only a small proportion of noncases are chosen as controls, ideally representing the population of interest (Merrill, 2013; Webb et al., 2020). Unfortunately, this is not an easy task; in fact, making a selection of appropriate controls is a major challenge and source of bias in case-control studies (Pirkis et al., 2020; Schulz & Grimes, 2002; Webb et al., 2020). Controls can be sampled from different registers (e.g., population registers, lists of GPs, and electoral rolls). Other options include neighborhood or friend controls, hospital controls, or dead controls (could be justifiable if cases are decedents). When choosing a specific type of control group, we need to be cognizant of their limitations. Nevertheless, controls should be selected independently of their exposure status (Rothman, Greenland, & Lash, 2008b; Webb et al., 2020).

In suicide research, the majority of case-control studies analyze suicides and use the PA method to collect information. Although the majority of studies use living controls (Milner, Sveticic, & De Leo, 2013; Pirkis et al., 2020), we must consider potential information bias in data collection when using suicide cases and living controls. Data collection on the suicide cases would involve a higher possibility of recall bias because information is derived from a third person (e.g., a relative), and traditionally the data are collected 3 to 12 months after the suicide. In addition, bereaved relatives are more likely to focus on factors they consider as potential causes of suicide (Pirkis et al., 2020). Therefore, some PA case-control studies have used alternative types of deaths as controls, including those from natural causes (Harwood, Hawton, Hope, Harriss, & Jacoby, 2006), sudden deaths (De Leo, Draper, Snowdon, & Kõlves, 2013), or injury mortality categories other than suicide (Phillips et al., 2002). The last two are considered, similarly to suicides, as acute, unexpected, and with comparable adverse impacts on informants. However, use of decedents as controls is likely to underestimate the true association between an exposure and outcome, because they share some similar risk factor or factors for (premature) death – for example, a physical illnesses such as cancer was found to be a risk factor for suicide in older adults in a study using living controls (Waern et al., 2002), but not in a study using sudden deaths as controls (De Leo et al., 2013). As noted by Webb and associates (2020), epidemiological studies rarely occur under ideal circumstances, and multiple control groups can be considered. However, their utilization is time and resource intensive (Celentano & Moyses, 2018; Merrill, 2013; Rothman et al., 2008b).

Similar to other types of analytical studies, case-control studies need to address the risk of confounding (Schulz & Grimes, 2002). *Matching* is one option for controlling some well-known confounders, such as sex, age, and area of residence (Merrill, 2013; Webb et al., 2020). This involves selecting one or more controls with the same characteristics (of a confounding variable) as the case for individual matching or for frequency matching. We aim for controls to share a similar distribution in a potential confounding variable as the cases (e.g., 80 % males; Webb et al., 2020). Another option to control for confounding variables is through multivariable statistical modeling. An example of a matched case-control study, using living controls with data collected from relatives, is described in Box 6.4.

Box 6.4. Example of a case-control study from Hong Kong

An increase in suicide rates in Hong Kong in the early 2000s motivated researchers to conduct a psychological autopsy case-control study. They focused on suicide in people with ethnic Chinese background who were aged 15–59 years in Hong Kong in 2002–2004. The procedures were approved by the relevant ethics committees.

Information about suicide cases was identified from the coroner and recruited through the forensic pathology service and the Coroner's Court. The next-of-kin of the suicide deceased were invited to an interview between 6 weeks to 12 months after the event to avoid recall limitations. Out of a total of 1,038 people approached, the first 150 informants who consented to the study were interviewed.

The control group was recruited from another nationally representative epidemiological study. One hundred and fifty age and gender matched subjects were selected and their closest relatives were invited to participate in the interviews.

Trained interviewers used a semi-structured interview schedule including different scales to collect information about various sociodemographic factors, life events, and clinical and psychological conditions from both groups. Detailed case discussions were conducted to systematically handle discrepant information from multiple sources, including consultations to reach consensus diagnoses for psychiatric conditions. Univariate and multivariate logistic regression was used for the statistical analyses.

The cases included 96 male and 54 female suicides with a mean age of 38.7 years. There was no significant difference in the gender or age distributions between the sample and all suicides aged 15–59 years in 2003. A number of significant differences between the suicide cases and their living controls were detected. Their final multivariable model included six factors that remained significantly associated with suicide, including psychiatric illness, previous suicide attempt, unmanageable debts, unemployment or underemployment, being single, and lack of social support. The final model explained 80 % of the variance between the suicide and the control groups. Significant interaction effects were not identified.

The authors noted the potential recall bias of psychological autopsy studies and justified their choice of living controls. They emphasized the importance of both psychosocial and clinical factors for suicide in Hong Kong in their conclusion.

Based on Chen, E.Y., Chan, W.S., Wong, P.W., Chan, S.S., Chan, C.L., Law, Y., ... Liu, K.Y. (2006). Suicide in Hong Kong: A case-control psychological autopsy study. *Psychological Medicine, 36*, 815–825.

As previously noted, we can compare the frequency of exposure in cases and controls. We can also compare the odds and calculate the odds ratio, which is the most common measure used in estimating the strength of association in case-control studies (see Box 6.3). The most widely used statistical method in the utilization of this measure is multiple logistic regression analysis. If the cases and controls are matched, then conditional logistic regression is the appropriate statistical procedure.

Case-control studies have a number of advantages. They are particularly efficient concerning cost, time, and sample size compared with other analytical study designs (Bonita et al., 2006; Manja & Lakshminrusimha, 2014). However, note the following caveat from Schulz and Grimes (2002) concerning the use of case-control studies: "Although easier to do they are also easier to do wrong" (p. 431). As previously described, there is a need for caution about different possible biases when interpreting the results of such a study.

Case-Crossover Studies

A *case-crossover study* is a relatively new study design that is suitable for investigating time-varying exposures on acute outcomes. For example, the effect of sexual activity on cardiac infarction was analyzed by Maclure (1991) in his formative study. In case-crossover studies, cases serve as their own controls (Maclure, 1991; Maclure & Mittleman, 2000; Rothman et al., 2008b). More specifically, rather than selecting controls and comparing occurrence of exposure in cases and controls, we select different time periods for each case: a case period – a relatively short time before the outcome (e.g., a day or a month) – and one or more control periods, and measure the exposure during these time intervals. Frequency of exposure during the case period is compared with the exposure frequency during the control period(s) (Maclure & Mittleman, 2000; Rothman et al., 2008b). Different options exist for selecting the control period and measuring exposure; for example, exposure status on a previous day(s)–pair matching or usual frequency of exposure in the past month (Maclure & Mittleman, 2000). Nevertheless, case-crossover studies are comparable to matched case-control studies when we do not need suitable controls, and when fixed confounders, such as gender, genetic, and chronic health conditions, are controlled (Maclure, 1991; Maclure & Mittleman, 2000). The traditional statistical method to analyze case-crossover studies is conditional logistic regression.

Although the case-crossover study design is appropriate for studying suicidal behavior (as a sudden outcome), particularly for proximal risk factors such as life events and acute use of alcohol, it is rarely used in suicide research. The first studies using the case-crossover

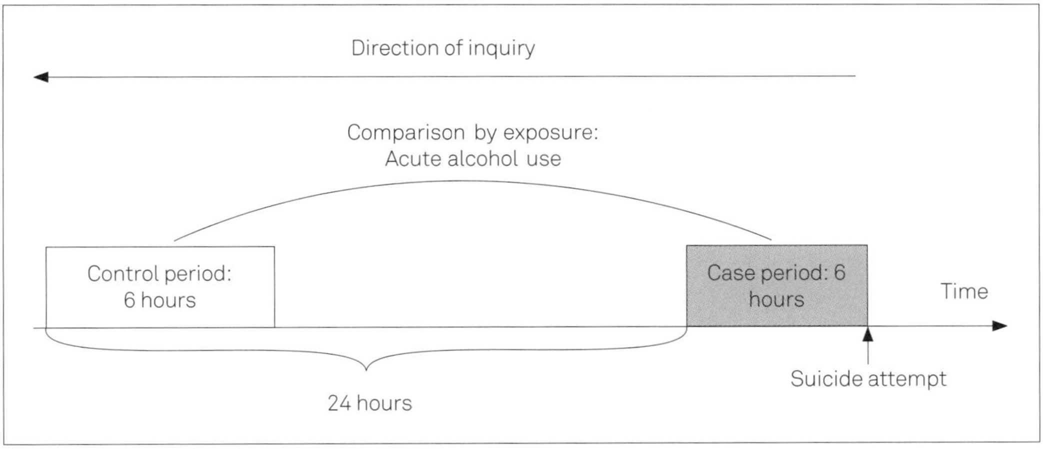

Figure 6.5 An example of a case-crossover study design. Based on Bagge, C. L., Lee, H.-J., Schumacher, J. A., Gratz, K. L., Krull, J. L., & Holloman, G., Jr. (2013). Alcohol as an acute risk factor for recent suicide attempts: A case-crossover analysis. *Journal of Studies on Alcohol and Drugs, 74*, 552–558.

design for that purpose have mainly analyzed the potential impact of time-varying exposures, such as acute alcohol use (Borges et al., 2004) or the initiation of medicines (e.g., antiepileptic drugs, in a study by Olesen et al., 2010) on the risk for suicide attempt and suicide. There has been a recent increase in use of the case-crossover design to analyze the association between climatic exposures, such as temperature (e.g., Kim et al., 2019) and air pollution, and suicide (e.g., Casas et al., 2017). Figure 6.5 illustrates the use of the case-crossover design in an analysis of acute alcohol use among 192 suicide attempters presenting to a trauma hospital in the state of Mississippi in the US (Bagge et al., 2013). The authors used pair matching in comparing alcohol use during the 6-hr period prior (case period) to suicide attempts with their alcohol use 1 day earlier (control period). In addition to fixed covariates, which were controlled for in the study design, they adjusted for other drug use and negative life events during the case period. Suicide attempters manifested 6.3 times (95% confidence interval, 2.1–19.3) higher odds of acute alcohol use during the case period compared with the control period, indicating that acute alcohol use is a proximal risk factor for a suicide attempt.

Case-crossover studies are time efficient, cheap to conduct, and control for fixed confounders. However, only a limited number of exposures can be investigated (Rothman et al., 2008b). There is also the potential for recall bias, if people are interviewed about prior exposures.

Cohort Studies

A *cohort study*, also called an incidence, longitudinal, or follow-up study, is the best observational study design to identify causal factors because it provides the most direct measurement of the risk of developing disease or becoming injured. In contrast to cross-sectional and case-control studies, cohort studies follow people from exposure to outcome. Thus, we can establish the temporal sequence needed to avoid reverse causality. A traditional prospective cohort study follows exposed and nonexposed cohorts of people over a period of time to measure incidence – that is, the first occurrence of the outcome(s) of interest (Figure 6.6.;

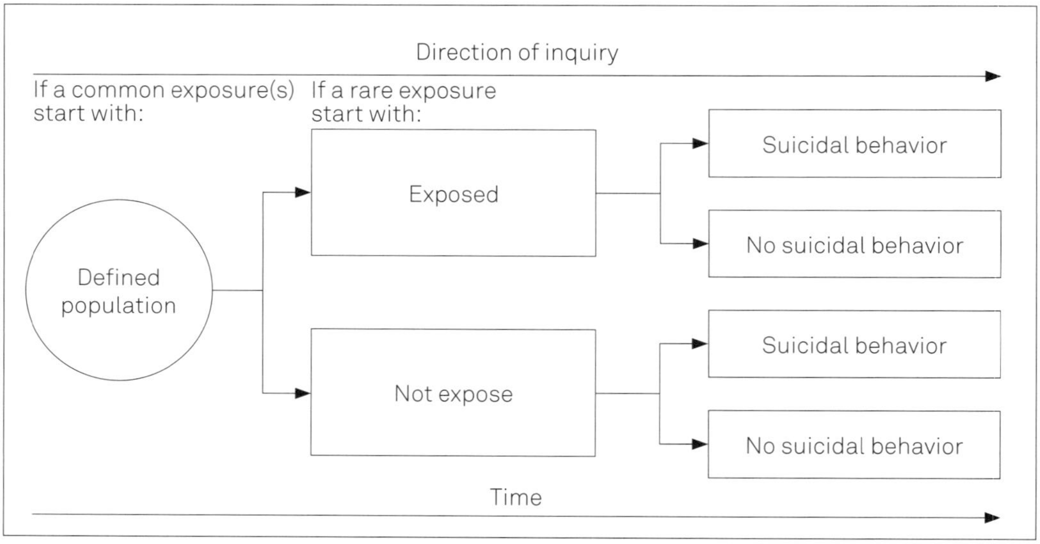

Figure 6.6 The cohort study design. Adapted with permission from "Basic Epidemiology," by R. Bonita, R. Beaglehole, & T. Kjellström, 2006, p. 47. © 2006 by the World Health Organization.

Grimes & Schulz, 2002b; Webb et al., 2020). The incidence in the two groups is compared. In suicide research we could, for example, study alcohol use, with an exposed group comprising multiple cohorts – heavy and regular users and abstainers (no exposure). We would then follow them to a first suicide attempt or suicide as our outcomes of interest. Since cohort studies measure the incidence of the outcome of interest, they need to commence with a defined population (healthy people without an outcome), and may require long periods of follow-up until the outcome of interest occurs (Celentano & Moyses, 2018; Webb et al., 2020). Therefore, they are not well suited for the study of rare outcomes, such as suicides, and thus cohort studies more frequently examine suicide attempts or suicidal ideation.

Another challenge for cohort studies is the long follow-up period if information was only collected at baseline (initiation of the cohort). If people subsequently changed their health behavior (e.g., modified their drinking habits), misclassification would ensue (Webb et al., 2020).

Selecting the Study Populations

Selection of a study cohort(s) depends on whether the exposure is common or rare:

With a *common exposure*, we can start by selecting a defined population and then dividing people into cohorts as the exposure is identified or they become exposed (see Figure 6.6). We can select a population based on some factor other than exposure (e.g., same community or time of birth; Celentano & Moyses, 2018). In this instance, we are using an *internal comparison* group(s), since both the exposed and unexposed emanate from the same population (Grimes & Schulz, 2002b; Woodward, 2005).

A good example of a cohort study of an internal comparison group is the Avon Longitudinal Study of Parents and Children (ALSPAC), a population-based birth cohort study that investigated influences on health and development across the life course. The study started with an initial sample of 14,541 pregnancies from the southwest of England in the period

1991–1992 (Boyd et al., 2013). Children and mothers or their primary caregivers were regularly followed up. Children were first asked about their suicidality at age 11 years (Winsper, Lereya, Zanarini, & Wolke, 2012). Several analyses have been conducted since then to link suicidality with different exposures, such as bullying (Winsper et al., 2012), birth order (Easey, Mars, Pearson, Heron, & Gunnell, 2019), autistic traits (Culpin et al., 2018), and parental suicidal behavior (Geulayov, Metcalfe, Heron, Kidger, & Gunnell, 2014).

With a *rare exposure*, the sample drawn from a population might be too small to generate a sufficient number of exposed persons (Celentano & Moyses, 2018). So we should start with respective groups of exposed and unexposed people. In this instance, we need to consider selecting a suitable *external comparison* group(s) – that is, those without the exposure (Grimes & Schulz, 2002b; Woodward, 2005). For example, a suicide death can also be an exposure for those left behind, the survivors. We can follow people bereaved by suicide over time to measure different outcomes, and to compare them with those not bereaved by suicide. Traditionally, this bereaved group is compared with a cohort of people bereaved by other types of death. However, this group could also be compared with non-bereaved (Brent, Melhem, Donohoe, & Walker, 2009). Nevertheless, selection of a comparison group depends on the aims of the study. Different types of selection bias should be considered.

In addition to selecting cohort(s), a crucial aspect of cohort studies is attrition of participants during follow-up. Common reasons for attrition are migration, death, and withdrawal from participation in the study. As loss to follow-up is unlikely to be random, it may potentially bias the results. Potential attrition and how to address it must be considered at the time of project planning – for example, the study would include the collection of contact details of next of kin or of a GP (Grimes & Schulz, 2002b). Information about death can also be obtained through linkage with official death records.

Cohort studies enable us to measure incidence and calculate risk and rate ratios (Box 6.3), and measure survival time. Several statistical methods are utilized for complex analyses to adjust for potential confounding. A few examples include Cox regression to calculate and compare hazard ratios and Poisson regression to calculate incidence rate ratios.

Prognostic Studies

Cohort studies can also start with an outcome (e.g., suicide attempt), in which case, they are called *survival studies* or prognostic studies. They then investigate what happens subsequent to the outcome – for example, recurrence or death (Dekkers et al., 2012; Webb et al., 2020). People with the condition (inception cohort) are followed for the same duration. As event occurrence (repeated suicide attempt or suicide) is relatively high, these studies can be conducted with smaller sample sizes. In suicide research, we can utilize surveillance systems to design similar studies to estimate risk factors for repeated suicide attempts or suicide death. See Box 6.5 for an example of a prognostic cohort study from Sri Lanka that analyzed determinants of repeated suicide attempts and suicide up to 2 years following the index suicide attempt (Knipe et al., 2019).

Box 6.5. Example of a prognostic cohort study from Sri Lanka

There is lack of studies about the risk of repeat self-harm and suicide from low and middle-income countries (LMICs). Therefore, the authors aimed to examine the risk of repeated self-harm and suicide among people presenting to the hospital with self-harm, and what factors were associated with an increased risk of repeated self-harm in rural Sri Lanka.

Information from a comprehensive suicide and self-harm surveillance system established in the frames of a large-scale randomized trial, including 223,861 people from 53,382 households, was utilized for this cohort study. Information collected through face-to-face interviews in the local language in the frames of the trial formed a baseline. All episodes of nonfatal and fatal self-harm (regardless of intent) presenting to 13 hospitals in rural Sri Lanka (11 small peripheral hospitals and two larger referral hospitals) over the 3–5 year follow-up period between 29 July 2011 and 12 May 2016 were included. For quality assurance, additional information about self-harm (fatal and non-fatal) was collected at the household level 3 years after the start of follow-up. Deaths were identified through the systematic surveys of police records and coroners' records. Ethical clearance was received from the relevant research ethics committees. Statistical analyses included Kaplan-Meier survival analysis, Cox proportional hazard and adjusted logistic regression models.

Analysis included 2,259 individuals with eligible index episodes of self-harm that were linked back to the baseline survey, they were older than 10 years and did not die during the first episode. Risk of repeated self-harm in first 12 months was 3.1 % and 5.2 % in 24 months; and risk of suicide was 0.6 % in 12 months and 0.8 % in 24 months. Risk of repeated self-harm (both fatal and nonfatal) was higher in men than in women, in older adults (56 years and older), and in those who used methods other than poisoning in their index presentation.

Risk of repeated self-harm, both fatal and non-fatal, was much lower compared to the high-income countries. The focus on repeated self-harm might have less impact in preventing suicides, and the targeting of other risk factors should be prioritized in rural areas in south Asia.

The authors noted some study deficiencies. They included the focus on hospitalized non-fatal self-harm only; limited demographic and clinical data available in the surveillance system; the possibility that people could have presented to a hospital outside the study area; and the small number of suicides that limited the statistical power of the relevant analyses. The results were not generalizable to the LMIC urban areas, where pesticides are not easily accessible as a means of suicide.

Based on Knipe, D., Metcalfe, C., Hawton, K., Pearson, M., Dawson, A., Jayamanne, S., ... Gunnell, D. (2019). Risk of suicide and repeat self-harm after hospital attendance for non-fatal self-harm in Sri Lanka: A cohort study. *Lancet Psychiatry, 6*, 659–666.

Historical or Retrospective Cohort Studies

While conducting prospective cohort studies is time-consuming and expensive, there is also the option of conducting *retrospective cohort studies*, also called *historical cohort studies* (Webb et al., 2020). In retrospective cohort studies, we identify information about the past exposure using records or data collected historically (Bonita et al., 2006; Webb et al., 2020). Despite tracking exposure retrospectively, our observation period still extends from exposure to outcome (the opposite direction of inquiry to case-control studies; Celentano & Moyses,

2018). The majority of large-scale retrospective cohort studies have been conducted in Scandinavian countries using national registries, which enable linkage of information and follow-up of cohorts over longer periods (Erlangsen, Qin, & Mittendorfer-Rutz, 2018). (For more about data linkage studies, see Chapter 8).

Nested Case-Control Studies and Case-Cohort Studies

Nested case-control and *case-cohort studies* are other options to reduce the costs of cohort studies (Celentano & Moyses, 2018; Webb et al., 2020). A nested case-control study is a case-control study embedded within a cohort study. Therefore, some epidemiologists consider them a subtype of case-control study, whereas others consider them a cohort study. More specifically, cases from an existing cohort are selected as the exposure of interest occurs (e.g., suicide). Controls are chosen from the same cohort. For a nested case-control study, one or more matched controls are selected simultaneously with cases. However, in case-cohort design studies, controls are selected randomly from the cohort at baseline (Celentano & Moyses, 2018; Webb et al., 2020). In addition to the compiled information on exposures at baseline, additional information can be collected and analyzed. In suicide research, nested case-control studies frequently utilize register-based data linkages (see Chapter 8 about data linkages for an example).

Ethical Considerations

Important ethical principles, applicable to all studies involving human subjects, include informed consent, privacy protection, and confidentiality for study participants, and respect for human rights and scientific integrity (Bonita et al., 2006). Protocols for all epidemiological studies, involving direct contact with human subjects, must be reviewed and approved by a human research ethics committee (for more on ethical aspects of suicide research, see Chapter 4).

Validity in Observational Studies

Validity measures the degree to which a measurement captures what it purports to measure. In the context of analytical research, there are two aspects to it: internal and external validity.

Internal Validity

Internal validity reflects whether the results of a study are true representations of reality (Figure 6.7). There are three major threats to internal validity that need to be considered in research studies: random error (chance), systematic error, and confounding. Both systematic error and confounding are forms of bias (Choi & Pak, 2005), and are sometimes referred to as *alternative explanations* for the results (Webb et al., 2020).

Random error refers to the degree to which the study's results are due to chance alone, which can lead to an incorrect estimate of the association between the exposure and outcome. One way to assess whether the association between exposure and outcome occurred

Figure 6.7 Internal and external validity.

by chance is to test a statistical hypothesis and calculate the probability (*p*) of a chance result (Grimes & Schulz, 2002a). The other, more preferred option is to calculate 95% confidence intervals around measures – narrower confidence intervals indicate greater precision (Grimes & Schulz, 2002a; Webb et al., 2020). The main sources of random error are sampling error, measurement error, and individual differences (Bonita et al., 2006). While we cannot completely avoid random error, we can increase our precision by increasing our sample size and improving the accuracy of our measurements (Bonita et al., 2006; Webb et al., 2020).

Systematic error occurs when study results differ systematically from the true values (Bonita et al., 2006). There are several different sources of related bias that researchers and participants can introduce at any stage of a study – during the study design, data collection, analysis, or interpretation. We previously addressed some of these under specific observational study designs. Systematic errors can lead to underestimation or overestimation of the true association, produce nonexistent associations, or mask true associations. There are two main types of bias associated with systematic error in observational epidemiological research. They are selection bias and information bias (Celentano & Moyses, 2018).

Selection bias refers to systematic artifactual differences in the characteristics of participants and nonparticipants and the study and comparison groups related to the selection of the study subjects, which can distort study findings (Bonita et al., 2006; Webb et al., 2020). There are a number of reasons for selection bias, including the use of convenience sampling (volunteers) and low response rates, resulting in exposure to self-selection of study participants. For example, people are more likely to participate in suicide research when they have been exposed to, or are particularly concerned about, suicidal behavior. Another source of selection bias is referred to as the *healthy worker effect*, which occurs in occupational studies if a specific occupational group is compared with a general population, because working people are in general healthier than others in the general population (Webb et al., 2020). In cohort studies, reasons for selection bias also include loss to follow-up.

Information bias (also known as *measurement bias* or *classification bias*) pertains to the quality of information, and more specifically to inaccuracies in the collection of information about exposures and outcomes, resulting in misclassification (Grimes & Schulz, 2002a; Rothman, Greenland, & Lash, 2008a). There are several sources of measurement error, including *recall bias*, which is a major obstacle to conducting PAs and a general obstacle for case-control studies. Another source is *observer bias*, where a researcher, clinician, or participant knows the exposure or outcome status. This knowledge may influence measurement. For instance, if an investigator knows a case was a suicide in a case-control study, they might be more inclined to diagnose a psychiatric disorder postmortem. Additionally, measurement error can occur if we use variable data collection methods – phone versus face-to-face interview or self-report versus interview (Grimes & Schulz, 2002a).

The effect of information bias on the association between an exposure and outcome of interest depends on whether or not classification was uniform for different groups. *Differential misclassification* refers to variable misclassification between groups. This may lead to underestimation or overestimation of the association. For example, collecting information from relatives who have lost their loved one to suicide, and using living controls, is likely to cause differential misclassification. *Nondifferential misclassification* refers to misclassification (e.g., problems with a specific scale) that is proportionally the same for all participants, and is more likely to attenuate or underestimate the strength of an association (Grimes & Schulz, 2002a; Webb et al., 2020).

To avoid systematic error, study protocols are needed that include clear definitions, inclusion and exclusion criteria, carefully chosen instruments, training of interviewers, and standard data collection methods (Webb et al., 2020). We should measure differences between participants and nonparticipants, and collect information about the reasons for attrition of subjects during follow-up (e.g., from a next of kin or GP).

Confounding occurs when the true association between the exposure and outcome is distorted by a third factor – a confounder – leading to a spurious effect. We need to test for potential confounders. They must be identified at the time of study design to ensure the relevant information is collected. Confounding occurs when (1) the exposure and confounder are both associated with the outcome; (2) the confounder is associated with the exposure; and (3) the confounder does not lie on the causal pathway between the exposure and outcome. In suicide research, the association between physical illness and suicide, for example, can be confounded by some other factor such as age (Figure 6.8). The confounding does not necessarily explain the relationship, but it may induce underestimation or overestimation of the true association, or obscure it completely (Bonita et al., 2006; Webb et al., 2020).

In observational studies, confounding can be controlled by restriction (e.g., including only males), matching (described previously in the section Selecting Cases and Controls), or a particular method of statistical analysis (e.g., using multivariable modeling).

External Validity

External validity refers to the generalizability of study results. Are the study findings applicable to the larger population or other groups, places, or times? Although internal validity is necessary, it does not guarantee external validity, and there are no rules for assessment. Such

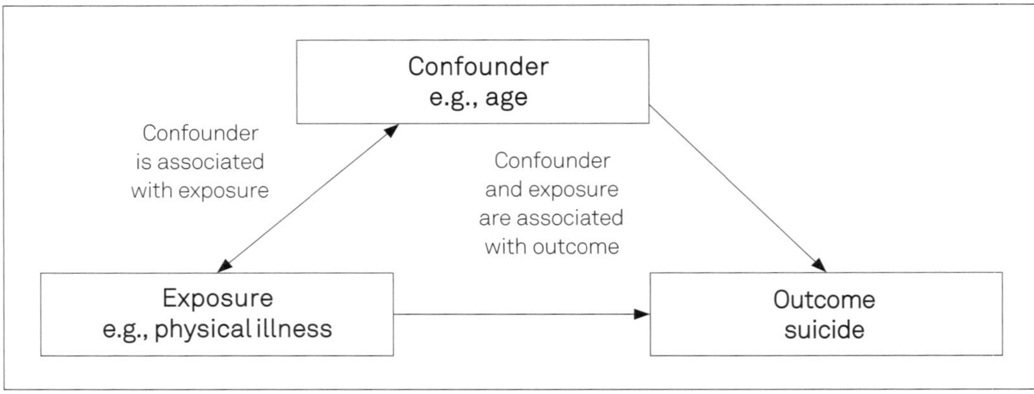

Figure 6.8 An example of a potential confounding effect.

assessment can therefore be considered more subjective than that for internal validity (Grimes & Schulz, 2002a; Webb et al., 2020). Webb and associates (2020) recommend considering whether results from the source population might be applicable to other populations (e.g., other countries). Thus, external validity can be further supported by similar findings from studies of other groups or countries (Bonita et al., 2006).

Causation

The ultimate goal of epidemiological studies is to determine causal relationships between the exposure and outcome, to support public health activities to prevent a condition of interest (Bonita et al., 2006; Parascandola, 2011). Although suicide is not a disease, it is an important public health problem, and a similar approach is necessary to prevent suicidal behavior (Franklin et al., 2017; Turecki et al., 2019). The concept of *cause* has changed over time. Until the mid-20th century, the prevailing understanding in epidemiology was that there was a single cause of a disease. After World War II, there was a need for adjustment to change the focus from communicable (infectious and parasitic) diseases as the major killers, to chronic diseases and related conditions. Current public health research argues that cause is not necessarily universal, and a multifactorial approach is now the predominant paradigm in epidemiology (De Vreese, 2009; Parascandola, 2011). Nevertheless, there is ongoing debate about the definition of cause, and different concepts of causation exist with a divide between deterministic and probabilistic approaches (De Vreese, 2009). Although some authors have called for a shared agreement on understanding causality and use of a singular approach (Parascandola, 2011; Rothman & Greenland, 2008), others encourage acceptance of pluralistic views to avoid restricting study questions and designs (Vandenbroucke, Broadbent, & Pearce, 2016). Some recommend avoidance of the notion of causation altogether (Lipton & Ødegaard, 2005).

Regardless, associations measured in observational studies are not necessarily causal. The first step is to establish whether an emergent association is valid (described above in the section Validity in Observational Studies). The next step involves assessing the association based on available information, which is not a straightforward process (Celentano & Moyses, 2018). Although a number of guidelines exist to evaluate causal inference, the most commonly referred to are those proposed by the medical statistician, Sir Austin Bradford Hill, as flexible guidelines or considerations (Fedak, Bernal, Capshaw, & Gross, 2015; Grimes & Schulz, 2002a). Widely known as the Bradford Hill criteria, they include:

- Strength of association – the stronger the association between the exposure and outcome, the more likely there is a causal relationship between the exposure and outcome (measured by risk ratio or odds ratio).
- Consistency of association – repeated results using different study designs, locations, and populations are more likely to indicate causation.
- Specificity – the association is more likely to be causal if it is specific – one exposure causes one outcome.
- Temporality – exposure has to precede outcome.
- Biological gradient – association is likely to be causal if an increase in the exposure results in an increase in the outcome (dose-response relationship).
- Biological plausibility – scientific plausibility of the association, which depends on the current state of knowledge.
- Coherence – an apparent causal association should not conflict with wider scientific knowledge (similar to biological plausibility).
- Experiment – evidence from an experiment showing that removing exposure reduces the likelihood of the outcome.
- Analogy – something similar established earlier – a similar exposure is causing a similar condition.

Bradford Hill did not propose his criteria as a strict checklist (Fedak et al., 2015; Rothman, Greenland, & Lash, 2008a). But over 50 years later, it remains a useful tool for making judgments about causality (Fedak et al., 2015). Some of the criteria are considered inarguable (e.g., especially temporality), and some others are less helpful (e.g., specificity; Fedak et al., 2015; Grimes & Schulz, 2002a). Therefore, we need to remain critical in our judgments about causation. The more the Bradford Hill and kindred criteria are affirmed in assessing causality – with temporality being essential – the more compelling the case.

More research into causal risk factors is necessary. As indicated by Franklin and colleagues (2017) there is a paucity of research on causal risk factors in suicide research. One word of caution in assessing causality in an observed association between an exposure and outcome of interest stems from the thinking of the philosopher of science Karl Popper (1962). He prudently argued that we can falsify a theory or hypothesis but never prove one. Moreover, also salient is the fact that "absence of evidence is not evidence of absence" (Altman & Bland, 1995, p. 485).

Extended Direction

A relatively new approach for conducting observational research on suicidal behavior is referred to as *mixed methods*, which blends the qualitative with the quantitative (Ross, 2012). For example, use of focus groups (a qualitative method) which comprise first responders to death scenes, such as police and emergency medical technicians, together with a facilitator, such as the researcher, could yield a useful hypothesis about initial responses of next of kin to the possible suicide of a family member. In turn, this hypothesis could be preliminarily tested in case-control studies, and subsequently in cohort studies, if that is justified (see Chapter 10 for mixed methods). In closing, a takeaway message in the context of this example of a mixed methods approach is a quotation from the 19th-century physicist Lord Kelvin:

I often say that when you can measure what you are speaking about, and express it in numbers, you know something about it; but when you cannot express it in numbers, your knowledge is of a meager and unsatisfactory kind; it may be the beginning of knowledge, but you have scarcely, in your thoughts, advanced to the stage of *Science*, whatever the matter may be. (Thomson, 1891, p. 73)

References

Almeida, O. P., Draper, B., Snowdon, J., Lautenschlager, N. T., Pirkis, J., Byrne, G., ... Pfaff, J. J. (2012). Factors associated with suicidal thoughts in a large community study of older adults. *British Journal of Psychiatry, 201*(6), 466–472. https://doi.org/10.1192/bjp.bp.112.110130

Altman, D. G., & Bland, J. M. (1995). Statistics notes: Absence of evidence is not evidence of absence. *BMJ, 311*(7003), 485.https://doi.org/10.1136/bmj.311.7003.485

Bagge, C. L., Lee, H.-J., Schumacher, J. A., Gratz, K. L., Krull, J. L., & Holloman, G., Jr. (2013). Alcohol as an acute risk factor for recent suicide attempts: a case-crossover analysis. *Journal of Studies on Alcohol and Drugs, 74*, 552–558. https://doi.org/10.15288/jsad.2013.74.552

Bertolote, J. M., Fleischmann, A., De Leo, D., Bolhari, J., Botega, N., De Silva, D., ... Värnik, A. (2005). Suicide attempts, plans, and ideation in culturally diverse sites: the WHO SUPRE-MISS community survey. *Psychological Medicine, 35*, 1457–1465. https://doi.org/10.1017/S0033291705005404

Bonita, R., Beaglehole, R., & Kjellström, T. (2006). *Basic epidemiology*. Geneva, Switzerland: World Health Organization.

Borges, G., Cherpitel, C. J., MacDonald, S., Giesbrecht, N., Stockwell, T., & Wilcox, H. C. (2004). A case-crossover study of acute alcohol use and suicide attempt. *Journal of Studies on Alcohol, 65*(6), 708–714. https://doi.org/10.15288/jsa.2004.65.708

Boyd, A., Golding, J., Macleod, J., Lawlor, D. A., Fraser, A., Henderson, J., ... Davey Smith, G. (2013). Cohort profile: the 'children of the 90s' – the index offspring of the Avon Longitudinal Study of Parents and Children. *International Journal of Epidemiology, 42*(1), 111–127. https://doi.org/10.1093/ije/dys064

Brent, D., Melhem, N., Donohoe, M. B., & Walker, M. (2009). The incidence and course of depression in bereaved youth 21 months after the loss of a parent to suicide, accident, or sudden natural death. *American Journal of Psychiatry, 166*, 786–794. https://doi.org/10.1176/appi.ajp.2009.08081244

Casas, L., Cox, B., Bauwelinck, M., Nemery, B., Deboosere, P., & Nawrot, T. S. (2017). Does air pollution trigger suicide? A case-crossover analysis of suicide deaths over the life span. *European Journal of Epidemiology, 32*(11), 973–981. https://doi.org/10.1007/s10654-017-0273-8

Celentano, D. D., & Moyses, S. (2018). *Gordis epidemiology* (6th ed.). Philadelphia, PA: Elsevier.

Centers for Disease Control and Prevention. (2012). *Principles of epidemiology in public health practice. An introduction to applied epidemiology and biostatistics* (3rd ed.). Atlanta, GA: U.S. Department of Health and Human Services.

Centini, F., Fiore, C., Riezzo, I., Rossi, G., & Fineschi, V. (2007). Suicide due to oral ingestion of lidocaine: A case report and review of the literature. *Forensic Science International, 171*(1), 57–62. https://doi.org/10.1016/j.forsciint.2006.05.003

Chen, E. Y., Chan, W. S., Wong, P. W., Chan, S. S., Chan, C. L., Law, Y., ... Liu, K. Y. (2006). Suicide in Hong Kong: A case-control psychological autopsy study. *Psychological Medicine, 36*, 815–825. https://doi.org/10.1017/S0033291706007240

Choi, B. C., & Pak, A. W. (2005). Understanding and minimizing epidemiologic bias in public health research. *Canadian Journal of Public Health, 96*(4), 284–286. https://doi.org/10.1007/BF03405165

Culpin, I., Mars, B., Pearson, R. M., Golding, J., Heron, J., Bubak, I., ... Rai, D. (2018). Autistic traits and suicidal thoughts, plans, and self-harm in late adolescence: Population-based cohort study. *Journal of the American Academy of Child & Adolescent Psychiatry, 57*(5), 313–320. e316. https://doi.org/10.1101/165860

Dekkers, O. M., Egger, M., Altman, D. G., & Vandenbroucke, J. P. (2012). Distinguishing case series from cohort studies. *Annals of Internal Medicine, 156*(1), 37–40. https://doi.org/10.7326/0003-4819-156-1-201201030-00006

De Leo, D., Draper, B.M., Snowdon, J., & Kõlves, K. (2013). Suicides in older adults: A case-control psychological autopsy study in Australia. *Journal of Psychiatric Research, 47*(7), 980–988. https://doi.org/10.1016/j.jpsychires.2013.02.009

De Vreese, L. (2009). Epidemiology and causation. *Medicine, Health Care and Philosophy, 12*(3), 345–353. https://doi.org/10.1007/s11019-009-9184-0

Durkheim, E. (1897/2002). *Suicide: A study in sociology*. London, UK: Routledge.

Easey, K.E., Mars, B., Pearson, R., Heron, J., & Gunnell, D. (2019). Association of birth order with adolescent mental health and suicide attempts: a population-based longitudinal study. *European Child & Adolescent Psychiatry, 28*, 1079–1086. https://doi.org/10.1007/s00787-018-1266-1

Erlangsen, A., Qin, P., & Mittendorfer-Rutz, E. (2018). Studies of suicidal behavior using national registers: An adventure without boundaries? *Crisis, 39*(3), 153–158. https://doi.org/10.1027/0227-5910/a000552

Fadnes, L.T., Taube, A., & Tylleskär, T. (2009). How to identify information bias due to self-reporting in epidemiological research. *Internet Journal of Epidemiology, 7*(2), 28–38.

Fedak, K.M., Bernal, A., Capshaw, Z.A., & Gross, S. (2015). Applying the Bradford Hill criteria in the 21st century: How data integration has changed causal inference in molecular epidemiology. *Emerging Themes in Epidemiology, 12*(1), 14. https://doi.org/10.1186/s12982-015-0037-4

Franklin, J.C., Ribeiro, J.D., Fox, K.R., Bentley, K.H., Kleiman, E.M., Huang, X., ... Nock, M.K. (2017). Risk factors for suicidal thoughts and behaviors: A meta-analysis of 50 years of research. *Psychological Bulletin, 143*(2), 187. https://doi.org/10.1037/bul0000084

Geulayov, G., Metcalfe, C., Heron, J., Kidger, J., & Gunnell, D. (2014). Parental suicide attempt and offspring self-harm and suicidal thoughts: Results from the Avon Longitudinal Study of Parents and Children (ALSPAC) birth cohort. *Journal of the American Academy of Child & Adolescent Psychiatry, 53*, 509–517. e502. https://doi.org/10.1016/j.jaac.2013.12.022

Glenn, C.R., Franklin, J.C., Kearns, J.C., Lanzillo, E.C., & Nock, M.K. (2016). Suicide research methods and designs. In R. O'Connor & J. Pirkis (Eds.), *The international handbook of suicide prevention* (pp. 710–724). Chichester, UK: Wiley.

Goodfellow, B., Kõlves, K., Selefen, A.-C., Massain, T., Amadéo, S., & De Leo, D. (2020). The WHO/START study in New Caledonia: A psychological autopsy case series. *Journal of Affective Disorders, 262*, 366–372. https://doi.org/10.1016/j.jad.2019.11.020

Grimes, D.A., & Schulz, K.F. (2002a). Bias and causal associations in observational research. *Lancet, 359*(9302), 248–252.

Grimes, D.A., & Schulz, K.F. (2002b). Cohort studies: Marching towards outcomes. *Lancet, 359*(9303), 341–345.

Grimes, D.A., & Schulz, K.F. (2002c). Descriptive studies: What they can and cannot do. *Lancet, 359*(9301), 145–149.

Grimes, D.A., & Schulz, K.F. (2002d). An overview of clinical research: The lay of the land. *Lancet, 359*(9300), 57–61.

Harwood, D.M.J., Hawton, K., Hope, T., Harriss, L., & Jacoby, R. (2006). Life problems and physical illness as risk factors for suicide in older people: A descriptive and case-control study. *Psychological Medicine, 36*(9), 1265–1274. https://doi.org/10.1017/S0033291706007872

Haut, F., & Morrison, A. (1998). The Internet and the future of psychiatry. *Psychiatric Bulletin, 22*, 641–642. https://doi.org/10.1192/pb.22.10.641-a

Jones, D.R. (1977). Suicide by aircraft: A case report. *Aviation, Space, and Environmental Medicine, 48*, 454–459.

Kaess, M., Durkee, T., Brunner, R., Carli, V., Parzer, P., Wasserman, C., ... Balazs, J. (2014). Pathological Internet use among European adolescents: Psychopathology and self-destructive behaviours. *European Child & Adolescent Psychiatry, 23*, 1093–1102. https://doi.org/10.1007/s00787-014-0562-7

Kim, Y., Kim, H., Gasparrini, A., Armstrong, B., Honda, Y., Chung, Y., ... Lavigne, E. (2019). Suicide and ambient temperature: A multi-country multi-city study. *Environmental Health Perspectives, 127*(11), 117007. https://doi.org/10.1289/EHP4898

Knipe, D., Metcalfe, C., Hawton, K., Pearson, M., Dawson, A., Jayamanne, S., ... Gunnell, D. (2019). Risk of suicide and repeat self-harm after hospital attendance for non-fatal self-harm in Sri Lanka: A cohort study. *Lancet Psychiatry, 6*, 659–666. https://doi.org/10.1016/S2215-0366(19)30214-7

Kõlves, K., Värnik, A., Tooding, L.-M., & Wasserman, D. (2006). The role of alcohol in suicide: A case-control psychological autopsy study. *Psychological Medicine, 36*(7), 923–930. https://doi.org/10.1017/S0033291706007707

Lipton, R., & Ødegaard, T. (2005). Causal thinking and causal language in epidemiology: It's in the details. *Epidemiologic Perspectives & Innovations, 2*(1), 8.https://doi.org/10.1186/1742-5573-2-8

Maclure, M. (1991). The case-crossover design: A method for studying transient effects on the risk of acute events. *American Journal of Epidemiology, 133*(2), 144–153. https://doi.org/10.1093/oxfordjournals.aje.a115853

Maclure, M., & Mittleman, M. (2000). Should we use a case-crossover design? *Annual Review of Public Health, 21*(1), 193–221. https://doi.org/10.1146/annurev.publhealth.21.1.193

Madentzoglou, M.S., Kastanaki, A.E., Nathena, D., Kranioti, E.F., & Michalodimitrakis, M. (2013). Nitrogen–plastic bag suicide: A case report. *American Journal of Forensic Medicine and Pathology, 34*, 311–314. https://doi.org/10.1097/PAF.0000000000000049

Manja, V., & Lakshminrusimha, S. (2014). Epidemiology and clinical research design: Part 1: Study types. *NeoReviews, 15*(12), e558–e569. https://doi.org/10.1542/neo.15-12-e558

Martin, C.D. (2006). Ernest Hemingway: A psychological autopsy of a suicide. *Psychiatry: Interpersonal and Biological Processes, 69*, 351–361. https://doi.org/10.1521/psyc.2006.69.4.351

Merrill, R.M. (2013). *Introduction to epidemiology* (6th ed.). Burlington, MA: Jones & Bartlett Learning.

Milner, A., Spittal, M.J., Pirkis, J., Chastang, J.-F., Niedhammer, I., & LaMontagne, A.D. (2017). Low control and high demands at work as risk factors for suicide: An Australian national population-level case-control study. *Psychosomatic Medicine, 79*, 358–364. https://doi.org/10.1097/PSY.0000000000000389

Milner, A., Sveticic, J., & De Leo, D. (2013). Suicide in the absence of mental disorder? A review of psychological autopsy studies across countries. *International Journal of Social Psychiatry, 59*, 545–554. https://doi.org/10.1177/0020764012444259

Morgenstern, H. (1995). Ecologic studies in epidemiology: Concepts, principles, and methods. *Annual Review of Public Health, 16*(1), 61–81. https://doi.org/10.1146/annurev.pu.16.050195.000425

Morgenstern, H. (2008). Ecologic studies. In K.J. Rothman, S. Greenland, & T.L. Lash (Eds.), *Modern epidemiology* (3rd ed., pp. 511–531). Philadelphia, PA: Lippincott Williams & Wilkins.

Olesen, J.B., Hansen, P.R., Erdal, J., Abildstrøm, S.Z., Weeke, P., Fosbøl, E.L., ... Gislason, G.H. (2010). Antiepileptic drugs and risk of suicide: A nationwide study. *Pharmacoepidemiology and Drug Safety, 19*, 518–524. https://doi.org/10.1002/pds.1932

Page, A., Milner, A., Morrell, S., & Taylor, R. (2013). The role of under-employment and unemployment in recent birth cohort effects in Australian suicide. *Social Science & Medicine, 93*, 155–162. https://doi.org/10.1016/j.socscimed.2013.03.039

Parascandola, M. (2011). Causes, risks, and probabilities: Probabilistic concepts of causation in chronic disease epidemiology. *Preventive Medicine, 53*(4–5), 232–234. https://doi.org/10.1016/j.ypmed.2011.09.007

Phillips, M.R., Yang, G., Zhang, Y., Wang, L., Ji, H., & Zhou, M. (2002). Risk factors for suicide in China: A national case-control psychological autopsy study. *Lancet, 360*(9347), 1728–1736.

Pirkis, J., Nicholas, A., & Gunnell, D. (2020). The case for case–control studies in the field of suicide prevention. *Epidemiology and Psychiatric Sciences, 29*, e62. https://doi.org/10.1017/S2045796019000581

Popper, K.R. (1962). *Conjectures and refutations: The growth of scientific knowledge*. New York, NY: Basic Books.

Porta, M. (2008). *A dictionary of epidemiology* (5 ed.). New York, NY: Oxford University Press.

Rockett, I.R. (1999). *Population and health: An introduction to epidemiology* (2nd ed). *Population Bulletin, 54*(4), 1–44.

Ross, T. (2012). *A survival guide for health research methods*. Maidenhead, UK: Open University Press.

Rothman, K.J., & Greenland, S. (2008). Cohort studies. In K.J. Rothman, S. Greenland, & T.L. Lash (Eds.), *Modern epidemiology* (3rd ed., pp. 100–110). Philadelphia, PA: Lippincott Williams & Wilkins.

Rothman, K.J., Greenland, S., & Lash, T.L. (2008a). Validity of epidemiologic studies. In K.J. Rothman, S. Greenland, & T.L. Lash (Eds.), *Modern epidemiology* (3rd ed., pp. 128–147). Philadelphia, PA: Lippincott Williams & Wilkins.

Rothman, K.J., Greenland, S., & Lash, T.L. (2008b). Case-control studies. In K.J. Rothman, S. Greenland, & T.L. Lash (Eds.), *Modern epidemiology* (3rd ed., pp. 111–127). Philadelphia, PA: Lippincott Williams & Wilkins.

Saarinen, P.I., Lehtonen, J., & Lönnqvist, J. (1999). Suicide risk in schizophrenia: An analysis of 17 consecutive suicides. *Schizophrenia Bulletin, 25*, 533–542. https://doi.org/10.1093/oxfordjournals.schbul.a033399

Schulz, K.F., & Grimes, D.A. (2002). Case-control studies: Research in reverse. *Lancet, 359*(9304), 431–434.

Sisask, M., Värnik, A., Kõlves, K., Bertolote, J.M., Bolhari, J., Botega, N.J., ... Wasserman, D. (2010). Is religiosity a protective factor against attempted suicide: A cross-cultural case-control study. *Archives of Suicide Research, 14*(1), 44–55. https://doi.org/10.1080/13811110903479052

Slade, J., Teesson, W., & Burgess, P. (2009). *The mental health of Australians 2: report on the 2007 National Survey of Mental Health and Wellbeing.* Retrieved from https://www1.health.gov.au/internet/main/publishing.nsf/content/A24556C814804A99CA257BF0001CAC45/$File/mha2hig.pdf

Stevenson, M., & McClure, R. (2005). Use of ecological study designs for injury prevention. *Injury Prevention, 11*(1), 2–4. https://doi.org/10.1136/ip.2003.003384

Stuckler, D., Basu, S., Suhrcke, M., Coutts, A., & McKee, M. (2009). The public health effect of economic crises and alternative policy responses in Europe: An empirical analysis. *Lancet, 374*(9686), 315–323.

Thomson, W. (1891). Electrical units of measurement. In *Popular lectures and addresses* (Vol. 1). (originally delivered on May 3, 1883).

Turecki, G., Brent, D.A., Gunnell, D., O'Connor, R.C., Oquendo, M.A., Pirkis, J., & Stanley, B.H. (2019). Suicide and suicide risk. *Nature Reviews Disease Primers, 5*(1), 74. https://doi.org/10.1038/s41572-019-0121-0

Vandenbroucke, J.P., Broadbent, A., & Pearce, N. (2016). Causality and causal inference in epidemiology: The need for a pluralistic approach. *International Journal of Epidemiology, 45*(6), 1776–1786. https://doi.org/10.1093/ije/dyv341

Värnik, A., Maris, R., & Maltsberger, J.T. (2003). Laur's final display: Suicide by fire. *Suicide and Life-Threatening Behavior, 33*, 448–451.

Waern, M., Rubenowitz, E., Runeson, B., Skoog, I., Wilhelmson, K., & Allebeck, P. (2002). Burden of illness and suicide in elderly people: Case-control study. *BMJ, 324*(7350), 1355. https://doi.org/10.1136/bmj.324.7350.1355

Webb, P., Bain, C., & Page, A. (2020). *Essential epidemiology: An introduction for students and health professionals* (4th ed.). New York, NY: Cambridge University Press.

Winsper, C., Lereya, T., Zanarini, M., & Wolke, D. (2012). Involvement in bullying and suicide-related behavior at 11 years: A prospective birth cohort study. *Journal of the American Academy of Child & Adolescent Psychiatry, 51*, 271–282. e273. https://doi.org/10.1016/j.jaac.2012.01.001

Woodward, M. (2005). *Epidemiology: Study design and data analysis* (2nd ed.). Boca Raton, FL: Chapman and Hall/CRC.

World Health Organization. (2004). *International statistical classification of diseases and related health problems* (10 ed., Vol. 1). Geneva, Switzerland: Author.

Wray, M., Colen, C., & Pescosolido, B. (2011). The sociology of suicide. *Annual Review of Sociology, 37*, 505–528. https://doi.org/10.1146/annurev-soc-081309-150058

Chapter 7

Intervention Studies in Suicide Research

Merike Sisask, Kairi Kõlves, and Ulrich Hegerl

Summary

This chapter presents an overview of different types of intervention studies, where participants can be either individuals, groups, or entire communities. Intervention studies include randomized controlled trials (RCTs), crossover trials, field trials, community trials, cluster RCTs (cRCTs), and non-randomized study designs. Different study designs have unique advantages and disadvantages, but the ultimate goal of any intervention study in the field of suicide research is to determine effective interventions for reducing suicidal behaviors. Important aspects of planning, implementing, and evaluating suicide preventive interventions (with an emphasis on a public health approach) are described and analyzed. Theoretical and methodological reflections are illustrated with practical examples of intervention studies in the field of suicide research (SUPRE-MISS, EAAD and OSPI-Europe, SEYLE).

The two main epidemiological study types are *observational studies* and *intervention studies* (also known as experimental studies). Observational study designs were detailed in Chapter 6, and this chapter describes various intervention study designs.

The goal of an intervention study in suicide research is to determine effective interventions for reducing suicidal behaviors (suicides, suicide attempts, and suicidal ideation). Although this target may appear self-explanatory and straightforward, it is not simple to estimate achievement of the effect. There are several reasons determining causality and reducing suicidal behavior can be challenging. First, the primary outcome measures – suicides and suicide attempts – are relatively rare events, and the effects of short interventions within limited populations cannot be predicted. Second, the secondary outcome measures – such as referrals to specialists, depression treatment, and attitudes toward suicidal behaviors – may not be specific enough or reflect the desired effects. Third, interventions for suicide prevention are implemented in real-life situations where researchers have only limited information and ability to control or influence conditions.

This chapter focuses on the critical aspects of planning, implementing, and evaluating intervention studies, with a focus on suicide prevention from a public health approach. The theoretical insights are illustrated with practical examples of the studies implemented and evaluated in diverse settings and different contexts. Intervention studies have notable similarities with observational studies regarding study quality (internal and external validity, causality, confounding factors, and other sources of bias). As these aspects were discussed in Chapter 6, they will not be repeated here, although specific features of intervention studies will be highlighted.

Types of Intervention Studies

In epidemiology, the terms *intervention study* and *experimental study* are used interchangeably. Also, *trial* is synonymous with terms for these kinds of studies (Rothman, Lash, & Greenland, 2013). Suicide researchers predominantly refer to intervention studies when discussing community-level trials (public health interventions) or when applying psychosocial interventions.

An intervention study is considered the ideal option to examine whether an *exposure* (intervention, experiment, or treatment) is causally related to an *outcome* (suicidal behaviors). However, for practical reasons, an intervention study is not always a viable option (Webb & Bain, 2011). Once there is sufficient evidence that an exposure – action or factor – might improve the situation and prevent suicidal behaviors, then it is desirable to conduct an intervention study. In contrast to observational studies, intervention studies, as reflected in their name, allow researchers to actively manipulate an exposure and estimate its effect on the occurrence of suicidal behaviors (Porta, 2008; Webb, Bain, & Page, 2020).

In intervention studies, participants are traditionally allocated to an *intervention group* (exposed to the intervention being tested) or a *control group* (not exposed to the intervention) (Celentano & Szklo, 2019; Porta, 2008; Rothman et al., 2013; Webb et al., 2020). Similar to a cohort study, an intervention study prospectively follows both groups to observe the outcome (Pencheon, Guest, Melzer, & Gray, 2006). Traditionally, random allocation is used; however, researchers cannot always control the allocation and timing of the experiment. Based on the allocation of the study participants – random or nonrandom – intervention studies are divided into randomized or nonrandomized designs. Study participants, also called *intervention units*, can be individuals, defined population groups, or whole communities. The following types of intervention studies will be introduced and described below (Bonita, Beaglehole, & Kjellström, 2006; Celentano & Szklo, 2019; Rothman et al., 2013; Webb et al., 2020):

- Clinical trials, including randomized controlled trials (RCTs) – targeted to individuals;
- Crossover trials – targeted to individuals;
- Field trials – targeted to groups;
- Cluster randomized controlled trials (cRCTs) – targeted to groups;
- Community trials – targeted to communities;
- Nonrandomized designs.

Clinical Trials and Randomized Controlled Trials

When appropriately designed, conducted, and reported, RCTs represent the gold standard of study designs. An RCT is essentially an experiment under the control of the researcher (Celentano & Szklo, 2019; Schulz, Altman, Moher, & the CONSORT Group, 2010). RCTs provide strong evidence about causality (Pencheon et al., 2006) and are considered the ideal design for evaluating both the efficacy and side effects of a new intervention (Celentano & Szklo, 2019). RCTs can be used to evaluate new drugs and other treatments of disease (clinical trials). Also, RCTs can be employed in preventive interventions such as assessing screening programs for early detection (selected prevention) or novel ways of organizing and delivering services for treatment and rehabilitation (indicated prevention) (Celentano & Szklo, 2019). The design of an RCT is illustrated in Figure 7.1.

In RCTs, participants with the same condition (e.g., suicide attempt) are allocated randomly into groups so that each person has an equal chance of being allocated to the intervention group (e.g., see the SUPRE-MISS study described in detail in Box 7.1; Bertolote et al.,

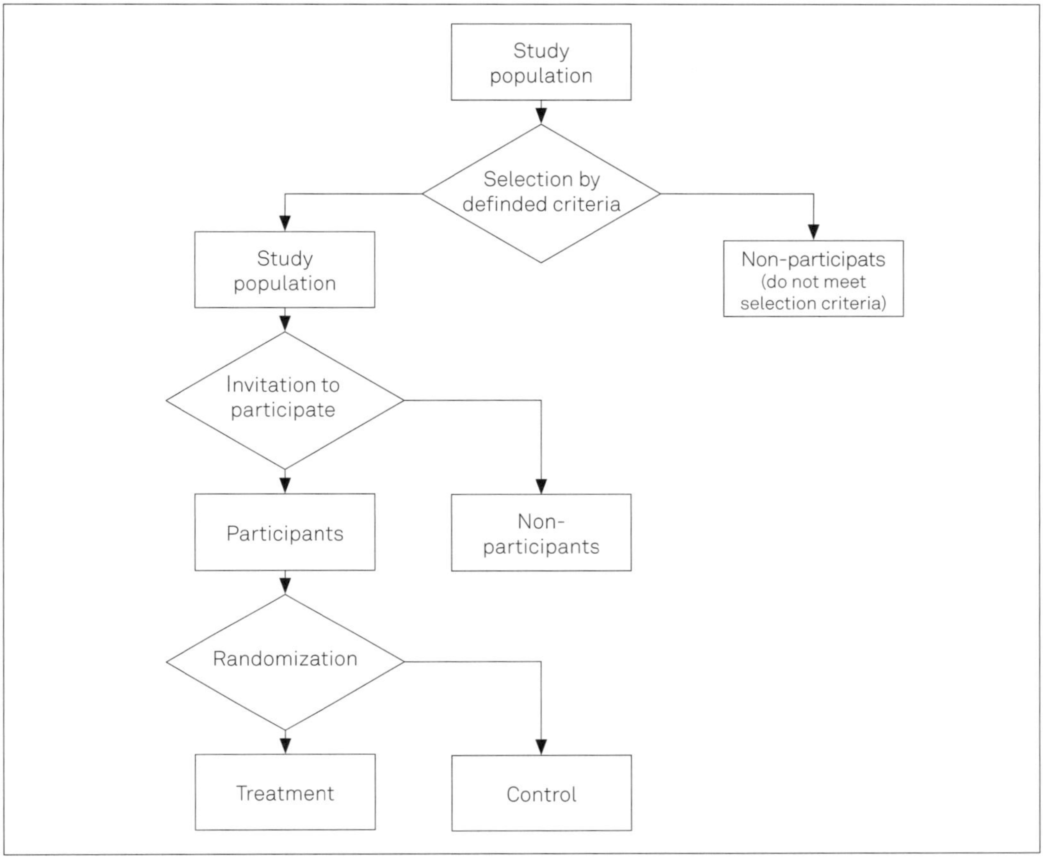

Figure 7.1 Design of a randomized controlled trial (RCT). Reprinted with permission from "Basic Epidemiology," by R. Beaglehole, R. Bonita, & T. Kjellström, p. 41. © 1993 by the World Health Organization.

2010; Fleischmann et al., 2008). The key factor in RCTs is randomization, which means, in the ordinary sense, tossing a coin to decide the allocation of a person to a study group. The critical element of randomization is the unpredictability of the subsequent allocation (Celentano & Szklo, 2019; Schulz & Grimes, 2002c). Generation of a randomization sequence takes a little time and effort but is rewarded with scientific accuracy and credibility of the RCT (Schulz & Grimes, 2002c).

Randomization has two main objectives. First, it ensures that the allocation to intervention and control groups (exposure to experimental manipulations) is unbiased. Second, randomization produces comparability between study groups for factors that might affect comparison by the outcome (i.e., it makes the study groups interchangeable at the start of the study; Bonita et al., 2006; Pencheon et al., 2006; Webb et al., 2020). If the allocation of participants to groups is random and blinded, therefore presumably having no effect on the outcome except through the treatment, any systematic (nonrandom) variation in outcome could be attributable to the treatment effect (Rothman et al., 2013). Randomization also ensures that personal views and preferences (conscious or unconscious) of the researchers do not bias the allocation (Bonita et al., 2006; Porta, 2008). It also eliminates the problem of selection bias that results from self-selection by participants (Celentano & Szklo, 2019).

Box 7.1. Example of an RCT:
WHO Multisite Intervention Study on Suicidal Behaviors

The Multisite Intervention Study on Suicidal Behaviors (SUPRE-MISS) was launched by the WHO for evaluation of an innovative brief intervention in a large multisite RCT. The study used suicides (Fleischmann et al., 2008) and repeated suicide attempts (Bertolote et al., 2010) as primary outcome measures.

Between January 2002 and April 2004, five participating sites in Brazil, India, Sri Lanka, Islamic Republic of Iran, and China applied the same study protocol and enrolled in total 1,867 suicide attempters identified by medical staff in emergency care departments (ECDs) within defined catchment areas. The study attempted to include all suicide attempters seen at the ECDs. However, as estimated later, approximately 5 % of all cases were lost before eligibility assessment, for various reasons. In total, 2,973 suicide attempters were assessed for eligibility, but 37 % of them were not enrolled, because of different impediments (e.g., death, clinical condition).

All enrolled suicide attempters were *randomly allocated* to a brief intervention and contact group (BIC; n = 922) or a treatment as usual group (TAU; n = 945). Allocation was based on a random-number table; the allocation sequence was stored in a separate location to prevent clinician bias. The study participants were blinded for their allocation to specific study groups. This information about follow-up contacts was given only after randomization.

The *follow-up period* was 18 months from enrollment (until 31 October 2005). The TAU group was handled according to the regular norms of the respective ECD. The BIC group included, in addition to TAU, a 1-hr individual information session as close to the time of discharge as possible. After discharge, nine follow-up contacts (phone calls or visits; more often within the first 3 months, less frequently afterwards) were conducted by a person with clinical experience (e.g., doctor, nurse, or psychologist). Referrals to more intensive care were made, if necessary and available. The overall dropout rate was 9.0 % (5.4 % for BIC and 12.5 % for TAU).

During the follow-up period across sites, significantly more (χ^2 = 13.83; $p < .001$) study participants had died by suicide in the TAU (2.2 %; n = 18) than in the BIC (0.2 %; n = 2) group. Across sites, there were no statistically significant differences in the rate of repeated suicide attempts between the TAU (7.5 %) and BIC groups (7.6 %), but there were substantial differences between sites in the overall repeat rates (from 1 % in Yuncheng to 23 % in Campinas).

The results of the BIC demonstrated that a suicide prevention strategy providing psychosocial counseling and supportive, ongoing contact with suicide attempters could significantly reduce mortality from suicide (Fleischmann et al., 2008). These encouraging results were not supported by any evidence of a similar nature for subsequent repetitions of suicide attempts in the BIC group (Bertolote et al., 2010). However, it must be considered that the SUPRE-MISS study had several important limitations, which are carefully analyzed and reflected in the articles published.

Randomization can be achieved only by proper concealment of allocation and *blinding* (Schulz & Grimes, 2002a, 2002b). In an ideal, *double-blind study* (or masked study), both the researchers (those deciding on the eligibility of participants and those conducting the intervention) and the participants themselves remain unaware of the intervention group to which the participants are assigned. If only the participant or the researcher is unaware of the allocation, it is a *single-blind study* (Webb et al., 2020). It is also recommended that the assessors (those collecting outcome data and analyzing it) are blinded – that is, unaware of the allocated intervention (Schulz & Grimes, 2002b).

The complete unpredictability of the allocation of study participants into study groups is guaranteed by simple (unrestricted) randomization. However, in some situations, *restricted randomization* is necessary (Schulz & Grimes, 2002c). For example, researchers might need intervention groups of equal sizes or groups that avoid imbalances on some important prognostic factors. A subtype of restricted randomization is *stratified randomization*, which is an allocation method that can increase the likelihood of comparability of the study groups in a subgroup analysis. In stratified randomization, a stratum (layer) is first stratified from the target population (e.g., site in a multicenter study, gender, or age group). Then, participants are randomized into study groups within each stratum (Celentano & Szklo, 2019). For example, an RCT testing the effectiveness of a web-based self-help intervention to reduce suicidal thoughts randomized the study participants after stratification for gender (van Spijker, van Straten, & Kerkhof, 2015).

Although randomization increases the comparability of study groups, it does not always work perfectly or guarantee comparability. For example, the quality of the groups at baseline is highly dependent on group size. If the groups are small (even if participants are allocated to them randomly), it is unlikely that the factors that could affect the outcome will be evenly distributed across the groups (Webb et al., 2020). Additionally, chance may play a role in the process of random allocation. Still, if the randomized study groups are large enough, and the randomization procedure is free of bias, the groups will tend to be similar (Celentano & Szklo, 2019). Finally, RCTs may suffer from a severe lack of generalizability due to the nonrepresentativeness of those who consent to participate – that is, participants who are ethically and practically eligible and chosen for RCTs are often highly selected groups of volunteers (Webb et al., 2020).

Most of the clinical trials for new drug treatments are RCTs (Canuso et al., 2018; Cipriani et al., 2018; Grunebaum et al., 2018). An example of an RCT is the World Health Organization (WHO) multisite intervention study on suicidal behaviors (SUPRE-MISS). This study tested a brief psychosocial intervention versus treatment as usual (TAU) among people hospitalized after a suicide attempt (Bertolote et al., 2010; Fleischmann et al., 2008). The study is described in more detail in Box 7.1.

Of equal importance to designing and conducting a high-quality RCT protocol is correctly reporting the results of the RCT. To improve the quality and transparency of RCT reporting, the Consolidated Standards of Reporting Trials (CONSORT) Statement was developed in 1996 and revised in 2010 (Schulz et al., 2010). The CONSORT 2010 Statement is freely available on the CONSORT website (http://www.consort-statement.org/) and includes a 25-item checklist of information to include when reporting an RCT. It also includes a flow diagram of the progress through the phases of an RCT of two study groups (enrollment, intervention allocation, follow-up, and data analysis).

Crossover Trials

A relatively new intervention design is the *crossover trial*, where the participants serve as their own controls (Webb et al., 2020). The same people are observed twice under conditions that are identical except for the intervention, which is the exposure of interest in intervention studies. Crossover trials need fewer participants to demonstrate statistically and clinically valid results than RCTs with parallel study groups, but they require a more extended study period. One of the most significant advantages of the crossover design is that it removes much of the variability inherent in comparing different study groups, which cannot be eliminated by randomization. The groups in crossover trials are fully controlled from a genetic perspective and for other demographic and personal factors that do not change over time. However, considering the length of the study, it is unlikely that nothing else has changed (e.g., in a psychosocial environment). The crossover trial has many methodological similarities with the case-crossover study design, described under observational studies in Chapter 6.

In a simple, two-period crossover study design, participants can be randomly allocated for a specified period to either an intervention group (new treatment) or a control group (TAU), and then vice versa for a similar period (Celentano & Szklo, 2019; Webb et al., 2020). However, if the effects of the new treatment are likely to carry over from the first period of the intervention to the other, then this design is obviously inappropriate (Webb et al., 2020). The carryover effect can sometimes (e.g., for drug interventions) be diminished by a *wash-out* period between the two interventions, when the participants do not receive any treatment. However, when the effects of an intervention tend to last for a longer period of time (e.g., psychosocial interventions), this may not be feasible or effective (Celentano & Szklo, 2019).

Special cautions for crossover trials include the order in which interventions are implemented, which may elicit participants' psychological responses (enthusiasm may diminish over time). A crossover design is also not suitable if the new treatment cures the health condition (Celentano & Szklo, 2019). Unfortunately, most interventions in suicide research are not suitable for this type of assessment. Crossover trials are appropriate to assess factors that have rapid effects that diminish quickly when the exposure is removed (Webb et al., 2020). For suicidal behaviors, the development of the condition may be a longitudinal continuum fluctuating between milder ideation and more severe behaviors. Occasionally, the outcomes are irreversible (e.g., suicide). An example of an intervention using a double-blind, placebo-controlled, randomized crossover study design is presented by Nugent et al. (2019), who successfully tested the effects of ketamine on a sample of subjects with major depressive disorder and healthy controls.

Field Trials

Field trials are conducted to study the effects of universal prevention of a condition (Pencheon et al., 2006) with the main focus on the incidence (initial occurrence of a condition – e.g., the first suicide attempt). The participants in field trials are not defined by the presence of disease or by presentation for clinical care: The people involved in field trials are healthy but presumed to be at risk. Data collection takes place *in the field*, usually among the general population who are disease-free (Bonita et al., 2006; Rothman et al., 2013).

Considering the target group and the desire to prevent diseases, it is likely that the incidence is relatively low. Thus, field trials usually require a much larger number of participants than clinical trials and are, therefore, usually much more expensive and logistically complicated (Bonita et al., 2006; Rothman et al., 2013). Furthermore, because the participants are not under active health care and are not accessible in a central location for treatment, a field trial often requires visiting study participants at their everyday settings (work, home, or school) or establishing special settings for conducting the study, which in turn adds to the cost.

As for clinical trials, random allocation of participants is an ideal choice, but the difficulties of implementing randomization in a large-scale field trial can outweigh the advantages (Rothman et al., 2013). Randomization protocols can be slightly modified for practical reasons (e.g., using cluster randomization), but because such modifications can seriously affect the validity and interpretation of findings, the advantages and disadvantages need to be weighed carefully.

Community Trials and Cluster Randomized Controlled Trials

The *community trial* (or community intervention) is an extension of the field trial that involves intervention targeted primarily to universal prevention on a community-wide basis. The main difference between a community trial and a field trial is whether the intervention is implemented (or exposure assigned) for each individual or for a cluster of individuals (communities) (Pencheon et al., 2006; Rothman et al., 2013). For many public health and policy interventions, it is impossible to conduct interventions (or evaluations) at the individual level. However, it is still possible to conduct a community trial (Webb et al., 2020). The cRCTs also target group behaviors, but the unit of study is a group (school, clan, workplace, etc.), not a whole community (Bonita et al., 2006)

In community trials, the units of allocation to receive an intervention are entire communities (Bonita et al., 2006; Porta, 2008). This is particularly appropriate for health conditions that are highly influenced by psychosocial environments and for which prevention efforts target group behavior. For example, the youth suicide prevention program Connect included a public campaign to improve knowledge and attitudes about suicide to increase belief in the usefulness of mental health care and reduce the stigma associated with help seeking (Bean & Baber, 2011). Moreover, testing the effect of restriction of access to suicide means, on reducing suicidal behaviors can be done using a community trial. For example, a Sri Lanka study conducted a test of the effectiveness of a lockable household pesticide storage unit to prevent self-poisoning, although no evidence was found (Pearson et al., 2017).

Ideally, intervention in community trials is allocated randomly to parallel groups of participants (Rothman et al., 2013). However, for practical reasons, random allocation is not always feasible or even meaningful. For example, if only two communities are involved in a study (intervention and control community), the differences in the baseline characteristics will have the same effect whatever the method of allocation (random or not). However, when one community is highly motivated and enthusiastic to implement the intervention, the outcome for them is likely to be better than in the other community who does it for other reasons (e.g., for extra money or because local politicians decided on it). When the number of randomized parallel groups is large (or at least greater than two), randomization is likely to produce similar distributions of baseline characteristics among the intervention groups (Rothman et al., 2013).

Analysis of community trials and cRCTs should always involve methods that consider the clustering, which is essential to properly estimate the amount of variability introduced by the randomization (Rothman et al., 2013). If randomization is not performed, other analysis methods are required to ensure that any differences found at the end of the study can be attributed to the intervention rather than to inherent differences between communities (Bonita et al., 2006).

When using the community trial and cRCT design, it is practically impossible (and perhaps even not desirable) to isolate the intervention communities from possible general social changes that also may impact the control community. As a result, definitive conclusions about the overall effectiveness of community-wide efforts are not always possible (Bonita et al., 2006), and thorough analysis of contextual factors is necessary (Denyer, Tranfield, & Van Aken, 2008; Moore et al., 2015; Rychetnik, Frommer, Hawe, & Shiell, 2002).

Box 7.2 below describes a four-level, community-based intervention study, which is one of the most frequently implemented and carefully evaluated community-based interventions worldwide. The four-level study represents a multifaceted intervention design, which is most likely to be efficient because of synergistic and catalytic effects.

Box 7.2. Example of a controlled, community-based intervention: The European Alliance Against Depression and Optimizing Suicide Prevention Programs and Their Implementation in Europe

The European Alliance Against Depression (EAAD) is an international, nonprofit organization based in Germany, with a wide network of European, global, and regional partners. The EAAD multifaceted four-level community intervention program combines two independent but partly overlapping aims: to improve the care for people with depressive disorders and to prevent suicidal behaviors.

The history of the EAAD goes back to 2000, when the Nurnberg Alliance Against Depression implemented the four-level intervention model in Germany and managed to reduce suicidal acts by 24% compared with a baseline year and a control region (Hegerl, Althaus, Schmidtke, & Niklewski, 2006), with a sustainable effect (Hegerl et al., 2010). Further evidence for the preventive effect on suicidal behavior was provided in additional regions in Germany and in Hungary (Hübner-Liebermann, Neuner, Hegerl, Hajak, & Spiessl, 2010; Székely et al., 2013). This promising intervention model was further optimized and implemented in 117 regions inside and outside Europe, and within the Optimizing Suicide Prevention Programs and Their Implementation in Europe (OSPI-Europe) project in 2008–2012 (Hegerl et al., 2009).

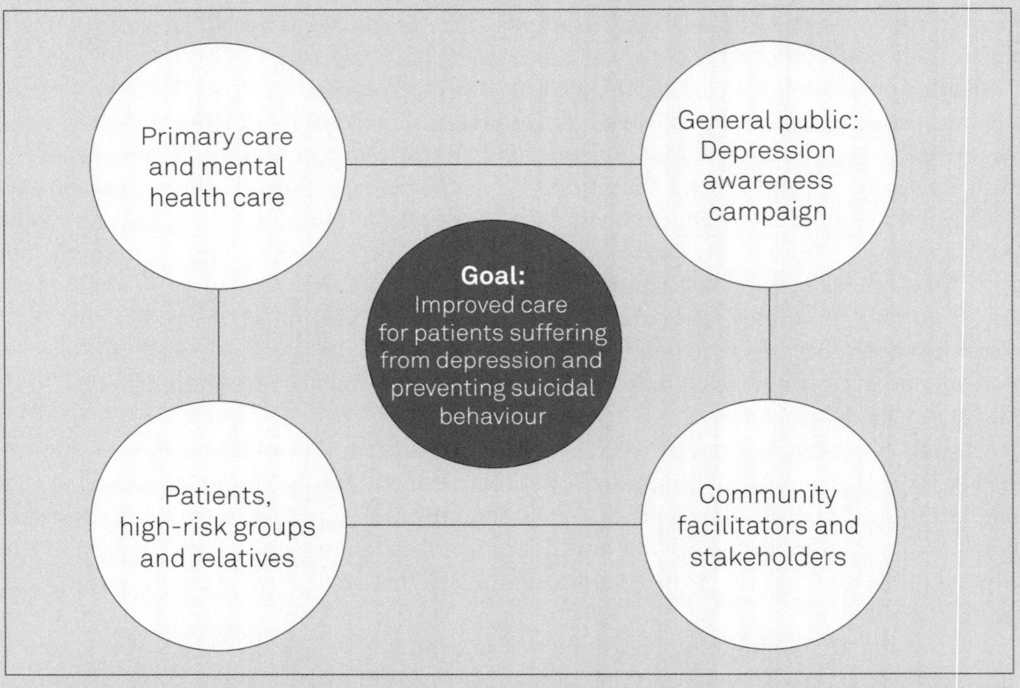

Reprinted with permission from the European Alliance Against Depression. Available at http://www.eaad.net/eaad-project/4-level-approach

The four levels in the EAAD intervention program include (Hegerl et al., 2008; see also https://www.eaad.net):

1. *General practitioners* (GPs): Cooperation with primary and mental health care providers, focusing on training for general practitioners
2. *The public:* Public relations activities and education of the broader public through a depression awareness campaign

3. *Community facilitators and gatekeepers:* Cooperation with community facilitators and gatekeepers and other stakeholders, with improvement of their mental health literacy
4. *Patients, their relatives, and high-risk groups:* Support for suicidal and depressive patients, survivors of suicide attempts, other high-risk-groups, and their relatives

Systematic implementation research and process analysis has shown that combining the four intervention levels yields not only additive but synergistic and catalytic effects (Harris et al., 2016; Hegerl et al., 2013).

Within the OSPI-Europe project, the EAAD four-level intervention was carefully implemented and rigorously evaluated in four European communities (cities) in Germany, Hungary, Portugal, and Ireland, with matched control communities (Hegerl et al., 2019). The selection criteria for the communities were population size (at least 150,000 inhabitants), regional interest in hosting the interventions, and that no previous similar program had taken place in those regions. A 1-year baseline period and a 2-year index period after inception of the interventions were used for evaluation.

The primary outcome measure was the number of completed and attempted suicides (combined and defined as *suicidal acts*). Evaluation of various types of secondary outcome measures are presented in other publications (Coppens et al., 2014, 2013; Kohls et al., 2017).

The OSPI-Europe outcome analysis showed that a decrease in suicidal acts compared with the baseline in the intervention regions (−3.26 %) did not differ significantly ($\chi^2 = 0.13; p = .72$) from the results in the control regions (−1.40 %). However, intervention effects differed between countries. A thorough process evaluation analysis detected the mechanisms of action for successful implementation and drivers for *added value:* strong local partnership, *in-kind* contributions, valuing existing partnership strengths, and synergies across intervention levels. Several limitations of the OSPI-Europe study have been highlighted for critical interpretation of the study results and for planning similar studies in the future (Hegerl et al., 2019).

An example of a cRCT is presented in Box 7.3, which is the well-known, school-based intervention study Saving and Empowering Young Lives in Europe (SEYLE), which tested four different intervention arms in comparison with a control group.

Box 7.3. Example of a cRCT: Saving and Empowering Young Lives in Europe

The Saving and Empowering Young Lives in Europe (SEYLE) was a multisite cRCT designed to investigate the efficacy, cost-effectiveness, and cultural adaptability of three different school-based suicide-preventive interventions. Study participants for follow-up assessment were adolescents from schools in 10 European countries (Austria, Estonia, France, Germany, Hungary, Ireland, Italy, Romania, Slovenia, and Spain), with Sweden serving as a scientific coordinating center (Carli et al., 2013; Wasserman et al., 2010, 2015).

The SEYLE study sample for follow-up consisted of 11,110 adolescents, median age 15 years, recruited from 168 schools. In each site, a catchment area was identified, and a list of eligible schools was generated. Clear inclusion criteria were determined for schools. Every class where 15-year-old pupils made up a majority was included for each school selected. All pupils in the participating classes were approached for enrollment (Carli et al., 2013; Wasserman et al., 2010, 2015).

Within each study site, the cluster design first led to randomization of eligible schools to one of three intervention arms or a control group. Schools (and pupils) were only informed about the intervention arm implemented at their school. Randomization of schools in all study sites was made by independent researchers from Columbia University (New York, USA) (Wasserman et al., 2015).

The SEYLE interventions were undertaken during an intense 4-week period after a baseline assessment.

The three intervention arms in the SEYLE study were:

1. *Question, Persuade, and Refer (QPR):* Gatekeeper training involving intervening and referrals by teachers and school staff after identifying pupils engaged in risky behaviors
2. *Youths Aware of Mental Health (YAM):* Awareness training in mental health promotion targeting adolescents, designed to promote knowledge of mental health, increase healthy lifestyles and behaviors, diminish unhealthy behaviors, and encourage pupils' self-referral
3. *Professional Screening (ProfScreen):* Screening by professionals for identification and clinical referral of pupils at high risk for mental illness or suicidal behavior at baseline (Carli et al., 2013; Wasserman et al., 2012; Wasserman et al., 2010, 2015)

Control group: For ethical reasons, the control group was exposed to minimal intervention that comprised self-referral.

Evaluation of outcomes was performed by comparing each intervention arm with a control group. Structured questionnaires were utilized at baseline and 3- and 12-month follow-ups to assess the change (Carli et al., 2013; Wasserman et al., 2010, 2015).

The primary outcome measure was suicide attempt – all new cases identified during the 3- and 12-month follow-ups. Another outcome measure was severe suicidal ideation in the 2 weeks preceding the follow-ups (Wasserman et al., 2015).

No significant differences between intervention groups and the control group were recorded at the 3-month follow-up. At the 12-month follow-up, the YAM was associated with a significant reduction of incident suicide attempts (odd ratio [OR] = 0.45, 95 % confidence interval [95 % CI], 0.24–0.85; p = .014) and severe suicidal ideation (OR = 0.50, 95 % CI, 0.27–0.92; p = .025), compared with the control group. No participants completed suicide during the study period (D. Wasserman et al., 2015). A cost-effectiveness analysis indicated that, based on the incremental cost-effectiveness ratios (ICERs), the YAM had the lowest incremental cost per 1 % point reduction in incidents for both outcomes and per quality adjusted life year (QALY) gained versus the control group (Ahern et al., 2018). These findings support the suggestion that the universal suicide preventive intervention YAM is both the most efficient and cost-effective of the SEYLE interventions, although several limitations to consider have also been highlighted.

Nonrandomized Designs

Nonrandomized study designs are also necessary as they provide valuable information for the evaluation of interventions (Celentano & Szklo, 2019). Sometimes this type of study design (somewhat similar to observational studies) may represent the most feasible, acceptable, and appropriate study design for evaluating health interventions, including public health interventions (Rychetnik et al., 2002).

Many health interventions cannot be subjected to randomization for several reasons (Celentano & Szklo, 2019). First, such trials are often logistically complex and extremely expensive, as many different health care measures are in use simultaneously. Second, ethical problems may occur because randomization may be viewed as an unacceptable process by many patients and health care providers. Third, RCTs take a long time to complete and as health care programs and health problems change over time, the results of the study may no longer be entirely relevant. These are the main reasons researchers look for alternative approaches that may provide some information.

One practical nonrandomized study design that complements clinical trial research is *outcomes research*, which refers to the use of the data from studies that often use large existing data sets (so-called big data) (Celentano & Szklo, 2019; Goodwin, Wessely, & Fear, 2015). The data and methodologies commonly used in outcome research are measures to assess well-being and satisfaction, economic analysis, decision analysis, administrative and clinical databases, disease registries, censuses, and more. Outcome research may benefit health care consumers, providers, managers, and policymakers in different ways (Jefford, Stockler, & Tattersall, 2003). Technological innovations such as machine learning and artificial intelligence have great potential to improve future data collection to reach underserved populations at risk (Jaroszewski, Morris, & Nock, 2019; Torous et al., 2018; see Chapter 16 in current work).

Perhaps the most common nonrandomized design in the health setting is the pre-post (or before-after) study design. Such a study design uses *historical controls* – people who were treated as usual before a program was established (or before a certain health care measure became available) and who are compared with those who received the intervention from the program after it was established (or after the measure became available) (Celentano & Szklo, 2019; Webb et al., 2020). When the change in the risk of the outcome is dramatic, the before-after design is akin to the so-called natural experiment (Celentano & Szklo, 2019). The term *natural experiment* refers to the nonrandom study design called a *quasiexperiment*, where the researcher lacks control over the participants' allocation (nonrandom) and timing of intervention (Porta, 2008; Rothman et al., 2013). An example of a large scale natural experiment was published by D. Wasserman and Värnik (1998), in which they described a sharp decrease in suicide rates in the former USSR, which could obviously be attributed to a strict alcohol policy with restrictions on sales and administrative control over consumption (during the period 1984–1990), but perhaps also to some extent to hope-inspiring changes in the social and political climate.

The main problem with the pre-post study design is that it assumes that the only (or most important) factor that has changed is the introduction of the new treatment (or new health care measures), which may not necessarily be the case (Webb et al., 2020). Structural circumstances and psychosocial factors may have changed over time, as well (such as housing, nutrition, and/or other aspects of lifestyle), and participants may have used other health services. Additionally, the data obtained in each of the two periods (before and after) are frequently not comparable in either quality or completeness. A problem of selection bias exists as well (Celentano & Szklo, 2019).

Feasibility and Pilot Studies

While RCTs (in particular cRCTs) can be designed to evaluate quite complex public health intervention programs, they are not always feasible or affordable, because of practical, ethical, or resource constraints (Rychetnik et al., 2002; Webb et al., 2020). Often, before planning and implementing a complex and resource-intensive intervention study at full scale, it is practical to conduct a simpler and cheaper design – a feasibility or pilot study of the planned intervention. During a feasibility or pilot study, the viability, practicability, or workability of the intervention or program will be assessed, as well as the ethical and cultural aspects (Porta, 2008). Within these studies, the assurance will be obtained that the measuring instruments satisfactorily capture the intervention's implementation processes and outcomes (Rychetnik et al., 2002). Feasibility and pilot studies are described in detail in Chapter 12.

Enrollment of Study Participants

In all intervention studies, it is vital to clearly define the target population: the study participants for whom an intervention is planned (Porta, 2008; Webb et al., 2020). In the absence of clear definitions of the conditions and exposure that define the target population, it is challenging to interpret the data afterward (Bonita et al., 2006). In suicide research, the target population with the *condition* can be the people medically treated in emergency care after a suicide attempt, people screened for suicidal ideation in primary health care, people bereaved by a suicide loss, and others. The use of definitions in suicide research is described in detail in Chapter 2.

A good study also has clearly defined *inclusion* and *exclusion* criteria to determine whether specific individuals should be enrolled or not. For example, these eligibility criteria might require people to fall within a certain age range (e.g., adult population 18+, 14- to 18-year-old adolescents, older adults 65+) or those who reside in a defined area or have been admitted to hospitals within a specified catchment area (Webb et al., 2020). These criteria must be determined as precisely as possible and fixed in the study protocol before the study begins. Subjective decisions made by a researcher in choosing who is included must be avoided. Any study procedure must be replicable by other researchers (Celentano & Szklo, 2019).

A major challenge is to recruit enough eligible volunteers who agree to be randomized. Failure to recruit a sufficient number of volunteers can leave a well-designed trial without enough participants to yield statistically valid results (Celentano & Szklo, 2019). Furthermore, participants may agree to be randomized, but following randomization, they may not comply with the intervention. Noncompliance may be overt (direct refusal to comply, or stopping participation in the study) or covert (e.g., stopping to take the drugs without admitting it). Overt noncompliers are also called *dropouts* from the study. Losses during follow-up and other forms of noncompliance are one of the major concerns in intervention studies. Participants may lose their interest in the study over time, particularly if the follow-up period is quite long (lasts for years). It is the responsibility of the research group to establish a system of checks on potential noncompliance and determine the reasons for the participants dropping out. Also, researchers must develop appropriate measures to motivate participants to continue (Celentano & Szklo, 2019).

In intervention studies, participants will be allocated either to an intervention or a control group so that the outcomes can be compared between the two groups (Bonita et al., 2006; Webb et al., 2020). Different allocation options (randomized, nonrandomized) have already been described under the specific intervention study designs. Sometimes the study participants in the control group receive no intervention at all; however, the majority of study participants are provided a placebo (a *pretend treatment*), which resembles the intervention but is not active (a common approach in drug trials). From an ethical perspective, the control group must receive at least an available standard treatment (i.e., TAU) or minimal intervention (e.g., information where to get help in an emergency) (Webb et al., 2020).

Intervention studies can have multiple study arms whose outcomes are compared (Porta, 2008). One such example is the SEYLE study (see Box 7.3). Usually, the study arms are categorized as intervention and control groups and compared against each other; however, researchers can choose to compare more groups receiving different interventions (Celentano & Szklo, 2019).

Planning and Implementing an Intervention

An *intervention* is defined as a set of actions with a coherent objective to bring about change or produce measurable outcomes (Rychetnik et al., 2002). The intervention must be clearly stated, with the duration and scope of the intervention and how long the study will last as a whole (Celentano & Szklo, 2019).

Public health interventions are intended to promote or protect health or prevent ill health in communities or populations; they are distinguished from clinical interventions, which are intended to prevent or treat illness in individuals. Planning public health interventions should be built on evidence from previous studies and driven by practical experience. The importance of the public health approach to suicide research and prevention and recommendations for how to implement suicide prevention programs in practice are thoroughly addressed in Chapter 3.

Public health interventions in suicide prevention rely on three types of prevention – universal, selective, and indicated (summarized as USI), based on their target groups (Gordon, 1983; Turecki et al., 2019). *Universal prevention* is targeted to the general population regardless of risk level. *Selected prevention* is targeted to people with identifiable risk factors, and *indicated prevention* is targeted to high-risk individuals. These various types of interventions are explained in more detail in Chapter 3 (Public Health Approach to Suicide Research) and Chapter 14 (Evaluating Suicide Prevention Approaches). It is quite common or even an ideal solution to combine different USI preventive efforts to reduce suicide deaths (Bonita et al., 2006; Celentano & Szklo, 2019; Turecki et al., 2019). Examples of interventions where different prevention levels have been combined either as a multifaceted intervention or as different intervention arms are given in Box 7.2. – European Alliance Against Depression (EAAD) and Optimizing Suicide Prevention Programs and Their Implementation in Europe (OSPI-Europe) – and Box 7.3. – Saving and Empowering Young Lives in Europe (SEYLE).

In fact, public health interventions are rarely a standard package, and the multiple components and contextual factors of an intervention should be described in full detail in the study protocol (Rychetnik et al., 2002). Currently, it is common to publish the study protocol in a peer-reviewed journal to add reliability to the implementation process and to ensure the process of publishing the results is smoother. For example, the study protocols of the SEYLE (D. Wasserman et al., 2010) and OSPI-Europe (Hegerl et al., 2009) were published in the journal *BMC Public Health* at the beginning of the studies. Contextual factors often interact with interventions, which can complicate the evaluation and affect the transferability of the intervention (Rychetnik et al., 2002).

Measuring the Outcome of an Intervention

As noted earlier, public health interventions tend to be complex and context-dependent, which should be reflected in the complexity of the evaluation plan (Rychetnik et al., 2002). Outcomes of the intervention are the possible results and identified changes in the defined condition (e.g., suicidal behaviors) that may stem from exposure to the intervention (Porta, 2008). During the evaluation process, the researcher is trying to find evidence on the implementation and outcomes of the intervention to ensure that the intervention can be defined as an evidence-based practice (Rychetnik et al., 2002). If the intervention and control groups are identical (which is the ideal) and the intervention has no effect, identical outcomes would be observed across the groups (Rothman et al., 2013). However, if the intervention is associated with a better outcome than the control situation (e.g., defined by TAU), better outcomes would be found in the intervention group than in the control group (Celentano & Szklo, 2019).

With unsuccessful interventions, the evidence should help to determine whether the intervention was inherently faulty (i.e., a failure of the intervention concept or theory), or poorly delivered (failure of implementation) (Rychetnik et al., 2002). For that purpose, researchers need to incorporate both the outcome and process evaluation into the study. Adequate interpretation of the evidence depends on the availability of sufficient descriptive information on the intervention and its context (e.g., living standard, cultural values, access to services), so that the transferability of the evidence can be determined (Rychetnik et al., 2002).

The evaluation criteria in general, and outcome measures in particular, should be clearly defined to help determine whether the interventions serve the interests of people involved in the interventions (both those affected by it and those delivering it), what the effects of interventions are (anticipated or unanticipated, beneficial or not), and whether the intervention is efficient as well as effective (Rychetnik et al., 2002). There are some general guidelines for selecting appropriate outcome measures for the evaluation of interventions (Celentano & Szklo, 2019): The measure must be clearly quantifiable to enable the expression of its effects in quantitative terms, the outcome measures should be relatively easy to define, the measure must be accessible for study purposes without unnecessarily complicated and expensive procedures, and the intervention group and the control group must be at risk for the same condition for which an intervention is being evaluated.

The outcome measures in suicide research are often divided into primary outcome measures and secondary outcome measures. *Primary outcome measures* are the main measures of the impact of the study. In suicide research, the primary outcome measures are indicators of suicidal behaviors. Measures directly related to suicidal behaviors can be a first suicide attempt (measuring incidence), people who have attempted suicide during their lifetime (measuring prevalence), repeated suicide attempts (measuring recurrence), and suicide (measuring mortality). However, as suicidal acts are rare events, it might be difficult to have a sufficient sample size to reach the desired statistical power. *Secondary outcome measures* are not as important as primary outcome measures but are still of interest in evaluating the impact of intervention. In suicide research, secondary outcome measures include suicidal ideation, risk and protective factors of suicidal behavior, public attitudes toward suicidality, quality of care for people with depression and other psychiatric disorders, stigma and attitudes toward help seeking, and visits to primary care physicians or psychiatrists.

There are several data sources that may be used for evaluation purposes in intervention studies. Regularly available data such as mortality and hospitalization data are often used. Such data can be obtained from different sources, which may differ in important ways (Celentano & Szklo, 2019). In suicide research, the main data sources in use are official statistics (e.g., suicides, external causes of death with undetermined intent), surveillance data (e.g., hospitalized suicide attempts, and sometimes events of self-harm with unclear intent are chosen to be added in a blind manner), monitoring data (e.g., monitoring of media coverage), screening data (e.g., primary care patients with depressive symptoms), and survey data (e.g., awareness about and attitudes toward suicidal behaviors). Specifics regarding official statistics, surveillance systems, and measures in suicide research are described in detail in Chapter 5.

To determine the impact of the intervention within an RCT, three main concepts that should be distinguished are efficacy, effectiveness, and efficiency (Celentano & Szklo, 2019; Porta, 2008):

- *Efficacy* refers to the extent to which the intervention *works* and produces beneficial results under ideal *laboratory* conditions; it is a measure in a situation where all conditions are controlled to maximize the effect of the intervention.
- *Effectiveness* refers to the extent to which the intervention does what it is intended to do for a specified population when administered in the field in usual circumstances, in a *real-life situation*; it is a measure of how intervention fulfills its objectives in practice.
- *Efficiency* refers to the extent to which the resources used to provide an intervention of known efficacy and effectiveness are minimized (cost-benefit ratio); the costs include not only money, but also time, discomfort, pain, absenteeism, disability, and social stigma; it is a measure of economy, the process of making the best use of scare resources. For details, see Chapter 15.

As the interventions targeted to suicide prevention are complex and context-dependent, it is highly recommended to allocate recourses for process evaluation. One possible guidance for systematic process evaluation is the Medical Research Council, UK (MRC) process evaluation framework, which is built on the three main themes: implementation (what is implemented and how), mechanisms of impact (how the delivered intervention produces change), and context (how context affects the implementation and outcomes (Moore et al., 2015). The MRC guidance also summarizes the key recommendations for process evaluation, divided into four distinct areas – planning, design and conduct, analysis, and reporting. Another model useful for conceptualizing process evaluation is *CIMO logic*, driven by the theory of change (Denyer et al., 2008):

- Context (C) – the surrounding factors and the nature of human actors who influence change;
- Interventions (I) – the nature of intervention and how it is implemented;
- Mechanisms (M) – the mechanism that in a certain context is triggered by the intervention;
- Outcome (O) – the outcome of the intervention in its various aspects.

A good example of thorough process evaluation of a suicide prevention program is the OSPI-Europe study (Harris et al., 2013; Hegerl et al., 2019).

An important aspect of evaluation is the economic measurement of interventions. Economic measures may reflect direct or indirect costs, and can include hospitalization rates, rehospitalization for the same condition within a certain time period after discharge, outpatient and emergency room visits, lost days of work, child care, and days of restricted activity (Celentano & Szklo, 2019). The economic aspects of suicide prevention are described in detail in Chapter 15.

For those planning and evaluating multifaceted, community-based interventions, a controversial effect of public relations (PR) campaigns should be noted. A PR campaign is a central element in community-based interventions. However, it is a matter of debate what the cost-benefit ratios are of an antisuicidal campaign addressing the broader public. Destigmatizing suicidal behavior and making suicide a topic of public debate will have a positive effect (e.g., encouraging help seeking), but destigmatizing and normalizing suicide will also reduce the threshold of reaching the decision to end one's life (e.g., for those depressed and feeling as if they are a burden to their family). Lowering the threshold is therefore likely to increase suicide risk in these patients, and the balance between costs and benefits remains unclear. The crucial advantage of the multifaceted, four-level intervention (see Box 7.2 for details) is that two goals are combined – improving care for people with depressive disorders and preventing suicidal behaviors. The topic of depression is focused on when addressing the public. Such campaigns about depression are likely to have high resonance in the community because almost half of the population is directly affected or impacted via an affected relative. The topic of suicide prevention is focused on when working with GPs and other health professionals and community facilitators. Moreover, improving knowledge about suicidal behaviors among those professionals responsible for diagnosing and recording cases (e.g., GPs, policemen) is likely to increase the number of recorded suicide attempts and suicides, which can lead to false negative findings and significant bias.

More considerations about rigorous evaluation – planning, choice of outcome measures and data sources, importance of contextual factors, quantitative and qualitative methods, external or internal evaluation – are presented in Chapter 14 (Evaluating Suicide Prevention Approaches).

Possible Biases in Intervention Studies

There are many biases that can occur in intervention studies that reduce the credibility of the measured outcomes. For internal and external validity issues and confounding see Chapter 6 (Observational Studies in Suicide Research). Briefly, the sources of error can be random or systematic:

- *Random error* is when the value of the sample measurement differs from the true population value (due to chance) and causes inaccurate measures of association. There are three major sources of random error: individual biological variation, sampling error, and measurement error. Random error can never be completely eliminated, because it is possible to study only a sample of the population (Bonita et al., 2006).
- *Systematic error* (or *bias*) occurs when results differ in a systematic manner from the true values. Bias is any systematic error in the design, conduct, or analysis of the study that results in a mistaken estimate of an exposure (intervention) effect on the outcome. Accuracy is not affected by sample size, and a study with a small systematic error is said to have a high accuracy (Bonita et al., 2006; Celentano & Szklo, 2019). Bias cannot be avoided simply by increasing the size of the sample – the problem persists no matter how large the sample is (Webb et al., 2020).

The possible sources of systematic error (bias) are many and varied. For a more detailed overview of various types of biases in RCTs, see Chapter 13, Table 13.5 (The Cochrane Collaboration's tool for assessing risk of bias in RCTs). Biases relevant to intervention studies are described below.

Selection bias occurs when there is a systematic difference between the characteristics of the people selected for a study (study participants) and of those who are not (demographic, socioeconomic, cultural, lifestyle, and health status factors). An obvious source of selection bias is self-selection, when participants select themselves for a study, either because of their condition or because they are or are not interested in the intervention (Bonita et al., 2006). Some specific sources of selection bias include volunteers, the healthy worker effect, low response rate, loss of participants to follow-up (selection out of the study participants or dropout) (Webb et al., 2020). Selection bias is described in more detail in Chapter 6 (Observational Studies in Suicide Research). Loss of participants to follow-up during the study is called also *attrition bias* (Porta, 2008).

Allocation bias is an effect caused by the failure to implement valid procedures for random allocation of study participants to intervention and control groups (Porta, 2008). Ideally, the two groups are as similar as possible to each other in every respect except the exposure status (i.e., allocation to the intervention or control group), which means they must be exchangeable. Maximizing similarities (i.e., exchangeability) between two groups also reduces the potential for confounding (Webb et al., 2020).

It is recommended that to avoid selection and allocation bias, randomization should be performed by an independent researcher who is not involved in developing and implementing the interventions (Schulz & Grimes, 2002a, 2002c). To avoid selection bias in a large, multicentered study, randomization is not executed by each participating center but is done by a neutral, independent coordinating center (Celentano & Szklo, 2019). An example of such a procedure is given in Box 7.3 for the SEYLE study, where Columbia University (New York, USA) randomized schools for all 12 European intervention sites.

Performance bias can be caused by systematic differences or inaccuracy in implementing the intervention activities. Examples of performance bias are study participants handled differently according to what study group they are in, the intervention actually received differs substantially from the intervention that was intended or planned by the study protocol, a *contamination effect* occurs between different study groups (a control group receives some intervention and an intervention group fails to get the intervention that was planned for them), and finally, study participants who know they are in the control group may be more likely to use other forms of care than study participants in the intervention group, who may be more likely to experience placebo effects (Porta, 2008).

Measurement bias (*also information or misclassification* bias) refers to any systematic error caused by inaccurate individual measurements, inaccuracies in methods of data acquisition, and misclassifications of conditions or exposures (Bonita et al., 2006; Celentano & Szklo, 2019). As this bias is outlined in detail in Chapter 6 (Observational Studies in Suicide Research), the information will not be repeated here.

Ethical Considerations

There are several ethical issues that are crucial for consideration when planning, implementing, and evaluating intervention studies targeting suicide prevention. In this chapter, only a selection of ethical considerations relevant to intervention studies is described. The ethical issues are described in detail in Chapter 4 (Ethical Aspects of Suicide Research).

In that interventions are strictly determined by the study protocol, ethical considerations are of paramount importance in the design of these studies. Experiments on human subjects are ethically permissible only when adherence to the scientific protocol does not conflict with the subject's best interests (Rothman et al., 2013). Study participants should not be denied appropriate intervention. The intervention being tested (a new treatment) must be acceptable in light of current knowledge (Bonita et al., 2006). Study participants should not be deprived of some preferable form of treatment or intervention that is not included in the study (Rothman et al., 2013). Sometimes the study participants in the control group without intervention are offered the opportunity to stay on a waiting list and receive the intervention after the study period is over.

Informed consent from study participants is required in almost all circumstances (Bonita et al., 2006), except for interventions targeted to whole communities. However, a further question is whether truly informed consent can be obtained for a study. As the study participants in an RCT are often enrolled into the study immediately after diagnosis (or after hospitalization), they may be capable of giving consent, and the family may be so shocked that they have difficulty in understanding what an agreement to be randomized entails (Celentano & Szklo, 2019). This may be an especially relevant concern after a young person's suicide attempt.

In community-based trials and cRCTs targeting suicide prevention where the randomization unit is a group of people or a community, it is vital to ensure that the available health care facilities in the community are identified. Furthermore, information about psychological, psychiatric, or crisis help and support must be made available for the general public and in particular for highly vulnerable individuals. In the SEYLE study (see Box 7.3 for details), screening out acutely suicidal pupils (emergency cases) was a prerequisite to guarantee them quick access to child psychiatric services (Cotter et al., 2015; D. Wasserman et al., 2010). To make this process run smoothly, a preliminary cooperation agreement was concluded between the research team and child psychiatric services, and an informed consent form was included in the conditional confidentiality in case of acute suicidality.

Conclusions

The aim of this chapter was to give an overview of the theoretical and methodological aspects of intervention (experimental) studies. The theoretical description was illustrated by several examples of intervention studies in the field of suicide research (SUPRE-MISS, EAAD and OSPI-Europe, and SEYLE). As conducting an intervention study is usually the best way to obtain evidence about causality, this is often a preferred choice by authorities when making funding decisions. As described in the current chapter, it is essential to remember that different types of intervention studies have advantages and disadvantages. The *gold standard* of intervention studies is an RCT, but other types of intervention study designs can be useful or even preferred in certain conditions. Multifaceted, community-based intervention programs can be designed in a manner such that more than additive effects of the different measures are generated by synergetic and catalytic effects, which, however, can make it difficult to disentangle the contribution of each single intervention to the total effect.

The choice of intervention study design should be driven by earlier evidence, research questions, practical experience, and resources available for implementation and evaluation. It is of utmost importance to carefully plan the target population, enrollment procedures, and allocation of study participants (individuals or communities) into intervention and control groups (preferably by randomization). Careful planning, implementation, and evaluation of interventions, while considering possible sources of biases and ethical issues, are essential. These aspects were described in the current chapter, with an emphasis on suicide prevention interventions from a public health approach.

References

Ahern, S., Burke, L.-A., McElroy, B., Corcoran, P., McMahon, E.M., Keeley, H., ... Wasserman, D. (2018). A cost-effectiveness analysis of school-based suicide prevention programmes. *European Child & Adolescent Psychiatry, 27*(10), 1295–1304. https://doi.org/10.1007/s00787-018-1120-5

Beaglehole, R., Bonita, R., & Kjellström, T. (1993). *Basic epidemiology*. Geneva, Switzerland: World Health Organization.

Bean, G., & Baber, K.M. (2011). Connect: An effective community-based youth suicide prevention program. *Suicide and Life-Threatening Behavior, 41*(1), 87–97. https://doi.org/10.1111/j.1943-278X.2010.00006.x

Bertolote, J.M., Fleischmann, A., De Leo, D., Phillips, M.R., Botega, N.J., Vijayakumar, L., ... Wasserman, D. (2010). Repetition of suicide attempts: Data from emergency care settings in five culturally different low- and middle-income countries participating in the WHO SUPRE-MISS study. *Crisis, 31*(4), 194–201. https://doi.org/10.1027/0027-5910/a000052

Bonita, R., Beaglehole, R., & Kjellström, T. (2006). *Basic epidemiology* (2nd ed.). Geneva, Switzerland: World Health Organization.

Canuso, C.M., Singh, J.B., Fedgchin, M., Alphs, L., Lane, R., Lim, P., ... Drevets, W.C. (2018). Efficacy and safety of intranasal esketamine for the rapid reduction of symptoms of depression and suicidality in patients at imminent risk for suicide: Results of a double-blind, randomized, placebo-controlled study. *American Journal of Psychiatry, 175*(7), 620–630. https://doi.org/10.1176/appi.ajp.2018.17060720

Carli, V., Wasserman, C., Wasserman, D., Sarchiapone, M., Apter, A., Balazs, J., ... Hoven, C.W. (2013). The Saving and Empowering Young Lives in Europe (SEYLE) randomized controlled trial (RCT): Methodological issues and participant characteristics. *BMC Public Health, 13,* 479. https://doi.org/10.1186/1471-2458-13-479

Celentano, D.D., & Szklo, M. (2019). *Gordis epidemiology* (6th ed.). Philadelphia, PA: Elsevier.

Cipriani, A., Furukawa, T.A., Salanti, G., Chaimani, A., Atkinson, L.Z., Ogawa, Y., ... Geddes, J.R. (2018). Comparative efficacy and acceptability of 21 antidepressant drugs for the acute treatment of adults with major depressive disorder: A systematic review and network meta-analysis. *Lancet, 391*(10128), 1357–1366. https://doi.org/10.1016/S0140-6736(17)32802-7

Coppens, E., Van Audenhove, C., Iddi, S., Arensman, E., Gottlebe, K., Koburger, N., ... Hegerl, U. (2014). Effectiveness of community facilitator training in improving knowledge, attitudes, and confidence in relation to depression and suicidal behavior: Results of the OSPI-Europe intervention in four European countries. *Journal of Affective Disorders, 165*, 142–150. https://doi.org/10.1016/j.jad.2014.04.052

Coppens, E., Van Audenhove, C., Scheerder, G., Arensman, E., Coffey, C., Costa, S., ... Hegerl, U. (2013). Public attitudes toward depression and help-seeking in four European countries baseline survey prior to the OSPI-Europe intervention. *Journal of Affective Disorders, 150*, 320–329. https://doi.org/10.1016/j.jad.2013.04.013

Cotter, P., Kaess, M., Corcoran, P., Parzer, P., Brunner, R., Keeley, H., ... Wasserman, D. (2015). Help-seeking behaviour following school-based screening for current suicidality among European adolescents. *Social Psychiatry and Psychiatric Epidemiology, 50*(6), 973–982. https://doi.org/10.1007/s00127-015-1016-3

Denyer, D., Tranfield, D., & Van Aken, J.E. (2008). Developing design propositions through research synthesis. *Organization Studies, 29*(3), 393–413. https://doi.org/10.1177/0170840607088020

Fleischmann, A., Bertolote, J.M., Wasserman, D., De Leo, D., Bolhari, J., Botega, N.J., ... Thanh, H.T.T. (2008). Effectiveness of brief intervention and contact for suicide attempters: A randomized controlled trial in five countries. *Bulletin of the World Health Organization, 86*(9), 703–709. https://doi.org/10.2471/BLT.07.046995

Goodwin, L., Wessely, S., & Fear, N.T. (2015). The future of "Big Data" in suicide behaviors research: Can we compare the experiences of the U.S. and U.K. armed forces? *Psychiatry, 78*(1), 25–28. https://doi.org/10.1080/00332747.2015.1016783

Gordon, R.S. (1983). An operational classification of disease prevention. *Public Health Reports, 98*(2), 107–109.

Grunebaum, M.F., Galfalvy, H.C., Choo, T.-H., Keilp, J.G., Moitra, V.K., Parris, M.S., ... Mann, J.J. (2018). Ketamine for rapid reduction of suicidal thoughts in major depression: A midazolam-controlled randomized clinical trial. *American Journal of Psychiatry, 175*(4), 327–335. https://doi.org/10.1176/appi.ajp.2017.17060647

Harris, F.M., Maxwell, M., O'Connor, R., Coyne, J.C., Arensman, E., Coffey, C., ... Hegerl, U. (2016). Exploring synergistic interactions and catalysts in complex interventions: Longitudinal, mixed methods case studies of an optimised multi-level suicide prevention intervention in four European countries (Ospi-Europe). *BMC Public Health, 16*, 268. https://doi.org/10.1186/s12889-016-2942-z

Harris, F.M., Maxwell, M., O'Connor, R.C., Coyne, J., Arensman, E., Székely, A., ... Hegerl, U. (2013). Developing social capital in implementing a complex intervention: A process evaluation of the early implementation of a suicide prevention intervention in four European countries. *BMC Public Health, 13,* 158. https://doi.org/10.1186/1471-2458-13-158

Hegerl, U., Althaus, D., Schmidtke, A., & Niklewski, G. (2006). The alliance against depression: 2-year evaluation of a community-based intervention to reduce suicidality. *Psychological Medicine, 36*(9), 1225–1233. https://doi.org/10.1017/S003329170600780X

Hegerl, U., Maxwell, M., Harris, F., Koburger, N., Mergl, R., Székely, A., ... on behalf of The OSPI-Europe Consortium. (2019). Prevention of suicidal behaviour: Results of a controlled community-based intervention study in four European countries. *PLOS One, 14*(11), e0224602. https://doi.org/10.1371/journal.pone.0224602

Hegerl, U., Mergl, R., Havers, I., Schmidtke, A., Lehfeld, H., Niklewski, G., & Althaus, D. (2010). Sustainable effects on suicidality were found for the Nuremberg alliance against depression. *European Archives of Psychiatry and Clinical Neuroscience, 260*(5), 401–406. https://doi.org/10.1007/s00406-009-0088-z

Hegerl, U., Rummel-Kluge, C., Värnik, A., Arensman, E., & Koburger, N. (2013). Alliances against depression – A community based approach to target depression and to prevent suicidal behaviour. *Neuroscience and Biobehavioral Reviews, 37*(Part 1), 2404–2409. https://doi.org/10.1016/j.neubiorev.2013.02.009

Hegerl, U., Wittenburg, L., Arensman, E., Van Audenhove, C., Coyne, J.C., McDaid, D., ... Bramesfeld, A. (2009). Optimizing Suicide Prevention Programs and Their Implementation in Europe (OSPI Europe): An evidence-based multi-level approach. *BMC Public Health, 9,* 428–435. https://doi.org/10.1186/1471-2458-9-428

Hegerl, U., Wittmann, M., Arensman, E., Van Audenhove, C., Bouleau, J.-H., Van Der Feltz-Cornelis, C., ... Pfeiffer-Gerschel, T. (2008). The "European Alliance Against Depression (EAAD)": A multifaceted, community-based action programme against depression and suicidality. *World Journal of Biological Psychiatry, 9*(1), 51–58. https://doi.org/10.1080/15622970701216681

Hübner-Liebermann, B., Neuner, T., Hegerl, U., Hajak, G., & Spiessl, H. (2010). Reducing suicides through an alliance against depression? *General Hospital Psychiatry, 32*(5), 514–518. https://doi.org/10.1016/j.genhosppsych.2010.06.008

Jaroszewski, A.C., Morris, R.R., & Nock, M.K. (2019). Randomized controlled trial of an online machine learning-driven risk assessment and intervention platform for increasing the use of crisis services. *Journal of Consulting and Clinical Psychology, 87*(4), 370–379. https://doi.org/10.1037/ccp0000389

Jefford, M., Stockler, M.R., & Tattersall, M.H.N. (2003). Outcomes research: What is it and why does it matter? *Internal Medicine Journal, 33*(3), 110–118. https://doi.org/10.1046/j.1445-5994.2003.00302.x

Kohls, E., Coppens, E., Hug, J., Wittevrongel, E., Van Audenhove, C., Koburger, N., ... Hegerl, U. (2017). Public attitudes toward depression and help-seeking: Impact of the OSPI-Europe depression awareness campaign in four European regions. *Journal of Affective Disorders, 217,* 252–259. https://doi.org/10.1016/j.jad.2017.04.006

Moore, G., Audrey, S., Barker, M., Bond, L., Bonell, C., Hardeman, W., ... Baird, J. (2015). Process evaluation of complex interventions: Medical Research Council guidance. *BMJ, 350,* h1258. https://doi.org/10.1136/bmj.h1258

Nugent, A.C., Ballard, E., Gould, T.D., Park, L.T., Moaddel, R., Brutsche, N.E., & Zarate, C.A. (2019). Ketamine has distinct electrophysiological and behavioral effects in depressed and healthy subjects. *Molecular Psychiatry, 24*(7), 1040–1052. https://doi.org/10.1038/s41380-018-0028-2

Pearson, M., Metcalfe, C., Jayamanne, S., Gunnell, D., Weerasinghe, M., Pieris, R., ... Konradsen, F. (2017). Effectiveness of household lockable pesticide storage to reduce pesticide self-poisoning in rural Asia: A community-based, cluster-randomised controlled trial. *Lancet, 390*(10105), 1863–1872. https://doi.org/10.1016/S0140-6736(17)31961-X

Pencheon, D., Guest, C., Melzer, D., & Gray, M. (Eds.). (2006). *Oxford handbook of public health practice* (2nd ed.). Oxford, UK: Oxford University Press. https://doi.org/10.1093/med/9780198566557.001.0001

Porta, M. (Ed.). (2008). *A dictionary of epidemiology* (5th ed.). Oxford, UK: Oxford University Press.

Rothman, K.J., Lash, T.L., & Greenland, S. (2013). *Modern epidemiology* (3rd mid-cycle revised ed.). Philadelphia, PA: Lippincott Williams and Wilkins.

Rychetnik, L., Frommer, M., Hawe, P., & Shiell, A. (2002). Criteria for evaluating evidence on public health interventions. *Journal of Epidemiology & Community Health, 56*(2), 119–127. https://doi.org/10.1136/jech.56.2.119

Schulz, K.F., Altman, D.G., Moher, D., & the CONSORT Group. (2010). CONSORT 2010 Statement: Updated guidelines for reporting parallel group randomised trials. *BMC Medicine, 8*(1), 18. https://doi.org/10.1186/1741-7015-8-18

Schulz, K.F., & Grimes, D.A. (2002a). Allocation concealment in randomised trials: Defending against deciphering. *Lancet, 359*(9306), 614–618. https://doi.org/10.1016/S0140-6736(02)07750-4

Schulz, K.F., & Grimes, D.A. (2002b). Blinding in randomised trials: Hiding who got what. *Lancet, 359*(9307), 696–700. https://doi.org/10.1016/S0140-6736(02)07816-9

Schulz, K.F., & Grimes, D.A. (2002c). Generation of allocation sequences in randomised trials: Chance, not choice. *Lancet, 359*(9305), 515–519. https://doi.org/10.1016/S0140-6736(02)07683-3

Székely, A., Konkolÿ Thege, B., Mergl, R., Birkás, E., Rózsa, S., Purebl, G., & Hegerl, U. (2013). How to decrease suicide rates in both genders? An effectiveness study of a community-based intervention (EAAD). *PLOS One, 8*(9), e75081–e75081. https://doi.org/10.1371/journal.pone.0075081

Torous, J., Larsen, M.E., Depp, C., Cosco, T.D., Barnett, I., Nock, M.K., & Firth, J. (2018). Smartphones, sensors, and machine learning to advance real-time prediction and interventions for suicide prevention: A review of current progress and next steps. *Current Psychiatry Reports, 20*(7), 51. https://doi.org/10.1007/s11920-018-0914-y

Turecki, G., Brent, D.A., Gunnell, D., O'Connor, R.C., Oquendo, M.A., Pirkis, J., & Stanley, B.H. (2019). Suicide and suicide risk. *Nature Reviews Disease Primers, 5*(1), 1–22. https://doi.org/10.1038/s41572-019-0121-0

van Spijker, B.A.J., van Straten, A., & Kerkhof, A.J.F.M. (2015). Online self-help for suicidal thoughts: 3-month follow-up results and participant evaluation. *Internet Interventions, 2,* 283–288. https://doi.org/10.1016/j.invent.2015.07.001

Wasserman, C., Hoven, C.W., Wasserman, D., Carli, V., Sarchiapone, M., Al-Halabí, S., ... Poštuvan, V. (2012). Suicide prevention for youth – a mental health awareness program: Lessons learned from the Saving and Empowering Young Lives in Europe (SEYLE) intervention study. *BMC Public Health, 12*(1), 776. https://doi.org/10.1186/1471-2458-12-776

Wasserman, D., Carli, V., Wasserman, C., Apter, A., Balazs, J., Bobes, J., ... Hoven, C.W. (2010). Saving and Empowering Young Lives in Europe (SEYLE): A randomized controlled trial. *BMC Public Health, 10*(1), 192–205. https://doi.org/10.1186/1471-2458-10-192

Wasserman, D., Hoven, C.W., Wasserman, C., Wall, M., Eisenberg, R., Hadlaczky, G., ... Carli, V. (2015). School-based suicide prevention programmes: The SEYLE cluster-randomised, controlled trial. *Lancet, 385*(9977), 1536–1544. https://doi.org/10.1016/S0140-6736(14)61213-7

Wasserman, D., & Varnik, A. (1998). Suicide-preventive effects of perestroika in the former USSR: The role of alcohol restriction. *Acta Psychiatrica Scandinavica, Supplement, 98*(394), 1–4.https://doi.org/10.1111/j.1600-0447.1998.tb10758.x

Webb, P., & Bain, C. (2011). *Essential epidemiology: An introduction for students and health professionals* (2nd ed.). Cambridge, UK: Cambridge University Press.

Webb, P., Bain, C., & Page, A. (2020). *Essential epidemiology: An introduction for students and health professionals* (4th ed.). Cambridge, UK: Cambridge University Press.

Chapter 8

Data Linkage and Studies of Suicidal Behavior

Annette Erlangsen, Ping Qin, and Ellenor Mittendorfer-Rutz

Summary

National administrative databases offer extensive options for research and exist in many countries. In the Nordic countries, this data source has been applied extensively to studies of suicidal behavior. This chapter provides an overview of the basic principles for linkage of administrative databases and describes some of the registers used in this type of research. Using examples from current studies, the options for different methodological applications are reviewed, as well as strengths and limitations of this data source.

(This chapter is based on an editorial: Erlangsen, A., Qin, P., & Mittendorfer-Rutz, E., 2018, Studies of suicidal behavior using national registers. *Crisis, 39*(3), 153–158. https://doi.org/10.1027/0227-5910/a000552. The text has been revised and updated.)

Suicide is a relatively rare event. In most countries, fewer than 20 suicide deaths are observed per 100,000 inhabitants on a yearly basis. Although this is good from a preventive perspective, it presents a challenge with respect to research on suicide, and large data samples are needed to identify risk factors or evaluate whether interventions are effective in reducing deaths by suicide. It has, for instance, been estimated that more than 40,000 person-years of data – equivalent of 40,000 persons followed over the course of 1 year or 80,000 followed over 6 months – are required to assess whether an intervention targeting people with self-harm is effective in reducing risk of suicide (Gunnell & Frankel, 1994). It is generally not feasible to conduct such large trials in standard clinical practice. Different strategies are employed to address this problem; studies may choose to focus on more frequent outcomes, such as suicide attempts, suicidal ideation, or levels of hopelessness. Using an alternate outcome implies that the findings will be only indirectly transferable to suicide. In other words, we cannot be certain that risk factors, which are also associated with suicide ideation, are present among those who die by suicide. Similarly, an intervention that prevents suicide attempts might not be effective at preventing suicide deaths. The best solution when studying rare outcomes is to use large data sets. For this reason, use of administrative data registers has gained momentum in suicide prevention research.

The purpose of this chapter is to illustrate the potential of national data linkage for suicide prevention research. This is achieved, first, by providing an overview of the principles for administrative databases and data linkage as well as practical aspects of this. Second, we will review some of the main contributions from register-based data to suicide research in terms of studies of risk predictors and evaluations of interventions. In addition, the strengths and limitations of register-based data are presented, as well as an exploration of future venues for research.

Administrative Databases

Administrative databases with national coverage exist in many countries, including the Nordic countries. They have proven their value as a data source for research within public health, and are particularly useful when studying rare events, such as suicide. In addition, administrative data are vital for studies of fatal outcomes where a direct data collection, such as interviews with the subject, is no longer an option.

Over recent years, administrative databases have become increasingly used to examine risk predictors of suicidal behavior. While many countries collect national data on vital events, such as births and deaths, national databases on health care provision, civil status, education, and other sociodemographic and socioeconomic information are less widespread (see Table 8.1). The possibility of linking data from different databases on an individual level is one of the key components in this type of research. Linkage based on a unique ID number brings advantages over linkage based on personal markers, such as date of birth and name, as these are less likely to secure a complete linkage. Nordic register data have, in this respect, contributed substantially to the knowledge base on suicidal behavior.

One Number

The key element in the Nordic registers, the personal identification (ID) number, is not a new invention; in 1947, the Swedish parliament introduced a personal ID number for all citizens. This was used as the backbone for a computerized Swedish population register in 1967 (Ludvigsson, Otterblad-Olausson, Pettersson, & Ekbom, 2009). Later the other Nordic countries followed suit, and a similar ID number and system was implemented in Norway in 1964, in Denmark in 1968, and Finland in 1969 (Population Register Centre, Finland, 2018; Kompetansesenter for IT i helsevesenet, 2010; Nielsen, 1991). Iceland had already introduced a personal ID number in 1952 but later opted for a name number that in 1980 was replaced by a 10-digit number (Watson, 2010).

The introduction of personal ID numbers meant that each citizen was given an ID card listing their personal ID number, and all newborns from this date onward were assigned a number at birth. Persons migrating into the country were also given an identifier. Each of the Nordic countries uses a different system, and those who move between the Nordic counties receive a different number in each country. Still, some similarities exist: The 10- to 11-digit number includes the person's birthdate and a marker for male or female sex. Each ID number is unique in the sense that no duplicates exist, and persons leaving the country maintain the same ID number upon reentry. Over recent decades, it has become possible to have one's ID number replaced – for instance, in cases of identity theft or for persons who change their sex.

The intention of the ID number was to have a better way of administering tax payments, accompanied by a wish to replace punch cards with the newly available options for electronic data processing in the late 1960s. However, across the public sector, several administrative systems quickly began using the identifier, including population, housing, hospital, and death registers, and the use of it has been mandatory for contacts with public authorities and services since the 1970s. It could be argued that the social welfare state with free public health care, numerous social transfer payments, and other public services provided an ideal setting for population-based registers. Still, probably nobody at that time realized that this would signify the beginning of a new era of public health research.

Table 8.1 Examples of administrative databases available for linkage in Denmark

Database	Available since[a]	Examples of available information
Sociodemographic databases		
Civil Registration System	1968	Date of birth, country of birth, civil status, household ID, family relations to people in same household, municipality
Migration	1980	Date and type of migration (immigration, migration)
Population's Education Register	1970	Highest obtained education
Worker Classification Module	1976	Job code (according to DISCO classifications), employer ID and socioeconomic status
Income Statistics Register	1980	Gross income, sick leave and unemployment benefits as well as other transfer payments
Social Pension Register	1994	Retirement and disability pension
Health-related databases		
National Health Service Register	1987	Number of contacts with primary care providers, including dentists and physiotherapists, as well as psychiatrists and psychologists in private practice
National Prescription Register	1995	Date of redeemed prescription, ATC code, type of drug, number of packages and pills
National Patient Register	1997	Date of admission and discharge, diagnoses (ICD-8 or ICD-10), patient type, different types of treatments offered, such as surgical procedures
National Patient Register – Treatment charges	2002	Prices for performed treatments in association with admission or contact with somatic hospital
Psychiatric Central Research Register	1969	Date of admission and discharge, diagnoses (ICD-8 or ICD-10), patient type, reason for contact, admission format (voluntary or involuntary)
Psychiatric Central Research Register – Treatment charges	2004	Prices associated with admission or contact with psychiatric hospital
Register of Causes of Death	1970	Date of death, primary (secondary and tertiary) cause of death (ICD-8 or ICD-10), manner of death

Note. ATC = anatomical therapeutic chemical; DISCO = Danish edition of the *International Standard Classification of Occupations*; ICD = World Health Organization's *International Classification of Diseases*.
[a]It may be that not all variables have been available since the start of the database, and some variables may have been converted into new measures over time.

Nowadays, the main health-related registers include nationwide data on all hospital admissions, prescriptions, clinical laboratory tests, and general practitioner visits, which can all be linked to high-quality, clinical databases on specific health conditions and disorders.

Types of Databases

The core component of the Nordic data linkage is the civil register, which is a complete database of all persons living in the country, including information on their date of birth, sex, civil status, address, and household ID. This type of register exists in all Nordic countries and is continuously updated so that information on newborn children, immigrants into the country, emigrants out of the country, and people dying is captured, with the date of these events. By using the civil register, it is possible to determine exactly how many people are alive and living in the country on any given date of the year. For this reason, none of the Nordic countries hold population censuses any longer. The exact name of the civil register in each of the countries varies slightly. In Denmark, it is called the Civil Registration System, while it is the Population Register in Norway and Sweden.

Studies on Suicidal Behavior

Much of the knowledge base for suicide research has been formed by clinical investigations, psychological autopsy studies, community-based sample surveys, and register-based studies. While clinical databases might provide more detailed data on biomarkers and scores from psychological scales, and the psychological autopsy studies gather information on traits and symptoms prior to death, representativeness and the possibility of data linkage are the main advantages of register-based data. Register-based studies offer the possibility of very long follow-ups, which may be explored in cohort studies as shown in Box 8.1 (Erlangsen, Stenager, et al., 2020), and large databases enable subgroup analyses (Mittendorfer-Rutz, Rasmussen, & Wasserman, 2004). Moreover, clinical studies on the prognosis after a suicide attempt may face the challenge of a low rate of compliance to treatment of this patient group. Here, the registers can contribute considerably to the existing knowledge base, as these studies have practically no loss to follow-up (Niederkrotenthaler et al., 2014).

Although many countries keep national databases – for instance, of causes of death – these do not always allow for individual-level linkage to other databases. As a consequence, studies using these might incur the ecological fallacy by being based on associations of aggregate data, such as national unemployment and suicide rates. Interestingly, multilevel analysis has shown that while aggregate-level data, such as area measures of unemployment rates, are significant predictors of suicide, individual-level characteristics, such as one's own unemployment, carry an even stronger association (Agerbo, Sterne, & Gunnell, 2007).

Box 8.1. Example of a cohort study from Denmark

Using national hospital data on disorders diagnosed and treated in hospital, authors examined whether people diagnosed with neurological disorders had higher suicide rates than persons not diagnosed with neurological disorders applying a cohort design.

All persons aged 15 years or older who were living in Denmark were followed from January 1, 1980, through December 31, 2016. People who migrated into the country were included on the date of immigration and people who reached the age of 15 years were included on the date of their birthday. Similarly, people who migrated out of the country or died by other causes of death were right-hand censored on the date of these events.

Neurological disorder were identified through ICD-8 or ICD-10 codes and date of onset for exposure was defined as date of first diagnosis. Somatic hospital registers date back to 1977 in

Denmark; hence, some individuals were already categorized as exposed at the start of the observation period. The outcome, death by suicide, was identified in the Cause of Death Register where the date of death marked the end of the 'at risk'-time for those who died by suicide.

In a cohort design, participants are followed from date of inclusion to end of follow-up marking the number of days being at risk of dying by suicide. Knowing the exact date of exposure for each individual, allows for calculation of suicide rates for those exposed and those not exposed. In Poisson regressions, adjusted estimates for the incidence rate ratio between exposed and not exposed were calculated.

Findings from this study revealed a suicide rate of 44.0 per 100,000 person-years for people with neurological disorders, compared with 20.1 per 100,000 person-years for people not diagnosed with a neurological disorder. Those with a neurological disorder had an incidence rate ratio of 1.8 (95% CI, 1.7–1.8) compared with those not diagnosed in adjusted analysis.

The limitations of the study were that estimates were based on hospital-diagnosed disorders only and that patients exclusively seen in primary care would not be identified as exposed. The strengths include the representativeness of the findings and that estimates were adjusted for relevant confounders, such as mental disorders or deliberate self-harm proceeding neurological disorders.

Based on Erlangsen, A., Stenager, E., Conwell, Y., Andersen, P.K., Hawton, K., Benros, M.E., ... Stenager, E. (2020). Association between neurological disorders and death by suicide in Denmark. *JAMA, 323*(5), 444–454.

Clinical interviews and surveys enable the possibility of asking for relevant background details and instant access to information, such as exposure to suicidal behavior in the social network (e.g., suicide by family members or friends). While these options are not available in register-based data, impressive multigenerational studies compensate by not being subject to informer bias, as illustrated in Box 8.2 (Mittendorfer-Rutz, Rasmussen, & Lange, 2012). Linkage with a multigeneration register and detailed data for a large study population offers also the possibility of bereavement studies using intraindividual designs (Mogensen, Möller, Hultin, & Mittendorfer-Rutz, 2016). These study designs inherently control for all time-stable confounding factors and thereby limit the risk of unmeasured residual confounding.

Box 8.2. Example of a study using a multigeneration register

Multigeneration registers can link information on family members – that is, parents, children, and siblings. For this reason, they offer a unique source to study the etiology of suicidal behavior, and more specifically, they offer the possibility to investigate aspects such as familial clustering of suicidal behavior and the effect of the psychosocial family environment. By individual linkage of a multigeneration register with other registers, longitudinal data with exact dates of individual events and events of family members are available. The register also offers the opportunity to conceptualize suicidological studies with a life-course perspective.

According to the paradigm of life-course epidemiology, exposure during sensitive periods in life, such as childhood or adolescence, can have a more detrimental effect than if exposure occurs outside these time windows. To investigate such sensitive periods, the temporal relationship of parental morbidity and mortality with offspring's suicide attempt was analyzed. Moreover, the study investigated whether any such associations are modified by offspring's age at attempt.

A case-control study was designed through linkage of the Multigeneration Register with other Swedish registers, such as the National Patient Register, the Cause of Death Register, the Population and Housing Censuses, and the Longitudinal Integration Database for Health Insurance and Labor Market Studies (Mittendorfer-Rutz, Rasmussen, & Lange, 2012). Cases comprised all individuals in Sweden born 1973–1983 with inpatient care due to suicide attempt (15–31 years of age) and with information on both biological parents (N = 15,193). Ten controls were matched to each case. Conditional logistic and spline regressions were applied.

Particularly for young women, most parental markers showed the strongest effect sizes if exposure was short-term (within 2 years after exposure) and related to the mother. Especially short-term exposure to maternal inpatient care due to psychiatric diagnoses had a significantly stronger effect on suicide attempt risk in young women compared with men. Adolescence turned out to be a specific sensitive period as the effects of experiencing a parent's psychiatric hospitalization on their children's suicide attempt were strongest during adolescence, and decreased considerably after that.

By using the Multigeneration Register linked to other registers with national coverage, studies can contribute to the growing evidence using life-course approaches in suicidological research.

Source: Mittendorfer-Rutz, E., Rasmussen, F., & Lange, T. (2012). A life-course study on effects of parental markers of morbidity and mortality on offspring's suicide attempt. *PLoS One, 7*(12), e51585.

Other interesting opportunities arise from linking clinical data, including data from randomized controlled trials, to register-based data. This way, reporting bias may also be addressed. For instance, a recent study found a substantial bidirectional divergence between self-reported and hospital records of deliberate self-harm (Morthorst, Krogh, Erlangsen, Alberdi, & Nordentoft, 2012). Suicidal behavior can be repetitive, and advanced analytical methods based on register data can be used here to model repeated suicide attempts (Mittendorfer-Rutz, Alexanderson, Westerlund, & Lange, 2014).

Risk Predictor Studies

Register-based studies have quantified risks of suicidal behavior related to mental disorders and its association with many specific disorders, including schizophrenia, psychosis, affective (including bipolar) disorders, personality (including borderline) disorders, anxiety disorders, alcohol and substance misuse, attention-deficit/hyperactivity disorder (ADHD), autism spectrum disorders, and dementia (Erlangsen, Zarit, & Conwell, 2008; Ljung, Chen, Lichtenstein, & Larsson, 2014; Mortensen, Agerbo, Qin, & Westergaard-Nielsen, 2000; Qin, 2011; Qin & Nordentoft, 2005). Importantly, findings from register-based studies have demonstrated elevated risks at time of admission and discharge from a psychiatric hospital and therefore point out the need for intervention. Population-wide data have also been used to calculate the absolute risk of suicide among people with schizophrenia, for instance, varied between 6.6 (95% confidence interval [95% CI], 5.9–7.3) for men and 4.9 (95% CI, 4.0–6.0) for women (Nordentoft, Mortensen, & Pedersen, 2011). In addition, exposure to mental disorders or suicide in relatives has been confirmed as a predictor for suicidal behavior, in populationbased register studies (Christiansen, Larsen, Agerbo, Bilenberg, & Stenager, 2013; Mittendorfer-Rutz, Rasmussen, & Wasserman, 2008; Qin, Agerbo, & Mortensen, 2003).

Among the social and economic characteristics that have been associated with higher risks of suicide behavior are not being married or in a de facto relationship, receiving a disability pension, being retired, living in an urban area, changing residence, coming from an immigrant background, not having children, and being exposed to the death of significant others (Burrell, Mehlum, & Qin, 2017; Jonsson, Alexanderson, Kjeldgård, Westerlund, & Mittendorfer-Rutz, 2013; Mogensen et al., 2016; Puzo, Mehlum, & Qin, 2017; Qin, 2005; Qin et al., 2003). An example of a nested case-control study to identify risk predictors is shown in Box 8.3 (Puzo et al., 2017).

Inventive linkage between registers, furthermore, has allowed for examination of rarely studied associations, such as the relation between death by suicide and area-level recordings of air pollen (slightly elevated levels of pollen: relative risk [RR] = 1.07; 95% CI, 1.01–1.13) and silicone breast implants (standardized mortality ratio = 2.9; 95% CI, 1.6–4.8) (Koot, Peeters, Granath, Grobbee, & Nyren, 2003; Qin, Waltoft, Mortensen, & Postolache, 2013).

Box 8.3. Example of a nested case-control study from Norway

In light of the steady growth in the immigrant population in Norway, a nested case-control design was employed to examine suicide risk in people with immigration background and disentangling the risk differences by country of origin using interlinked data from Norwegian registries.

The cases comprised all individuals who died by suicide during the period from 1969 to 2012. Each case was matched on sex and date of birth with up to 20 individuals who were alive at the date of case suicide. This procedure yielded 373,178 comparison controls matched for the 23,073 suicide cases. The data were analysed with conditional logistic regression in which each match-set formed a stratum. By the design, the controls were sampled from individuals "at risk" for suicide at the date when the case occurred, an approach known as *incidence density sampling* or *risk-set sampling*, which makes the odds ratios produced from conditional logistic regression an unbiased estimation of the incidence rate ratio.

Suicide cases were identified from the Causes of Death Register using the diagnostic codes in ICD 8th, 9th, and 10th revision in respective periods. Demographic data including country of birth, date of immigration or emigration as well as sex, date of birth and links to parents were obtained from Norwegian Population Register. Personal socioeconomic status such as marital status, annual income, education attainment and place of residence were retrieved from the Statistics Norway's Events Database (FD-Trygd) which is a collection of running administrative data from a number of public authorities for all residents in the county.

The study showed that both first- and second-generation immigrants had a significantly lower risk of suicide compared with native Norwegians, whereas the risks for individuals with blended background were significantly higher, with notable differences by country group of origin. The reduced risk applied to first-generation immigrants from all but other Nordic countries and was most prominent for those from Asia and Africa. The increased risk was most pronounced among individuals born in Norway with one parent from Asia or Central and South America, and those born in Asia or Central and South America with at least one Norwegian-born parent. These findings remained also when adjusting for personal socioeconomic differences and underscore the importance of considering immigrants as a heterogeneous group with respect to suicide prevention.

The nested case-control design is very suitable to study a rare event like suicide because it can minimize the burden associated with a large sample and time-dependent confounding and explanatory variables. By matching controls to cases on sex and birthdate, we efficiently controlled the confounding effects of sex and age induced by their skewed distribution with respect to suicide occurrences and socioeconomic status. On the other hand, the matching made it impossible to assess the direct influence of sex and age on the risk for suicide, which may be considered a limitation.

Based on Puzo, Q., Mehlum, L., & Qin, P. (2017). Suicide among immigrant population in Norway: A national register-based study. *Acta Psychiatrica Scandinavica, 135*(6), 584–592.

Intervention Studies

In principle, new treatment regimens, both pharmacological and psychosocial therapies, can be evaluated using register-based data. For instance, a recent study has shown that temazepam and zopiclone/zolpidem from the group of benzodiazepines and hypnotics were considerably more toxic than diazepam (Geulayov et al., 2018). This might be of relevance for policy makers planning interventions to limit availability of means for suicide – that is, by restricting access to highly toxic drugs. However, the availability of long-term follow-up data also implies that one might study effects on outcomes not usually addressed in clinical interventions, such as death by suicide. By linkage between clinical and register data, it was feasible to generate a sufficiently large body of follow-up material on recipients of the psychosocial therapy provided in Danish suicide prevention clinics to have the statistical strength to evaluate the effect on death by suicide using propensity score matching as shown in Box 8.4 (Erlangsen et al., 2014).

Box 8.4. Example of study using propensity score matching

Intervention studies may benefit from combining a clinical database with national linkage data, for instance, to identify a comparison group. An example of this is found in the effect evaluation of the psychosocial therapy provided in the Suicide Prevention Clinics in Denmark.

Data on people treated after suicide attempt were provided from eight Suicide Prevention Clinics. People who had been recorded with a suicide attempt in the psychiatric or somatic hospital registers were used as a pool for identifying matched controls. Id-numbers were available for all persons who had received the intervention. It was, thus, possible to ensure that the same person was not a part of the comparison group by comparing id-numbers.

The strategy applied in propensity score matching is to select a comparison group who resemble the intervention group with respect to all relevant predictors of studied outcome, i.e., suicidal behaviour as well as factors influencing the likelihood of attending treatment. The underlying assumption is, thus, to assume that any difference observed for the studied outcome between the two groups is due to the intervention. In this study, a total of 31 factors were used to calculate the propensity score, ranging from sociodemographics characteristics to mental disorders, previous suicidal behaviour, and parental risk factors. Based on the propensity score, three comparisons with the closest match for each case were selected. Odds ratios (OR) for the studied outcomes were calculated.

In all, 5,678 recipients of psychosocial therapy in the Suicide Prevention Clinics were matched to 17,034 comparisons who had not received the intervention after having had a suicide attempt. After 1 year of follow-up, a lower risk of repeated self-harm was noticed in the intervention group when compared to the matched comparison group (OR: 0.7, 95 % CI 0.6–0.8). After 20 years of follow-up, recipients of the intervention had a lower risk of suicide compared with no psychosocial therapy (OR: 0.7, 95 % CI 0.6–0.9).

While this study design does not allow for causal inference as in randomized clinical trials, it allows for an evaluation of effects in already implemented interventions.

Based on Erlangsen, A., Lind, B., Stuart, E.A., Qin, P., Stenager, E., Larsen, K.J., ... Nordentoft, M. (2014). Short-term and long-term effects of psychosocial therapy for people after deliberate self-harm: A register-based, nationwide multicentre study using propensity score matching. *Lancet Psychiatry, 2*(1), 49–58.

Nordic Data Linkage

There are seemingly few boundaries to possible areas and study designs using register-based data. Theoretically, it would even be possible to obtain an individual-level database on 26+ million inhabitants by merging data across the Nordic countries. The relatively comparable social welfare systems of the Nordic countries would even support coherence in patterns across national borders. In practical terms, however, it seems less likely that this will happen, as data regulations in some countries prevent individual-level data from being stored physically outside the country. Although a lessening of the regulations has taken place over the last decades, it might take some time before this will be feasible.

Still, researchers have not been restricted by these measures. Given that aggregate results from data analyses may be taken out of the country, studies have used this opportunity to combine Danish, Finish, and Swedish register data – for instance, with respect to assessing risks of suicide after bereavement and among persons in same-sex marriages (Erlangsen, Drefahl, et al., 2020; Guldin et al., 2015). Obtaining aggregate data sets on number of events, such as suicide, and time of exposure (e.g., person-years), broken down by relevant covariates, is in some instances feasible. Such data sets may be considered as anonymous in aggregate, implying that it becomes possible to share these across borders with respect to conducting joint regression analysis for several countries.

Safety Considerations

Needless to say, sensitive data of this type are protected by heavy security restrictions. All Nordic countries, therefore, have sound legislation and regulations for utilization of personal data and privacy safeguarding. To obtain access to data, both projects and researchers have to be approved by national data protection agencies, ethical review boards and, in some cases, by the respective data providers or owners. Typically, researchers access data extracts through secured Internet portals while physically data is stored on a server in protected locations, such as national statistical offices or approved research institutes. It is, furthermore, often a requirement that the personal ID number is replaced by an anonymous linkage number before data are delivered to specific projects. After legal review, the data are only made available for researchers who meet the criteria for access to this type of sensitive data. These procedures follow the national ethical review acts, the personal data acts, and the administrative procedure acts of each country. As data are derived from different registers, no personal contact with the individuals is established. Furthermore, results are presented at a group level without any possibility of backward identification. The research groups working with register data also apply high standards of data safety.

Strengths and Limitations

Strengths of register-based studies are manifold. Those include nationwide coverage that ensures full representativeness. In general, data validity is evaluated favorably. This is supported by an administrative system where errors are corrected on a continuous and retrospective basis. In addition, having a study population of several million is beneficial in terms of statistical power when studying relatively rare events, such as death by suicide and deliberate self-harm. Precision in estimates of prevalence and risk is improved by uniformly collected measures and individual-level data. Furthermore, the longitudinal nature of the data and having dates for events allow not only inclusion of time-varying covariates but also time-to-event analysis.

Some limitations should be considered, however. First, one obstacle is the lack of information from general practitioners – for example, no national coverage in Sweden and no recording of diagnoses. In most Nordic countries, electronic records of diagnoses given in the general practitioner's office are not available, although this is likely to change in the near future. Next, only persons who actively seek treatment are captured by hospital or medical prescription records. In other words, those who are not diagnosed are not included in the exposure groups, suggesting that the actual population at risk is underestimated. This is likely to be a prevalent problem with respect to mental disorders and could potentially introduce selection bias to risk estimates. Also, the validity of diagnoses depends on clinical rigor and assessment tools, which might have improved over time. It is often praised as an advantage that exact dates are available in the registers; however, those dates are typically date of diagnosis and not onset of disorders.

Access From Abroad and Lessons Learned

Foreign researchers can obtain access to register-based data, depending on national regulations. In most cases, the easiest way of gaining access would be through collaborations with research institutions in the respective countries. While data in some countries have to remain stored physically within the borders of the country, the exact regulations vary from one country to the next. One of the most important lessons learned from the Nordic register research is the importance of regulated access to, and safe storage of, data in order to minimize risk of misuse.

Starting register-based studies is time-consuming; from the first initial plan to actually having access to a data extract is likely to take 12 months or more. The first effort is to obtain permission for the study; in Denmark, the Data Protection Agency distributes permissions through institutional review boards. The next step is to select the variables from the different registers that will be needed for the project. Here, the national statistical offices might have consultants who will advise regarding which variables are available. Data extracts from the registers may be ordered either through the national statistical office or directly from the authorities who administer the individual registers. Storage of individual-level data is protected by security regulations, and different rules apply, such as storage on a protected server or two-factor logon requirements. As a rule, identifiable data may not be made public, which includes specifications that any cell in a published table may not consist of fewer than three observations.

Future Avenues

A lot of ingenuity has gone into examining statistical associations using register-based data, and this will certainly continue in coming decades. While international studies have begun to employ machine-learning algorithms and big data, these avenues have yet to be explored in a Nordic setting; it will be interesting to see what data linkage can contribute in this respect. Genetic data has been gathered, also on a population level, in several of the Nordic countries. In the Danish iPSYCH project, genetic chips have been coded for a population-based sample as well as for all individuals who have been diagnosed with severe mental disorders, allowing for comprehensive studies of genetic predictors and later epigenetics (Pedersen et al., 2018). Other avenues might lie in the possibility of linkage to yet relatively unexplored registers, such as hospital lab tests or electronic patient journals, including analyses of free text fields.

Conclusions

Register data, such as those available in the Nordic countries, have contributed substantially to the existing knowledge on high-risk groups with respect to suicidal behavior. It is likely that similar data sources might be further explored in more countries in the future; even linkage of relatively few registries might generate a more complete and less biased database than what can be secured through other data sources. The boundaries for register-based research are set by the necessary data protection laws. However, it seems that there are no limits in sight for research options using register-based data to address studies regarding the etiology and prevention of suicidal behavior.

References

Agerbo, E., Sterne, J. A., & Gunnell, D. J. (2007). Combining individual and ecological data to determine compositional and contextual socio-economic risk factors for suicide. *Social Science and Medicine, 64*(2), 451–461. https://doi.org/10.1016/j.socscimed.2006.08.043

Burrell, L. V., Mehlum, L., & Qin, P. (2017). Risk factors for suicide in offspring bereaved by sudden parental death from external causes. *Journal of Affective Disorders, 222,* 71–78. https://doi.org/10.1016/j.jad.2017.06.064

Christiansen, E., Larsen, K. J., Agerbo, E., Bilenberg, N., & Stenager, E. (2013). Incidence and risk factors for suicide attempts in a general population of young people: A Danish register-based study. *Australian and New Zealand Journal of Psychiatry, 47*(3), 259–270. https://doi.org/10.1177/0004867412463737

Erlangsen, A., Drefahl, S., Haas, A., Bjorkenstam, C., Nordentoft, M., & Andersson, G. (2020). Suicide among persons who entered same-sex and opposite-sex marriage in Denmark and Sweden, 1989–2016: A binational, register-based cohort study. *Journal of Epidemiology and Community Health, 74*(1), 78–83. https://doi.org/10.1136/jech-2019-213009

Erlangsen, A., Lind, B., Stuart, E. A., Qin, P., Stenager, E., Larsen, K. J., ... Nordentoft, M. (2014). Short-term and long-term effects of psychosocial therapy for people after self-harm: A register-based, nationwide multicentre study using propensity score matching. *Lancet Psychiatry, 2*(1), 47–58. https://doi.org/10.1016/S2215-0366(14)00083-2

Erlangsen, A., Stenager, E., Conwell, Y., Andersen, P.K., Hawton, K., Benros, M.E., ... Stenager, E. (2020). Association between neurological disorders and death by suicide in Denmark. *JAMA, 323*(5), 444–454. https://doi.org/10.1001/jama.2019.21834

Erlangsen, A., Qin, P., & Mittendorfer-Rutz, E. (2018). Studies of suicidal behavior using national registers. *Crisis, 39*(3), 153–158. https://doi.org/10.1027/0227-5910/a000552

Erlangsen, A., Zarit, S.H., & Conwell, Y. (2008). Hospital-diagnosed dementia and suicide: A longitudinal study using prospective, nationwide register data. *American Journal of Geriatric Psychiatry, 16*, 220–228. https://doi.org/10.1097/01.JGP.0000302930.75387.7e

Geulayov, G., Ferrey, A., Casey, D., Wells, C., Fuller, A., Bankhead, C., ... Hawton, K. (2018). Relative toxicity of benzodiazepines and hypnotics commonly used for self-poisoning. *Journal of Psychopharmacology, 32*(6), 654–662. https://doi.org/10.1177/0269881118754734

Guldin, M.B., Li, J., Pedersen, H.S., Obel, C., Agerbo, E., Gissler, M., ... Vestergaard, M. (2015). Incidence of suicide among persons who had a parent who died during their childhood: a population-based cohort study. *JAMA Psychiatry, 72*(12), 1227–1234. https://doi.org/10.1001/jamapsychiatry.2015.2094

Gunnell, D., & Frankel, S. (1994). Prevention of suicide: aspirations and evidence. *BMJ, 308*(6938), 1227–1233.

Jonsson, U., Alexanderson, K., Kjeldgård, L., Westerlund, H., & Mittendorfer-Rutz, E. (2013). Diagnosis-specific disability pension predicts suicidal behaviour and mortality in young adults: A nationwide prospective cohort study. *BMJ Open, 3*(2). https://doi.org/10.1136/bmjopen-2012-002286

Kompetansesenter for IT i helsevesenet. (2010). *Identifikatorer for personer* [Identifiers for people].

Koot, V.C. M., Peeters, P.H. M., Granath, F., Grobbee, D.E., & Nyren, O. (2003). Total and cause specific mortality among Swedish women with cosmetic breast implants: Prospective study. *BMJ, 326*, 527–528. https://doi.org/10.1136/bmj.326.7388.527

Ljung, T., Chen, Q., Lichtenstein, P., & Larsson, H. (2014). Common etiological factors of attention-deficit/hyperactivity disorder and suicidal behavior: A population-based study in Sweden. *JAMA Psychiatry, 71*(8), 958–964. https://doi.org/10.1001/jamapsychiatry.2014.363

Ludvigsson, J.F., Otterblad-Olausson, P., Pettersson, B.U., & Ekbom, A. (2009). The Swedish personal identity number: Possibilities and pitfalls in healthcare and medical research. *European Journal of Epidemiology, 24*(11), 659–667. https://doi.org/10.1007/s10654-009-9350-y

Mittendorfer-Rutz, E., Alexanderson, K., Westerlund, H., & Lange, T. (2014). Is transition to disability pension in young people associated with changes in risk of attempted suicide? *Psychological Medicine, 44*(11), 2331–2338. https://doi.org/10.1017/S0033291713003097

Mittendorfer-Rutz, E., Rasmussen, F., & Lange, T. (2012). A life-course study on effects of parental markers of morbidity and mortality on offspring's suicide attempt. *PLoS One, 7*(12), e51585. https://doi.org/10.1371/journal.pone.0051585

Mittendorfer-Rutz, E., Rasmussen, F., & Wasserman, D. (2004). Restricted fetal growth and adverse maternal psychosocial and socioeconomic conditions as risk factors for suicidal behaviour of offspring: A cohort study. *Lancet, 364*(9440), 1135–1140. https://doi.org/10.1016/S0140-6736(04)17099-2

Mittendorfer-Rutz, E., Rasmussen, F., & Wasserman, D. (2008). Familial clustering of suicidal behaviour and psychopathology in young suicide attempters. *Social Psychiatry and Psychiatric Epidemiology, 43*(1), 28–36. https://doi.org/10.1007/s00127-007-0266-0

Mogensen, H., Möller, J., Hultin, H., & Mittendorfer-Rutz, E. (2016). Death of a close relative and the risk of suicide in Sweden: A large scale register-based case-crossover Study. *PLoS One, 11*(10), e0164274. https://doi.org/10.1371/journal.pone.0164274

Mortensen, P.B., Agerbo, E., Qin, P., & Westergaard-Nielsen, N. (2000). Psychiatric illness and risk factors for suicide in Denmark. *Lancet, 355*, 9–12. https://doi.org/10.1016/S0140-6736(99)06376-X

Morthorst, B., Krogh, J., Erlangsen, A., Alberdi, F., & Nordentoft, M. (2012). Effect of assertive outreach after suicide attempt in the AID (assertive intervention for deliberate self harm) trial: Randomised controlled trial. *BMJ, 345*, e4972. https://doi.org/10.1136/bmj.e4972

Niederkrotenthaler, T., Tinghög, P., Alexanderson, K., Dahlin, M., Wang, M., Beckman, K., ... Mittendorfer-Rutz, E. (2014). Future risk of labour market marginalization in young suicide attempters: A population-based prospective cohort study. *International Journal of Epidemiology, 43*(5), 1520–1530. https://doi.org/10.1093/ije/dyu155

Nielsen, H. (1991). *CPR – Danmarks Folkeregister* [The Centralized Civil Register: The population register of Denmark]. Retrieved from https://cpr.dk/cpr-systemet/historie/

Nordentoft, M., Mortensen, P. B., & Pedersen, C. B. (2011). Absolute risk of suicide after first hospital contact in mental disorder. *Archives of General Psychiatry, 68*, 1058–1064. https://doi.org/10.1001/archgenpsychiatry.2011.113

Pedersen, C. B., Bybjerg-Grauholm, J., Pedersen, M. G., Grove, J., Agerbo, E., Baekvad-Hansen, M., ... Mortensen, P. B. (2018). The iPSYCH2012 case-cohort sample: New directions for unravelling genetic and environmental architectures of severe mental disorders. *Molecular Psychiatry, 23*(1), 6–14. https://doi.org/10.1101/146670

Population Register Centre, Finland. (2018). *History of the Finnish population information system.* Retrieved from https://vrk.fi/en/history

Puzo, Q., Mehlum, L., & Qin, P. (2017). Suicide among immigrant population in Norway: A national register-based study. *Acta Psychiatrica Scandinavica, 135*, 584–592. https://doi.org/10.1111/acps.12732

Qin, P. (2005). Suicide risk in relation to level of urbanicity: A population-based linkage study. *International Journal of Epidemiology, 34*, 846–852. https://doi.org/10.1093/ije/dyi085

Qin, P. (2011). The impact of psychiatric illness on suicide: Differences by diagnosis of disorders and by sex and age of subjects. *Journal of Psychiatric Research, 45*, 1445–1452. https://doi.org/10.1016/j.jpsychires.2011.06.002

Qin, P., Agerbo, E., & Mortensen, P. B. (2003). Suicide risk in relation to socioeconomic, demographic, psychiatric and familial factors: A national register-based study of all suicides in Denmark, 1981–1997. *American Journal of Psychiatry, 160*, 765–772. https://doi.org/10.1176/appi.ajp.160.4.765

Qin, P., & Nordentoft, M. (2005). Suicide risk in relation to psychiatric hospitalization: Evidence based on longitudinal registers. *Archives of General Psychiatry, 62*(4), 427–432. https://doi.org/10.1001/archpsyc.62.4.427

Qin, P., Waltoft, B. L., Mortensen, P. B., & Postolache, T. T. (2013). Suicide risk in relation to air pollen counts: A study based on data from Danish registers. *BMJ Open, 3*(5). https://doi.org/10.1136/bmjopen-2012-002462

Watson, I. (2010). A short history of national identification numbering in Iceland. *Bifröst Journal of Social Science, 4*, 51–88. https://doi.org/10.12742/bjss.2010.3

Chapter 9
The Words to Say It – Qualitative Suicide Research

Ines Testoni, Ciro De Vincenzo, and Adriano Zamperini

Summary

This chapter presents an overview of qualitative research methods, with examples from suicide research. The chapter is divided into four sections including (1) a description of the basic theoretical assumptions of qualitative research; (2) sampling in qualitative research; (3) frequently used data collection methods and their characteristics, including a description of the types of qualitative data sources; and (4) analysis of qualitative data, how it is conducted, and the available software. The chapter will conclude with a brief glimpse into qualitative secondary analysis and ethical concerns in qualitative research.

Traditionally, suicide research has been described predominantly from a quantitative perspective (Fitzpatrick, 2011; Goldney, 2002; Hjelmeland & Knizek, 2010; Hjelmeland, 2011). Over the last two decades, however, qualitative methods have become more prominent in the field of psychology, but also in public health research, and in suicide research (Lester, 2002, 2009, 2010). In response to the growing call for more flexible and open ways to study the complexity of suicidal behavior, both *idiographic* (methodology aimed at obtaining particular and specific descriptions) and *nomothetic* (methodology aimed at achieving universal results) approaches have been interwoven into qualitative (*understanding*) and quantitative (*explaining*) methods in suicide research (Bantjes & Swartz, 2017; Cutcliffe, 2005; Gerisch, 2002; Leenars, 2002). Qualitative methods are based on hermeneutics and phenomenology, which are generally framed within constructivist and interpretative theories, and were developed as a confutation of the neopositivistic quantitative paradigm (Rennie, 2012). This means there is not a single unitary reality that can be fully distinguished from individuals' worldviews, and therefore it is not feasible to establish validity in any objective sense, as it is not possible to separate research assumptions from the way data are collected. Discovery, rather than verification and generalization, is the major purpose, resulting from a deep understanding of human behavior and from questioning why people behave in a certain manner. Indeed, narrations are emphasized through the depiction of circular interactions between different dimensions of meanings as they are reflected in language. The strength of the qualitative approach is the interpretative processes and insights it can offer, as quantification is not possible without qualification, since all phenomena need to be recognized through interpretation before their enumeration (Bauer, Gaskell, & Allum, 2000).

In suicide research, which addresses complex biographical and social factors, the application of qualitative methods makes it easier to consider issues such as intentionality, for example, by interviewing people who have attempted suicide and exploring their interpretation of events. Although phenomenological issues and their relevance for understanding the various meanings of suicide in different human contexts have been raised (Bell, 2001; Schlimme, 2013), research reasoning the existential dimensions have historically been ignored. In recent years, this gap has been addressed through qualitative studies that focus on the idiographic aspects implied in any suicidal experience (Hjelmeland & Knizek, 2011, 2016).

In this chapter, we will present the theoretical underpinnings of qualitative methods and their varied applications in suicide research, with attention to the collection and analysis of textual rather than visual data, illustrated with qualitative suicide research examples.

Key Steps in Qualitative Research

Any qualitative study requires that the specific method used should be driven by the subject matter being investigated, conceivably based on a set of theoretical assumptions, and that the research questions are asked through a constructive dialogue with participants. To achieve this, three fundamental aspects, which are often interconnected and transversal but sometimes also idiosyncratic, should be considered: the *interpretative standpoint*, the *data collection*, and the *data analysis*.

Indeed, qualitative research traditionally includes the following steps (Tong, Sainsbury, & Craig, 2007):

- The *definition of the initial research question*, which can be progressively transformed into a wider and deeper problem. For instance, a researcher could be interested in how the personal life history of a loved one who died by suicide has changed in the family's narratives. Starting from this research question, the researcher faces a broader problem – that is, what role that suicide has had in modifying the narrative of the life course.
- The *definition of the group of research participants* describes the selection criteria – for example, age or type of relationship with the deceased.
- The *selection of the data collection method(s)* suitable for the research question and data collection. There are several methods of data collection. For example, the researcher might choose to collect data via interviews, asking participants a set of questions, or through the use of focus groups, creating a dialogue with participants.
- The *construction of the corpus of data* for the analyzes. Data collected will be transcribed to obtain the text which composes the *corpus* to be analyzed.
- The *choice of the analysis techniques*. For example, bottom-up or top-down strategies, where the researcher decides on a theory-driven or a data-driven approach to analysis.
- The *interpretation of the data* and the *development of answers* related to the research question are completed.
- The *write-up* of the findings is completed for dissemination to the public and the scientific community.

Nevertheless, different approaches and methods of conducting qualitative research may produce differences which can become the subject of debate among academics. As the consensus process is still being developed, the widely accepted aspects of qualitative research design are the following: It is not possible to generalize the results; qualitative research is useful for discovery and developing preliminary and pilot research; and it allows for definition of the relationship, on the one hand, between *etic* (researcher's point of view) and *emic* (social actors' point of view) aspects, and, on the other hand, between idiographic and nomothetic strategies (de Sardan, 2015).

Qualitative Approaches

There are numerous qualitative approaches (Given, 2008; Howitt 2010). Our literature review of qualitative suicide research over the last two decades identified that the most-utilized qualitative approaches have been *grounded theory* (GT), *ethnographic* or *ethnomethodological approaches*, *interpretative phenomenological analysis* (IPA), *narrative methods*, and *case studies*. These approaches have been considered as the most common across all fields using qualitative enquiry (Creswell & Poth, 2017). We will provide a brief description of these approaches, with examples from suicide research.

Grounded Theory

GT aims to create a new theory and is therefore very useful in describing understudied and new experiences and events to understand the important aspects (Glaser & Strauss 1967; Strauss & Corbin, 1994, 1998). GT has its roots in symbolic interactionism, which studies the interrelationship between the meaning of the perception of subjects and their actions (Blumer, 1969). It is mainly utilized in sociology and psychology and is characterized by a *bottom-up* process, because the researcher starts from a *tabula rasa* position.

GT requires a flexible strategy in the selection of the sample because it is constructed while the project progresses. This means that data collection runs concurrently with the analysis, permitting the researcher to make real-time judgments about the involvement of further participants (Strauss & Corbin, 1998).GT aims first to examine data closely, remaining *grounded* to what the data shows, and second, to build up more coherent and general frames (theory) which make sense of the data (Denzin & Lincoln, 2013). Structured and semistructured interviews to collect data are developed in a circular process, where the phases of hypothesizing and interpreting develop progressively together. Participants are selected on the basis of a specific issue or topic (e.g., people who indicated that a precipitating factor in their self-harm included financial, employment, or other difficulties related to economic hardship or austerity; see Barnes et al., 2016), and the final number of participants depends on the *saturation* of the emerging contents (Francis et al., 2010). When the topics begin to be repetitive, this indicates that the problem has been sufficiently observed.

The use of GT in qualitative suicide research has been growing in popularity in the last two decades (i.e., Aherne et al., 2018; Morrissey & Higgins, 2019; Vandewalle et al., 2019). For example, in Iran, Rahimipour Anaraki and Boostani (2014) interviewed 16 imprisoned mothers about their children's conditions. They used a purposive sample strategy (explained below in the section Sampling and Target Populations) and recruited until saturation was reached. Due to the lack of research on this topic in Iran, the researchers applied GT, which allowed them to develop concepts and categories within the data, constantly comparing similarities and differences between different interviews. This process of constant comparison should lead to more abstract themes, which are a result of what was present in the data. The results highlighted that many children had suicide experiences (ideation or attempts), and mothers were constantly emotionally challenged in order to manage those aspects. Sanger and Veach (2008) also used a GT approach to analyze the suicide notes of 138 individuals who died by suicide, to highlight the interpersonal nature of suicidal behavior. As there was no preexisting theory about the interpersonal relationships in the context of suicidal behavior, the selection of GT was justified. The coding process permitted descriptions of interpersonal problems and difficulties rather than the use of preexisting theory.

Ethnographic Methods

Ethnographic methods have developed in anthropology, sociology, and cultural psychology, which focus on studying cultures, ethnicities, and other groups. It is an extremely broad area with a great variety of practices and methods, characterized by the active involvement of the researcher in the real life of the environment they are studying. The aim is to understand the culture, interactions, and values that characterize the relationships between the people, investigating every aspect through *participant observations* (Reeves, Kuper, & Hodges, 2008). Ethnographic approaches are mainly based on three concepts (Reeves, Kuper, & Hodges, 2008):

- *indexicality* (no statement can have a meaning independent of its context, so generalization is impossible);
- *reflexivity* (each statement is referable only to itself and does not refer to any reality other than itself); and
- *accountability* (action is considered as an expression of actors' intentionality and of their meaning making process).

Given these characteristics are linked to contexts and actions, the number of participants in the research cannot be predefined a priori. *Field research*, *action research*, and *research in the real world* can be considered as derivations of the ethnographic method, since they assume the best way to understand any phenomenon is to view it in its context and to be immersed in it (see Reed, 2007).

In suicide research, ethnographic approaches emphasize the role of cultural factors, as discussed by Staples and Widger (2012), who consider suicide as a social relationship, through which people create meaning in their own lives. Similarly, Kuruvilla and Jacob (2012) note the increase of studies in suicide research and explain the importance of ethnographic qualitative methods in giving a greater understanding of differences and in the process of comparison among cultures, with respect to factors related to suicidal behavior. For example, DiStefano (2008) explored suicidal and nonsuicidal self-harm among sexual minorities in Japan, which is relatively undocumented from a qualitative perspective due to stigma. The author participated by joining the community to better understand such sensitive experiences. The selection of the participants was conducted through snowball sampling that requires key contacts who ask other people in the community to take part in the research. In total, 84 individuals participated in the study until data saturation was reached and the data was analyzed. Results showed that suicidality and self-harm were serious problems among sexual minorities in Japan with the homophobic and transphobic environment being one of the main themes.

Another study, by Miller (1995), adopted an ethnographic approach to explore the intergenerational messages of women across generations involved in suicide attempts. Specifically, she aimed to understand how the mother–daughter relationship is built, and how the meaning of suicide is constructed within the family. On that basis, four generations of women of the same family (seven women participated in the study), who had all attempted suicide except for one, took part in the research. Consistent with the ethnographic methodology, the researcher was an active observer of the household of the target family, participating in and generating debates. Results highlighted the themes of differentiation, generational curse, matriarchy, men as an out-group, failures, and powerlessness. An exhaustive overview of the studies carried out in the area of ethnomethodology applied in suicide research is presented in the volume edited by Shrivastava, Kimbrell, and Lester (2012).

Interpretative Phenomenological Analysis

The *phenomenological approach* was developed from the philosophical contributions of Edmund Husserl and Martin Heidegger at the end of 19th and the early 20th century. After an initial phase of theoretical and methodological inquiry, the phenomenological method moved to other domains, such as sociology and psychology. Its application in these fields can be considered to be a specific development and transformation of the ethnographic method (which, in those years, was almost exclusively used in anthropology), since its aim is to describe a phenomenon in its complexity, assuming a nonjudgmental perspective (Smith, Jarman, & Osborn, 1999; Larkin, Watts, & Clifton, 2006). Phenomenology is a school of thought that emphasizes a focus on people's subjective experiences and interpretations of the world. It means that phenomenologists aim to understand how the world appears to others, and their well-established methods include descriptive and hermeneutic work, based on critiques of essentialism and in-depth exploration of personal and social phenomena, through the investigation of human experience as it becomes expressed in spontaneous productions of speech or writing (Wertz, Nosek, McNiesh, & Marlow, 2011).

Interpretative phenomenological analysis (IPA) fully shares all of these fundamental aspects and is based on an idiographic approach (Smith & Shinebourne, 2012). IPA uses homogenous samples, composed of 3–16 participants for a single study, selected according to the research questions and the point of view consciously taken by the researcher (Smith, Flowers, & Larkin, 2009). Data collection does not set out to test hypotheses, but to answer a fundamental question (e.g., Orri et al., 2014), which should be maintained during the entire data analysis. IPA's hermeneutic is dialectical, because it is the result of the interpretation of the point of view of the researcher and those of the participants, since they can offer the researcher some meaningful insight into the topic of the study (Smith, Flowers, & Larkin, 2009).

IPA has become relatively popular in qualitative suicide research in recent years. Begley and Quayle (2007) aimed to understand the lived experience of people who had lost a family member by suicide in Ireland. Analyzing data from in-depth interviews with eight individuals, they found that the bereavement experience was strongly connected with the relationship that one had had with the deceased. Specifically, common themes emerged, defining a pathway through the grief of suicide: controlling the impact of death, attempting to make sense of it, social uneasiness, and a renovated sense of purposefulness. The research focused on the importance of meaning-making processes, suggesting that this plays a fundamental role in shaping how individuals experience their bereavement.

In Ghana, Osafo, Hjelmeland, Akotia, and Knizek (2011a) explored psychology students' attitudes toward suicide and its meaning. The sample was composed of 15 students, all Christians, who were interviewed. IPA fits well with the scope of their research of gaining better understanding of a specific cultural context and social meanings. Analyses showed that participants had negative attitudes toward suicide, which was strongly influenced by their religious beliefs.

A number of other experiences have been analyzed using IPA, for example the effects of traumatic grief (Smith, Joseph, & Nair, 2011), the attitude toward suicides of lay persons (Osafo, Hjelmeland, Akotia, & Knizek, 2011b), suicide ideation in older adults (Kim & Sok, 2017), and perspectives of adolescents who had pursued suicidal intentions (Orri et al., 2014).

Narrative and Biographical Methods

The *narrative methods* and biographical approaches emerged from feminist studies and from cultural psychology (Roth, 2000). They hinge on a dialogical space between the researcher and the participant, and aim to deepen how the participant develops and narrates a story about important themes of their life, such as turning points, fundamental historical or social events, and/or ruptures in relationships. The final description consistently links between the past history and the present in a storyline that uses both discursive and affective resources (e.g., specific rhetoric or narrative frames and feelings or memories), grounded in the person's experience or in the broader sociocultural context, which helps to understand how the meaning-making process emerges (Bruner, 1990). The researcher follows a range of topics placing themselves in a position of authentic listening when interviewing participants. The sequence of topics can be more or less structured, based on the objectives of the research (Tracy, 2014). Thus, the focus of research using narrative and biographical methods is on the participant as a storyteller, who constantly molds their past, present, and future description of their life. Therefore, what emerges from studies adopting narrative and biographical methods are the different ways through which participants organize their own report schemas or frames that help to structure participants' position toward themselves, and their life and feelings involved in liminal moments, rather than a core subjective experience (as in the IPA).

There are good examples of studies using narrative and biographical strategies in suicide research. For example, Binnix, Rambo, Abrutyn, and Mueller (2018) in their study from the US, tried to gain a better understanding of how individuals who attempted or contemplated suicide narrate the experience of being tempted to kill themselves. The participants were recruited through snowball sampling with the final convenience sample comprising 20 participants. Consistent with a biographical approach, during the interviews, individuals were invited to speak about their life before the moment in which suicide seemed to be an alternative, trying to focus also on how significant relationships changed across their lifespan and how friends' and relatives' attitudes changed once they became suicidal. Thus, the core of narrative and biographical methods is to collect biographies of the participants to understand the general background of their life events. From the analysis, it emerged that stigma has an important role in further relations with significant others and that it is a strong barrier to seeking future help.

Owens and Lambert (2012) used a narrative approach to understand how 66 people bereaved by suicide in England made sense of a family member's suicide. Authors used data obtained from a previous study which used a psychology autopsy method and interviews (see Chapter 11). As is typical in the narrative and biographical approaches and in other qualitative studies, their interviews began with open questions, allowing both researcher and participants to further describe episodes of the deceased's life and death, and of their own lives. The results suggested that the qualitative narrative approach can help to deepen psychological autopsy studies and helps to widen the understanding of suicide and the sense making of relatives.

Case Study

A *case study* (also called a *case review* or *case report*) is a systematic enquiry into an event or a situation, aimed at explaining the phenomenon of interest (Bromley, 1986). A case study is supposed to include an outline of its purpose, which may be exploratory, descriptive, or interpretive, from which the possible actions and products of the study derive (Stake, 1995).

This perspective emphasizes the effort to understand the meaning of contingent, unique, and often cultural or subjective phenomena (Thomae, 1999). Case study design specific to suicide research is said to differ from any other qualitative approach. It may utilize IPA and a narrative and biographical approach, along with different methods and instruments of collective data, such as archive documentation, focus groups, and interviews.

There are a number of examples of case studies in suicide research. With the aim of understanding the relationship between substance abuse and self-harm, Breet and Bantjes (2017) carried out a multiple-case study. A multiple-case study is a further development of the single-case study, where multiple cases are analyzed rather than one. The goal is to discover, by comparing multiple-case replications of a single phenomenon, how differences and commonalities between the cases form a coherent event or phenomenon. Moreover, both single-case and multiple-case studies largely use different sources of data, thus strengthening the analysis. Specifically, the researchers conducted interviews with 80 patients, and the results showed that substance use and self-harm were embedded in a process of poor decision making, which facilitated self-harming behavior as a result of the failure of coping mechanisms (Breet & Bantjes, 2017).

Sampling and Target Populations

Sampling is an important component of qualitative research design that has been given limited attention in the majority of studies (Robinson, 2014). Robinson presents important points to be considered for sampling in qualitative studies:

- Setting a *sample universe* (also called the *study* or *target population*), that identifies the totality of persons from which cases used in the research can be extracted. A sample universe should be created by identifying the set of inclusion and/or exclusion criteria: demographic, geographical, physical, psychological, and/or life-story homogeneity. The stricter the criteria the more homogeneous the *universe* sample.
- Selecting a *sample size* or *size range*, by considering what is ideal and what is practical.
- Devising a *sampling strategy* by selecting a purposive or a convenience sampling strategy to specify categories of people to be included in the sample.
- Sourcing the sample by *recruiting participants* from the target population.

Qualitative research that has a specific idiographic aim typically involves a small sample size to permit an intensive analysis of the contribution of each participant. Indeed, a small sample size range permits individuals within the sample to be given a defined identity, rather than being subsumed into an anonymous role (Robinson & Smith, 2010). There are several different sampling strategies (Robinson, 2014):

- Random sampling – randomly selecting cases from a list of all or most cases of the population – is used in quantitative research.
- Convenience sampling – nonrandomly selecting cases from a nearby convenient population (e.g., psychology students) – is used in both quantitative and qualitative research.
- Purposive sampling – nonrandom ways to ensure that the particular categories of cases are represented in the sample, based on a priori theoretical assumption. There are different purposive sampling strategies:
  - *Stratified* – the group is divided up into categories, and a fixed number of participants is allocated to each one;
  - *Cell* – sampling is provided for a series of a priori categories that must be filled;

- *Quota* – a flexible stratified sample with a series of categories and a minimum number of cases required for each one; and
- *Theoretical* sampling takes place during the collection and analysis of data and parallel interpretation – for example, while analyzing the results, it may become necessary to involve specific participants who can address the lack of information.

The most common target groups in qualitative suicide research are people bereaved by suicide (e.g., Ross et al., 2018; Begley & Quayle, 2007) and people who have attempted suicide (Binnix, Rambo, Abrutyn, & Mueller, 2018; Miller, 1995). The importance of the latter in suicide research is obviously paramount, because their first-person narratives allow clinicians and psychotherapists to shed light on deep and very personal aspects, not always accessible through standardized tools (e.g., Orri et al., 2014; Rivlin, Fazel, Marzano, & Hawton, 2013). Moreover, very important in qualitative research is the consideration of the impact of the research on participants, and how vulnerable populations (e.g., individuals who have attempted suicide) feel about taking part in research. Biddle et al. (2013) used data derived from four of their previously conducted qualitative studies in the UK to explore the issue of the impact of research on vulnerable populations. Participants of all studies (N = 63) were asked to complete a visual analogue scale measuring their emotional state before and after the interview and to reflect on the change. It was found that the majority of participants experienced a general increase in well-being and that any negative feelings tended to be transient.

Data Collection Methods

A variety of different data collection methods are utilized in qualitative studies, including interviews, focus groups, documents (e.g., police and coronial forms, medical records), diaries, letters, and observations. The most frequently used instruments for gathering data are qualitative interviews, focus groups, diaries, and letters, and these will be described in the suicide research context below.

The Interview

The interview is the most common method used by researchers to collect qualitative data, because it provides more detailed information than other data collection methods (Creswell, 2003, 2007; Kvale, 2007). An interview has great flexibility in that it gives a chance to have an open dialogue with the participant or can be more prestructured by the interviewer. The degree to which an interview is more or less open versus structured is based on different research design decisions (e.g., how a specific field has already been explored; whether a topic is well-defined or needs more in-depth analyses). Moreover, interviews are not only sources of experiences or narratives by participants, but they can also provide fruitful information about nonverbal communication, gestures, posture, and tone – all of which can be analyzed.

There are four common formats of an interview:

- An *informal conversation*, which is conducted face to face, to learn more about a specific issue without having a predetermined set of structured questions. This is often used in ethnographic studies. Indeed, it is useful when the researcher aims to understand how a specific topic is perceived, for example, within a community (e.g., suicidal behavior among sexual minorities in Japan, in the study by DiStefano, 2008).

- A *semistructured interview* can be carried out face to face or by computer or telephone, presenting open questions and following a framework for topics to be explored, prepared in advance by developing a guide with a list of informal groupings of topics that the interviewer can ask about in different ways. GT and IPA traditionally utilize semistructured interviews. Sometimes the biographical approach utilizes this strategy, especially when the research question is focused on critical issues, as is required in a narrative psychological autopsy, and so interviews should be prepared accurately, to maintain an unambiguous focus (Orri et al., 2014; Rivlin et al., 2013).
- An *open-ended interview* can be undertaken in the same way as the semistructured interview and is composed of questions on a specific topic. It is used especially in clinical and ethnographic studies (i.e., Fontanella, Campos, & Turato, 2006).
- An *in-depth interview* is traditionally carried out face to face, in a relaxed atmosphere, so that a positive relationship can be created with the participant (Zhang, Dong, Delprino, & Zhou, 2009). The core of the in-depth interview is to understand a topic directly from the point of view of the participant. Thus, in-depth interviews are essentially interactive and oriented to obtain rich information in terms of explanation and exploration. That is why in-depth interviews are conducted with a sample of no more than 10 participants, each interviewed individually.

All types of interviews should include an careful choice of setting with few distractions; a clear explanation given to participants of the interview's purposes, its format, and its timing; an opportunity to ask if they have any questions before starting the interview, and the acquisition of informed consent; and information for the participants regarding how they can contact the interviewer later if they wish (Frey & Oishi, 1995).

The Focus Group

The second most commonly used data collection method in qualitative research in the suicide research context is the *focus group*. Focus groups consist of a group interview that gives the researcher the ability to capture the views of more people at the same time, therefore being more cost-effective than individual interviews, and providing insights into what people think of the phenomena being studied (Wilkinson, 1998). In addition, group interaction between members may encourage them to make connections to various concepts through the discussion, while the facilitator (also called the FG leader or moderator) improves the communication, to provide a more comprehensive understanding of the issue being considered (Seal, Bogart, & Ehrhardt, 1998). Indeed, when well-facilitated, group discussion generates data rarely accessible without group interaction, which produces an avalanche effects on ideation and reflection (Greenbaum, 2000; Lindlof & Taylor, 2002; Box 9.1).

Box 9.1. Focus Group as a strategy for data collection

A focus group (FG) is a method of collecting rich data from a group of people in a topic-driven discussion. Unlike a one-to-one interview, an FG involves interactions between the researcher (or an FG facilitator, leader, or moderator) and the members of the group (usually 6 to 10). As with an interview, the discussion should be recorded and transcribed verbatim. The researcher should be helped by one or two assistants who focus their attention on how members interact and their nonverbal communication. Their observations will strengthen the results of data analysis.

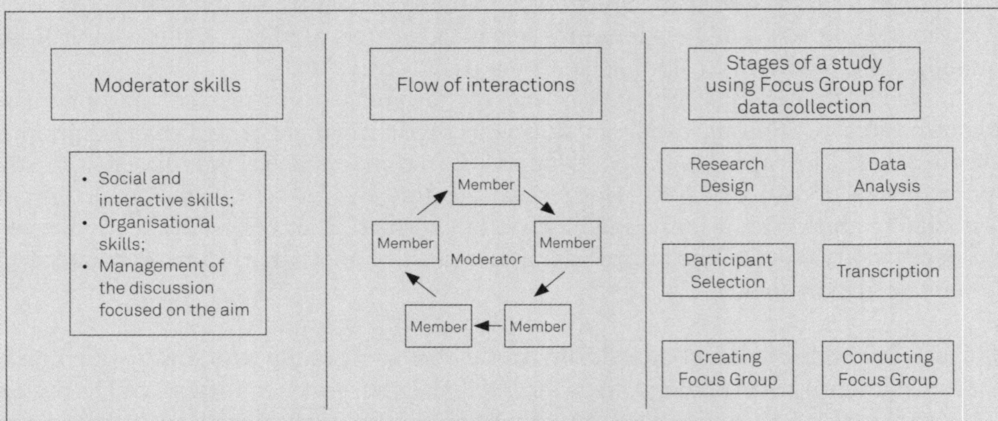

Stages of a study using FGs for data collections:

- Define the research problem and the aim of the study and ensure FGs are the most appropriate data collection method
- Prepare general guideline questions for your FGs. You can identify three general questions:
  - Introductory questions. Aim: "to break the ice"
  - Transitional questions. Aim: guide the discussion through the key element
  - Key questions. Aim: to promote the discussion about your research topic

Participant selection:

- Define what type of participants you would like to include in your study and argue your point

Creating FGs:

- Identify the sufficient number of FGs and participants
- Ensure relatively equal numbers of participants to have balanced groups
- Conduct a pilot FG with the aim of testing your guideline questions

Conducting FGs:

1. Welcome your participants and give a general overview of the topic
2. Start with your general guideline questions
3. Ensure that everyone participates in the group discussion

Do not give your personal opinions, and do try to manage possible conflicts.

Focus groups are often utilized for specific aspects involved in suicide experiences. For example, Perceval, Kõlves, Reddy, and De Leo (2017) used focus groups to investigate risk and protective factors and attitudes toward suicide and help seeking among farmers living and working in Australia. Yang and colleagues (2018) used focus groups in California to study the factors that affect suicide in the Laotian community, showing the importance of understanding the impact of how community affects service use, in helping to prevent suicide. Focus groups can be used also in combination with interviews. In another Australian study, Rimkeviciene, Hawgood, O'Gorman, and De Leo (2015), exploring suicide attempters' experiences of personal stigma, used semistructured interviews, and included in their research design, a focus group to check the clinician's perceptions of the problem.

Diaries and Letters

Another relatively common form of data collection is of diaries and letters. This type of data collection has become a consolidated practice in psychological and psychosocial research. The diaries and letters are considered an expression of personal narrative, and they provide the material for a helpful strategy of data collection to gain an objective account of how a specific phenomenon unfolds over time (Bolger, Davis, & Rafaeli, 2003; Reis & Gable, 2000; Takarangi, Garry, & Loftus, 2006). Implicit in the understanding of personal journals is the epistemological and ontological assumption that language acts as a mediator between an observer and a preexisting reality (MacLure, 2013; Rouse, 1996). In particular, the study of the diaries of people who died by suicide is an important opportunity for greater insight into the psychodynamics of this final choice. Kramer (2002) employed diaries to study the psychobiographical profile of a young woman who died by suicide more than 50 years ago. Among the documents analyzed were her letters, a secondary school diary, creative writing works, college newspaper book reviews, and academic papers. Using both an Eriksonian and object-relational theoretical framework, the roles of faith, hope, and despair in suicide were scrutinized. De Âvila Berni et al. (2018) utilized a proof-of-concept study using Virginia Woolf's personal writings (letters and diaries) to create a text classification to predict individual suicidal behavior. Barnes, Lawal-Solarin, and Lester (2007) analyzed a series of letters to a friend from a young man who died by suicide. They found several trends over time, including a decrease in the number and the type of words used, indicating negative emotions, and an increase of words referring to death.

Qualitative Data Analysis and Interpretation

Preparing and Organizing Data

The final phase in qualitative research involves analysis and interpretation of data, which are challenging tasks. Considering the various types of data sources, the first step of qualitative analysis is preparing and organizing the information collected. Some data require work to be processed and elaborated in a textual manner – for example, interviews and focus groups need to be transcribed verbatim. Furthermore, this step is not just about transcription but includes the definition of the *data set* too. The data set is the part of the data that the researcher has collected (the *data corpus*) that is used in the specific analysis. The analysis of texts is a component of the wider area of qualitative analysis, which can be directed to examine different artefacts (not just texts of various formats, but also pictures, audio, video, photos, gestures, and movements). We will focus on textual data as the most common in qualitative suicide research. Moreover, the analysis of data directly obtained by the researcher can be called primary analysis (secondary analysis will be illustrated in the section Secondary Qualitative Analysis in Suicide Research).

Selecting Method for Analysis

Once the researcher has extracted a set of textual data from its data sources and corpus, there are different procedures or methods that guide the analysis. The overall aim of all procedures or methods is to make sense of what was uncovered, and to apply more general, abstracted, and intertwined ways of looking at the data. For example, thematic analysis refers to *themes* (sometimes considered and referred to also as *codes*, whereas at other times the term *codes* is used to refer to the result of the first phase of the analysis), which are consistent concepts and ideas that are common in the texts (e.g., Harper & Thompson, 2012; Lune & Berg, 2017).

There are a number of choices available for qualitative data analysis. Sometimes the method of analysis can be directly deduced from the research design – for example, if the aim was to explore how roles change during a conversation, an appropriate method could be conversation analysis; or if the aim was to explore how participants' discourse was constructed, one could choose discourse analysis. However, the research is often designed to use a broader approach such as GT or IPA, which usually requires a precise way to conduct the analysis that is internal to theoretical and methodological assumptions of the research design. Nevertheless, often the researcher has to choose what to extract from the data and where to focus, without being forced into rigid schemes by either the research design or the data collection method. In that case, there are two main options available: to conduct a *content analysis* or a *thematic analysis*. Content analysis traditionally explores patterns of content quantitatively using statistical methods, focusing more directly on data and attempting to reduce any interferences by the researcher. Thematic analysis, as described in the next section, is an umbrella concept including techniques and strategies through which to extract codes, categories, and themes from the data.

Thematic Analysis

Thematic analysis is the most commonly used method in qualitative research. It is useful as it is focused on recognizing and examining themes within texts (Testoni et al., 2016), which are considered significant to the description of a phenomenon and associated with the research question (Braun & Clarke, 2006), and it can be applied to data following many different procedures. Braun and Clarke (2006) recommend a six-phase process for performing a thematic analysis:

1. *Familiarization with the data*: in this phase, the researcher reads the data set several times to grasp some global meanings and gain a sense of what the data are about.
2. *Generating preliminary codes*: in this phase, the researcher starts assigning codes to interesting features throughout the data set. A code must be as close as possible to the sense of the parts of the text it represents.
3. *Searching for themes*: in this phase, the researcher's attention shifts toward trying to merge the codes into a set of themes.
4. *Reviewing themes*: in this phase, the researcher should *test* the generated themes, trying to evaluate if they work throughout the entire data set and the precedent codes.
5. *Defining and naming themes*: once the review of themes is over, the aim is to refine the themes generated and try to give a definition and a name that grasps the deeper meanings of the data.
6. *Producing the report*: in which the researcher communicates the results. It is important to appropriately select examples of each code and theme. Moreover, the researcher should discuss the results in light of the literature and critically evaluate how they fill the gap identified by the research question.

It is important to note that according to Braun and Clarke (2006), many qualitative studies tend to use the principles of thematic analysis (searching for a theme that can describe the sense, meaning, and the importance of a topic); however, they do so without explicitly describing the methodology used.

The overall procedure of qualitative data analysis usually follows two strategies that can be used individually or in parallel:

- The first strategy is to follow a *bottom-up approach* (data-driven, inductive) – the process of coding occurs without fitting a preexisting theoretical framework. This is more descriptive and uses quotations as expressions that convey meanings. For example, once the texts have been collated, during the first reading, it is important to highlight the most important sentences and try to understand what they reveal. During the second reading, the researcher can review their notes to explore possible links in the data.
- The second strategy is the *top-down approach* (theory-driven, deductive), which tends to interpret the meaning of quotations based on preconceived frames. The results focus on specific aspects that are useful to answer the research question. For example, once the core that can offer a unity to the texts has been hypothesized, it may be useful to consider it in light of the literature and check any possible further interpretations. Once useful theories have been found, the texts can be reconsidered in the light of such information.

The biggest challenge in the qualitative analysis of data is the validity of inferences extracted from the text, which require that coding is consistent, such that different people can code, categorize, and thematize the same text similarly (Weber, 1990). To solve this problem, different methodological strategies have been created, which include *computer-supported textual analysis*. The computer programs used for content analysis can be divided into two groups: *computer-aided qualitative data analysis software* (also known as CAQDAS), which allows the manual labeling of portions of text with alphanumeric codes referring to concepts that researchers want to highlight (examples include Atlas.ti and NVivo), and which is very useful for texts that are not too large; and software aimed at *semiautomatic analysis* using statistical and lexical techniques (examples include SPAD and Wordmapper), which is useful for very large texts. Box 9.2 describes a qualitative study using thematic analysis, with texts being processed by Atlas.ti, to analyze suicide bereavement group meeting reports over 4 years.

Box 9.2. Example of a qualitative study design and its results from Italy

This study presents a qualitative analysis of reports of people bereaved by suicide during self-help group meetings. The aims of the research were:

- verify whether a forgiveness process spontaneously emerges within a group of people bereaved by suicide, and how this is related to blame processes; and,
- evaluate the effects of being part of a self-help group, specifically if processes of self/other blaming and acceptance of the relative's suicide are promoted.

The target population were people who participated in the self-help group activities of the De Leo Fund (Padua, Italy), an organization that helps grieving people, by offering different kinds of support activities. The group was composed of two men and eight women, and the group sessions took place on average once per week in 2013–2016. Every session lasted one and a half hours and was conducted by two trained professional psychologists.

The data consisted of the narratives of the group members collected through the official reports of meetings by two psychologists leading the group sessions, over a four-year period. The research was approved by the Ethics Commission of the Department of Psychology of the University of Padua and followed APA Ethical Principles of Psychologists and Code of Conduct and the principles of the Declaration of Helsinki.

The data analysis process was driven by a top-down approach and divided into six main phases: preparatory organization, generation of categories or themes, coding data, testing emergent ideas, searching for alternative explanations, and writing up the report.

To extract principal concepts or themes from the sources, data were analyzed using thematic analysis. Thematic analysis was performed in two steps: top-down and bottom up. In the first phase (top down), three main categories were identified: self/other blame, forgiveness, and guilt. These categories constituted the predetermined themes, object of the main researchers' interest. The frequency of their appearance was assessed along the period of observation. The second phase (bottom up) consisted of retracing other different important categories and their relationships with the predetermined ones. This second step permitted to deepen the understanding of the predetermined categories.

The software program Atlas.ti was used to analyse the texts. Finally, figures and graphs were created to help to represent and describe the relationships between the findings.

The main findings showed the persistence of self-blame during the four year period and highlighted the increasing of self-blame every time new participants joined the group. This indicates that self-blame is a typical emotion characterizing the beginning of a bereavement support group journey.

Based on Testoni, I., Francescon, E., De Leo, D., Santini, A., & Zamperini, A. (2019). Forgiveness and blame among suicide survivors: A qualitative analysis on reports of 4-year self-help-group meetings. *Community Mental Health Journal, 55*, 360–368.

Software Programs Supporting Qualitative Analysis: Atlas.ti and NVivo

Different software programs exist to help researchers to carry out and monitor meticulous analysis (e.g., Willig & Rogers, 2008). Two of the most widely used are Atlas.ti (Friese, 2012) and NVivo (Bazeley & Jackson, 2013). Atlas.ti is software that enables researchers to gather and organize all of their data, as well as to group and code it in a specific manner and within an established procedure (e.g., Braun & Clarke, 2006). Indeed, identifying networks between data is both a subjective and objective practice, and Atlas.ti provides researchers with useful tools, such as "memos," to register all of their thoughts and ideas (e.g., Testoni, Francescon, De Leo, Santini, & Zamperini, 2019; Testoni, Pesci, De Vincenzo, Dal Corso, & Zamperini, 2019; Testoni, Ghellar, Rodelli, De Cataldo, & Zamperini, 2017). The main steps of the analysis process are (Hwang, 2008):

- Creation of a hermeneutical unit (i.e., a container containing the imported documents, codes, and annotations).
- Insertion of the documents (written texts, such as diaries, interviews, etc.) into the hermeneutical container. The documents imported into the program are called *primary documents*.
- Coding process: documents are read, and the relevant sentences identified are called *quotations*. Codes are then assigned to significant portions of quotations.

- Creation of *families*, which are superordinate categories that contain several codes considered to be assimilable (themes).
- It is possible to establish relationships between the various elements (mainly between the codes) to support the emerging theory that allows a hierarchical order between the objects and the existing links.
- Creation of a *network*: it is possible to recognize the relationships between codes (which can be one of the following: belong to, imply, cause, or in opposition to) and detect the frequency with which each code appears. Networks allow researchers to sort the data visually and choose to display only some objects of the analysis; and they represent the theory developed by the analysis.

The advantages of using Atlas.ti are that it facilitates the organization of data, offers a summary of the results, facilitates comparisons between documents, simplifies the process of parallel analysis between meanings that emerge in texts, and allows a coding similar to that made with paper and pencil.

NVivo can be used for both qualitative and in mixed methods analysis. With NVivo, it is possible to identify themes or concepts as a *node*, which researchers can relate to some of their material. Nodes are blocks of meanings emerging from the source of analysis and related to research units of analysis. Nodes can be either a parent or a child, depending on the hierarchy the researcher wants to highlight within the data. One of the main characteristics of NVivo is that researchers can work with *cases* too, and they can apply *attributes* to their units of analysis. A case is a sort of container that represents and distinguishes the unit that is being analyzed (it could be, e.g., university students; see, e.g., Testoni, Iacona, et al., 2018). Attributes are ways of classifying data, giving them specifications and different values. As in Atlas.ti, in NVivo there is a useful tool, called a *code book*, which can contains all of the coding rules used by the analyst.

Secondary Qualitative Analysis in Suicide Research

If primary analysis is used with original first-hand materials, *secondary analysis*, by contrast, utilizes data which were produced by others, such as studies, records data, editorials, research articles, reviews, and databases. Indeed, a large volume of data is collected through research activities across the world, and the Internet permits access to much of this accumulated information. Three types of secondary data analysis are widely discussed in the literature: *appended studies*, *meta-analyses*, and *qualitative secondary analysis* (QSA) (Gilbert, 1993). The first of these is usually a piece added to a study designed by another researcher, while the second is a statistical analysis that combines the results of multiple scientific studies. QSA is the use of qualitative data that was collected by someone else or to answer a different research question. Although it is aimed at optimizing data utility with difficult-to-reach participants, this method requires an explicit description to best evaluate the research results, because many misunderstandings could weaken the outcome (Szabo & Strang, 1997). QSA uncovers aspects that need further elaboration, either by revisiting parts of the method or through further exploration, improving explanations and interpretations of the primary sources.

For example, in suicide research, Fogarty et al. (2018) used QSA for a secondary analysis of qualitative interview and focus group data to explore the views of at-risk men, friends, and family about the tensions inherent in suicide prevention and to consider how prevention may be improved. Their results highlighted that there are negative tensions in at-risk men's and family members' perspectives, which weaken the possibilities of detecting risk behaviors and prevention. Specifically, there are two main tensions: one with their support system (including between respect for privacy and vigilant risk monitoring, differentiating normal vs. risky behavioral change, familiarity vs. anonymity in risk monitoring, and respecting autonomy vs. imposing constraints), and the other with the service system (including dependence on vs. perceived failures of community services).

Another example of the application of a secondary qualitative analysis can be narrative literature reviews, in which the researcher can apply a thematic analysis to the collected papers to get a broader and more general result (Lakeman & FitzGerald, 2008). For example, Shields, Kavanagh, and Russo (2017) conducted a qualitative systematic review of the suicide bereavement process using thematic analysis.

Checklists

The purpose of qualitative checklists is to guide researchers and evaluators in determining when qualitative methods are appropriate, to improve the quality of the reporting, and to allow readers to better understand the design, conduct, analysis, and findings of qualitative studies. The most widely used qualitative worksheet is the Consolidated Criteria for Reporting Qualitative (COREQ) studies checklist, which was developed to promote comprehensive reporting of qualitative studies (Tong, Sainsbury, & Craig, 2007). The COREQ checklist consists of specific items that cover the necessary components of study design that should be reported. This should help researchers to describe important aspects of the research team, study methods, context of the study, findings, analysis, and interpretations, emphasizing the value of transparency and the possibility of duplicating the study methods (Tong, Sainsbury, & Craig, 2007). In recent years, it has also become widely followed in suicide research (e.g., Morrissey & Higgins, 2019; Testoni, Francescon, De Leo, Santini, & Zamperini, 2019).

Commonly, COREQ and other checklists are aimed at evaluating the following elements, which are considered essential in any qualitative study (Patton, 2002):

- *Research team reflexivity* – is the research question correctly formulated, and are the positions of researchers sufficiently considered (e.g., whether the theoretical background has been clearly stated, and the general epistemological assumptions have been specified)?
- *Study design* – are the adopted approach and method (participants, instruments, procedure, legitimation, analysis, results, and discussion) exhaustively described, and, in particular, did the researcher make first-hand observations of activities and interactions, as a participating observer?
- *Method* – is the data collection explained in detail and the experience transformed into words, so that fieldwork descriptions of activities and interpersonal interactions, or any other observable aspect, are correctly considered, and data consist of verbatim quotations with sufficient context to be interpretable? Is the interview questionnaire or topic guide correctly reported, and are they systematically reported? Do written materials (organizational or clinical documents or records, official publications, reports, diaries, letters, written responses to open-ended surveys, and so on) preserve integrity and context?
- *Data analysis* – whether and how the data are organized into readable narrative descriptions with major themes, categories, and illustrative case examples extracted through the analysis; are the themes, patterns, understandings, insights, and subsequent analysis the result of qualitative enquiry?

- *Outcomes* – are qualitative findings reliable, and do the results generate useful and credible findings?

Ethical Considerations

Qualitative research enters people's lives to understand their experiences, and recognize their latent and explicit convictions, observing their behavior often in their everyday life settings. This requires special attention to research ethics, including careful consideration of how this information is collected, treated, and managed. Furthermore, additional consideration should be given to the management of relationships, because researchers are at risk of being intrusive or collusive or unable to respect the private realm of people and their personal universe of beliefs. As a result of these factors, qualitative inquiry raises distinctive ethical issues which must be considered. All research processes followed need to receive ethical clearance from the relevant human research committees. For more on ethics in suicide research, see Chapter 4.

Conclusions

In this chapter, we have addressed the topic of qualitative research in the field of suicide research, describing a wide range of approaches, methods of data collection, and illustrative studies. It is important to note that this area is growing very rapidly, and therefore, it was necessary to limit our chapter to the most consolidated methodologies. Nevertheless, the growing number of qualitative studies in recent years seems to reflect the popularity of qualitative research in suicide research. We encourage readers to further familiarize themselves with the literature on qualitative research methods to fully master this art.

References

Aherne, C., Coughlan, B., Surgenor, P. (2018). Therapists' perspectives on suicide: A conceptual model of connectedness. *Psychotherapy Research, 28*(5), 803–819. https://doi.org/10.1080/10503307.2017.1359428

Bantjes, J., & Swartz, L. (2017). The cultural turn in critical suicidology: What can we claim and what do we know? *Death Studies, 41*, 512–520. https://doi.org/10.1080/07481187.2017.1333355

Barnes, D.H., Lawal-Solarin, F.W., & Lester, D. (2007). Letters from a suicide. *Death Studies, 31,* 671–678. https://doi.org/10.1080/07481180701405212

Barnes, M.C., Gunnell, D., Davies, R., Hawton, K., Kapur, N., Potokar, J., & Donovan, J.L. (2016). Understanding vulnerability to self-harm in times of economic hardship and austerity: A qualitative study. *BMJ Open, 6*(2), e010131. https://doi.org/10.1136/bmjopen-2015-010131

Bauer, M.W., Gaskell, J., & Allum, N.C. (2000). Quality, quantity and knowledge interests: Avoiding confusions. In M.W. Bauer & G. Gaskell (Eds.), *Qualitative researching with test, image, and sound: A practical handbook* (pp. 3–17). London, UK: Sage.

Bazeley, P., & Jackson, K. (2013). *Qualitative data analysis with NVivo*. Thousand Oaks, CA: Sage.

Begley, M., & Quayle, E. (2007). The lived experience of adults bereaved by suicide. *Crisis, 28*, 26–34. http://https://doi.org/10.1027/0227-5910.28.1.26

Bell, D. (2001). Who is killing what or whom? *Psychoanalytic Psychotherapy, 15*(1), 21–37, https://doi.org/10.1080/02668730100700021

Biddle, L., Cooper, J., Owen-Smith, A., Klineberg, E., Bennewith, O., Hawton, K., ... Gunnell, D. (2013). Qualitative interviewing with vulnerable populations: Individuals' experiences of participating in suicide and self-harm based research. *Journal of Affective Disorders, 145*(3), 356–362. https://doi.org/10.1016/j.jad.2012.08.024

Binnix, T.M., Rambo, C., Abrutyn, S., & Mueller, A.S. (2018). The dialectics of stigma, silence, and misunderstanding in suicidality survival narratives. *Deviant Behavior, 39,* 1095–1106. https://doi.org/10.1080/01639625.2017.1399753

Blumer, H. (1969). *Symbolic interactionism: Perspective and method*. Englewood Cliffs, NJ: Prentice-Hall.

Bolger, N., Davis, A., & Rafaeli, E. (2003). Diary methods: Capturing life as it is lived. *Annual Review of Psychology, 54*(1), 579–616. https://doi.org/10.1146/annurev.psych.54.101601.145030

Braun, V., & Clarke, V. (2006). Using thematic analysis in psychology. *Qualitative Research in Psychology, 3,* 77–101. https://doi.org/10.1191/1478088706qp063oa

Breet, E., & Bantjes, J. (2017). Substance use and self-harm: Case studies from patients admitted to an urban hospital following medically serious self-harm. *Qualitative Health Research, 27,* 2201–2210. https://doi.org/10.1177/1049732317728052

Bromley, D.B. (1986). *The case-study method in psychology and related-disciplines*. Chichester, UK: Wiley.

Bruner, J.S. (1990). *Acts of meaning.* Cambridge, MA: Harvard University Press.

Creswell, J.W. (2003). *Research design: Qualitative, quantitative, and mixed methods approaches.* Thousand Oaks, CA: Sage.

Creswell, J.W. (2007). *Qualitative inquiry & research design: Choosing among five approaches* (2nd ed.). Thousand Oaks, CA: Sage.

Creswell, J.W., & Poth, C.N. (2017). *Qualitative inquiry & research design: Choosing among five approaches.* Los Angeles, CA: Sage.

Cutcliffe, J.R. (2005). Toward an understanding of suicide in first-nation Canadians. *Crisis, 26,* 141–145. https://doi.org/10.1027/0227-5910.26.3.141

de Âvila Berni, G., Rabelo-da-Ponte, F.D., Librenza-Garcia, D., Boeira, M.V., Kauer-Sant'Anna, M., Cavalcante Passos, I., & Kapczinsk, F. (2018). Correction: Potential use of text classification tools as signatures of suicidal behavior: A proof-of-concept study using Virginia Woolf's personal writings. *PLoS ONE, 13*(11), e0207963. https://doi.org/10.1371/journal.pone.0207963

de Sardan, J.P.O. (2015). Emic and the actors' point of view. In *Epistemology, fieldwork, and anthropology* (pp. 65–82). New York, NY: Palgrave Macmillan.

Denzin, N.K., & Lincoln, Y.S. (2013). *Collecting and interpreting qualitative materials* (4th ed.). London, UK: Sage.

DiStefano, A.S. (2008). Suicidality and self-harm among sexual minorities in Japan. *Qualitative Health Research, 18,* 1429–1441. https://doi.org/10.1177/1049732308322605

Fitzpatrick, S. (2011). Looking beyond the qualitative and quantitative divide: Narrative, ethics and representation in suicidology. *Suicidology Online, 2,* 29–37.

Fogarty, A.S., Spurrier, M., Player, M.J., Wilhelm, K., Whittle, E.L., Shand, F., ... Proudfoot, J. (2018). Tensions in perspectives on suicide prevention between men who have attempted suicide and their support networks: Secondary analysis of qualitative data. *Health Expectations, 21,* 261–269. https://doi.org/10.1111/hex.12611

Fontanella, B.J.B., Campos, C.J. G., & Turato, E.R. (2006). Data collection in clinical-qualitative research: Use of non-directed interviews with open-ended questions by health professionals. *Revista Latino-Americana de Enfermagem, 14*(5), 812–820. https://doi.org/10.1590/S0104-11692006000500025

Francis, J.J., Johnston, M., Robertson, C., Glidewell, L., Entwistle, V., Eccles, M.P., & Grimshaw, J.M. (2010). What is an adequate sample size? Operationalising data saturation for theory-based interview studies. *Psychology & Health, 25*(10), 1229–1245. https://doi.org/10.1080/08870440903194015

Frey, J.H., & Oishi, S.M. (1995). *How to conduct interviews by telephone and in person. The survey kit* (Vol. 4). Thousand Oaks, CA: Sage.

Friese, S. (2012). *Doing qualitative research with ATLAS.ti.* London, UK: Sage.

Gerisch, B. (2002). Aspects of qualitative research in suicidology. *Archives of Suicide Research, 6,* 31–39. https://doi.org/10.1080/13811110213118

Gilbert, N. (1993). *Researching social life.* Thousand Oaks, CA: Sage.

Given, L. (Ed.). (2008). *The Sage encyclopedia of qualitative research methods*. Thousand Oaks, CA: Sage. https://doi.org/10.4135/9781412963909

Glaser, B.G., & Strauss, A.L. (1967). *The discovery of grounded theory: Strategies for qualitative research*. Chicago, IL: Aldine.

Goldney, R.D. (2002). Qualitative and quantitative approaches in suicidology: Commentary. *Archives of Suicide Research, 6*, 69–73. https://doi.org/10.1080/13811110213117

Greenbaum, T. (2000). *Moderating focus groups*. Thousand Oaks, CA: Sage.

Harper, D., & Thompson, A.R. (2012). *Qualitative research methods in mental health and psychotherapy: A guide for students and practitioners*. Oxford, UK: Wiley.

Hjelmeland, H. (2011). Cultural context is crucial in suicide research and prevention. *Crisis, 32*, 61–64. https://doi.org/10.1111/hex.12611

Hjelmeland, H., & Knizek, B.L. (2010). Why we need qualitative research in suicidology. *Suicide and Life-Threatening Behavior, 40*, 74–80. https://doi.org/10.1521/suli.2010.40.1.74

Hjelmeland, H., & Knizek, B.L. (2011). What kind of research do we need in suicidology today? In R. O'Connor & J. Pirkins (Eds.), *The international handbook of suicide prevention* (pp. 591–608). New York, NY: Wiley.

Hjelmeland, H., & Knizek, B.L. (2016). Time to change direction in suicide research. In R. O'Connor & J. Pirkins (Eds.), *The international handbook of suicide prevention* (2nd ed., pp. 696–709). New York, NY: Wiley. https://doi.org/10.1002/9781118903223.ch3

Howitt, D. (2010). *Introduction to qualitative methods in psychology*. London, UK: Pearson.

Hwang, S. (2008). Utilizing qualitative data analysis software: A review of Atlas.ti. *Social Science Computer Review, 26*(4), 519–527. https://doi.org/10.1177/0894439307312485

Kim, O.S., & Sok, S.R. (2017). Life experiences of elderly people with suicide ideation at the long-term care hospitals in South Korea. *International Journal of Nursing Practice, 23*(6), e12597. https://doi.org/10.1111/ijn.12597

Kramer, D.A. (2002). A psychobiographical analysis of faith, hope, and despair in suicide. *Journal of Adult Development, 9*, 117–126. https://doi.org/10.1023/A:1015785313076

Kuruvilla, A., & Jacob, K.S. (2012). Outcome and implications of research in suicidology from developing countries. In A. Shrivastava, M. Kimbrell, & D. Lester (Eds.), *Suicide from a global perspective: Psychosocial approaches* (pp. 205–214). Hauppauge, NY: Nova Science.

Kvale, S. (2007). *Doing interviews*. Thousand Oaks, CA: Sage. https://doi.org/10.4135/9781849208963

Lakeman, R., & FitzGerald, M. (2008). How people live with or get over being suicidal: A review of qualitative studies. *Journal of Advanced Nursing, 64*, 114–126. https://doi.org/10.1111/j.1365-2648.2008.04773.x

Larkin, M., Watts, S., & Clifton, E. (2006). Giving voice and making sense in interpretative phenomenological analysis. *Qualitative Research in Psychology, 3*(2), 102–120. https://doi.org/10.1191/1478088706qp062oa

Leenars, A.A. (2002). In defence of the idiographic approach: Studies of suicide notes and personal documents. *Archives of Suicide Research, 6*, 19–30. https://doi.org/10.1080/13811110213125

Lester, D. (2002). Qualitative versus quantitative studies in psychiatry: Two examples of cooperation from suicidology. *Archives of Suicide Research, 6*, 15–18. https://doi.org/10.1080/13811110213124

Lester, D. (2009). Learning about suicide from the diary of Cesare Pavese. *Crisis, 30*, 222–224. https://doi.org/10.1027/0227-5910.30.4.222

Lester, D. (2010). Qualitative research in suicidology: Thoughts on Hjelmeland and Knizek's "Why we need qualitative research in suicidology". *Suicidology Online, 1*, 76–78.

Lindlof, T.R., & Taylor, B.C. (2002). *Qualitative communication research methods* (2nd ed.). Thousand Oaks, CA: Sage.

Lune, H., & Berg, B.L. (2017). *Qualitative research methods for the social sciences* (9th ed.). London, UK: Pearson.

MacLure, M. (2013). Researching without representation? Language and materiality in post-qualitative methodology. *International Journal of Qualitative Studies in Education, 26*(6), 658–667. https://doi.org/10.1080/09518398.2013.788755

Miller, M. (1995). An intergenerational case study of suicidal tradition and mother-daughter communication. *Journal of Applied Communication Research, 23*, 247–270. https://doi.org/10.1080/00909889509365430

Morrissey, J., & Higgins, A. (2019). "Attenuating anxieties": A grounded theory study of mental health nurses' responses to clients with suicidal behaviour. *Journal of Clinical Nursing, 28*, 947–958. https://doi.org/10.1111/jocn.14717

Orri, M., Paduanello, M., Lachal, J., Falissard, B., Sibeoni, J., & Revah-Levy, A. (2014). Qualitative approach to attempted suicide by adolescents and young adults: The (neglected) role of revenge. *PLoS ONE, 9*(5), e96716. http://doi.org/10.1371/journal.pone.0096716

Osafo, J., Hjelmeland, H., Akotia, C.S., & Knizek, B.L. (2011a). Social injury: An interpretative phenomenological analysis of the attitudes towards suicide of lay persons in Ghana. *International Journal of Qualitative Studies on Health and Well-Being, 6,* 8708. https://doi.org/10.3402/qhw.v6i4.8708

Osafo, J., Hjelmeland, H., Akotia, C.S., & Knizek, B.L. (2011b). The meanings of suicidal behaviour to psychology students in Ghana: A qualitative approach. *Transcultural Psychiatry, 48*, 643–659. https://doi.org/10.1177/1363461511417319

Owens, C., & Lambert, H. (2012). Mad, bad or heroic? Gender, identity and accountability in lay portrayals of suicide in late twentieth-century England. *Culture, Medicine and Psychiatry, 36*, 348–371. http://doi.org/10.1007/s11013-012-9259-x

Patton, M.Q. (2002). *Qualitative research and evaluation methods* (3rd ed.). Thousand Oaks, CA: Sage.

Perceval, M., Kõlves, K., Reddy, P., & De Leo, D. (2017). Farmer suicides: A qualitative study from Australia. *Occupational Medicine, 67,* 383–388. https://doi.org/10.1093/occmed/kqx055

Rahimipour Anaraki, N., & Boostani, D. (2014). Living in and living out: A qualitative study of incarcerated mothers' narratives of their children's living condition. *Quality and Quantity, 48*, 3093–3107. http://doi.org/10.1007/s11135-013-9943-0

Reed, J. (2007). *Appreciative inquiry: Research for change*. Thousand Oaks, CA: Sage. https://doi.org/10.4135/9781412983464

Reeves, S., Kuper, A., & Hodges, B.D. (2008). Qualitative research methodologies: Ethnography. *BMJ, 337,* a1020. https://doi.org/10.1136/bmj.a1020

Reis, H.T., & Gable, S.L. (2000). Event-sampling and other methods for studying everyday experience. In H.T. Reis & C.M. Judd (Eds.), *Handbook of research methods in social and personality psychology* (pp. 190–222). New York, NY: Cambridge University Press.

Rennie, D.L. (2012). Qualitative research as methodical hermeneutics. *Psychological Methods, 17*, 385–398. https://doi.org/10.1037/a0029250

Rimkeviciene, J., Hawgood, J., O'Gorman, J., & De Leo, D. (2015). Personal stigma in suicide attempters. *Death Studies, 39,* 592–599. https://doi.org/10.1080/07481187.2015.1037972

Rivlin, A., Fazel, S., Marzano, L., & Hawton, K. (2013). The suicidal process in male prisoners making near-lethal suicide attempts. *Psychology, Crime and Law, 19*, 305–327. https://doi.org/10.1080/1068316X.2011.631540

Robinson, O.C. (2014). Sampling in interview-based qualitative research: A theoretical and practical guide. *Qualitative Research in Psychology, 11,* 25–41. https://doi.org/10.1080/14780887.2013.801543

Robinson, O.C., & Smith, J.A. (2010). Investigating the form and dynamics of crisis episodes in early adulthood: The application of a composite qualitative method. *Qualitative Research in Psychology, 7,* 170–91. https://doi.org/10.1080/14780880802699084

Ross, V., Kõlves, K., Kunde, L., & De Leo, D. (2018). Parents' experiences of suicide-bereavement: A qualitative study at 6 and 12 months after loss. *International Journal of Environmental Research and Public Health, 15*(4), 618. https://doi.org/10.3390/ijerph15040618

Roth, S. (2000). Developing working-class feminism: A biographical approach to social movement participation. In S. Stryker, T.J. Owens, & R.W. White (Eds.), *Self, identity, and social movements* (pp. 300–323). Minneapolis, MN: University of Minnesota Press.

Rouse, J. (1996). Feminism and the social construction of scientific knowledge. In L.H. Nelson & J. Nelson (Eds.), *Feminism, science, and the philosophy of science*. Dordrecht, The Netherlands: Springer.

Sanger, S., & Veach, P.M. (2008). The interpersonal nature of suicide: A qualitative investigation of suicide notes. *Archives of Suicide Research, 12*, 352–365. https://doi.org/10.1080/13811110802325232

Schlimme, J.E. (2013). Sense of self-determination and the suicidal experience. A phenomenological approach. *Medicine, Health Care and Philosophy, 16*(2), 211–223. https://doi.org/10.1007/s11019-011-9358-4

Seal, D.W., Bogart, L.M., & Ehrhardt, A.A. (1998). Small group dynamics: The utility of focus group discussions as a research method. *Group Dynamics: Theory, Research, and Practice, 2*(4), 253–266. https://doi.org/10.1037/1089-2699.2.4.253

Shields, C., Kavanagh, M., & Russo, K. (2017). A qualitative systematic review of the bereavement process following suicide. *OMEGA-Journal of death and dying, 74*(4), 426–454. https://doi.org/10.1177/0030222815612281

Shrivastava, A., Kimbrell, M., & Lester, D. (Eds.). (2012). *Suicide from a global perspective: Psychosocial approaches.* Hauppauge, NY: Nova Science.

Smith, J.A., Jarman, M., & Osborn, M. (1999). Doing interpretative phenomenological analysis. In M. Murray & K. Chamberlain (Eds.), *Qualitative health psychology: theories and methods* (pp. 218–240). London, UK: Sage. https://doi.org/10.4135/9781446217870.n14

Smith, A., Joseph, S., & Nair, R.D. (2011). An interpretative phenomenological analysis of posttraumatic growth in adults bereaved by suicide. *Journal of Loss and Trauma, 16,* 413–430. https://doi.org/10.1080/15325024.2011.572047

Smith, J.A., Flowers, P., & Larkin, M. (2009). *Interpretative phenomenological analysis: Theory, method and research.* London, UK: Sage.

Smith, J.A., & Shinebourne, P. (2012). Interpretative phenomenological analysis. In H. Cooper, P.M. Camic, D.L. Long, A.T. Panter, D. Rindskopf, & K.J. Sher (Eds.), *APA handbook of research methods in psychology, Vol. 2. Research designs: Quantitative, qualitative, neuropsychological, and biological* (pp. 73–82). Washington, DC: American Psychological Association. https://doi.org/10.1037/13620-005

Stake, R. (1995). *The art of case study research.* Thousand Oaks, CA: Sage.

Staples, J., & Widger, T. (2012). Situating suicide as an anthropological problem: Ethnographic approaches to understanding self-harm and self-inflicted death. *Culture, Medicine, and Psychiatry, 36,* 183–203. https://doi.org/10.1007/s11013-012-9255-1

Strauss, A., & Corbin, J. (1994). Grounded theory methodology: An overview. In N.K. Denzin & Y.S. Lincoln (Eds.), *Handbook of qualitative research* (pp. 1–18). London, UK: Sage.

Strauss, A.L., & Corbin, J. (1998). *Basics of qualitative research: Techniques and procedures for developing grounded theory.* London, UK: Sage.

Szabo, V., & Strang, V.R. (1997). Secondary analysis of qualitative data. *Advances in Nursing Science, 20,* 66–74. https://doi.org/10.1097/00012272-199712000-00008

Takarangi, M.K., Garry, M., & Loftus, E.F. (2006). Dear diary, is plastic better than paper? I can't remember: Comment on Green, Rafaeli, Bolger, Shrout, and Reis (2006). *Psychological Methods, 11*(1), 119–122. https://doi.org/10.1037/1082-989X.11.1.119

Testoni, I., Francescon, E., De Leo, D., Santini, A., & Zamperini, A. (2019). Forgiveness and blame among suicide survivors: A qualitative analysis on reports of 4-year self-help-group meetings. *Community Mental Health Journal, 55,* 360–368. https://doi.org/10.1007/s10597-018-0291-3

Testoni, I., Ghellar, T., Rodelli, M., De Cataldo, L., & Zamperini, A. (2017). Representations of death among Italian vegetarians: An ethnographic research on environment, disgust and transcendence. *Europe's Journal of Psychology, 13,* 378–395. https://doi.org/10.5964/ejop.v13i3.1301

Testoni, I., Iacona, E., Fusina, S., Floriani, M., Crippa, M., Maccarini, A., & Zamperini, A. (2018). "Before I die I want to ...": An experience of death education among university students of social service and psychology. *Health Psychology Open, 5*(2). https://doi.org/10.1177/2055102918809759

Testoni, I., Parise, G., Zamperini, A., Visintin, E.P., Toniolo, E., Vicentini, S., & De Leo, D. (2016). The "sick-lit" question and the death education answer. Papageno versus werther effects in adolescent suicide prevention. *Human Affairs, 26*(2), 153–166. https://doi.org/10.1515/humaff-2016-0016

Testoni, I., Pesci, S., De Vincenzo, C., Dal Corso, L., & Zamperini, A. (2019). Work and spirituality among people with Asperger syndrome: An exploratory study. *Journal of Disability & Religion, 23*(2), 178–196. https://doi.org/10.1080/23312521.2019.1580174

Thomae, H. (1999). The nomothetic-idiographic issue: Some roots and recent trends. *International Journal of Group Tensions, 28*(1), 187–215. https://doi.org/10.1023/A:1021891506378

Tong, A., Sainsbury, P., & Craig, J. (2007). Consolidated criteria for reporting qualitative research (COREQ): A 32-item checklist for interviews and focus groups. *International Journal for Quality in Health Care, 19,* 349–357. http://doi.org/10.1093/intqhc/mzm042

Tracy, S.J. (2014). *Qualitative research methods: Collecting evidence, crafting analysis, communicating impact.* Chichester, UK: Wiley-Blackwell.

Vandewalle, J., Beeckman, D., Van Hecke, A., Debyser, B., Deproost, E., Verhaeghe, S. (2019). Contact and communication with patients experiencing suicidal ideation: A qualitative study of nurses' perspectives. *Journal of Advanced Nursing, 75*(11), 2867–2877. https://doi.org/10.1111/jan.14113

Weber, R.P. (1990). *Basic content analysis* (2nd ed.). Newbury Park, CA: Sage. https://doi.org/10.4135/9781412983488

Wertz, M.S., Nosek, M., McNiesh, S., & Marlow, E. (2011). The composite first person narrative: Texture, structure, and meaning in writing phenomenological descriptions. *International Journal of Qualitative Studies on Health and Well-Being, 6*(2), 5882. https://doi.org/10.3402/qhw.v6i2.5882

Wilkinson, S. (1998). Focus group methodology: A review. *International Journal of Social Research Methodology, 1*(3), 181–203. https://doi.org/10.1080/13645579.1998.10846874

Willig, C., & Rogers, W.S. (Eds.). (2008). *The SAGE handbook of qualitative research in psychology.* Thousand Oaks, CA: Sage. https://doi.org/10.4135/9781848607927

Yang, L.H., Lam, J., Vega, E., Martinez, M., Botcheva, L., Hong, J.E., ... Lewis, S.E. (2018). Understanding the impact of community on the experience of suicide within the Lao community: An expansion of the cultural model of suicide. *Asian American Journal of Psychology, 9*(4), 284–295. https://doi.org/10.1037/aap0000131

Zhang, J., Dong, N., Delprino, R., & Zhou, L. (2009). Psychological strains found from in-depth interviews with 105 Chinese rural youth suicides. *Archives of Suicide Research, 13*(2), 185–194. https://doi.org/10.1080/13811110902835155

Chapter 10

Mixed Methods in Suicide Research

Victoria Ross and Kairi Kõlves

Summary

Mixed methods offer a valuable *third paradigm* in suicide research that can address the limitations of quantitative and qualitative research methods. This chapter describes how the application of mixed methods can enable researchers to gain a more substantive understanding of suicide. We discuss the range of mixed method designs available, depending on why, how, and where the quantitative and qualitative components will be applied and integrated. Examples are also provided of how mixed methods have been applied in suicide research.

Mixed methods approaches are becoming increasingly popular in suicide research. In this chapter we give a brief outline of the evolution of mixed methods research and describe how mixed methods are currently defined and conceptualized. We discuss some the limitations of traditional quantitative methods in enhancing our understanding of suicidal behaviors, and how mixed methods play an important role in addressing these gaps. We also present the main mixed methods designs and provide some examples of how different types of mixed method studies have been successfully applied to suicide research.

Evolution of Mixed Methods Research

Although mixed research is traditionally thought to have its origins in the social and behavioral sciences (e.g., Johnson, Onwuegbuzie, & Turner, 2007), it has been argued that the integration of qualitative and quantitative approaches was applied in the natural sciences as far back as the 1600s, long before this approach was labeled as mixed methods research (Maxwell, 2016). Maxwell cites Galileo's application of both observational descriptions and mathematical calculations (in demonstrating sunspots were features of the sun, rather than planets), as an early example of linking qualitative and quantitative data to support a conclusion. Combined qualitative and quantitative methods were also applied in medicine and epidemiology since at least the mid-19th century, and mixed research was seen in the community studies of cultural anthropologists and fieldwork sociologists in the early 20th century (Johnson et al., 2007; Maxwell, 2016).

In the social science methodological literature, Campbell and Fiske (1959) are credited as being the first researchers to apply multiple research methods in their work on *convergent validation* or *triangulation*, where more than one method is used as part of a validation process (Harris et al., 2016; Johnson et al., 2007). Their work was extended further by Webb, Campbell, Schwartz, and Sechrest (1966), who argued that confirmation by two or more independent measurement processes greatly reduces uncertainty in the interpretation of results. Similarly, Bouchard (1976) believed that the convergence of findings from two or more methods enhances confidence in the validity of findings, giving evidence against the possibility that they are a *methodological artefact* (Johnson et al., 2007).

Although mixed methods research is not new, it is recognized as a new research paradigm that is becoming increasingly popular in research practice. In fact, methodological experts such as Johnson et al. (2007) have argued for a *three-paradigm methodological world*, comprising quantitative, qualitative, and mixed methods, because each approach has its strengths and weaknesses and times and places of need (Johnson et al., 2007). However, as it is an emerging research paradigm, there is still much debate around how mixed methods should be conceptualized and defined, particularly with regard to exactly how and where quantitative and qualitative methods should be integrated (Creswell & Tashakkori, 2007). We discuss these concepts in more detail in the following sections.

Conceptualizing and Defining Mixed Methods

Creswell and Tashakkori (2007) have highlighted the importance of distinguishing between mixed methods as a collection and analysis of quantitative and qualitative data, and mixed methods as the integration of the two approaches to research. Early conceptualizations of mixed methods as merely the combination of quantitative and qualitative methods or two types of data collection techniques have been justly criticized as overly simplistic, or as indicating a *quasimixed* approach (Creswell & Tashakkori, 2007; Teddlie & Tashakkori, 2006). There is much debate on how mixed methods should be conceptualized, particularly in terms of how this approach impacts on all aspects and dimensions of the research process. Creswell and Tashakkori (2007) examined the various ways that mixed methods are viewed by researchers and identified the following four key perspectives:

- The *method perspective*, where the focus is on the process and outcomes of using quantitative and qualitative data.
- The *methodological perspective*, which views mixed methods as a distinct methodology and larger process of research that integrates research processes such as worldview, questions, methods, inferences, or conclusions.
- The *paradigm perspective*, which argues that mixed methods research is more about philosophical assumptions and less about methods or the process of research.
- The *practice perspective*, where mixed methods is viewed pragmatically as a means or set of procedures that follow a bottom-up approach to research.

Creswell and Tashakkori (2007) suggest that most researchers using mixed methods are likely to have embraced each of these four perspectives at various times, rather than adhering to one particular perspective.

There have been numerous terms which have been applied to describe mixed methods; for example, multiple operationalism, triangulation, blended research, integrative research, multimethod research, multiple methods, triangulated studies, ethnographic residual analysis, and mixed research (Johnson et al., 2007). As with initial conceptualizations of mixed methods, early definitions merely emphasized the mixing of quantitative and qualitative approaches that were not necessarily linked to a particular type of enquiry. For example, Greene, Caracelli, and Graham (1989) defined mixed methods as "those that include at least one quantitative method (designed to collect numbers) and one qualitative method (designed to collect words), where neither type of method is inherently linked to any particular inquiry paradigm" (p. 256). A decade later, definitions began to shift from the mixing of two methods, to integration at all phases of the research process (Creswell & Plano Clark, 2011), such as the definition by Tashakkori and Teddlie (1998), that mixed methods "combine qualitative and quantitative approaches in the methodology of a study" (p. ix).

In an effort to gain consensus on a definition for mixed methods research, Johnson et al. (2007) asked leaders in mixed methods research to provide their own definitions. The 19 definitions obtained differed in terms of *what is mixed* (e.g., methods or methodologies, or types of research), *when or where* in the mixing occurs (e.g., data collection, analysis), the *breadth* of the mixed research (e.g., from the collection of two types of data, to mixing at all stages), and finally, the *purpose* of the mixing. Based on their review of the definitions and common themes obtained, Johnson et al. (2007) compiled the following composite definition:

> Mixed methods research is the type of research in which a researcher or team of researchers combines elements of qualitative and quantitative research approaches (e.g., use of qualitative and quantitative viewpoints, data collection, analysis, inference techniques) for the purposes of breadth and depth of understanding and corroboration. (Johnson et al., 2007, p. 123)

As highlighted by Tashakkori and Creswell (2007), given the constant evolution of mixed methods, it will be important to continue to keep the discussion regarding definitions open.

Why Mixed Methods Are Important in Suicide Research

Researchers have highlighted the fact that despite many years of research in the field, little is known about the effectiveness of suicide prevention activities, and although various risk factors for suicide have been identified, it is still impossible to predict suicide risk in clients (Kral, Links, & Bergmans, 2012). Given the lack of significant progress in suicide prevention research, scholars have called for the need for greater methodological diversity in addressing the complex problem of suicide; in particular, the inclusion of more qualitative and mixed methods approaches (Hjelmeland & Knizek, 2010; Kral et al., 2012; Rogers & Apel, 2010).

Traditionally, research methods applied to the study of suicide prevention have been primarily quantitative. Hjelmeland and Knizek (2010) calculated that in the period 2005–2007, less than 3% of research articles published in three key international suicidology journals had used qualitative methods. The authors argue that the main quantitative suicide research methods – observational studies, (neuro)biological research, and intervention studies – have many weaknesses. They point out that while each of these approaches can explain different aspects of suicidal behavior, none of them can provide a complete understanding. To expand our knowledge and understanding of suicide, researchers have therefore argued for the increased use of mixed methods in suicide research to allow for broadening of research questions and more substantive understanding (Hjelmeland & Knizek, 2010; Kral et al., 2012).

According to Kral et al. (2012), to understand suicidal behavior, we need to consider both the complexity of the phenomenon of suicide and the perspectives of suicidal individuals, through the application of a variety of research methods and models. They emphasize the value of asking research participants to talk about their lives, suicidal states, motivation for suicide, and their experiences of recovery. In this way, the subjective experiences of suicidal people can assist our understanding of the complex factors at play and the unique support needs of suicidal individuals, and help inform the support services provided (Kral et al., 2012; Ross, Kõlves, & De Leo, 2019). Qualitative enquiry can also provide important contextual factors that can be integrated with quantitative data to enhance understanding and interpretation in a specific context for suicide (e.g., Ross, Koo, & Kõlves, 2020).

Mixed methods research can thus be applied to strategically harness the strengths and complement the weaknesses of quantitative and qualitative methods: a powerful approach to addressing the complex and multifaceted problem of suicide (Johnson et al., 2007; Tariq & Woodman, 2013). As outlined previously, the integration or triangulation of mixed methods results also provides readers and reviewers with more confidence in the results and conclusions that can be drawn from the study (McKim, 2017). However, McKim also cautions that it is important to be clear about the perceived value of combining two such distinct methods, given that conducting a mixed methods study requires significant additional resources, time, and expertise.

Mixed Method Designs

Creswell and Plano Clark (2011) recommend that prior to designing a mixed methods study, it is important to consider how the quantitative and qualitative aspects of the study will interact, how they will be prioritized, their timing in the study, and how they will be mixed and/or integrated. Once these decisions have been made, there are a range of mixed methods designs available. Creswell and Plano Clark (2011) provide a comprehensive description of mixed methods studies and identify the following four main mixed methods designs:

- The *convergent parallel design*. The researcher uses concurrent timing to implement the quantitative and qualitative components, prioritizes the methods equally, analyses each component separately, and then integrates the results at the interpretation stage.
- The *explanatory sequential design*. This comprises two distinct interactive phases. The first phase is the quantitative collection and analysis of data, which aims to address the research questions. The second, qualitative phase is designed to enhance understanding of the findings from the first phase.
- The *exploratory sequential design*. The first phase prioritizes the collection and analysis of qualitative data. The second, quantitative phase is conducted to test and generalize the initial findings.
- The *embedded design*. Using this design, the researcher may embed a qualitative strand within a quantitative design, or embed a quantitative strand within a qualitative design. The purpose of including the embedded strand is to enhance the overall study design in some way.

Figure 10.1 illustrates the four main mixed methods study designs. Using these four basic designs as a framework, more complex designs bringing multiple design elements together, such as a *transformative design* and a *multiphase design*, can be developed (see Creswell & Plano Clark, 2011).

Application of Mixed Methods in Suicide Research

In recent years, mixed methods approaches have become increasingly popular in suicide research. We conducted searches of the available literature where mixed methods have been applied in suicide research and identified four major themes: factors associated with suicidal

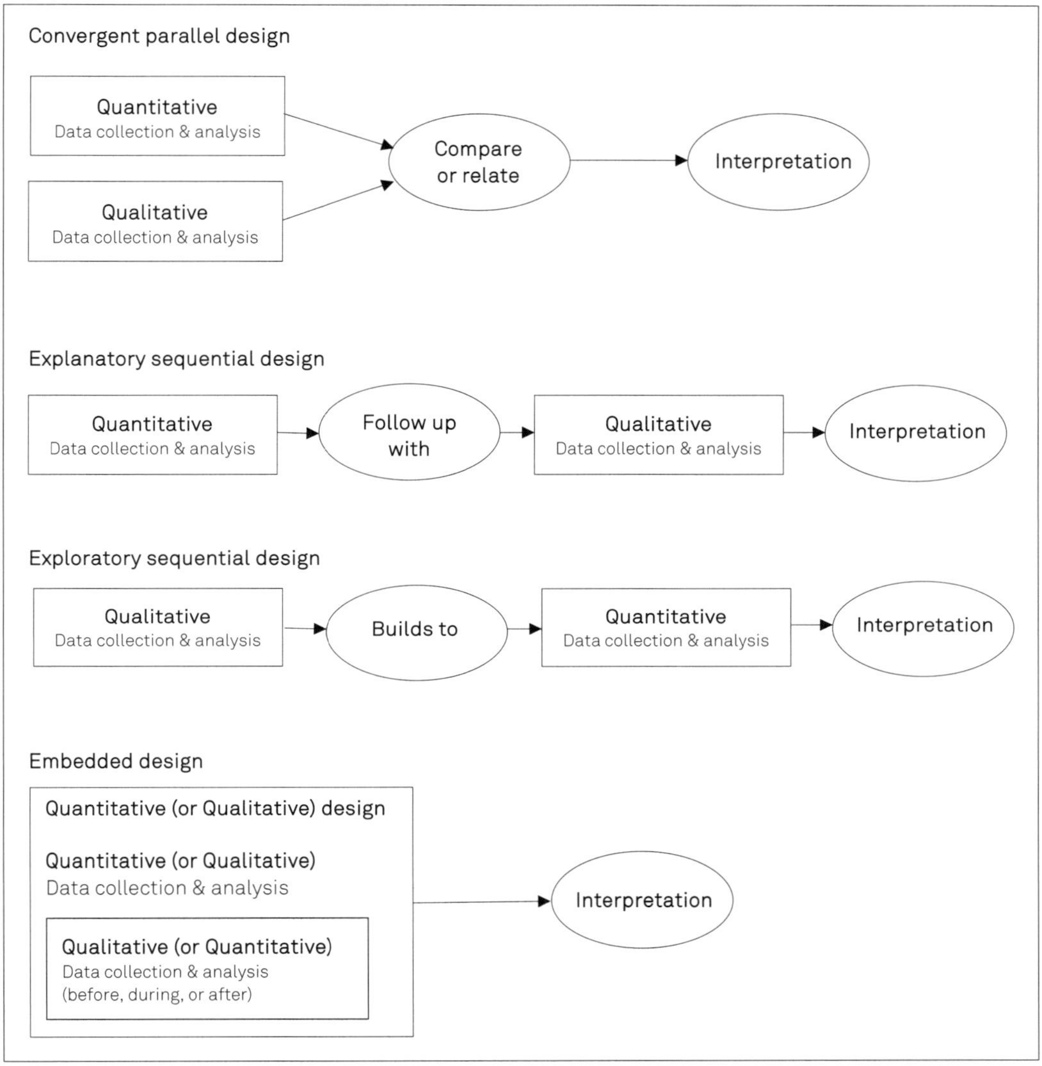

Figure 10.1. Four main mixed methods research designs. Reprinted with permission from "Designing and Conducting Mixed Methods Research" (2nd ed.), by J. W. Creswell & V. L. Planco Clark, pp. 69–70, Thousand Oaks, CA: Sage. © 2011 by SAGE.

behaviors, reactions to suicide bereavement and help seeking, stigma, and evaluating suicide prevention interventions.

Our brief review indicated that the most common topic in mixed methods suicide research was *factors associated with suicidal behaviors*. Several studies obtained data from the US National Violent Death Reporting System (NVDRS), a database that comprises quantitative and qualitative data including age, race and cause of death, toxicology reports, coroners' reports, police reports, and transcribed interviews from the decedents' family and friends regarding life stressors, school problems, emotional problems, and mental health issues. For example, Holland and colleagues (2017) examined a comprehensive list of variables that may contribute to suicide in youths aged 11 to 15, while Schiff and colleagues (2015) used NVDRS data to identify relationships between suicide and partner problems, criminal and legal troubles, job or financial problems, and health issues. In Australia, Fitzpatrick and colleagues (2019) used data from the National Coronial Information System, including demographic information and details of death (time, location, cause of death). They also obtained police and coroners' reports which included information on social factors (housing and economic circumstances, family violence, legal issues, interpersonal relationships and supports, etc.). Other mixed methods approaches have included the application of questionnaires to obtain both quantitative and qualitative data on why Asian American college students consider suicide (Wong, Koo, Tran, Chiu, & Mok, 2011), and the combined use of cognitive therapy transcriptions and quantitative diagnostic interview data to identify cognitive warning signs for suicide attempts (Adler et al., 2016).

Another key theme in mixed methods suicide research was *suicide bereavement and subsequent help-seeking behaviors*. Lubens and Silver (2019) examined both risk and protective factors regarding grief in veterans following the loss of a comrade to suicide. Online surveys were administered to measure quantitative concepts such as grief, anger, combat exposure, unit cohesion, depression, and posttraumatic stress symptoms, and interviews were conducted to obtain qualitative information about military history, relationships with other members of their unit, and descriptions of any losses of comrades. Spillane, Matvienko-Sikar, Larkin, Corcoran, and Arensman (2018) investigated the physical and psychological health effects of suicide bereavement on family members. The Depression, Anxiety, and Stress Scale (DASS) was used in conjunction with a semistructured interview to explore emotional, physical, and social impacts, as well as the support services accessed. Maple and colleagues (2019) used a combination of data from the client contact database of an Australian national suicide postvention service, StandBy (e.g., service use, client demographics, and deceased data), and semistructured interviews, to examine help-seeking behaviors in the suicide bereaved.

Another common theme in mixed methods suicide research is *stigma* regarding suicide and those who engage in suicidal behaviors. Bartik, Maple, and McKay (2015) examined the stigma surrounding suicide in a sample of young people who had lost a friend to suicide. Stigma was measured quantitatively using a standardized stigma questionnaire, and qualitative interviews allowed the researchers to identify young people's perceptions of stigma associated with suicide in their rural communities. In another study, Farrelly and colleagues (2015) conducted interviews to collect both quantitative and qualitative data to examine how stigma toward mental illness affects suicidality in mentally ill individuals. A qualitative model derived from the interview data suggested that the experience of discrimination is a stressor which leads to difficulty coping, negative self-image, and a perception of decreased social support. The anticipation of further negative events, and the perception of a lack of supportive networks led individuals in the study to feelings of hopelessness and suicidality. Quantitative analyses provided support for the model.

The use of mixed methods in evaluating *suicide prevention interventions* was also a key theme. Harris et al. (2016) applied a mixed methods approach to explore the interactions between components of a multilevel suicide intervention program in four European countries Optimised Multi-Level Suicide Prevention Intervention (OSPI-Europe). A longitudinal, mixed method case study design was applied to a process evaluation of the program, where four waves of qualitative and quantitative data were collected at 6-monthly intervals. This novel approach to the evaluation of a complex intervention enabled the identification of synergistic interactions that added value beyond the sum of individual intervention levels or components of the program in isolation. The growing application of mixed methods in the field of evaluation is not surprising, given the practical nature of evaluation research and the need for multiple sources of evidence when assessing programs (Johnson et al., 2007). Another example of the value of the application of mixed methods in evaluation research is provided in an evaluation study of a suicide prevention initiative at a jumping site in Australia (Box 10.1; Ross et al., 2020).

Box 10.1. Example of a mixed methods evaluation study from Australia

Gap Park in Sydney, Australia, has long been recognized as a suicide jumping site. In 2010–2011 a series of suicide prevention measures were implemented as part of the Gap Park Masterplan. In order to evaluate its effectiveness in reducing suicides, this study applied a mixed methods design. Data was obtained from the Australian National Coronial Information System (NCIS) to examine suicide numbers at Gap Park before and after the Masterplan was implemented. Qualitative data was obtained from individual interviews with police officers who were experienced in responding to suicidal behaviors at Gap Park. Joinpoint analysis of NCIS data showed a nonsignificant upward trend in jumping suicides across the study period. A significant upward trend in suicides was seen for females before the implementation of the Masterplan (2000–2010). This was followed by a significant downward trend for females from the implementation period onwards (2010–2016); however, a nonsignificant upward trend was observed for males.

Qualitative analysis of police interview data identified six key themes: romanticism and attraction at hotspots; profiles and behavioral patterns of suicidal individuals; responding to a person in a suicidal crisis; repeated attempts; means restriction; and personal impacts on police officers. The results of this study provided important insights, suggesting the Gap Park Masterplan has contributed to a reduction in female but not in male suicides. Information obtained from police officers provided important contextual factors which enhanced the understanding of the quantitative results, particularly in terms of how specific aspects of the Gap Park Masterplan appear to be working. For example, officers noted the CCTV and alarms were very effective in saving lives through detection and location of suicide attempters, but stressed that the fencing at Gap Park is not difficult to climb and is likely to be more of a visual or psychological barrier. The significant reduction in female suicides may suggest that the fencing is more of a physical, or even psychological barrier, for females than for males.

Police officers also provided valuable insights into the profiles and behaviors of suicidal individuals, and the most effective techniques for intervening in suicide attempts. It was also reported that suicide attempters often cited information available on the Internet as influencing their decisions to jump from Gap Park. In addition, police officers spoke of the significant personal stressors involved in responding to suicides and suicide attempts, and how the stigma of mental health issues was a barrier to seeking help.

To the best of our knowledge, this study is one of the first reported mixed method evaluations of suicide prevention hotspot initiatives. A major strength of the study is the integration of suicide trend analysis with qualitative police interviews, which has enabled a deeper understanding of how the suicide prevention initiatives are working, and thus enhanced the validity of the results. The study is also the first to apply in-depth interviews with police officers: A method that has provided important insights from the considerable expertise of front-line officers intervening in suicide attempts. A limitation of the study is that due to suicide being a rare event, the small number in the analysis made it difficult to detect statistically significant changes in trends.

Based on Ross, V., Koo, Y. W., & Kõlves, K. (2020). A suicide prevention initiative at a jumping site: A mixed-methods evaluation. *EClinicalMedicine, 19*, 100278.

Ethical Considerations

The nature of ethical issues in the application of mixed methods research is broadly similar to that of the ethical problems associated with suicide research in general, given the sensitive nature of the research and vulnerability of participants who have been exposed to or have experienced suicidal behaviors. The inclusion of qualitative data collection methods such as interviews and focus groups bring additional concerns, such as exacerbating suicidality by bringing attention to suicidal thoughts and feelings, or potential disclosure to other group members who might become distressed (Lakeman & FitzGerald, 2009). More on ethical considerations in suicide research can be found in Chapter 4.

Conclusions

Mixed methods offer a powerful option to address the gaps found in other sociological approaches, by harnessing the strengths and minimizing the weaknesses of quantitative and qualitative approaches. The convergence of the two methods provides confidence in the validity of the findings and in the conclusions that can be drawn from the study. For these reasons, we strongly encourage the wider application of mixed methods in suicide research. However, when considering a mixed methods design, it is important to consider how the integration of quantitative and qualitative methods will add value, given the significant expertise, time, and resources required (McKim, 2017). In this chapter, we have provided a brief introduction to mixed methods. For more comprehensive information on designing and conducting mixed methods studies we recommend Creswell and Plano Clark (2011). For more specific details regarding quantitative and qualitative approaches individually, please see Chapter 6 for observational studies, Chapter 7 for intervention studies, and Chapter 9 for qualitative studies.

References

Adler, A., Bush, A., Barg, F.K., Weissinger, G., Beck, A.T., & Brown, G.K. (2016). A mixed methods approach to identify cognitive warning signs for suicide attempts. *Archives of Suicide Research, 20*(4), 528–538. https://doi.org/10.1080/13811118.2015.1136717

Bartik, W., Maple, M., & McKay, K. (2015). Suicide bereavement and stigma for young people in rural Australia: a mixed methods study. *Advances in Mental Health, 13*(1), 84–95. https://doi.org/10.1080/18374905.2015.1026301

Bouchard, T.J., Jr. (1976). Unobtrusive measures: An inventory of uses. *Sociological Methods & Research, 4*(3), 267–300. https://doi.org/10.1177/004912417600400301

Campbell, D.T., & Fiske, D.W. (1959). Convergent and discriminant validation by the multitrait-multimethod matrix. *Psychological Bulletin, 56*, 81–105. https://doi.org/10.1037/h0046016

Creswell, J.W., & Plano Clark, V.L. (2011). *Designing and conducting mixed methods research* (2nd ed.). Thousand Oaks, CA: Sage.

Creswell, J.W., & Tashakkori, A. (2007). Differing perspectives on mixed methods research. *Journal of Mixed Methods Research, 1*(4), 303–308. https://doi.org/10.1177/1558689807306132

Farrelly, S., Jeffery, D., Ruesch, N., Williams, P., Thornicroft, G., & Clement, S. (2015). The link between mental health-related discrimination and suicidality: Service user perspectives. *Psychological Medicine, 45*(10), 2013–2022. https://doi.org/10.1017/S0033291714003158

Fitzpatrick, S.J., Brew, B.K., Read, D.M., Inder, K.J., Hayes, A., & Perkins, D. (2019). Rethinking suicide in rural Australia: A study protocol for examining and applying knowledge of the social determinants to improve prevention in non-Indigenous populations. *International Journal of Environmental Research and Public Health, 16*(16), 2944. https://doi.org/10.3390/ijerph16162944

Greene, J.C., Caracelli, V.J., & Graham, W.F. (1989). Toward a conceptual framework for mixed-method evaluation designs. *Educational Evaluation and Policy Analysis, 11*(3), 255–274. https://doi.org/10.3102/01623737011003255

Harris, F.M., Maxwell, M., O'Connor, R., Coyne, J.C., Arensman, E., Coffey, C., ... Székely, A. (2016). Exploring synergistic interactions and catalysts in complex interventions: Longitudinal, mixed methods case studies of an optimised multi-level suicide prevention intervention in four European countries (Ospi-Europe). *BMC Public Health, 16*(1), 268. https://doi.org/10.1186/s12889-016-2942-z

Hjelmeland, H., & Knizek, B.L. (2010). Why we need qualitative research in suicidology. *Suicide and Life-Threatening Behavior, 40*(1), 74–80. https://doi.org/10.1521/suli.2010.40.1.74

Holland, K.M., Vivolo-Kantor, A.M., Logan, J.E., & Leemis, R.W. (2017). Antecedents of suicide among youth aged 11–15: A multistate mixed methods analysis. *Journal of Youth and Adolescence, 46*(7), 1598–1610. https://doi.org/10.1007/s10964-016-0610-3

Johnson, R.B., Onwuegbuzie, A.J., & Turner, L.A. (2007). Toward a definition of mixed methods research. *Journal of Mixed Methods Research, 1*(2), 112–133. https://doi.org/10.1177/1558689806298224

Kral, M.J., Links, P.S., & Bergmans, Y. (2012). Suicide studies and the need for mixed methods research. *Journal of Mixed Methods Research, 6*, 236–249. https://doi.org/10.1177/1558689811423914

Lakeman, R., & FitzGerald, M. (2009). The ethics of suicide research: The views of ethics committee members. *Crisis, 30*(1), 13–19. https://doi.org/10.1027/0227-5910.30.1.13

Lubens, P., & Silver, R.C. (2019). US combat veterans' responses to suicide and combat deaths: A mixed-methods study. *Social Science & Medicine, 236*, 112341. https://doi.org/10.1016/j.socscimed.2019.05.046

Maple, M., McKay, K., Hess, N.C., Wayland, S., & Pearce, T. (2019). Providing support following exposure to suicide: A mixed method study. *Health & Social Care in the Community, 27*(4), 965–972. https://doi.org/10.1111/hsc.12713

Maxwell, J.A. (2016). Expanding the history and range of mixed methods research. *Journal of Mixed Methods Research, 10*(1), 12–27. https://doi.org/10.1177/1558689815571132

McKim, C.A. (2017). The value of mixed methods research: A mixed methods study. *Journal of Mixed Methods Research, 11*(2), 202–222. https://doi.org/10.1177/1558689815607096

Rogers, J.R., & Apel, S. (2010). Revitalizing suicidology: A call for mixed methods designs. *Suicidology Online, 1*, 92–94.

Ross, V., Kõlves, K., & De Leo, D. (2019). Exploring the support needs of people bereaved by suicide: a qualitative study. *OMEGA – Journal of Death and Dying.* Advance online publication. https://doi.org/10.1177/0030222819825775

Ross, V., Koo, Y.W., & Kõlves, K. (2020). A suicide prevention initiative at a jumping site: A mixed-methods evaluation. *EClinicalMedicine, 19*, 100278. https://doi.org/10.1016/j.eclinm.2020.100265

Schiff, L.B., Holland, K.M., Stone, D.M., Logan, J., Marshall, K.J., Martell, B., & Bartholow, B. (2015). Acute and chronic risk preceding suicidal crises among middle-aged men without known mental health and/or substance abuse problems: An exploratory mixed-methods analysis. *Crisis, 36*(5), 304. https://doi.org/10.1027/0227-5910/a000329

Spillane, A., Matvienko-Sikar, K., Larkin, C., Corcoran, P., & Arensman, E. (2018). What are the physical and psychological health effects of suicide bereavement on family members? An observational and interview mixed-methods study in Ireland. *BMJ Open, 8*(1), e019472. https://doi.org/10.1136/bmjopen-2017-019472

Tariq, S., & Woodman, J. (2013). Using mixed methods in health research. *JRSM Short Reports, 4*(6). https://doi.org/10.1177/2042533313479197

Tashakkori, A., & Creswell, J.W. (2007). The new era of mixed methods. *Journal of Mixed Methods Research, 1*(1), 3–7. https://doi.org/10.1177/2345678906293042

Tashakkori, A., & Teddlie, C. (1998). *Mixed methodology: Combining qualitative and quantitative approaches* (Vol. 46). Thousand Oaks, CA: Sage.

Teddlie, C., & Tashakkori, A. (2006). A general typology of research designs featuring mixed methods. *Research in the Schools, 13*(1), 12–28.

Webb, E., Campbell, D., Schwartz, R., & Sechrest, L. (1966). *Unobtrusive measures.* Chicago, IL: Rand McNally.

Wong, Y.J., Koo, K., Tran, K.K., Chiu, Y.-C., & Mok, Y. (2011). Asian American college students' suicide ideation: A mixed-methods study. *Journal of Counseling Psychology, 58*(2), 197. https://doi.org/10.1037/a0023040

Chapter 11
Psychological Autopsy – A Tool in Suicide Research

Kairi Kõlves, Elice Tucholski, Airi Värnik, and Diego De Leo

Summary

The psychological autopsy (PA) method has been extensively used in suicide research. The term *psychological autopsy* was coined by the father of modern suicidology, Edwin Shneidman. Since its development in the 1950s, PA has made a significant contribution to suicide research, bereavement and postvention, legal areas, and forensic investigations (from which it originates). The current chapter will give a brief overview of the history of PA and the development of qualitative and quantitative approaches. We will look further into its methodology and shortcomings, with examples focused on a suicide research perspective.

Psychological autopsy (PA) refers to a procedure that retrospectively reconstructs a person's life cycle, with special attention to behaviors, thoughts, or feelings, which may have manifested in the days or weeks immediately preceding the person's death (Bartol & Bartol, 2008; Botello et al., 2013; Leenaars, 2017). This is traditionally achieved through a review of collateral records (e.g., police, coronial, and medical reports), and interviews with relatives, friends, colleagues, or health care professionals. The PA has been found to be a useful tool in suicide research and additionally in forensic and legal systems globally. The aim of the current chapter is to provide a brief overview of the history of PA, its methodology, and its shortcomings, by illustrating them with examples focused on suicide research perspective.

A Brief History of the PA

Shneidman and Psychological Autopsy

PA studies grew out of the need to determine the manner of death in equivocal deaths in the US in the 1950s. The PA was conceived in response to requests from the Los Angeles Coroner's Office during the late 1950s (Botello et al., 2013; Diller, 1979; Leenaars, 2017). At that time, the chief medical examiner was seeking an accurate procedure to assist with certifying the manner of death when uncertainty arose in declaring an accident or suicide on death certificates (Botello et al., 2013; Diller, 1979; Leenaars, 2017). American researchers Edwin Shneidman, Robert Litman, and Norman Farberow from the Los Angeles Suicide Prevention Center developed and subsequently practiced the procedure. However, Shneidman is acknowledged as having named the procedure in 1958 (Shneidman, 1981). Shneidman (1994) held that through investigating a decedent's lifestyle, behavioral elements, degree of psychic pain, and cognitive functioning, the PA serves as a consultation for the coroner or medical examiner to make a reasoned judgment of the psychological, motivational, and intentional properties of a death.

> The primary purpose of the psychological autopsy is quite simple: to assist the coroner in making decisions for the death certificate as to the most appropriate mode of death – the modes of death are natural, accident, suicide and homicide (the so called NASH categories) – in cases which the mode of death, at first look, seems equivocal or uncertain. (Shneidman, 2004, p. 31)

To reach such a conclusion, factors which may have accelerated one's death through unconscious or conscious actions are carefully analyzed, considering motive, intent, and lethality (Scott et al., 2006; Shneidman, 1994).

It is important to note to international readers that terms such as *mode* and *manner of death* are foundational within the PA concept and are of US origin. They are comparable expressions often used interchangeability to refer to the circumstances leading to the cause of death (Simmons, 2007). Generally, these terms are extrinsically linked with the so-called NASH classification system, where the categories include natural death, accident, suicide, and homicide (Bartol & Bartol, 2008; Leenaars, 2017; Scott et al., 2006; Young, 1992). *Equivocal death* is also an Americanism specific to the PA. Lacks et al. (2008) defined equivocal death as "any death where there is doubt or uncertainty clouding any obvious conviction as to whether the death occurred due to natural forces, an accident, was self-inflicted or malicious" (p. 150).

Since its inception in 1958, PA has transcended the forensic arena. Despite PA's initial purpose to identify manner (mode) of death, the use of the PA started to change, as noted by Shneidman (1969). After some work of their own group, Litman et al. (1963) published an analysis of 100 consecutive cases of equivocal suicides, raising also the question, how accurate are suicide statistics? In Shneidman's view (1969), there were three main questions to which the PA could respond:

- Why did the individual do it?
- How did the individual die?
- What is the most accurate mode of death?

The two first questions can be responded to only after the manner (or mode) of death is already determined. As Shneidman (2004) noted: "in cases in which death is clearly suicidal (with suicide notes). In these few cases, the goal of the procedure is to help understand the why of the suicidal death" (p. 32), while the last question is behind the initial development of the PA. Based mainly on Shneidman's work, Ebert (1987) noted four main purposes of the PA: (1) explaining the manner of death; (2) scrutinizing why the death occurred at a particular time; (3) accessing data useful in the prediction of suicide and in the assessment of lethality; and (4) for therapeutic purposes, to help the grieving processes of the bereaved relatives and friends. Jacobs and Klein (1993) added also the purpose of the PA as a research tool to help us to understand and prevent suicides.

Clinical Psychological Autopsy

Simultaneously with the work by Shneidman and his colleagues in Los Angeles, a similar approach to studying people who had died by suicide was utilized by other US researchers in St. Louis County, Missouri (Robins et al., 1959) and in the Seattle area (Dorpat & Ripley, 1960). Their studies were also conducted in the second part of the 1950s and collected information by interviewing relatives of people who had died by suicide and postmortem review documents (Clark & Horton-Deutsch, 1992). Different from the traditional PA, their aim was to identify clinical features of people who died by suicide, using a narrative style.

They utilized structured interviews with the main focus on recognizing (diagnosing) psychiatric conditions. A number of reviews have considered these studies as the first psychological autopsies (Clark & Horton-Deutsch, 1992; Conner et al., 2011; Isometsä, 2001). Nevertheless, they do not use the term PA, as they were conducted prior to its development and the coining of the term by Shneidman in 1958, and they were subsequently called *clinical psychological autopsies* (Robins, 1981). However, some researchers have suggested that the use of the term *psychiatric autopsy* would have been more appropriate (e.g., Pridmore & Walter, 2013).

This approach was later widened into case-control studies by the inclusion of the control group(s) (Isometsä, 2001; see Chapter 6 for more on case-control studies) and also adding psychometric scales (e.g., life event inventories and personality questionnaires), with the focus remaining on psychiatric disorders. The overemphasis of psychiatric conditions has been criticized as causing (over)medicalization (De Leo, 2002), with an almost unique focus on psychiatric conditions in suicide research and prevention (Gavin & Rogers, 2006; Pouliot & De Leo, 2006; Pridmore, 2015). Furthermore, the ability of PA studies to determine postmortem diagnosis using third-person information and a structured format has been considered flawed by some authors (Hjelmeland et al., 2012; Leenaars, 2017). It is also important to note that this stream of the PA in suicide research was not proposed by Shneidman (Leenaars, 2017).

Forensic Versus Research Approach

LaFon (1999, 2008) proposed a simple distinction between two main types of PA: forensic – in an *equivocal death psychological autopsy* – and research – the *suicide psychological autopsy* (SPA). While both utilize the PA concept, the equivocal death psychological autopsy follows traditional forensic lines of inquiries to assist with determining the manner of death, and to assist with criminal proceedings if applicable (LaFon, 1999). The SPA should be conducted when the manner of death as suicide has been determined. Important knowledge concerning psychosocial, mental health, or other factors that may have contributed to a suicidal death can be understood through the SPA. For further clarification, we can also distinguish between qualitative and quantitative PA.

Over the years, the PA has been extensively utilized by forensic systems to determine manner (or mode) of death, and also in suicide research. The PA is well-established in the US and is admissible as evidence in a court in some states – for example, Minnesota (Caulkins, 2019), including in high-level cases such as the death of Marilyn Monroe (Botello et al., 2013; Litman, 1996). The PA has also been adopted abroad, and is currently practiced in the courts of countries such as Australia, Canada, France, India, and the UK (Aquila et al., 2018; Botello et al., 2013; Saxena & Saini, 2017).

Suicide research has also extensively used the PA for both narrative (qualitative) and structured (quantitative) approaches to analyze why people die by suicide in order to support preventive activities. Based on our Scopus searches of the peer-reviewed research papers on the *psychological autopsy*, it seems that it became more widely popular in suicide research from the end of the 1980s (Figure 11.1). There has been a notable increase in its use in non-Western countries: while papers come from nearly 30 countries, the majority of the studies were conducted in China (Figure 11.1).

The wider use of the PA comes with differences in professional adoption, terminology, classification systems, and diagnostic instruments, but also the question of cross-cultural adoptability, which have made understanding the modern methodology increasingly difficult (Ebert, 1987). Such confusion leaves the technique open to interpretation and continued criticism. A number of authors, writing from both forensic and research perspectives, have noted the absence of a standardized protocol, which has led practitioners to rely on their own assumptions and/or experience based on evidence in the literature (Ebert, 1987; Snider et al., 2006). We will take a further look at the development of the methodology of the PA with the main focus on the research approach.

Methodology

Qualitative Versus Quantitative Approaches

As noted earlier, when it comes to data gathering, there are two streams of PA studies, a factor that also influences the data analysis. On the one hand, there is the traditional narrative style as proposed by Shneidman, and on the other hand, the structured quantitative style from clinical PAs.

Early procedural guidelines by Shneidman (1969) were qualitative and consisted of a 16-item recommended outline of the PA (see Box 11.1), also referred to as *Shneidman technique* (e.g., by Lacks et al., 2008). The importance of narratives in the forensic field was emphasized (Bullis, 2012). However, a number of researchers have noted a lack of guidance in the literature about how to conduct a PA, and called for the standardization of PA procedures. For example, Ebert (1987) proposed a 26-item guideline categorized against the components

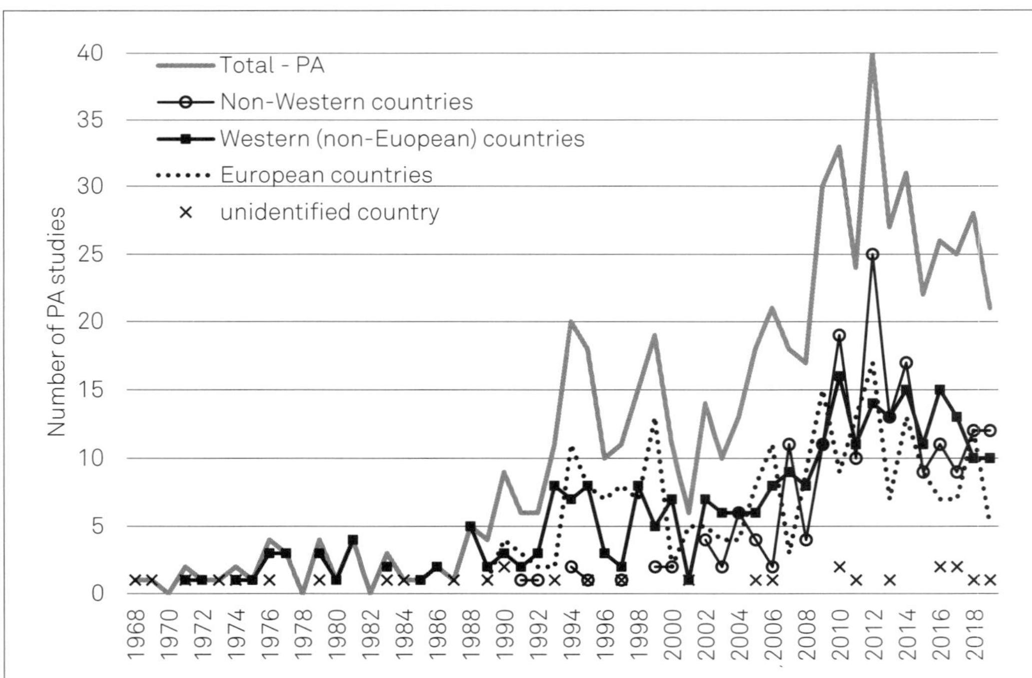

Figure 11.1 Annual number of psychological autopsy (PA) studies in different regions. Based on data collected on Scopus on January 10, 2020.

he held as crucial for the administration of the PA. While his guide was more detailed and extensive compared with Shneidman's, other researchers have pushed for further standardization, noting the existing guidelines are too general (Werlang & Botega, 2003). Other attempts at standardization and quantification include the evolution of the Operational Criteria for the Determination of Suicide (OCDS; Rosenberg et al., 1988); the Empirical Criteria for the Determination of Suicide (ECDS; Jobes et al., 1991); the Semistructured Interview for Psychological Autopsy (SIPA; Werlang & Botega, 2003), which is a standardized protocol based on a survey of suicidologist-forensic experts (Snider et al., 2006); and the use of base rates and predictive modeling (Simmons, 2007). Nevertheless, those standardization attempts are mainly focused on determining the manner of death.

Box 11.1. Outline for psychological autopsy by Shneidman

1. Identifying information (including name, age, address, marital status, religious practices, and occupation)
2. Details of the death (including cause of death if known)
3. Outline of decedent's history (siblings, medical issues, medical treatment, psychotherapy, previous suicide attempts)
4. Death history of decedent's family (suicides, cancer, other fatal illnesses, ages at death, and other details)
5. Description of lifestyle and personality
6. Typical patterns of reactions to stress, emotional upsets, and periods of disequilibrium
7. Any recent (within the 12 months prior to death) upsets, pressures, tensions, or anticipated trouble
8. Role of alcohol and drugs in (a) overall lifestyle of decedent and (b) their death
9. Nature of decedent's interpersonal relationships (including physicians)
10. Fantasies, dreams, thoughts, premonitions, or fears of decedent relating to death, accident, or suicide
11. Changes in decedent before death (of habits, hobbies, eating, sexual patterns, and other life routines)
12. Information relating to the life side of the decedent (upswings, successes, plans)
13. Assessment of intentions (i.e., role of the decedent in their demise)
14. Rating of lethality
15. Reactions of informants to decedent's death
16. Comments, special features, etc.

Reprinted from Shneidman, E.S., (1969). Suicide, lethality, and the psychological autopsy. *International Psychiatry Clinics, 6*(2), pp. 246–247.

Qualitative studies may have been underutilized in suicide research (Hjelmeland & Knizek, 2010; see Chapter 9 for qualitative methods). However, there has been an increase in qualitative research in the last decade. For example, the 16-item outline by Shneidman, as an interview guide, has been used in some recent PA studies utilizing mainly modified interpretative phenomenological analysis (Andoh-Arthur et al., 2018; Kizza et al., 2012; Rasmussen et al., 2018). Nevertheless, other qualitative analysis methods have also been utilized in combination with the PA. For example, Kjølseth et al. (2010) used the systematic text condensation method (including features from phenomenological and grounded theory) for qualitative analysis of a PA study about older adult suicides in Norway. See Box 11.2 for an example of a qualitative PA study from Uganda.

Box 11.2. Example of a qualitative psychological autopsy study from Uganda

Research has found links between suicide and alcohol use. Alcohol abuse and intoxication have both been found to increase the risk of suicide. Alcohol consumption has increased especially in low- and middle-income countries in recent decades. Over 2 decades (1986–2006), northern Uganda was impacted by civil conflict between the Ugandan Government armed forces and rebel groups. Internally displaced people (IDP) camps and forced inactivity are likely to have increased alcohol consumption in the country. Therefore, the authors aimed to analyze in-depth the role of alcohol in suicides in postconflict northern Uganda (Acholi subregion).

The qualitative psychological autopsy method was utilized with interviews including both narrative- and problem-focused elements. The main narrative question was describing the circumstances that surrounded the suicidal death of their loved one. The problem-focused questions were guided by Shneidman's (1969) 16-item outline for a psychological autopsy (see Box 11.1). Researchers identified 20 people who died by suicide (17 men and 3 women) with alcohol use being a feature prior to suicide in 16 out of the 20 decedents (80 %; 14 men and 2 women). They were divided into four groups: one-time drinkers of alcohol, social drinkers, problem drinkers, and *victims* of others' alcohol use. Two to five informants over the age 18 (close or extended family members or friends) were interviewed. Informants were identified through local leaders followed by snowballing technique.

As suicides and suicide attempts are a criminal offence, suicides for the study were identified mainly through police records and local leaders. The families, or informants, were first approached by a coordinator and a local leader to request their participation and set an appointment for the interview. The interviewer was introduced to the family by the coordinator. Individual interviews were conducted with individuals who were eligible and consented to the study. Interviews were mainly conducted in IDP camps, but also at a health facility, or at home within 5.5 to 19 months after suicide. Data was collected by a clinical psychologist who is Ugandan, but from another ethnic group, therefore interviews were conducted in English (the official language of Uganda). As the majority of informants spoke only their mother tongue (Acholi), the study used interpreters. The interpreters were carefully selected and trained. For a smooth flow, the interpreter just summarized the responses.

All interviews were recorded and transcribed. A modified interpretative phenomenological analysis (IPA) was used for data analysis to get an in-depth understanding of the role of alcohol in the decedents' suicides. The approach was modified as information came from relatives, but in the original IPA, the units of analysis should be the participants themselves. Ethical clearance was obtained from all relevant ethics committees.

Alcohol use had direct and indirect impacts on suicides. Main themes included alcohol as a facilitator, alcohol as means to suicide, and alcohol's influence on the lifestyle impacting suicide directly; indirectly, alcohol was also found to influence the suicidal process of though the drinking of significant others.

Based on Kizza, D., Hjelmeland, H. M., Kinyanda, E., & Knizek, B. L. (2012). Alcohol and suicide in postconflict northern Uganda. *Crisis, 33*(2), 95–105.

As previously noted, the use of standardized tools with the focus on psychiatric conditions in quantitative PA studies stems from the early clinical PA studies (Conner et al., 2011; Hawton et al., 1998; Isometsä, 2001; Pouliot & De Leo, 2006). The most frequently used questionnaires to measure psychiatric disorders include versions of Structured Clinical Interview

(SCID) for DSM-III and DSM-IV, Mini International Neuropsychiatric Interview (MINI), and Schedule for Affective Disorders and Schizophrenia (SADS; Conner et al., 2011; Pouliot & De Leo, 2006). However, the use of those measures has not been properly tested for their use in proxies and potential for misclassification by practitioners, including interviewer fallacy, which is likely to lead to overdiagnosing of psychiatric disorders (Hjelmeland et al., 2012; Leenaars, 2017; Pouliot & De Leo, 2006).

The majority of clinical PA studies include enquires about life events utilizing a variety of different scales about varying time periods (Conner et al., 2011; Pouliot & De Leo, 2006). There have been calls to expand the number of factors studied (Conner et al., 2011), including also socioenvironmental factors (Pouliot & De Leo, 2006). Over time, different approaches to the PA have shown some blending, and other studies have been able to utilize the information collected for a quantitative PA for further qualitative analyses. For example, Owens and Lambert (2012) have used narrative information initially collected in the framework of a PA case-control study (Owens et al., 2003) in a further qualitative analysis.

Information Sources

Considering that the main goals of PA studies are to reconstruct a person's life trajectory, and biography and circumstances of death, various forms of data are collected, reviewed, and synthesized. As noted earlier, the two main information sources include (1) the review of collateral records and (2) interviews with informants including relatives, friends, and colleagues, but also with health care professionals and other related officials. There has been no notable addition or subtraction to these practices since their introduction in the late 1950s (Botello et al., 2013; Shneidman, 1981).

Collateral Records

A review of collateral records is defined as the analysis of combinations of various information sources – that is, police and coronial reports, medical reports, personal diaries, financial records (Leenaars, 2017; Snider et al., 2006), mobile phones, and social media accounts (Aquila et al., 2018). Both the forensic and research approaches utilize medical and police or coronial records as essential information sources. However, there is a lack of standard procedure for how to use different sources. Some researchers have pointed out that practitioners are left to rely on their own experience and assumptions when considering relevant sources to evaluate (Snider et al., 2006). Considering the development of new technologies, Aquila and colleagues (2018) proposed analyzing information from mobile phones and social media, calling this a *social-mobile autopsy*.

Informants

Following Shneidman (1981), the PA "is done by talking to some key persons – spouse, lover, parent, grown child, friend, colleague, physician, supervisor, co-worker – who knew the decedent" (p. 330). As noted by Leenaars (2017), "Regardless of whether we use Shneidman' paradigm or not, many informants must be used in PA studies." Traditionally, research studies have included close and extended family members, friends, and physicians (Brent, 1989; Hawton et al., 1998; Knoll, 2008; Pouliot & De Leo, 2006). Involving multiple informants is important considering that close family members can be impacted by different feelings including self-blame and anger, which may influence their narratives. This is especially the case for parents (Dieserud et al., 2015). In addition to interviews with parents of adolescents, information from their siblings or friends should be sought, as parents may be unaware of aspects related to their children's drug problems or sex life (Brent, 1989; Hawton et al., 1998; Leenaars, 2017). Furthermore, close family members may also minimize the impact of family quarrels.

An additional issue is contradictory information from different sources (Dieserud et al., 2015; Leenaars, 2017). This is a major challenge and potential cause of bias in quantitative PA studies, where information from different informants needs to be synthesized into one suicide case. How to unify the information from the different informants is a complex problem (Pouliot & De Leo, 2006; Zhang et al., 2018). A few techniques have been recommended, such as the use of a *rate-up* strategy for symptoms and life events, and averaging for scales (Conner et al., 2012; Phillips et al., 2002; Zhang et al., 2018). Nevertheless, the use of different methods to synthesize information obtained is likely to produce different results.

Timing

While the timing of contacting bereaved informants to conduct the interview varies, there is general agreement that it should not occur too early during the intensive grief period (Conner et al., 2011; Hawton et al., 2003; Pouliot & De Leo, 2006). Earlier studies seem to recommend shorter time frames – for example, Diller (1979) recommended that the first contact happen between 4 weeks and 2 months after death. Beskow et al. (1991) reported that they contacted informants as early as 4 weeks after their loss, in their PA studies, but noted that there did not seem to be an impairment in the quality of information if the interviews were conducted later. Brent (1989) collected information at between 2 and 6 months, and found no impact of timing. Based on their experiences, Hawton et al. (1998) recommended the optimal timeframe to be between 3 months and 1 year.

Identifying and Contacting Informants

The majority of studies have identified informants from coronial or police records. The first contact with a potential participant is crucial to participation rates (Rudestam, 1979). A high response rate has been reported for those studies where persons were directly contacted – knocking on their door or making a phone call, which was common practice in early studies. The currently accepted approach is sending a letter, which is followed by a phone contact 1–2 weeks afterwards (Hawton et al., 1998). It has also been noted that relatives of people who were under psychiatric care prior to suicide are more likely to participate in PA studies (Hawton et al., 1998).

Interview Process

Traditionally, interviews are conducted in a semistructured format, which may vary by the type of PA (qualitative or quantitative). While historically face-to-face interviews have been recommended, they can be also conducted over the phone to reduce the costs of travel. If possible, recording of interviews will guarantee quality control and avoid the need for note taking.

The interview should start with an introduction explaining the rationale of the study and the rights of the participants (e.g., to withdraw from the study, postpone the interview, and take breaks). Initial questions should be open questions offering the interviewee the opportunity to talk about their relationship with the deceased, what type of a person they were and the circumstances of their death. As the interview progresses, the interviewer can move to structured questionnaires, depending on the study type. The interview should end by thanking the participant and emphasizing the importance of their contribution (Conner et al., 2012; Hawton et al., 1998). It is also recommended to pilot test the interview content and order of questions (Cooper, 1999).

It has been advised that interviews should be conducted by interviewers who have some clinical background, including psychiatrists, psychologist, and nurses, but also social workers. Training of clinical interviewers is necessary, and interviewer guidelines for the study are also proposed. Ongoing supervision and support of interviewers is required (Conner et al., 2012; Cooper, 1999; Hawton et al., 1998; Pouliot & De Leo, 2006).

Impact of PA on Participants

Interviews with the bereaved by suicide may arouse emotional reactions, given their likely feelings of sadness, guilt, shame, and anger (Hawton et al., 2003). In Shneidman's opinion (1981), an additional purpose of the PA was to support the bereaved (*postvention)*, since he noted the therapeutic effect the PA interviews had on relatives. "This [PA] procedure also serves to assuage some of the feelings of guilt and shame of the survivors and has a therapeutic mental health effect in the community" (Shneidman, 2004, p. 32; NB: *Suicide survivor* in US terminology refers to people bereaved by suicide). Several studies have approached this point more systematically. Analyses from Sweden (Beskow et al., 1991) and the UK (Hawton et al., 2003) have confirmed that the majority of bereaved participants benefit from the interview, with only a few participants finding it a negative experience.

The qualitative approach has also been used to analyze the experience of PA participants. A PA study with 97 bereaved informants from Norway identified, through a qualitative analysis, that the majority considered the experience as overall positive (62%) (Dyregrov et al., 2011). The PA interview gave bereaved persons an opportunity to vent their feelings, such as sadness and anger; it seems that the interview eased their distress. Some even called it a therapy, which increased their insight and understanding capabilities and gave them the opportunity to have something positive to come out of negative. Less than a third (28%) considered it *a positive but painful experience* – they were concerned about their reactions beforehand and insecure about expressing themselves during the interview – while the remaining 10% considered the PA interview to be a neutral and an unproblematic experience (Dyregrov et al., 2011). Another PA study from Montreal (35 relatives interviewed about adolescent and young adult suicide cases), reported that PA helped relatives to find a meaning and reduced feelings of guilt (63%). It was also perceived as an altruistic gesture (34%) to prevent suicides by contributing to scientific knowledge and receiving support (26%). The PA interview gave the bereaved the opportunity to talk about their loss and could serve to alleviate their sense of isolation (Henry & Greenfield, 2009).

Control Groups

Different observational study designs can be utilized for PA studies, including case reports, case series, and case-control studies (for more more details, see Chapter 6). A number of reviews have emphasized the importance of including a control group (Clark & Horton-Deutsch, 1992; Conner et al., 2011; Hawton et al., 1998; Pouliot & De Leo, 2006). However, case-control studies are subject to a number of different biases, and choosing a suitable control group can be a challenging task, as discussed in Chapter 6 with an example of a case-control PA study from Hong Kong.

Cultural Adaptability

As noted earlier, to better understand suicide, the use of the PA has spread across the globe, to different continents and ethnic and cultural groups. However, the acceptability of a Western-developed tool in other cultural contexts is an important question, and adaptation to a different cultural context is very important. While the use of a qualitative approach might be more acceptable, for the quantitative PA approach utilizing different scales, it is advisable to first conduct a feasibility study to test the methodology, questionnaires, and ethical and cultural acceptability. For example, Zhang et al. (2002) conducted a feasibility study in China to test the PA methodology with the focus on its social and cultural acceptability. Nevertheless, full comparability across different cultures is not achievable (Conner et al., 2011).

Ethical Considerations

There are numerous ethical considerations that need to be addressed when designing and conducting PA studies (Beskow et al., 1990, 1991; Cooper, 1999). Is it ethical to contact bereaved people? When and how should we do it? Who should conduct interviews and how? The majority of these questions have been addressed throughout this chapter. However, similar to all types of research, it is a central issue to ensure that the rights of participants are completely respected. To participate in the study, all participants have to be given full details about the study, and they need to sign a consent form. They have the right to withdraw from the study at any point or postpone the interview, without this causing any guilt or harm to the bereaved. It is also important to give information about sources of help in the area, if participants need it, and the possibility of contacting the study team after the interview, if required, or to provide a follow-up call to participants a few weeks later (Beskow et al., 1991; Hawton et al., 2003). As noted by Beskow et al. (1990), in PA studies, we need to keep in mind that we have to also respect the integrity of the deceased.

Conclusions

The PA has provided significant value in suicide research, bereavement, and postvention, and in legal areas and forensic investigations. Nevertheless, undertaking a PA study is time-consuming and expensive. Therefore, it is important to consider carefully and in detail: What is your research question? What are the new factors that should be looked at? What aspects already identified may need a fresh look? What subgroups should be studied? Should we utilize a qualitative or quantitative approach?

References

Andoh-Arthur, J., Knizek, B. L., Osafo, J., & Hjelmeland, H. M. (2018). Suicide among men in Ghana: The burden of masculinity. *Death Studies, 42*, 658–666. https://doi.org/10.1080/07481187.2018.1426655

Aquila, I., Sacco, M., Gratteri, S., Sirianni, M., De Fazio, P., & Ricci, P. (2018). The "Social-mobile autopsy": The evolution of psychological autopsy with new technologies in forensic investigations on suicide. *Legal Medicine, 32*, 79–82. https://doi.org/10.1016/j.legalmed.2017.12.008

Bartol, C. R., & Bartol, A. M. (2008). *Introduction to forensic psychology: Research and application.* Thousand Oaks, CA, US: Sage Publications.

Beskow, J., Runeson, B., & Åsgård, U. (1990). Psychological autopsies: Methods and ethics. *Suicide and Life-Threatening Behavior, 20*(4), 307–320.

Beskow, J., Runeson, B., & Åsgård, U. (1991). Ethical aspects of psychological autopsy. *Acta Psychiatrica Scandinavica, 84*(5), 482–487. https://doi.org/10.1111/j.1600-0447.1991.tb03181.x

Botello, T., Noguchi, T., Sathyavagiswaran, L., Weinberger, L. E., & Gross, B. H. (2013). Evolution of the psychological autopsy: Fifty years of experience at the Los Angeles County Chief Medical Examiner-Coroner's Office. *Journal of Forensic Sciences, 58*(4), 924–926. https://doi.org/10.1111/1556-4029.12138

Brent, D. A. (1989). The psychological autopsy: Methodological considerations for the study of adolescent suicide. *Suicide and Life-Threatening Behavior, 19*(1), 43–57. https://doi.org/10.1111/j.1943-278X.1989.tb00365.x

Bullis, R. K. (2012). Narrative approaches in psychological autopsies: Suggestions for methodologies and training. *Journal of Forensic Psychology Practice, 12*(2), 124–146. https://doi.org/10.1080/15228932.2012.650075

Caulkins, C. G. (2019). *The psychological autopsy: What, who, and why.* Retrieved from https://www.researchgate.net/publication/332835408_The_Psychological_Autopsy_What_Who_and_Why

Clark, D. C., & Horton-Deutsch, S. L. (1992). Assessment in absentia: The value of the psychological autopsy method for studying antecedents of suicide and predicting future suicides. In R. W. Maris, A. L. Berman, J. T. Maltsberger, & R. I. Yufit (Eds.), *Assessment & prediction of suicide* (pp. 144–182). New York, NY: Guilford Press.

Conner, K. R., Beautrais, A. L., Brent, D. A., Conwell, Y., Phillips, M. R., & Schneider, B. (2011). The next generation of psychological autopsy studies: Part I. Interview content. *Suicide and Life-Threatening Behavior, 41*, 594–613. https://doi.org/10.1111/j.1943-278X.2011.00057.x

Conner, K. R., Beautrais, A. L., Brent, D. A., Conwell, Y., Phillips, M. R., & Schneider, B. (2012). The next generation of psychological autopsy studies: Part II: Interview procedures. *Suicide and Life-Threatening Behavior, 42*, 86–103. https://doi.org/10.1111/j.1943-278X.2011.00073.x

Cooper, J. (1999). Ethical issues and their practical application in a psychological autopsy study of suicide. *Journal of Clinical Nursing, 8*(4), 467–475. https://doi.org/10.1046/j.1365-2702.1999.00276.x

De Leo, D. (2002). Why are we not getting any closer to preventing suicide? *British Journal of Psychiatry, 181*(5), 372–374. https://doi.org/10.1192/bjp.181.5.372

Dieserud, G., Leenaars, A. A., & Dyregrov, K. (2015). The importance of many informants in PA studies. *Suicidology Online, 6*(2), 47–55.

Diller, J. (1979). The psychological autopsy in equivocal deaths. *Perspectives in Psychiatric Care, 17*(4), 156–161. https://doi.org/10.1111/j.1744-6163.1979.tb00971.x

Dorpat, T. L., & Ripley, H. S. (1960). A study of suicide in the Seattle area. *Comprehensive Psychiatry, 1*(6), 349–359. https://doi.org/10.1016/S0010-440X(60)80058-2

Dyregrov, K. M., Dieserud, G., Hjelmeland, H. M., Straiton, M., Rasmussen, M. L., Knizek, B. L., & Leenaars, A. A. (2011). Meaning-making through psychological autopsy interviews: The value of participating in qualitative research for those bereaved by suicide. *Death Studies, 35*(8), 685–710. https://doi.org/10.1080/07481187.2011.553310

Ebert, B. W. (1987). Guide to conducting a psychological autopsy. *Professional Psychology: Research and Practice, 18*(1), 52. https://doi.org/10.1037/0735-7028.18.1.52

Gavin, M., & Rogers, A. (2006). Narratives of suicide in psychological autopsy: Bringing lay knowledge back in. *Journal of Mental Health, 15*(2), 135–144. https://doi.org/10.1080/09638230600608735

Hawton, K., Appleby, L., Platt, S., Foster, T., Cooper, J., Malmberg, A., & Simkin, S. (1998). The psychological autopsy approach to studying suicide: a review of methodological issues. *Journal of Affective Disorders, 50*(2–3), 269–276.

Hawton, K., Houston, K., Malmberg, A., & Simkin, S. (2003). Psychological autopsy interviews in suicide research: The reactions of informants. *Archives of Suicide Research, 7*(1), 73–82. https://doi.org/10.1080/13811110301566

Henry, M., & Greenfield, B.J. (2009). Therapeutic effects of psychological autopsies: The impact of investigating suicides on interviewees. *Crisis, 30*(1), 20. https://doi.org/10.1027/0227-5910.30.1.20

Hjelmeland, H.M., Dieserud, G., Dyregrov, K.M., Knizek, B.L., & Leenaars, A.A. (2012). Psychological autopsy studies as diagnostic tools: are they methodologically flawed? *Death Studies, 36*(7), 605–626. https://doi.org/10.1080/07481187.2011.584015

Hjelmeland, H.M., & Knizek, B.L. (2010). Why we need qualitative research in suicidology. *Suicide and Life-Threatening Behavior, 40*(1), 74–80. https://doi.org/10.1521/suli.2010.40.1.74

Isometsä, E. (2001). Psychological autopsy studies: A review. *European Psychiatry, 16*(7), 379–385. https://doi.org/10.1016/S0924-9338(01)00594-6

Jacobs, D., & Klein, M.E. (1993). The expanding role of psychological autopsies. In A. Leenaars (Ed.), *Suicidology: Essays in honor of Edwin S. Shneidman.* Northvale, NJ: Aronson.

Jobes, D.A., Casey, J.O., Berman, A.L., & Wright, D.G. (1991). Empirical criteria for the determination of suicide manner of death. *Journal of Forensic Science, 36*(1), 244–256. https://doi.org/10.1520/JFS13025J

Kizza, D., Hjelmeland, H.M., Kinyanda, E., & Knizek, B.L. (2012). Alcohol and suicide in postconflict northern Uganda. *Crisis, 33*(2), 95–105. https://doi.org/10.1027/0227-5910/a000119

Kjølseth, I., Ekeberg, Ø., & Steihaug, S. (2010). Why suicide? Elderly people who committed suicide and their experience of life in the period before their death. *International Psychogeriatrics, 22*(2), 209–218. https://doi.org/10.1017/S1041610209990949

Knoll, J.L. I. (2008). The psychological autopsy, part I: applications and methods. *Journal of Psychiatric Practice, 14*(6), 393–397. https://doi.org/10.1097/01.pra.0000341894.35877.1b

Lacks, R.D., Westveer, A.E., Dibble, A., & Clemente, J. (2008). Equivocal death investigation: Case study analyses. *Victims and Offenders, 3*(2–3), 150–164. https://doi.org/10.1080/15564880801938292

LaFon, D.S. (1999). Psychological autopsies for equivocal deaths. *International Journal of Emergency Mental Health, 1*(3), 183–188.

LaFon, D.S. (2008). The psychological autopsy. In B.E. Turvey (Ed.), *Criminal profiling: An introduction to behavioral evidence analysis* (3rd ed., pp. 419–429). Burlington, MA: Academic Press.

Leenaars, A.A. (2017). *The psychological autopsy: A roadmap for uncovering the barren bones of the suicide's mind.* New York, NY: Routledge. https://doi.org/10.4324/9781315266213

Litman, R.E. (1996). Suicidology: A look backward and ahead. *Suicide and Life-Threatening Behavior, 26*(1), 1–7.

Litman, R.E., Curphey, T., Shneidman, E.S., Farberow, N.L., & Tabachnick, N. (1963). Investigations of equivocal suicides. *JAMA, 184*(12), 924–929. https://doi.org/10.1001/jama.1963.03700250060008

Owens, C., Booth, N., Briscoe, M., Lawrence, C., & Lloyd, K. (2003). Suicide outside the care of mental health services: A case-controlled psychological autopsy study. *Crisis, 24*(3), 113. https://doi.org/10.1027//0227-5910.24.3.113

Owens, C., & Lambert, H. (2012). Mad, bad or heroic? Gender, identity and accountability in lay portrayals of suicide in late twentieth-century England. *Culture, Medicine, and Psychiatry, 36*(2), 348–371. https://doi.org/10.1007/s11013-012-9259-x

Phillips, M.R., Yang, G., Zhang, Y., Wang, L., Ji, H., & Zhou, M. (2002). Risk factors for suicide in China: A national case-control psychological autopsy study. *Lancet, 360*(9347), 1728–1736.

Pouliot, L., & De Leo, D. (2006). Critical issues in psychological autopsy studies. *Suicide and Life-Threatening Behavior, 36*(5), 491–510. https://doi.org/10.1521/suli.2006.36.5.491

Pridmore, S. (2015). Mental disorder and suicide: A faulty connection. *Australian & New Zealand Journal of Psychiatry, 49*(1), 18–20. https://doi.org/10.1177/0004867414548904

Pridmore, S., & Walter, G. (2013). Psychological autopsies. *Australian & New Zealand Journal of Psychiatry, 47*(9), 878–879. https://doi.org/10.1177/0004867413495929

Rasmussen, M.L., Haavind, H., & Dieserud, G. (2018). Young men, masculinities, and suicide. *Archives of Suicide Research, 22*(2), 327–343. https://doi.org/10.1080/13811118.2017.1340855

Robins, E. (1981). *The final months: A study of the lives of 134 persons who committed suicide.* New York, NY: Oxford University Press.

Robins, E., Murphy, G.E., Wilkinson, R.H., Jr. Gassner, S., & Kayes, J. (1959). Some clinical considerations in the prevention of suicide based on a study of 134 successful suicides. *American Journal of Public Health and the Nations Health, 49*(7), 888–899. https://doi.org/10.2105/AJPH.49.7.888

Rosenberg, M.L., Davidson, L.E., Smith, J.C., Berman, A.L., Buzbee, H., Gantner, G., ... Murray, D. (1988). Operational criteria for the determination of suicide. *Journal of Forensic Science, 33*(6), 1445–1456. https://doi.org/10.1520/JFS12589J

Rudestam, K.E. (1979). Some notes on conducting a psychological autopsy. *Suicide and Life-Threatening Behavior, 9*(3), 141–144.

Saxena, G., & Saini, V. (2017). Psychological autopsy: A way to revealing the enigma of equivocal death. *International Journal of Forensic Sciences, 2*(2), 1–8.

Scott, C.L., Swartz, E., & Warburton, K. (2006). The psychological autopsy: Solving the mysteries of death. *Psychiatric Clinics, 29*, 805–822. https://doi.org/10.1016/j.psc.2006.04.003

Shneidman, E.S. (1969). Suicide, lethality, and the psychological autopsy. *International Psychiatry Clinics, 6*(2), 225–250.

Shneidman, E.S. (1981). The psychological autopsy. *Suicide and Life-Threatening Behavior, 11*, 325–340.

Shneidman, E.S. (1994). The psychological autopsy. *American Psychologist, 49*(1), 75–76. https://doi.org/10.1037/0003-066X.49.1.75

Shneidman, E.S. (2004). *Autopsy of a suicidal mind.* New York, NY: Oxford University Press.

Simmons, S. (2007). Dead mean walking: The use of base rates as an adjunct to psychological autopsy. *American Journal of Forensic Psychiatry, 28*(2), 51–65.

Snider, J.E., Hane, S., & Berman, A.L. (2006). Standardizing the psychological autopsy: Addressing the Daubert standard. *Suicide and Life-Threatening Behavior, 36*, 511–518. https://doi.org/10.1521/suli.2006.36.5.511

Werlang, B.G., & Botega, N.J. (2003). A semi-structured interview for psychological autopsy in suicide cases. *Brazilian Journal of Psychiatry, 25*(4), 212–219. https://doi.org/10.1590/S1516-44462003000400006

Young, T.J. (1992). Personality assessment in equivocal deaths. *Journal of Personality Assessment, 58*, 430–431. https://doi.org/10.1207/s15327752jpa5802_19

Zhang, J., Wang, Y., & Fang, L. (2018). How to integrate proxy data from two informants in life event assessment in psychological autopsy. *BMC psychiatry, 18*(1), 115. https://doi.org/10.1186/s12888-018-1698-7

Zhang, J., Wieczorek, W.F., Jiang, C., Zhou, L., Jia, S., Sun, Y., ... Conwell, Y. (2002). Studying suicide with psychological autopsy: Social and cultural feasibilities of the methodology in China. *Suicide and Life-Threatening Behavior, 32*, 370–379. https://doi.org/10.1521/suli.32.4.370.22342

Chapter 12

Pilot and Feasibility Studies in Suicide Research

David Watling and Kairi Kõlves

Summary

Preliminary studies including feasibility and pilot studies are a critical component of research. Feasibility and pilot studies can identify methodological, practical, and ethical concerns prior to an expensive full-scale study. This chapter explores the differences and similarities between feasibility and pilot studies. In addition, key methodological (i.e., retention, sampling, outcome selection) and analysis considerations in preliminary research are discussed. Finally, researchers are provided with guidance for reporting standards and moving from feasibility and pilot studies to full-scale studies.

Preliminary research to determine the feasibility of an observational or an intervention study and its ability to answer a research question is an important step prior to an extensive, expensive full-scale study (Cope, 2015; Morris & Rosenbloom, 2017). Such preliminary research can be used to self-assess readiness; and identify ethical, practical, or participant sampling and retention issues, as well as refine the research question, determine the practicality of an intervention, and demonstrate the value of the intervention to funding agencies (Cope, 2015; Doody & Doody, 2015). This chapter will focus on preliminary research with attention paid to methodological considerations, analysis, reporting standards, and progressing from preliminary research into full-scale studies, with the main attention given to intervention studies. While the areas addressed are not unique to suicide research, and apply to preliminary research in multiple domains, we provide examples from suicide research to reinforce each topic. To begin our exploration into preliminary studies, we disentangle pilot and feasibility studies.

Feasibility or Pilot Study?

The terms *feasibility study* and *pilot study* have been used interchangeably to describe the preliminary stage of research (Arain, Campbell, Cooper, & Lancaster, 2010); however, each are unique phases and have unique requirements (Eldridge, Chan, et al., 2016; Eldridge, Lancaster, et al., 2016). Nonetheless, there is a degree of overlap in the outcomes measured between the two. In light of this, Eldridge, Lancaster, et al. (2016; among others; e.g., Arain et al., 2010) developed a conceptual framework to define and clarify the distinction between preliminary studies, informed by the UK's National Evaluation, Trials and Studies Coordinating Centre (NETSCC).

Importantly, the NETSCC reinforces the notion that preliminary studies (feasibility and pilot) ought to be conducted should there be uncertainty in the conduct of a new intervention study. Moreover, it stipulates that preliminary studies should be globally understood as feasibility studies, with three distinct types: *randomized pilot studies*, *nonrandomized pilot studies*, and *feasibility studies* that are not pilot studies (henceforth referred to simply as feasibility studies; Abbott, 2014). While it is commonplace for researchers to report both a feasibility and pilot study within the same paper, the two are still distinct. Indeed, the extended Consolidated Standards of Reporting Trials (CONSORT) guidelines suggest distinguishing between primary (feasibility) and secondary (pilot) objectives (Eldridge, Chan, et al., 2016).

Feasibility Study

A *feasibility study* has been defined as "research done to assist the design of the main study and to answer the question 'Can the study be done?'" (Billingham, Whitehead, & Julious, 2013, p. 2; see also Eldridge, Chan, et al., 2016; Eldridge, Lancaster, et al., 2016). In response to this question, a feasibility study may also be used to assess the acceptability of an intervention or a questionnaire. In suicide research, prototypical feasibility studies explore feasibility, including uptake, access, resources and time, training, and acceptability including engagement, attendance, therapeutic alliance, and satisfaction outcome (e.g., Haddock et al., 2019; Hill & Pettit, 2019; Tracey, Rowney, Pignatiello, Monga, & Korczak, 2018). Intervention eligibility and refusal rates, follow-up rates, and completion rates have also been suggested as potential outcomes (Eldridge, Chan, et al., 2016). Moreover, feasibility studies may describe characteristics of proposed outcomes and variance estimates (Arain et al., 2010). A feasibility study will assist in determining the fluency, potential issues, and outcome characteristics in each of these areas and in turn will assist later trial implementation.

Details on what will be measured and how, and a justification for the study should be clearly presented in published protocols or in the background documents of the study (e.g., Eldridge, Chan, et al., 2016; Haddock et al., 2016). In addition to having clear outcome measures a priori, it is important, intuitively, to have preexisting standards for what would be acceptable and feasible, based on previous research and clinical guidance. For example, Haddock et al. (2019) reported what they deemed to be an acceptable number of attended sessions (i.e., criteria) prior to the study (Haddock et al., 2016). Having preset criteria will ensure it is clear whether the study is feasible and acceptable (or not). An example is presented in Box 12.1.

Box 12.1. Example of feasibility and pilot study that assessed the acceptability of a cognitive behavior intervention in suicide prevention

The UK study INSITE (INpatient Suicide Intervention and Therapy Evaluation) was conducted to assess the feasibility and acceptability of a cognitive behavior intervention in suicide prevention (CBSP) intervention in people with psychosis in an inpatient setting (while also conducting a nonrandomized pilot trial) and compared treatment as usual versus the CBSP protocol.

Regarding feasibility, this study reported:

- the mean number of sessions attended;
- the breakdown of numbers of participants in relevant areas (i.e., employment status, age, marital status, and living arrangements);
- attrition rates, adverse events, and therapeutic alliance (quantitatively with validated measures; qualitatively with interviews).

Although 178 participants were referred to the study, only 70 were eligible and only 51 patients were randomized (19 were discharged prior to baseline). Just over half of the offered sessions were attended, and most sessions were delivered in an outpatient setting. Moreover, most patients (62 %) attended the minimum 10 sessions (86 % attended at least five). Reasons for non-attendance were also documented, with only a mean of 1.83 sessions not attended without a reason.

These outcomes were deemed most important to the authors in terms of demonstrating intervention feasibility. However, this list could be adapted to suit a range of areas relevant to the intervention (e.g., call-back rates in a phone follow-up service). In such studies, descriptive statistics (%, n, range) ensure outcomes are clearly reported, and in this study, they were reported either in the text or in tables.

In addition to assessing feasibility and acceptability, a pilot trial of the CBSP intervention was also conducted to compare a treatment as usual group (TAU) to a group with TAU and the new intervention (CBSP). In the pilot trial, a range of secondary measures were taken including measuring a range of secondary outcomes including suicidal ideation, psychopathology, functioning, service use, and psychological measures of suicide – similar measures to what were proposed to be explored in the eventual full-scale trial; plus cost effectiveness.

While statistical analyses were conducted to explore outcomes preintervention and postintervention, no direct hypothesis testing was performed. Instead, means and standard deviations for each outcome were presented separately for the groups (i.e., TAU and CBSP), and a cost-effectiveness analysis was conducted to answer the initial research question – is the study feasible? Based on the obtained outcomes, the study was deemed to be acceptable, feasible, and cost-effective, and would progress to a full-scale study.

Based on Haddock, G., Pratt, D., Gooding, P.A., Peters, S., Emsley, R., Evans, E., ... Awenat, Y. (2019). Feasibility and acceptability of suicide prevention therapy on acute psychiatric wards: Randomised controlled trial. *BJPsych Open, 5*(1), e14.

Pilot Study

Pilot studies are technically considered a subset of the broader feasibility term (Eldridge, Chan, et al., 2016; Eldridge, Lancaster, et al., 2016). As such, there is some overlap between pilot and feasibility studies (Arain et al., 2010). Even so, pilot studies are defined separately as "a version of the main study that is run in miniature to test whether the components of the study can all work together" (Arain et al., 2010, p. 5). For example, researchers may seek to explore the effectiveness of blinding procedures, selection bias, recruitment rates, and how well these processes run. Additional outcomes may include the numbers of participants that meet inclusion criteria, complete treatment requirements, or complete follow-up assessments. A specific type of pilot study, the *pilot trial*, is put in place to determine if components of a proposed randomized controlled trial (RCT) will work (or not) when undertaken. Due to their lacking power (because of their small sample size), pilot trials should not discuss treatment effectiveness but may present pre versus post or group outcome measures. We also distinguish briefly here between randomized and nonrandomized pilot studies. The former includes participants being randomized to distinct groups whereas the latter does not (Eldridge, Lancaster, et al., 2016).

Methodological Considerations

Ironing out potential issues prior to full-scale trials by implementing preliminary studies can be achieved by taking a close look at intervention methodology. The current section presents methodological aspects of feasibility and pilot studies, including procedures, outcomes, and issues faced.

Methodological Considerations in Feasibility Studies

Procedures

In line with the aims of preliminary research, there are multiple factors to consider around study procedures. These can be addressed in both feasibility and pilot studies, and facilitated by checklists or guidelines. In terms of a feasibility study, where the focus is on whether the trial can be conducted, procedures that need to be addressed include assessing appropriateness of study design, adequacy and availability of resources, expectations of study components (e.g., data collection; Boeije, Drabble, & O'Cathain, 2015), and ensuring the validity and reliability of measurement tools (Hazzi & Maldaon, 2015). In line with this, Morris and Rosenbloom (2017) provide an 11-stage step-by-step guide in conducting feasibility research (i.e., feasibility or pilot studies). The guidelines cover important aspects that ought to be considered, including setting, sample size, recruitment, and data analysis, as well as seeking approval from institutional review boards (see Box 12.2).

Box 12.2. Guidelines for conducting preliminary studies

1. Identify a problem and/or a question.
2. Review the literature.
3. Identify gaps in our knowledge.
4. Refine the general question, formulating a specific research question(s).
5. Consider your reasons for conducting preliminary research & determine the form it should take.
   Evaluate the feasibility of carrying out the planned protocols and interventions of an anticipated larger study.
   a. Randomization of participants? Conduct randomized pilot study.
   b. Without randomizing participants? Conduct nonrandomized pilot study.
      Evaluate aspects of data collection, data management, the adequacy of resources to carry out a study, or other processes to be undertaken in an anticipated future trial (excluding the specific intervention and exact protocol) with a small sample?
   c. Conduct a feasibility study that is not a pilot study.
6. Design the study.
   a. Choose a research design (cross-sectional, cohort, or correlation, for example).
   b. Determine setting, sample size, recruitment strategy, randomization (if appropriate), instruments, data analysis, and procedures.
   c. Ensure protection of human subjects (submit plan for institutional review board approval).
7. Collaborate with stakeholders at the setting to minimize disruptions and obtain support.
8. Carry out the study.
9. Analyze the results.
10. Relate the findings to plans for a future study.
    a. Do results suggest it is worthwhile to pursue the study as planned?

b. Do results provide data suggesting it would be important to modify aspects of this study to improve the anticipated larger study?
c. Do results provide the data needed to propose a larger study as planned?

11. Disseminate your findings.

Moving beyond preliminary planning of a feasibility study, checklists have been developed to assess the quality of feasibility studies after completion. For example, Bird et al. (2014) and Slade et al. (2017) developed a measure of the feasibility of a complex intervention in mental health services and constructed reporting guidelines to compliment the assessment (see extract in Box 12.3). The Structured Assessment of Feasibility (SAFE) guidelines were developed by synthesizing intervention papers' primary barriers to (i.e., blocks) and facilitators of (i.e., enablers) implementing an intervention. The blocks primarily focused on staffing skills and resources, whereas the enablers focused on intervention specifics (e.g., flexibility, manualized, applicable to population). Each item is presented as a question, with responses being yes, no, partial, or unable to rate, with examples provided for each response option. With this checklist, it is possible to assess the quality of the feasibility study and make appropriate changes to enhance the likelihood of success in the final full-scale study.

Box 12.3. SAFE guidelines for assessing feasibility of mental health intervention

Blocks subscale

1. Do staff require specific training to deliver the intervention?
2. Is the intervention complex?
3. Is the intervention time consuming to provide?
4. Does the intervention include/require ongoing support and supervision?
5. Does the intervention require additional human resources?
6. Does the intervention require additional material resources?
7. Is the intervention costly?
8. Are there known serious or adverse events associated with the intervention?

Enablers subscale

9. Is the intervention applicable to the population of interest (e.g., adults using community mental health teams)
10. Is the intervention manualized?
11. Is the intervention flexible (i.e., can it be tailored to the context and situation)?
12. Is the intervention likely to be effective (i.e., evidence based and expected to produce positive outcomes)?
13. Is the intervention cost-saving?
14. Do the intended goals of the intervention match the prioritized goals of the National Health Service?
15. Can the intervention be piloted?
16. Is the intervention reversible?

Note. SAFE = structured assessment of feasibility.

Methodological Considerations in Pilot Studies

Methodological considerations that can be addressed through pilot studies, where the focus is on determining if the components of the study will work together and the utility of techniques, methods, and questionnaires (Eldridge, Chan, et al., 2016). Pilot studies provide the opportunity to evaluate outcomes, evaluate screening and recruitment methods and potential issues in the intervention, conduct sample size estimates, and propose data analytic techniques (Bell, Whitehead, & Julious, 2018) – all to ensure methodological rigor in the full-scale trial.

Sample Size Estimates

A key outcome from pilot studies is informing sample size estimates for the full-scale study or trial. However, there is some debate around sample size estimates and recommendations in pilot studies, given their underpowered nature. Here we must distinguish between sample size estimates for the pilot study or trial and sample size estimate processes derived from the pilot trial to inform the full study or trial – both of which are important decision points in preliminary research. In the former, CONSORT pilot and feasibility guidelines do not stipulate a sample size *calculation*; however, sample size *justification* is required. For the latter, CONSORT trial guidelines require a sample size calculation. While distinct, the two estimates share a relationship, and it is important to understand the implications and interaction between each – a larger sample in the pilot may reduce the sample needed in the full-scale trial (Whitehead, Julious, Cooper, & Campbell, 2016). For more on this, Whitehead et al. (2016) provide a detailed discussion, while a brief overview is provided here.

Given the range of guidance available in this area, it is worthwhile exploring sample size calculation and justification. Available guidance on sample size estimates vary in methods, from power calculations, to rules of thumb. To estimate pilot *trial* sample size, some have suggested power-based calculations are not appropriate, as the pilot trial is not testing efficacy, only exploring how well an intervention fits together (Whitehead et al., 2016). As such, rules of thumb may be more useful in sample size justifications. It must be noted, however, that the resultant variance estimates (to guide full trial sample size calculations) are influenced by pilot sample size, and thus rules of thumb should be critically evaluated. Whitehead et al. (2016) have presented rule-of-thumb estimates ranging from 24 to 70 participants (total) but this may be best informed by estimating the standardized difference (based on previous related research) between groups in the pilot trial. They provide an optimal formula-based method to estimate pilot trial sample size and the full trial sample size (see Whitehead et al., 2016 for details).

However, given the underpowered nature of pilot studies, which may underestimate the required sample size in the full trial, an alternative strategy is to perform a *sensitivity analysis* (Bell et al., 2018). A sensitivity analysis is a method for determining outcome robustness in relation to changes in methods, confounders, and assumptions (Schneeweiss, 2006; Thabane et al., 2013); a "what-if-the-key-inputs-or-assumptions-changed-type of discussion" (Thabane et al., 2013, p. 1). Detailed guidance on performing such analyses is beyond the scope of this chapter, however, useful methods on a range of outcomes are explored by Bell et al. (2018), and a deeper discussion is provided in Thabane et al. (2013). Briefly, a sensitivity analysis will provide an understanding of variability in an outcome (i.e., sample size estimate) if variables in the study were to change (e.g., protocol changes, clinical cutoffs in outcomes). To bring these addressed areas together, a strong example of a feasibility study conducted in the UK by Fife et al. (2019) is provided in Box 12.4.

Box 12.4. Example of a feasibility study of a dialectical behavior therapy protocol for psychiatric patients

Based on recent evidence highlighting the efficacy of dialectical behavior therapy (DBT) in treating people who self-harm, a preliminary study was used to evaluate the feasibility of a DBT-informed protocol in psychiatric inpatients in the UK, focusing on self-harm and crisis management strategies.

Of note, the authors clearly:

- described purpose of study (to assess feasibility and acceptability of a new intervention);
- identified aims (determine number of eligible participants, identify retention rate guided by previous research, conduct outcome estimates for a pilot trial, and describe suitability for the protocol);
- provided sample size justification (based on previous related work);
- reported the study according to extended CONSORT guidelines (Eldridge et al., 2016).

These were achieved by:

- determining eligibility by setting an empirically informed retention window (6 months) with outcomes compared with the initially justified sample size estimate (achieved 80%);
- detailed above using the CONSORT flow diagram of participant recruitment with descriptions provided of participants who were identified ($n = 63$) but did not agree to participate ($n = 19$);
- described retention rates in terms of number of sessions attended and percentage of those who attended all sessions, and described nonattendance and final numbers analyzed ($n = 9$);
- provided descriptive statistics only as there were limited participants that completed all outcomes (e.g., self-report on self-injury);
- analyzed adverse events and participants' perspectives of intervention feasibility (i.e., aspects that were helpful vs. unhelpful) with an inductive content analysis;
- made no estimates of effect size, given the small sample size.

All nine patients who completed the postintervention measures also completed the qualitative interview. *Mindfulness* and *strategy* components were seen as useful in the intervention to 33% and 22% of patients, respectively. Given the limited sample size achieved, adaptations were made to the recruitment procedure, suggestions were made to monitor the effect of off-protocol effects (i.e., existing treatment and interpreting outcomes with caution), and recommendations for continued follow-up were made.

Based on Fife, S., Blumenfeld, F., Williams, C., & Wood, L. (2019). A feasibility study highlighting challenges in evaluating a structured, psychological treatment for self-harm in adult psychiatric inpatient settings. *Psychiatry Research, 282*, 112609.

Outcome Selection

While the range of possible outcomes have already been discussed, selection of which outcomes are to be used is critical to several areas. Outcome selection, as has been demonstrated throughout the examples provided in this chapter, is dependent on what is considered most important for each research project. If recruitment and retention are considered highly important, such as in the study by Fife et al. (2019), this can be included as an outcome. In turn, this will have an impact on sample size. In contrast, if a major consideration is adverse events, such as in the study by Haddock et al. (2019), these can be measured. In addition to quantitative outcomes, assessing feasibility and acceptability can be enhanced by incorporating qualitative measures – particularly when all data can be triangulated to form a comprehensive view of study feasibility. For example, brief interviews can be conducted to assess participants' recommendations for improvement (Fife et al., 2019), adverse events, and therapeutic alliance (Haddock et al., 2019), or to further explore mechanisms of how an intervention may operate to contribute to related theory (e.g., Rory et al., 2019).

Analysis Considerations

As with any study, analysis in feasibility and pilot studies must be guided by the research question using predefined outcomes with set levels of success or failure (Thabane et al., 2010). Recent recommendations strongly suggest feasibility and pilot studies should be used for learning about the methods rather than for confirming an effect, given their traditionally small sample size and underpowered nature (Eldridge, Chan, et al., 2016). As such, traditional hypothesis testing is discouraged in feasibility and pilot studies, where the purpose is to assist in the design, and determine whether study components will work together and should be expanded to a full-scale study (respectively) rather than to determine the effect of an intervention. This distinction stresses the importance in pilot studies of evaluating outcomes in relation to a minimally important difference in outcomes (e.g., in relation to clinical cutoffs or ranges) as opposed to a traditional statistically significant difference (e.g., $p<.05$; Hislop et al., 2014; Copay et al., 2007). For feasibility, this may be demonstrated by evaluating interventions in comparison to a predefined level of acceptability (i.e., participant satisfaction, maintenance), achievability (i.e., resources), or achieving proposed recruitment objectives (i.e., sample size).

In line with this recommendation against traditional hypothesis testing, Lee, Whitehead, Jacques, and Julious (2014) and Bell et al. (2018) present approaches for analyses that may be better suited for pilot studies by using significance thresholds and confidence intervals outside of the traditional 5% cutoff. Lee et al. (2014) and Bell et al. (2018) suggest interpreting the confidence interval (of the difference between treatment and control groups) in relation to the *minimum clinically important difference* (MCID) specified a priori and zero (i.e., no difference). While tradition dictates a 95% confidence interval, Lee et al. (2014) and Bell et al. (2018) also suggest preparing multiple intervals (75%, 80%, 85%, 90%, and 95%), which, when displayed together, can demonstrate the strength of the evidence.

In contrast, Bayesian methods employing a Go/No go decision criteria (*hurdles*, specified a priori) offer an alternative to calculating intervention effects (Lee et al., 2014). In this method, results obtained from the pilot trial are combined with prior beliefs and distributions of similar studies' results and compared with an empirically derived MCID (i.e., a hurdle). If the hurdle is cleared, the next hurdle can be assessed, and the intervention may continue (i.e., Go), alternatively it may need refinement if not cleared (i.e., Nogo; Lee et al. 2014). Caution is recommended with this method, however (e.g., Lee et al., 2014), due to sample size restrictions.

A good example from suicide research is presented by Sayal et al. (2019) in the UK, who implemented a problem-solving intervention to reduce repeat self-harm in suicidal individuals. Sayal et al. (2019) developed four criteria that would assist in determining whether their remotely delivered problem-solving cognitive behavior therapy (PSCBT) was feasible in preventing self-harm. The criteria included:

- Recruitment of 5 participants per month;
- Collection of data from 70% of participants on primary outcome at 6 months;

- Engagement of 80 % of participants allocated to the PSCBT intervention;
- Retention of 60 % of participants for 10–12 sessions of the PSCBT intervention.

An independent committee reviewed progress at 14 months and determined that recruitment should cease given three of the four criteria were not met. Rather than a decision based on statistical significance, this study was stopped due to not achieving prespecified feasibility criteria.

Nontreatment Outcome Analysis

Extending beyond analysis of outcomes is the process of estimating a target effect size; an important step informing full study sample size estimates. As per the recommendations by Haddock et al. (2019) for effect-size estimates, it is important to specify this a priori. A range of methods can be employed to generate an effect size, and these were the subject of a systematic review which identified seven distinct ways to estimate an effect size (Hislop et al., 2014). Common approaches addressed included rules of thumb (e.g., 0.3 to 0.5 standardized effect size), clinical experience (e.g., comparison with previous participants), economic impact (e.g., cost-benefit), or based on a review of empirical evidence in a related area (e.g., previous suicide intervention effects). Nonetheless, given the underpowered nature of pilot trials due to their small sample, it is important to understand that estimation may be imprecise, and again sensitivity analyses may prove useful (see the section Sample Size Estimates).

Noninferential Analyses

Beyond analyses that inform preliminary intervention efficacy, a range of researchers also stress the importance of reporting descriptive statistics and/or detailed qualitative reports (Eldridge, Chan, et al., 2016). This is particularly relevant for more traditional feasibility studies where authors explore the feasibility and acceptability of an intervention (e.g., Fife, 2018; Fife et al., 2019). For example, Fife et al. (2019) presented only descriptive and qualitative results to demonstrate feasibility and highlight components of the study that could be improved. These were compared with predefined levels of what would be deemed acceptable (i.e., 70 % retention rate).

In conclusion, pilot or feasibility study success (or failure) must be determined in relation to criteria and research objectives stated a priori. As discussed, this may refer to an MCID in outcomes, a recruitment rate based on sample size justifications, or participant satisfaction and acceptable levels of adverse events. This should guide researchers in their analysis plans and help ensure interpretations are valid given the limited power of small preliminary studies.

Reporting

A *guiding template* for the conduct and reporting of feasibility and pilot studies is a necessary resource to ensure studies are conducted and reported appropriately, and high standards are maintained (Eldridge, Chan, et al., 2016). In an extension of the CONSORT statement, Eldridge, Chan, et al. (2016) adapted the checklist of requirements to apply to feasibility and pilot studies. Across six stages of development involving discussion, testing, Delphi surveys, iterative reviews, and rewording, a draft checklist was created (see Eldridge, Chan, et al., 2016). The authors suggest the routine use of the adapted checklist will enhance the conduct, reporting, and quality of pilot studies. The guidelines extend from the title through to the discussion of limitations (e.g., Fife et al., 2019), generalizability, and interpretation of outcomes, as well as providing guidance around registering the study and providing access to the protocol and disclosing funding. The full guidelines can be found on the CONSORT website (http://www.consort-statement.org/extensions/overview/pilotandfeasibility).

To our knowledge there are no reviews assessing the reporting standards for feasibility and pilot studies in suicide research; however, recent studies have reviewed the quality of reporting according to these guidelines across other areas. These reviews cover a broad range of topics ranging from physiotherapy (e.g., Luiz Felicio Cadete et al., 2019) to anesthesia (Shanthanna et al., 2018) and a range of behavioral interventions (Bhatt et al., 2018). Reviews have often reported poor adherence to the extended CONSORT guidelines (e.g., Luiz Felicio Cadete et al., 2019; Shanthanna et al., 2018; Bhatt et al., 2018; Chan et al., 2017; Kosa et al., 2019). The importance of reporting according to predefined and well-recognized standards cannot be understated. In their final reporting standard (i.e., Standard 22a), Eldridge, Chan, et al. (2016) recommendations for progression from a pilot to a future definitive trial are discussed, along with proposed amendments.

Moving from Preliminary to Full-Scale Studies

Once a pilot study is complete, researchers must determine whether it should be progressed into a full-scale study. However, this decision process is not always straightforward and should be informed by progression criteria predetermined by the research team. In their literature review and expert workshops for progression criteria for pilot studies, Avery et al. (2017) identified three predominant issues: recruitment, protocol nonadherence, and outcome data – primary areas that were determined to affect the decision to progress to a full-scale study.

Recruitment, as a common outcome in preliminary research is a key concern that will determine trial progression. As discussed earlier (see the section Outcome Selection), this is the ability to recruit the predetermined number of participants during the specified time period to ensure the intervention is feasible. This may include estimating the expected number of participants available for eligibility screening, the number of participants screened who are eligible, and the number of participants who are eligible and will consent to randomization. These estimates can be informed by preexisting observational data (i.e., historical studies) or acquired from practicing clinicians, and they are with respect to the proposed pilot period (e.g., 18 months – reporting the pilot period is an important component). However, rather than setting an overall target recruitment number (e.g., 30 people within 6 months), Avery et al. (2017) suggest breaking this down (e.g., three people per month per site) on a *recruitment trajectory* to the final goal. The outcomes of the pilot study recruitment can then be used to inform the expected recruitment rates, with expectations adjusted and issues rectified where necessary. For example, a study from the UK by Fife et al. (2019) faced recruitment difficulties, and adaptions were made to this process (e.g., increase study team availability, screening, outcome clarification). Furthermore, areas that were helpful or unhelpful were discussed, and the authors suggested these areas would inform adjustments for the full-scale intervention. Similarly, an Australian longitudinal pilot study of suicide and other sudden death bereavement, experienced a lower than expected response rate and adjusted the name of their study (as introduced to the participants) to reduce potential bias in eligible participants and increase recruitment rates, especially in their comparison group (Kõlves & De Leo, 2018).

Protocol nonadherence concerns participants receiving an alternative intervention to their assigned intervention, or one not provided in the pilot. Such nonadherence can reduce power in the study by confounding the difference between groups. This can be reduced by adapting the full-scale trial to improve blinding, or improving the acceptability of the intervention (i.e., allowing more flexibility). Where it is feasible to measure off-protocol instances, Avery et al. (2017) advise that this can be useful information to either advise the trial or identify the need to halt progression to the trial and reevaluate the intervention design. An instance of protocol nonadherence was reported in a pilot study by Yen et al. (2019) of a Skills to Enhance Positivity (STEP) program for suicidal adolescents admitted to an emergency department in the US. In their two-phase STEP intervention, the first phase (consisting of four sessions) was conducted in person. However, when discharged after two sessions, many participants did not return for an in-person follow-up for sessions three and four. While some were accessible for the remaining sessions via phone, the intervention protocol was developed for the first phase to be conducted in person. This presented some concern as there might have been an increased chance of off-protocol or alternative protocol effects which could have had a confounding effect in the pilot intervention. A remedy is discussed by Yen et al. (2019) to increase feasibility and protocol adherence by implementing the intervention in the standard inpatient schedule rather than as a separate research protocol.

The example of the STEP intervention also applied for *outcome data*, which reflects the importance of collecting enough, valid data from participants: If an intervention is adhered to per protocol, the likelihood of collecting complete data may increase. A range of additional factors may also influence data completeness (e.g., attrition, poor acceptability, measure suitability), and ensuring these areas are addressed (if they present in the pilot trial) is critical to maintaining statistical power. Aside from increasing the likelihood of protocol adherence, ensuring that outcomes are appropriate and well-detailed is critical to increasing the quality of the data obtained.

This was highlighted briefly by Czyz, King, and Biermann (2019) who explored preliminary feasibility and acceptability of a motivational interview enhanced safety planning intervention for hospitalized suicidal teenagers in the US. As a measure of a range of proximal outcomes (e.g., safety plan use, self-efficacy, and motivation), the authors employed single-item measures of each construct to reduce the burden on the teens. Considering this, the authors do discuss the validity of single-item measures, particularly in the target population (i.e., suicidal teens in the US). Valid measures that are suited to the target population and are not overly cumbersome may increase the likelihood of obtaining reliable, valid, and complete data.

Guidelines to Inform Progression from Preliminary to Full-Scale Studies

As introduced in previous sections of this chapter where we have highlighted the utility of researchers using guidelines to ensure quality is adhered to in their research, progressing from pilot to full-scale studies may be similarly enhanced using guidelines (Avery et al., 2017). For example, Avery et al. (2017) developed a Top 10 list of tips to consider (see Box 12.5). When progressing from pilot to full-scale studies, the tips include codesigned (funders and steering committees) decision criteria for progressing study promotion and participant recruitment, protocols for assessment of treatment adherence and missing data, ensuring similarity between pilot and main study recruitment sites, consistently ensuring up-to-date technology is used, and reporting according to the CONSORT guidelines (Eldridge, Chan, et al., 2016). The authors also suggest having a *traffic light* system for each criterion whereby green allows progression, amber requires attention before progression, and red prevents progression. A similar decision process is articulated by Thabane et al. (2010). Such processes can ensure all aspects of the preliminary studies are addressed and refined where needed prior to moving to the full-scale study.

Box 12.5. Top 10 tips when progressing from preliminary research to full-scale trials

1. A traffic light system of green (go), amber (amend), and red (stop) might be preferable to a simple stop vs. go approach when specifying progression criteria for internal pilot studies.
2. Prespecified progression criteria agreed with funders need to strike a careful balance between being firm enough to promote ambition in the trial team yet being flexible enough to allow opportunities to remedy early problems.
3. Recruitment progression criteria should be based on rates per center per unit time (e.g., per month) that can be easily extrapolated, rather than specifying that an absolute number should be reached by a specific date, due to the unpredictability of opening sites.
4. When recruitment falls behind, it is essential to explore screening logs to determine whether insufficient participants were approached, insufficient participants passed eligibility criteria, or insufficient eligible participants agreed to randomization.
5. The assessment of intervention adherence, cross-over, and outcome event rates should take into account the duration from randomization to timing of primary outcomes if sufficient data are to be gleaned in time to inform progression.
6. When assessing missing data, it is important to explore the degree of missing data within key outcomes as well as the percentage of participants with missing data.
7. Trial teams should involve both their funders and their trial steering committee in assessing their progression criteria.
8. Pilot study recruitment sites should be representative of sites that recruit into the main study.
9. Trialists may be able to take the opportunity to assess whether changes to existing technologies have occurred since the original study was planned, so that new technologies can be considered with funders, such as using an adaptive design.
10. Pilot studies need to be reported fully. An extension to CONSORT guidelines for pilot and feasibility studies is now available.

Adapted from Avery et al. (2017). Informing efficient randomised controlled trials: Exploration of challenges in developing progression criteria for internal pilot studies. *BMJ Open, 7*(2), e013537, p. 9.

Conclusions

This chapter has explored feasibility and pilot studies, distinguishing between the two phases of research, and detailing some important aspects of each. Methodological and analysis considerations were addressed to guide researchers in their conducting of preliminary suicide research. Examples have been detailed to provide guidance in key areas, and the chapter concluded with detail on progressing from preliminary studies to full-scale studies. While it has not been discussed in this chapter, it is important to note additionally the requirement for ethical approval from relevant committees in preliminary research. This is discussed in greater detail in Chapter 4.

References

Abbott, J.H. (2014). The distinction between randomized clinical trials (RCTs) and preliminary feasibility and pilot studies: What they are and are not. *Journal of Orthopaedic & Sports Physical Therapy, 44*(8), 555–558. https://doi.org/10.2519/jospt.2014.0110

Arain, M., Campbell, M.J., Cooper, C.L., & Lancaster, G.A. (2010). What is a pilot or feasibility study? A review of current practice and editorial policy. *BMC Medical Research Methodology, 10*(1), 1–7. https://doi.org/10.1186/1471-2288-10-67

Avery, K.N., Williamson, P.R., Gamble, C., Francischetto, E.O. C., Metcalfe, C., Davidson, P., ... Blazeby, J.M. (2017). Informing efficient randomised controlled trials: Exploration of challenges in developing progression criteria for internal pilot studies. *BMJ Open, 7*(2), e013537. https://doi.org/10.1136/bmjopen-2016-013537

Bell, M.L., Whitehead, A.L., & Julious, S.A. (2018). Guidance for using pilot studies to inform the design of intervention trials with continuous outcomes. *Clinical Epidemiology, 10,* 153–157. https://doi.org/10.2147/CLEP.S146397

Bhatt, M., Zielinski, L., Sanger, N., Ieta, S., Luo, C., Bantoto, B., ... Samaan, Z. (2018). Evaluating completeness of reporting in behavioral interventions pilot trials. *Research on Social Work Practice, 28*, 577–584. https://doi.org/10.1177/1049731517720033

Billingham, S.A., Whitehead, A.L., & Julious, S.A. (2013). An audit of sample sizes for pilot and feasibility trials being undertaken in the United Kingdom registered in the United Kingdom Clinical Research Network database. *BMC Medical Research Methodology, 13*(1), *104*, 1–6. https://doi.org/10.1186/1471-2288-13-104

Bird, V.J., Le Boutillier, C., Leamy, M., Williams, J., Bradstreet, S., & Slade, M. (2014). Evaluating the feasibility of complex interventions in mental health services: Standardised measure and reporting guidelines. *British Journal of Psychiatry, 204*, 316–321. https://doi.org/10.1192/bjp.bp.113.128314

Boeije, H.R., Drabble, S.J., & O'Cathain, A. (2015). Methodological challenges of mixed methods intervention evaluations. *Special Issue: VI European Congress of Methodology, 11*(4), 119–125. https://doi.org/10.1027/1614-2241/a000101

Chan, C.L., Leyrat, C., & Eldridge, S.M. (2017). Quality of reporting of pilot and feasibility cluster randomised trials: A systematic review. *BMJ Open, 7*(11), 1–14. https://doi.org/10.1136/bmjopen-2017-016970

Copay, A.G., Subach, B.R., Glassman, S.D., Polly, J., & Schuler, T.C. (2007). Understanding the minimum clinically important difference: a review of concepts and methods. *Spine Journal, 7*, 541–546. https://doi.org/10.1016/j.spinee.2007.01.008

Cope, D.G. (2015). Conducting pilot and feasibility studies. *Oncology Nursing Forum, 42*, 196–197. https://doi.org/10.1188/15.ONF

Czyz, E.K., King, C.A., & Biermann, B.J. (2019). Motivational interviewing-enhanced safety planning for adolescents at high suicide risk: A pilot randomized controlled trial. *Journal of Clinical Child and Adolescent Psychology, 48*(2), 250–262. https://doi.org/10.1080/15374416.2018.1496442

Doody, O., & Doody, C.M. (2015). Conducting a pilot study: Case study of a novice researcher. *British Journal of Nursing, 24*, 1074–1078. https://doi.org/10.12968/bjon.2015.24.21.1074

Eldridge, S.M., Chan, C.L., Campbell, M.J., Bond, C.M., Hopewell, S., Thabane, L., & Lancaster, G.A. (2016). CONSORT 2010 statement: Extension to randomised pilot and feasibility trials. *Pilot and Feasibility Studies, 2*(1), 1–29. https://doi.org/10.1136/bmj.i5239

Eldridge, S.M., Lancaster, G.A., Campbell, M.J., Thabane, L., Hopewell, S., Coleman, C.L., & Bond, C.M. (2016). Defining feasibility and pilot studies in preparation for randomised controlled trials: Development of a conceptual framework. *PLoS One, 11*(3), e0150205, 1–22. https://doi.org/10.1371/journal.pone.0150205

Fife, S. (2018). *A feasibility study to evaluate a self-harm group in psychiatric inpatient settings* (Unpublished doctoral dissertation). University of Essex, UK.

Fife, S., Blumenfeld, F., Williams, C., & Wood, L. (2019). A feasibility study highlighting challenges in evaluating a structured, psychological treatment for self-harm in adult psychiatric inpatient settings. *Psychiatry Research, 282*, 112609. https://doi.org/10.1016/j.psychres.2019.112609

Haddock, G., Davies, L., Evans, E., Emsley, R., Gooding, P.A., Heaney, L., ... Awenat, Y. (2016). Investigating the feasibility and acceptability of a cognitive behavioural suicide prevention therapy for people in acute psychiatric wards (the 'INSITE' trial): Study protocol for a randomised controlled trial. *Trials, 17*, 1–8. https://doi.org/10.1186/s13063-016-1192-9

Haddock, G., Pratt, D., Gooding, P.A., Peters, S., Emsley, R., Evans, E., ... Awenat, Y. (2019). Feasibility and acceptability of suicide prevention therapy on acute psychiatric wards: Randomised controlled trial. *BJPsych Open, 5*, e14. https://doi.org/10.1192/bjo.2018.85

Hazzi, O., & Maldaon, I. (2015). A pilot study: Vital methodological issues. *Business: Theory and Practice, 16*, 53–62. https://doi.org/10.3846/btp.2015.437

Hill, R.M., & Pettit, J.W. (2019). Pilot randomized controlled trial of LEAP: A selective preventive intervention to reduce adolescents' perceived burdensomeness. *Journal of Clinical Child and Adolescent Psychology, 48*(Suppl 1), 45–56. https://doi.org/10.1080/15374416.2016.1188705

Hislop, J., Adewuyi, T.E., Vale, L.D., Harrild, K., Fraser, C., Gurung, T., ... for the DELTA Group. (2014). Methods for specifying the target difference in a randomised controlled trial: The Difference ELicitation in TriAls (DELTA) systematic review. *PLoS Medicine, 11*(5), e1001645, 1–16. https://doi.org/10.1371/journal.pmed.1001645

Kõlves, K., & De Leo, D. (2018). Suicide bereavement: Piloting a longitudinal study in Australia. *BMJ Open, 8*(1), e019504, 1–6. https://doi.org/10.1136/bmjopen-2017-019504

Kosa, S.D., Monize, J., Leenus, A., Selvin, L., Samra, S., Szwiega, S., ... Thabane, L. (2019). Reporting quality of pilot clinical trials in chronic kidney disease patients on hemodialysis: A methodological survey. *Pilot and Feasibility Studies, 5*, 1–8. https://doi.org/10.1186/s40814-019-0436-3

Lee, E.C., Whitehead, A.L., Jacques, R.M., & Julious, S.A. (2014). The statistical interpretation of pilot trials: Should significance thresholds be reconsidered? *BMC Medical Research Methodology, 14*(1), 41. https://doi.org/10.1186/1471-2288-14-41

Luiz Felicio Cadete, S., Moseley, A.M., Thabane, L., Almeida, M., & Lucíola da Cunha Menezes, C. (2019). A methodological survey on reporting of pilot and feasibility trials for physiotherapy interventions: A study protocol. *BMJ Open, 9*(5), 1–5. https://doi.org/10.1136/bmjopen-2017-020580

Morris, N.S., & Rosenbloom, D.A. (2017). CE: Defining and understanding pilot and other feasibility studies. *American Journal of Nursing, 117*(3), 38–45. https://doi.org/10.1097/01.NAJ.0000513261.75366.37

Rory, C.O.C., Lundy, J.-M., Stewart, C., Smillie, S., McClelland, H., Syrett, S., ... Simpson, S.A. (2019). SAFETEL randomised controlled feasibility trial of a safety planning intervention with follow-up telephone contact to reduce suicidal behaviour: study protocol. *BMJ Open, 9*(2), 1–11. https://doi.org/10.1136/bmjopen-2018-025591

Sayal, K., Roe, J., Ball, H., Atha, C., Kaylor-Hughes, C., Guo, B., ... Morriss, R. (2019). Feasibility of a randomised controlled trial of remotely delivered problem-solving cognitive behaviour therapy versus usual care for young people with depression and repeat self-harm: Lessons learnt (e-DASH). *BMC Psychiatry, 19*(1), 1–12. https://doi.org/10.1186/s12888-018-2005-3

Schneeweiss, S. (2006). Sensitivity analysis and external adjustment for unmeasured confounders in epidemiologic database studies of therapeutics. *Pharmacoepidemiology and Drug Safety, 15*(5), 291–303. https://doi.org/10.1002/pds.1200

Shanthanna, H., Kaushal, A., Mbuagbaw, L., Couban, R., Busse, J., & Thabane, L. (2018). A cross-sectional study of the reporting quality of pilot or feasibility trials in high-impact anesthesia journals. *Canadian Journal of Anesthesia, 65*, 1180–1195. https://doi.org/10.1007/s12630-018-1194-z

Slade, M., Bird, V., Chandler, R., Clarke, E., Craig, T., Larsen, J., ... Leamy, M. (2017). *REFOCUS: Developing a recovery focus in mental health services in England*. Nottingham, UK: Institute of Mental Health.

Thabane, L., Ma, J., Chu, R., Cheng, J., Ismaila, A., Rios, L.P., ... Goldsmith, C.H. (2010). A tutorial on pilot studies: The what, why and how. *BMC Medical Research Methodology, 10*(1), 1–10. https://doi.org/10.1186/1471-2288-10-1

Thabane, L., Mbuagbaw, L., Zhang, S., Samaan, Z., Marcucci, M., Ye, C., ... Debono, V.B. (2013). A tutorial on sensitivity analyses in clinical trials: the what, why, when and how. *BMC Medical Research Methodology, 13*(1), 1–12. https://doi.org/10.1186/1471-2288-13-92

Tracey, M., Rowney, G., Pignatiello, A., Monga, S., & Korczak, D. (2018). Feasibility of a manualized family-based suicide prevention strategy to reduce adolescent suicide risk among emergency department referred youth: A quality improvement project. *Paediatrics & Child Health, 23*, e54. https://doi.org/10.1093/pch/pxy054.136

Whitehead, A.L., Julious, S.A., Cooper, C.L., & Campbell, M.J. (2016). Estimating the sample size for a pilot randomised trial to minimise the overall trial sample size for the external pilot and main trial for a continuous outcome variable. *Statistical Methods in Medical Research, 25*(3), 1057–1073. https://doi.org/10.1177/0962280215588241

Yen, S., Ranney, M.L., Tezanos, K.M., Chuong, A., Kahler, C.W., Solomon, J.B., & Spirito, A. (2019). Skills to enhance positivity in suicidal adolescents: Results from an open development trial. *Behavior Modification, 43*(2), 202–221. https://doi.org/10.1177/0145445517748559

Chapter 13
Systematic Reviews and Meta-Analyses in Suicide Prevention Research

Katrina Witt, Allison Milner[†], and Matthew J. Spittal

Summary

With the increasing popularity of evidence synthesis in the field of self-harm and suicide prevention, this chapter aims to provide an introduction to the design and conduct of methodologically rigorous systematic reviews and meta-analyses. Examples from the field are used to provide specific guidance on how to formulate robust review questions, searching electronic databases for published and gray literature, and statistical models for meta-analysis.

With growing interest in the science behind the development, implementation, and evaluation of interventions to prevent self-harm and suicide, it has become more important than ever for clinicians, commissioners of clinical services, researchers, policy makers, and other relevant stakeholders to remain up-to-date with key developments in the field. Systematic reviews (both with and without meta-analysis) respond to this need by identifying all of the available evidence for a specific research question, appraising the quality of this evidence, synthesizing this evidence, and presenting this information in an accessible, easy-to-digest format (Mulrow, 1994).

However, systematic reviews and meta-analyses can themselves vary in their comprehensiveness and quality. The purpose of this chapter, therefore, is to provide general guidance and an introduction to the concepts behind conducting methodologically rigorous systematic reviews and meta-analyses in the field of self-harm and suicide prevention.

Review Formats

An overview of the most common review formats encountered in the field of self-harm and suicide prevention, alongside their relative advantages and limitations, is provided in Table 13.1.

The advantages of systematic reviews over narrative reviews can have important implications for clinical decision making in the field of psychiatry. For example, a 2003 meta-synthesis found that narrative reviews may overestimate the long-term effectiveness of atypical antipsychotic medications for the management of psychosis by downplaying the significance of any adverse effects of these medications. Systematic reviews, on the other hand, were characterized by greater conservatism; concluding that while atypical antipsychotic medications may be associated with less significant side-effect profiles, the trials that had been conducted were associated with a number of methodological limitations and that further study was required before valid evidence-based policy statements could be made about the safety and effectiveness of atypical antipsychotic medications as compared with typical antipsychotic medications (Cipriani & Geddes, 2003).

Table 13.1 Overview of common review formats in the field of self-harm and suicide prevention, their strengths and limitations

Review format	Definition	Advantages	Limitations
Narrative reviews	Often written by established experts in the field, these synthesize literature through the reviewer's own experiential and/or theoretical lens (Cook, Mulrow, & Haynes, 1997). The selection of studies is often unclear. The research question(s) may also be unfocused, aiming to provide an 'overview' of the field or of recent developments.	• Less stringent inclusion and exclusion criteria allow narrative reviews to provide more comprehensive coverage of a topic area, particularly where study designs and/or methods may have changed over time.	• Lack objective and reproducible methods describing how studies were identified and included. • Personal biases of the reviewer(s) may influence which studies are selected for inclusion and which are selected for exclusion. • Narrative reviews can be difficult for other researchers to reproduce.
Rapid evidence reviews	Typically prepared by or for policy makers, these reviews aim to balance the strengths of the systematic review process with the brevity of the narrative review process.	• These are typically conducted over the course of a few weeks, as compared with systematic reviews that can take months to complete.	• Rapid evidence reviews are subject to many of the same limitations as narrative reviews.
Systematic reviews	Conducted by a team of two or more researchers, these aim to answer a predefined research question, with clearly articulated participants, intervention(s), comparator(s), outcome(s) (PICOs); inclusion; and exclusion criteria. Standard, often publicly available, tools are also used to assist reviewers in rating the quality of each study included.	• Based on a comprehensive, systematic search of all available resources. • The search process is well-documented, using methods that can be reproduced by other researchers. • All studies that meet objective criteria for inclusion are included. • Role of the reviewer's own subjective bias in the selection of studies to include in the review is therefore minimized.	• Systematic reviews require considerable time investment. The average time to complete and publish a systematic review is around 67 weeks (Borah, Brown, Capers, & Kaiser, 2017).
Meta-analysis	Refers to the statistical synthesis of quantitative results from two or more studies. It is important to remember that a systematic review can be undertaken without a meta-analysis; however, a meta-analysis can never be undertaken without a systematic review to first identify relevant studies for inclusion in the analysis.	• Allows for the precise direction and magnitude of an effect to be quantified. • Enables statistical investigations of the consistency of the effect across studies or over time to be explored.	• Given their complexity, the time investment for meta-analyses is even greater than that for systematic reviews – up to 69 weeks (Allen & Olkin, 1999). • Reviewers must determine whether each study measures outcome(s) in a similar way, using similar tools, and in similar populations. Otherwise, heterogeneity between studies may be too high for meta-analysis to be meaningful. • Guidance from a biostatistician is recommended.

Searching the Literature

The cornerstone of any systematic review or meta-analysis is the comprehensiveness of the literature search undertaken to locate relevant studies for inclusion. This will influence the ultimate quality of the resultant review.

For first-time reviewers, the best way to accomplish this is to receive help from an information technician and/or librarian with expertise in systematic reviews, as early in the review process as possible (Charrois, 2015). This person can assist with:

- Formulating the research question
- Developing and refining keywords
- Identifying electronic databases to search
- Incorporating methods to improve the identification of gray literature
- Deduplicating results from the electronic search
- Organizing results of the electronic search in preparation for screening

Formulating the Research Question

Ideally summarized into a single-sentence statement, the research question encapsulates the primary purpose of the review. To assist in formulating the research question, the University of Oxford's Centre for Evidence-Based Medicine (Ho, Liew, Ng, Shunmugam, & Glasziou, 2016) promotes the use of the PICO method which restructures the research question into a clear format by breaking the research question into its component parts:

- P: participants, patients, population, or problem;
- I: intervention(s), or in the case of epidemiological studies, exposure(s);
- C: comparator(s); and
- O: outcome(s).

Examples of how to apply the PICO method to research questions within the field of self-harm and suicide prevention are provided in Table 13.2.

It is important to remember there is a trade-off between sensitivity and specificity; adding specific detail to any one of the PICO components will increase the specificity of the search, at the expense of its sensitivity. Additionally, depending on the review question, it may be necessary to omit the intervention and/or comparator components, if for example, the review is focused on establishing the prevalence of a condition without assessment of the effectiveness of any intervention.

Alternatively, a further field, typically indicated with an *S* to indicate *study design*, may be added where specification of the study design is important; this may particularly be the case for systematic reviews of qualitative literature (Methley, Campbell, Chew-Graham, McNally, & Cheraghi-Sohi, 2014).

Developing and Refining Keywords

In the next stage, keywords reflecting each PICO component of the review question are developed and tested in an iterative way to ascertain how well they perform in retrieving relevant studies. A good starting place is to collect together a number of studies known to be relevant to the review question and highlighting common keywords or phrases in their titles, abstracts, and/or methods sections.

Table 13.2 Applying the PICO method to an example of a research question

Example	Participants, patients, population, or problem	Intervention(s) (or exposure[s])	Comparator(s)	Outcome(s)
Is cognitive behavior therapy effective in reducing self-harm repetition in patients diagnosed with major depression?	**Patients diagnosed with major depression.** Consider adding any limits on how the diagnosis was made (e.g., self-report vs. clinician-determined) and/or the use of any structured tools (e.g., the Structured Clinical Interview for the Diagnostic and Statistical Manual of Mental Disorders, version 5) to assist in diagnosis.	**Cognitive behavior therapy.** Consider adding specific detail on whether or not therapy was manualized, and any relevant limits on the minimum number of sessions, length of treatment, and therapeutic dose.	**Treatment as usual (TAU).** It is important to remember that TAU is not a unitary construct; it will vary over time and between different treatment centers (Witt et al., 2018). Further detail on minimum number of sessions, length of treatment, and therapeutic dose may therefore be desirable.	**Self-harm repetition.** Consider adding limits to how repetition was determined (e.g., hospital admission, emergency department presentation, and/or from a psychometric scale such as the Columbia Suicide Severity Rating Scale).

Note. PICO = participants, patients, population, or problem; intervention(s) (or exposure[s]); comparator(s); and outcome(s).

While the PICO components can serve as an excellent starting point for identifying keywords, it is important to remember that limiting studies to those that mention the outcome(s) of interest within the title and/or abstract fields only may lead to the inadvertent exclusion of otherwise relevant studies, resulting in a lower overall sensitivity of the search (Eriksen & Frandsen, 2018). Therefore, it is generally recommended that the *outcome(s)* component is only used where keywords are searched throughout each study's full text, and not limited to the title and/or abstract.

At this stage, synonyms may also be identified and added to further improve the sensitivity of the systematic search. In the field of self-harm and suicide prevention, for example, it is important to remember that terminology has changed considerably over the past 60 years (Silverman, Berman, Sanddal, O'Carroll, & Joiner, 2007a, 2007b), and continues to evolve (Goodfellow, Kõlves, & De Leo, 2020). Therefore, depending on the research question and the time frame covered by the review, it may be necessary to incorporate obsolete terminology (e.g., *parasuicide*) along with emergent terms (e.g., *nonsuicidal self-injury*).

Identifying Electronic Databases to Search

As a multidisciplinary field, studies on self-harm and suicide prevention tend to be published in diverse journals linked to a broad range of disciplines, including allied health, nursing, medicine, implementation science, psychiatry, psychology, and the social sciences. Therefore, any comprehensive systematic review conducted in this field will require reviewers to search several electronic databases that index literature from a number of these disciplines.

An overview of the electronic databases commonly used in systematic reviews conducted in the field of self-harm and suicide is provided in Table 13.3.

Table 13.3 Electronic databases commonly searched in systematic reviews in the field of self-harm and suicide

Database	Description	Advantages	Limitations
CINAHL	Indexes over 4,000 journals as well as selected conference proceedings, and some theses and dissertations. **Discipline(s) covered:** allied health, nursing.	Reports of randomized controlled trials (RCT) indexed in CINAHL are not currently exported to CENTRAL.	Subscription required.
Cochrane Central Register of Controlled Trials (CENTRAL)	Comprehensive index of RCTs indexing over 530,000 (Lefebvre & Glanville, 2008). Updated quarterly from searches of Medline, EMBASE, ClinicalTrials.gov, and various trial registries such as the World Health Organization's International Clinical Trials Registry Platform (ICTRP) and International Standard Randomized Controlled Trials Number registry (ISRCTN), among others. **Discipline(s) covered:** cross-discipline, implementation science.	Access is available without subscription in most countries. Comprehensive index of RCTs. Searching a second database has been shown to lead to the identification of only 3.3 % additional RCTs not already indexed in CENTRAL (Royle & Milne, 2003).	Limited to RCTs.
Cochrane Database of Systematic Reviews	Indexes over 8,000 systematic reviews and meta-analyses, and over 2,500 systematic review protocols. **Discipline(s) covered:** cross-discipline, implementation science.	Access is available without subscription in most countries.	Limited to evidence reviews published by the Cochrane Collaboration.
EMBASE	Indexes over 8,500 journals. **Discipline(s) covered:** Medicine, including preclinical topics, drugs and pharmacy.	Across disciplines, EMBASE indexes the greatest number of unique studies not indexed in a second database (Bramer, Rethlefsen, Kleijnen, & Franco, 2017). Indexes around 67 % of the world's psychiatry journals (McDonald, Taylor, & Adams, 1999). Natural language searching allowed.	Subscription required (Lefebvre & Glanville, 2008).

continued on next page

Table 13.3 continued

Database	Description	Advantages	Limitations
Medline	Indexes over 5,800 biomedical journals, mainly from the US. **Discipline(s) covered:** Medicine, veterinary science, including preclinical topics.	Access is available without subscription, via PubMed.	Requires knowledge of the appropriate Medical Subject Heading (MeSH) terms for each keyword. Indexes around 47% of the world's psychiatry journals (McDonald et al., 1999). Mainly limited to US journals.
ProQuest	Indexes over 7,000 journals, and around 5 million theses and dissertations from a number of universities internationally (available through ProQuest Dissertations and Theses Global). **Discipline(s) covered:** cross-discipline.	Most comprehensive coverage of theses and dissertations (Lefebvre & Glanville, 2008)	Subscription required.
PsycINFO	Indexes over 2,000 books, book chapters, and journals internationally. **Discipline(s) covered:** Behavioral sciences, psychology.	Indexes around 73% of the world's psychiatry journals (McDonald et al., 1999).	Subscription required.
PubMed	Indexes over 29 million records. **Discipline(s) covered:** Medicine, biomedicine, and other life sciences.	Access available without a subscription. Includes recently published studies not yet indexed in MEDLINE by applying the "as supplied by publisher" filter (Lefebvre & Glanville, 2008). Automatic mapping of keywords against MeSH terms.	
SCOPUS	Indexes over 15,000 journals and 500 conference proceedings across a range of disciplines (Lefebvre & Glanville, 2008). **Discipline(s) covered:** cross-discipline.	Can also be used to obtain metrics of the scholarly influence of identified resources (e.g., Field Weighted Citation Impact [FWCI]).	Subscription required.

A specialist database, the Suicide Prevention Randomized Controlled Trials Database was developed in 2014 by the Australian Centre for Research Excellence for Suicide Prevention (CRESP; Christensen et al., 2014). This database indexes 154 randomized controlled trials (RCTs) of psychological interventions for the prevention of self-harm and suicide. However, although future updates of this database are planned, at the time of writing, only studies added up to 30 December 2014 had been indexed.

Ancestry Searching

In addition to conducting formal searches of several electronic databases, ancestry searching (i.e., hand-searching reference lists of studies identified as eligible for inclusion in the systematic review) is also recommended to identify relevant records that may have been inadvertently missed by the electronic search strategy, either because they were not indexed in any of the electronic databases searched, or because they were indexed with keywords that did not allow them to be easily identified as relevant to the review question (Lefebvre & Glanville, 2008). In suicide prevention, this may particularly be so where obsolete keywords (e.g., *parasuicide*) are used.

Incorporating Methods to Improve Identification of Gray Literature

A comprehensive literature search will also incorporate methods to identify and retrieve gray literature, such as unpublished studies and other relevant research that have not been formally published in a peer-reviewed academic journal. Gray literature can include academic theses and dissertations, annual reports, conference proceedings, clinical practice guidelines, government reports, and technical reports (Charrois, 2015).

Studies reporting positive (or significant) findings are significantly more likely to be submitted for publication (Song et al., 2009), and are more likely to be published (Dwan et al., 2008; Hopewell, Loudon, Clarke, Oxman, & Dickersin, 2009), compared with those reporting negative (or nonsignificant) findings. The failure to include gray literature in a systematic review may therefore be particularly problematic when conducting meta-analyses. Despite this, there are currently no standard recommendations to guide reviewers on how to systematically search for gray literature (Stansfield, Dickson, & Bangpan, 2016).

While conference abstracts and theses and dissertations can be retrieved from some electronic databases (e.g., EMBASE, ProQuest), and protocols of ongoing RCTs are readily available from a number of international clinical trial registries (e.g., Australian New Zealand Clinical Trials Registry [ANZCTR], ClinicalTrials.gov, International Clinical Trials Registry Platform [ICTRP], and the International Standard Randomized Controlled Trials Number registry [ISRCTN], among others), other forms of gray literature are rarely indexed in academic electronic databases.

Additional searches therefore often need to be conducted to locate gray literature. It has been estimated that of the time reviewers spend searching for literature, around 20 % will be dedicated to the identification of gray literature alone (Saleh, Ratajeski, & Bertolet, 2014).

General Purpose Search Engines

The use of general purpose search engines to assist with the identification of gray literature is generally not recommended. The search algorithm implemented by these general purpose search engines is influenced by popularity, relevancy, and other factors (Page, Brin, Motwani,

& Winograd, 1999) and can be easily manipulated to ensure a higher ranking (Bar-Ilan, 2007). Therefore, the relative ranking assigned to a record can change over time (Bramer, Giustini, & Kramer, 2016), thereby negatively affecting the reproducibility of the systematic review.

If using these search engines, reviewers are encouraged to log out of all personal accounts, clear their Internet search history, and delete all cookies in order to minimize the impact that personalization may have on the relative weighting assigned to identified records by the search algorithm. Using advanced search options can also assist with this (Ćurković, 2017).

Additionally, given that records identified from these general purpose search engines are liable to being either taken offline or substantially altered, reviewers should retain a cached version of all records identified.

Meta-Search Engines and Web Crawlers

Meta-search engines may be more appropriate for identifying gray literatures, as these combine the coverage of all general purpose engines to retrieve information. Where combined with a Web crawler, these meta-search engines can search for gray literature in a systematic and automated fashion, and can automatically create a cached version of each relevant record identified, thereby overcoming many of the limitations of general purpose search engines (Kausar, Dhaka, & Singh, 2013).

Deduplicating Results From the Electronic Search

Once the electronic search strategy has been executed, identified records (often termed *hits* at this stage) should be exported into an electronic reference management library. Care must be taken to ensure that all identified hits from across all electronic databases are exported. It is not sufficient to export only the top number or proportion of hits.

Once exported, reviewers will need to check for duplicated hits (i.e., studies that have been indexed by more than one electronic database). While all electronic reference management libraries do have in-built deduplication functions, these have known limitations, particularly where there are minor spelling or punctuation differences between hits of the same study (Qi et al., 2013). Therefore, a three-stage process is generally recommended (Kwon, Lemieux, McTavish, & Wathen, 2015):

- use of the in-built automated deduplication function,
- use of the in-built automated deduplication function in Microsoft® Excel®, and
- manual identification.

Organizing Results From the Electronic Search in Preparation for Screening

The final stage is to organize all deduplicated hits into a suitable format for screening against the review's inclusion and exclusion criteria. Once exported to an electronic reference management library, deduplicated hits can easily be exported into a number of software applications for screening. If working remotely in a team of reviewers, the reviewers may find Web-based screening management software to be particularly useful at this stage (MacDonald, Misener, Weeks, & Helwig, 2016).

Screening Studies for Inclusion in the Review

A key feature of systematic reviews, compared with narrative reviews, is the use of prespecified objective and reproducible criteria for determining which studies should be included in the review (O'Connor, Green, & Higgins, 2008). Determining which studies to include, and which to exclude, will therefore have important implications for the review's findings, generalizability, quality, and utility.

Developing Robust Inclusion and Exclusion Criteria

The inclusion and exclusion criteria applied to the review should reflect both the review's broader research question and each of the PICO components including, where relevant, any restrictions on study design. While the specific inclusion and exclusion criteria will vary between reviews as a consequence of the research question and the relative weighting assigned to each of the PICO components, as a general rule, some common inclusion and exclusion criteria are outlined in Table 13.4.

Table 13.4 Common inclusion and exclusion criteria

Criteria	Explanation
Comparators	Reflecting the *C* component of the PICO acronym, studies may be excluded on the basis of the comparison group or condition used. This may be particularly important for reviews where meta-analysis is planned (see Table 13.2).
Diagnosis	Reflecting the *P* component of the PICO acronym (i.e., participants, patients, population, or problem), limits may be placed on the diagnoses participants in the included studies are diagnosed with, as well as how these diagnoses were made (see Table 13.2).
Design	Excluding studies on the basis of their design can help to improve the homogeneity of the review. This may be particularly important for reviews in which meta-analysis is planned.
Time period	Where a previous systematic review has been published, reviewers may decide to update the field by including only studies published after the publication date of the previous systematic review. Also, where a treatment or intervention was only made available after a given date, reviewers may decide to include only studies published after this date.
Intervention(s) (or Exposure[s])	Reflecting the *I* component of the PICO acronym, studies may be excluded where participants did not receive the same intervention (or exposure), in the same dosage, and/or over the same intervention (or exposure) period (see Table 13.2).
Language	Limited resources may mean that reviewers are unable to access translation services. The inclusion of studies published in different languages may therefore not be possible. This should, nevertheless, be acknowledged as a potential limitation.
Outcome(s)	Reflecting the *O* component of the PICO acronym, studies that do not report information or data on the key outcome(s) of interest of the review may be excluded. Further limits may also be placed on how the outcome(s) were measured (e.g., self-report vs. objective measures), and how outcomes were operationalized (e.g., what psychometric tools were used to assess, for example, suicidal ideation) (see Table 13.2).

While some reviews also use inclusion and exclusion criteria that reflect study quality (Meline, 2006), the Cochrane Collaboration recommends all studies should be included in a systematic review irrespective of their quality; although study quality should nonetheless be assessed and reported for each study included in the review.

Screening Studies for Inclusion or Exclusion

Typically, a two-stage process is employed to screen studies for inclusion or exclusion:
- title and abstract screening and
- full-text screening.

Title and Abstract Screening

Concurrently screening each study's title and abstract together represents a more efficient strategy, and is also associated with greater precision, compared with a multistage process where study titles are screened first, followed by abstracts (Mateen, Oh, Tergas, Bhayani, & Kamdar, 2013).

At this stage, two reviewers work independently of one another to determine which studies may be eligible for inclusion based on the content contained in each study's title and abstract only. Eligibility criteria should be applied liberally, and studies should only be excluded if they clearly meet one or more of the exclusion criteria, to avoid prematurely excluding potentially relevant studies (Meline, 2006).

Full-Text Screening

At the next stage, the full texts of all studies identified as potentially relevant for inclusion on the basis of title and abstract screening should be downloaded and rescreened by at least two reviewers working independently of one another. Where the full text of a potentially relevant study cannot be readily located online, efforts should be made wherever possible to contact the senior (or corresponding) author of the primary study for a copy. Your institutional information technician and/or librarian may also be able to assist with requesting full-text copies of studies that cannot be located online.

Any disagreements between reviewers as to whether a specific study should be included or excluded from the review should, at this stage, be resolved either by deferring to a senior author with considerable expertise in the field or, preferably, through consensus discussions among the review team (Higgins & Deeks, 2008).

It may also be necessary to contact the senior (or corresponding) author of the primary study at this stage for clarification to assist in determining whether the study is relevant for inclusion in the review. For example, it may be that although data on a given outcome (e.g., suicide death) were not reported in the published study, these data are nonetheless available and can be provided by the senior (or corresponding author) on request. In a recent review of cognitive behavior-based interventions for the prevention of nonfatal self-harm, for example, although over three quarters of studies were able to provide information on suicide, these data had to be requested from the authors in the majority of cases (Witt, Townsend, et al., 2019).

Specific Issues

Identifying Duplicate (and Multiple) Studies Using the Same Sample

Duplicate (and multiple) studies are those in which data from the same pool of participants are published in two or more studies. The inclusion of data from the same pool of participants can introduce substantial bias into a review; particularly where meta-analysis is planned. This can have serious consequences as a result, up to and including a formal retraction of the review from publication (Parsaik, Singh, Khosh-Chashm, & Mascarenhas, 2015).

The extent of overlap between studies can range from complete to partial overlap. *Complete overlap* occurs when an identical study reporting the same outcomes in the same sample is published in two or more publications. The inclusion of these studies in any systematic review or meta-analysis is generally not justified. *Partial overlap* occurs when a similar study reporting either new outcomes, new data, or data from a subset of the original study sample is published in two or more publications. The inclusion of these studies may be justified, particularly if the secondary study is reporting data for a new outcome. Care must be taken to ensure that the overlapping studies are never pooled together into a single meta-analysis, however.

While there are no standard tools or procedures for detecting study overlap, asking yourself the following questions may assist in identifying such studies:

- Do the studies cross-reference one other?
- Do the studies share the same or similar authors?
- Were participants recruited from the same setting (e.g., clinic, hospital) over the same time period and with the same (or similar) diagnosis/exposure/intervention?
- Looking at the number of participants included and their demographic characteristics, are these the same or similar? Remember that if one paper was published a number of years before the overlapping study, the mean or median age of the sample will have advanced by the same number of years, but many other demographic characteristics will remain the same.
- For studies based on mortality registries, are the same outcome data being used across studies? Are the exposure data similar?

If the studies are RCTs or cluster randomized controlled trials (cRCTs), the following additional questions may also help:

- Are the clinical trials registration numbers the same?
- Additionally, if the study is an RCT or cRCT, access the clinical trials registration record online. Are the studies listed as multiple publications for the same registration record?

However, in the field of suicide prevention, even where the provision of a registered clinical trial number is a requirement under the Consolidated Standards of Reporting Trials (CONSORT) for RCTs, few studies provide such registration numbers, complicating the identification of overlapping studies in this field (Witt, Potts, et al., 2019).

Additionally, because suicide prevention is a relatively small field internationally, it is common to see the same authors collaborate with one another on different studies, further complicating the identification of overlapping studies. Consulting with senior reviewers with expertise in the field will therefore also help with the identification of studies suspected of overlapping with one another.

Extracting Data and Methodological Information From Studies Included

The most time-consuming aspect of any systematic review is the process of extracting data and information from the included studies in an objective and systematic manner. To assist with this, reviewers use a standard template for extracting information from included studies (*pro forma*), which they pilot test on a random proportion of all included studies to ensure it contains the various information fields needed to successfully answer the research question(s).

A number of examples of such pro formas are freely available online. At a minimum, however, these should contain fields to record information on:

- The study's first author and contact details
- Year of publication
- Study country
- Study setting (e.g., hospital, school, clinic)
- Study design
- Intervention or exposure duration
- Intervention or exposure dosage
- Sample age
- Sample sex or gender composition
- Any relevant diagnoses and information on the diagnostic criteria used to determine these
- Any relevant comorbidities and information on the criteria used to determine these
- Total number of participants at baseline
- Number of participants allocated to the intervention or exposure and control conditions
- Total number of participants at each relevant outcome assessment time point
- Number of participants in the intervention or exposure and control conditions
- Proportion of dropouts from baseline to the final follow-up assessment
- Proportion of dropouts in the intervention or exposure and control conditions
- Information on funding sources
- Any other relevant conflicts of interests (including, in the case of interventions, whether the person or persons who developed the intervention were also involved in their evaluation)

For each outcome included in the review, moreover, the following should be recorded:

- How the outcome was ascertained (e.g., self-report, other-report, or objective measure)
- If relevant, the tool used either to ascertain or measure the outcome (e.g., name of a standard psychometric scale)
- If relevant, information on anchor points and scale valence of the tool
- If relevant, units of measurement
- Total number of participants with data on the outcome at each relevant time point (including in the intervention or exposure, and control conditions)
- Number of participants with the outcome of interest at each relevant time point (including in the intervention or exposure, and control conditions)
- Number and proportion of participants with missing data for the outcome at each relevant time point (including in the intervention or exposure, and control conditions)
- Information on the time point (e.g., postintervention or follow-up assessment, and number of days, weeks, months, or years in the case of follow-up assessments)

Given that mistakes in extraction data represent the single largest source of error in a systematic review (Mathes, Klaßen, & Pieper 2017), and can lead to bias in the estimate of effect size where meta-analysis is used, guidelines recommend that a minimum of two reviewers extract data from included studies independently from one another (Buscemi, Hartling, Vandermeer, Tjosvold, & Klassen, 2006). Consensus discussions with a senior reviewer with expertise in the field can also help to resolve mistakes in data extraction.

Assessing Methodological Quality (Risk of Bias)

Assessing the methodological quality of the included studies involves critical appraisal and judgment regarding whether there were any potential risks of bias. Here *bias* refers to any "systematic error, or deviation from the truth, in results or inferences" (Higgins & Altman, 2008, p. 188) with the potential to lead to findings which may not reflect the true situation. Variability in bias can help to explain variation in results observed between the different studies included in a systematic review or meta-analysis.

Given that sources of bias will also vary between studies using different designs, several design-specific tools have been developed to assist reviewers with assessing risk of bias.

Randomized Controlled Trials

In the hierarchy of research designs, an RCT is considered the most robust study design for assessing the effectiveness of interventions (see Chapter 7 for a detailed description). Eligible participants are randomly allocated either to receive the intervention or the control. The process of randomization minimizes noncomparability between these two groups, and therefore any difference between the two groups at postintervention is hypothesized to arise from the effect of the intervention (Torgerson & Torgerson, 2008).

However, bias in the methods used either to select participants into the RCT or allocate participants to the intervention or control conditions, or inadequate blinding of participants, study personnel, and/or outcome assessors, as well as incomplete outcome reporting, can all still affect the quality of evidence from an RCT. For this reason, the Cochrane Collaboration recommends that consideration should be given to each of the biases outlined in Table 13.5 (Higgins et al., 2011; Sterne et al., 2019).

Highlighting the importance of assessing for methodological bias in the field of self-harm and suicide prevention, recent work suggests that RCTs characterized by inadequate allocation concealment and outcome assessor blinding, for example, may overestimate the effectiveness of cognitive behavior therapy (CBT) for the prevention of repeat self-harm, by as much as 63% (Witt, Townsend, et al., 2019).

Cluster Randomized Controlled Trials

In cRCTs (see Chapter 7 for a detailed description), the unit of randomization constitutes a group (or *cluster*) – for example, a school class or all those attending a particular general practitioner, clinic, or hospital, rather than an individual participant. This design is commonly used where it is considered likely that participants allocated to the control condition may be unintentionally exposed to the intervention, or aspects of the intervention (Torgerson & Torgerson, 2008).

Table 13.5 Version 2.0 of Cochrane Collaboration's tool for assessing risk of bias in RCTs

Domain	Source of bias	Explanation
Randomization process	Random sequence generation	Any systematic difference in the characteristics of the intervention and control groups at baseline (Higgins et al., 2011). While randomization should minimize selection bias, this can only be successfully achieved if participants are allocated to the intervention and control groups via a truly randomized process.
	Allocation concealment	Researchers should have no foreknowledge of allocations, to ensure the randomization sequence cannot be intentionally subverted (Higgins et al., 2011).
	Baseline differences between the intervention and control groups	Any differences between the intervention and control groups, particularly with regard to prognostic factors, may suggest a problem with the adequacy of the randomization process and may bias estimates of treatment effectiveness unless statistically controlled in analyses (Twisk et al., 2018).
Effect of assignment	Blinding of participants and clinical personnel	Any systematic difference between the intervention and control groups in terms of either the standard of care provided or in exposure to factors other than the intervention treatment (Higgins et al., 2011). Blinding (or masking) participants and study personnel is often used to reduce this risk; however, blinding may not always be possible. In self-harm and suicide prevention research, for example, it is generally not possible to blind participants and clinical personnel where a psychosocial therapy (e.g., CBT) is evaluated (Hawton et al., 2016).
	Deviation(s) from the intended intervention	Changes to the intervention that are inconsistent with what was proposed in the RCT's original trial protocol. This may be due to difficulties in recruitment or retention of participants, and/or where participants, clinical personnel, outcome assessors, or others undermine implementation of the intervention (Sterne et al., 2019). Further items require reviewers to assess the extent to which such deviations may have affected the outcome(s) and whether their effects were likely to have been balanced between the intervention and control groups.
	Use of appropriate analyses to estimate the treatment effect	Analyzing data by excluding participants who did not receive the assigned intervention (*per protocol analyses*) or by grouping participants according to the treatment they did receive, rather than the treatment to which they were assigned (*as treated analyses*) can bias the estimate of the treatment effect. Instead, the use of intention-to-treat analyses in which data from participants are analyzed according to allocation assignment are generally considered appropriate (Sterne et al., 2019).
Missing outcome data	Availability of outcome data	Data should generally not be missing for more than approximately 5 % of the participant pool, depending on the risks of the event (Sterne et al., 2019). Any systematic differences between the intervention and control groups in terms of differential levels of missing data between groups should also be considered.
	Evidence the treatment effect was not influenced by missing outcome data	Analyzing data in such a way as to minimize the risk that the result was influenced by missing outcome data by, for example, correcting for missing data statistically or by conducting sensitivity analyses to demonstrate the results changed little under a variety of different assumptions as to the causes and/or effects of the missing data (Sterne et al., 2019).

continued on next page

Table 13.5 continued

Domain	Source of bias	Explanation
	Dependency of missing outcome data on the *true* value	Missing data may be related to participants' health status, leading some participants to prematurely exit from the RCT. In these cases, missing data may be dependent on the true value and may therefore lead to bias in the assessment of the treatment effect (Sterne et al., 2019). Further questions require reviewers to reflect on the extent to which dependency of missing outcome data on the *true* value may be different for the intervention as compared with the control group.
Measurement of the outcome	Appropriateness of method(s) used to ascertain the outcome	Suitability of the method(s) used to measure the outcome(s) (Sterne et al., 2019).
	Differences in the ascertainment of the outcome(s) between groups.	Any systematic difference in the method(s) used to measure the outcome(s) between the intervention and control groups, including the timing of the outcome assessment(s) between groups (Sterne et al., 2019).
	Blinding of outcome assessors	Any systematic difference between the intervention and control groups in how the primary and secondary outcomes were measured (Higgins et al., 2011). Blinding (or masking) outcome assessors may reduce the risk that knowledge of which group a participant was assigned may affect outcome measurement and/or interpretation.
	Participant knowledge of the intervention received	Where self-reported outcome(s) are used, it is appropriate to consider the extent to which the participants' knowledge of the assigned intervention could influence their assessment of any participant-reported outcome(s) (Sterne et al., 2019). Further questions ask reviewers to reflect on the likelihood that assessment of the outcome was influenced by this knowledge.
Reporting bias	Selective outcome reporting	Occurs when there are systematic differences between the analyses that were planned (for example, in an RCT protocol) and those that are ultimately published (Sterne et al., 2019). This may occur, for example, where only statistically significant differences between the intervention and control groups are reported (Higgins & Altman, 2008).
	Selective reporting of multiple measurements of the same outcome	Occurs where a trial protocol indicates that a certain outcome (e.g., suicidal ideation) will be measured in multiple ways (e.g., using both self-reported and clinician-rated scales), and yet only data from one of these measurements is published. The concern here is that the choice may have been influenced by statistical significance (Sterne et al., 2019).
	Selective reporting of multiple eligible analyses of data	Occurs where a trial protocol indicates that, for example, data for both the unadjusted and adjusted models will be reported, but data for only one of these models is subsequently published. This may also occur where different models are proposed to account for missing data. Again, the concern here is that model choice may have been influenced by statistical significance (Sterne et al., 2019).
Any other biases		These may include particular sources of bias relevant to certain study types; for example, carry-over effects for crossover trials, and recruitment bias in cluster randomized trials. Other biases may also be of relevance to studies conducted in particular clinical settings.

In addition to the sources of bias as outlined in Table 13.5, cRCTs present unique sources of bias because data are structured on two levels: the individual participant level and the cluster level. Given that individuals within a cluster are likely to be more similar to one another than those between clusters, data from individuals included in a cRCT cannot be assumed to be independent. Therefore, unless statistical adjustment is made for the effects of clustering, data from cRCTs may overestimate the treatment effect (Donner & Klar, 2002).

For this reason, reviewers must obtain information on:

- the number of clusters,
- the average number of individual participants included in these clusters, and
- an estimate of the intracluster coefficient (ICC) between clusters.

While several methods are available for adjusting results for the effects of clustering (Donner & Klar, 2002), a simple approach is to use the above information to estimate the design effect which represents a value by which the total number of participants allocated to the intervention group, as well as the number of participants experiencing the outcome(s) of interest in the case of dichotomous (or binary) outcomes, is reduced. The formula to calculate the design effect is available elsewhere (Higgins, Deeks, & Altman, 2008). Where data on the ICC is not reported in the original study, reviewers should first contact the senior (or corresponding) author to ascertain whether this value can be provided on request or, failing this, use the ICC from another similar and reliable cRCT (Higgins et al., 2008).

cRCTs are also characterized by a higher risk of selection bias given that the recruitment of individual participants into cRCTs typically occurs after clusters have been allocated either to the intervention or control conditions. As a consequence, allocation can rarely, if ever, be concealed from participants and clinical personnel leading to biased recruitment into the trial. For example, participants with a more severe illness course may choose to attend the clinic randomized to the intervention condition. Participants may also differentially refuse consent to participate in the trial depending on which condition, intervention or control, their clinic was allocated (Hahn, Puffer, Torgerson, & Watson, 2005).

In recognition of these risks, an updated version of the Cochrane Collaboration's risk of bias tool is available for the assessment of risk of bias in cRCTs (Eldridge et al., 2016).

Crossover Trials

In *crossover trials* (see Chapter 7 for a detailed description), participants are randomized to receive a sequence of interventions – for example, a 6-week trial of CBT followed by 6 weeks of *treatment as usual* (TAU), and it is the ordering of this sequence that is randomized so that half the participants receive CBT first, and the remainder receive TAU first. Compared with RCTs, crossover trials may minimize between-participant variation, as each patient acts as their own control (Sibbald & Roberts, 1998).

In addition to the sources of bias outlined in Table 13.5, a particular source of bias in crossover trials is the *carry-over effect,* whereby the effect of the intervention may influence a participant's response to the control condition (Elbourne et al., 2002). This, in turn, may lead to an underestimation of the effectiveness of the intervention (Curtin, Elbourne, & Altman, 2002). While methods are available to statistically account for carry-over effects (Higgins et al., 2008), a simple solution involves extracting all outcome data from the first phase of the trial, prior to the point of crossover. However, review authors taking this approach should carefully assess any risk of bias that might be introduced as a consequence (Higgins, 2016).

A second unique source of bias in crossover trials occurs where there are systematic differences in the first phase of the trial as compared with the second phase of the trial beyond the effect of the intervention alone. Termed the *period effect,* this may occur where there is a major change in health care policy which affects the way in which persons at risk of suicide are treated or managed.

An updated version of the Cochrane Collaboration's risk of bias tool is available for crossover trials (Higgins, 2016).

Zelen's Postconsent Design

While rare, some studies in the field of self-harm and suicide prevention have implemented Zelen's postconsent design, whereby participants are randomized and allocated either to the intervention or control group of the RCT prior to their consent being sought (Zelen, 1979). It is not currently known what effect, if any, use of Zelen's postconsent design may have on estimates of treatment effectiveness in the field of self-harm and suicide prevention, as so few studies have used this design (Witt, Townsend, et al., 2019). One recent Cochrane review found that the addition of studies employing Zelen's postconsent design typically had little impact on the magnitude of the effect size for both CBT and brief postdischarge contact interventions for the prevention of repeat self-harm (Hawton et al., 2016).

Nonetheless, where studies employing this design are included in a meta-analysis, it is recommended that subgroup analyses are undertaken to investigate what impact the inclusion of studies using this design may have had on the magnitude of the treatment effect size.

Cohort Studies

In a *cohort study* a given population (*cohort*) is identified and followed up longitudinally over time (see Chapter 6 for a detailed description). Members of the cohort share a common exposure (e.g., an emergency department presentation following a suicide attempt, or CBT for suicidal ideation) or condition (e.g., a diagnosis of borderline personality disorder) and are then followed forward to determine which outcome(s) (e.g., suicide) occur as a result (Grimes & Schulz, 2002). The key difference between RCTs and cohort studies is that participants are not, and often cannot be, randomly allocated to experience the exposure of interest – one is an experimental and another an observational study (see Chapter 6 and Chapter 7 for details).

Traditionally two cohorts are included in these types of studies, one which experiences an event or condition or intervention hypothesized to be associated with the outcome(s) of interest (the *exposed cohort*); the other being an unexposed (or *reference* or *control*) cohort. The control cohort may either be followed up over the same time period as the exposed cohort (*concurrent controls*), or they may have been followed up at an earlier point in time (*historical controls*) (Grimes & Schulz, 2002).

Although the terminology used to refer to bias in RCTs and cohort, case-control, and other observational studies differs, many biases share a similar cause and similar impacts (Ali Mansournia, Higgins, Sterne, & Hernán, 2017). To assist reviewers in assessing risks of bias in controlled cohort studies, members of the Cochrane Collaboration have developed the Risk of Bias in Non-randomized Studies of Interventions (ROBINS-I) tool; an outline of which is provided in Table 13.6 (Sterne et al., 2016).

Table 13.6 Risk of Bias in Nonrandomized Studies of Interventions (ROBINS-I) tool for assessing risk of bias in nonrandomized cohort and case-control studies

Domain	Source of bias	Explanation
Preintervention	Baseline confounding	A confounder is a third variable which changes the association between the exposure or intervention and the outcome. To be a confounding factor, this third variable must be (1) associated with the exposure or intervention; (2) associated with the outcome, (3) not lie on the causal pathway between the exposure or intervention and the outcome. Baseline confounding is particularly problematic where this third factor is also prognostic such that it may influence the likelihood that an individual will receive the exposure or intervention (Sterne et al., 2016).
	Selection bias	Occurs where otherwise eligible participants are differentially excluded from the exposed or intervention as compared with control cohorts (Sterne et al., 2016). This bias is generally less problematic in prospective, as compared with retrospective, cohort studies, because participants are enrolled into the study before outcome status has been determined.
Intervention	Classification bias	Occurs where an individual's exposure or intervention status is inaccurately determined. Classification bias can be either differential or non-differential. *Differential classification bias* occurs where misclassification of exposure or intervention status is likely to be related to outcome status and is highly problematic. *Nondifferential classification bias* occurs where the misclassification of exposure or intervention status is unlikely to be related to outcome status and is therefore less problematic (Sterne et al., 2016).
Postintervention	Deviation from the intended intervention	Any systematic difference in the care received by the exposed or intervention and the control cohorts which represents a departure from the intended intervention (Sterne et al., 2016). Consideration should also be given to the effects of *contamination* whereby the standard of care changes during the follow-up period through, for example, the introduction of new clinical practice guidelines (Thompson, Craig, Hilton-Boon, Campbell, & Katikireddi, 2018). However, this may not always be clearly assessed or known. Contamination may also occur where the intervention is easily accessible by the public and does not require a prescription or referral from a health care professional (Thompson et al., 2018).
	Missing data	Occurs where otherwise eligible participants are excluded from analysis due to incomplete data on exposure or intervention status, confounders, or where there is differential loss to follow-up of participants in the exposed or intervention and the control cohorts that may be affected by prognostic factors (Sterne et al., 2016). While missing data is common in cohort studies as cohort members may die, move, or migrate out of the study's catchment area, and/or refuse to continue participating, it is particularly problematic where there are differential levels or reasons for missing data in the exposed or intervention and the control cohorts.
	Outcome measurement	Any systematic differences in the measurement of outcomes for the exposed or intervention and the control cohorts, including where outcome assessors are made aware of exposure or intervention status, if different methods are used to ascertain outcomes in the exposed or intervention and the control cohorts, and/or where there is a different rate of measurement error between the exposed or intervention and the control cohorts (Sterne et al., 2016).
	Selection of reported results	Occurs where outcome(s) are selectively reported for the exposed or intervention and the control cohorts (Sterne et al., 2016).

Case-Control Studies

In *case-control studies* (see Chapter 6 for a detailed description), participants who have experienced the outcome(s) of interest (e.g., a hospital admission for attempted suicide – that is, *cases*) are selected and matched to those who have not (*controls*). Researchers then track back in time to determine which cases and controls were exposed to the risk factor or intervention of interest, and which were not. The key difference between cohort and case-control studies is that the latter design moves backwards in time (i.e., determining outcome status first, before ascertaining participants' exposure status). Therefore, while case-control studies can provide valuable information on association, they should not be used to demonstrate causality (Miettinen, 1976).

Case-control studies are common in the field of self-harm and suicide prevention research, as many of the key outcomes assessed in this field, and particularly suicide, are uncommon (or rare). Case-control studies can therefore oversample cases to ensure analyses will have sufficient statistical power to detect treatment effects.

Reviewers can use the ROBINS-I tool to assess for risks of bias in case-control studies (Sterne et al., 2016).

Uncontrolled Study Designs

While other *uncontrolled study designs* are included in the hierarchy of research designs, including *case series* and *case reports* (see Chapter 6 for details), these are generally not included in systematic reviews and meta-analyses in the field of self-harm and suicide prevention research and will not be considered further.

Conducting a Meta-Analysis

Recall that a systematic review can be conducted without a meta-analysis, but that a meta-analysis cannot be conducted without a systematic review. The final (optional) step in the systematic review process is therefore to statistically combine results from studies included in the review into a meta-analysis.

A key advantage of a meta-analysis over a systematic review is that the magnitude of the effect size for a particular intervention – for example, CBT for the prevention of repeat self-harm – can be calculated and quantified by pooling together data from different studies. However, the process of conducting a meta-analysis is complex, and support from a biostatistician is strongly recommended, particularly for first-time reviewers. This person can assist in advising on:

- Choosing effect size(s)
- Choosing the correct statistical model
- Quantifying heterogeneity
- Detecting small study effects (publication bias)
- Other specific issues

Choosing Effect Size(s)

Effect sizes represent the magnitude or strength between two variables – for example, the effect of the exposure or intervention (e.g., CBT) on the outcome(s) of interest (e.g., repetition of self-harm or suicide death). For each study and each relevant outcome, therefore, the first step is to calculate effect sizes and their associated variance from the data reported in the original study (Borenstein, Hedges, Higgins, & Rothstein, 2009).

Choosing the effect size to use will depend on how the data from studies using different designs can be unified such that the effect size reported in one study will mean the same as (or be approximately similar to) that in another study, the type of data available to calculate the effect sizes, and how reviewers wish for effect sizes to be interpreted (Borenstein et al., 2009). In general, however, effect size choice will be guided by the type of data available within the original study reports, with different effect sizes preferred for dichotomous (or binary) outcomes as compared with continuous outcomes.

Dichotomous (or Binary) Outcomes

Dichotomous (or binary) *outcomes* are those in which only the presence or absence of the outcome is possible. A simple example is suicide; a participant has either died by suicide during the follow-up period, or they have not. Common effect sizes for dichotomous outcomes as used in the field of self-harm and suicide prevention are outlined in Table 13.7.

Table 13.7 Common effect sizes for dichotomous outcomes

Effect size	Interpretation	Guidance
Odds ratio	Ratio of the odds of the outcome of interest occurring in the intervention group as compared with the odds in the control group. Odds ratios are centered at 1.00 such that a value of 1.00 indicates no association. An odds ratio of greater than 1.00 indicates increased odds of the outcome occurring in the intervention group, while a value of less than 1.00 indicates decreased odds of the outcome occurring in the intervention group (Ranganathan, Aggarwal, & Pramesh, 2015).	Odds ratios and their standard errors must be log-transformed prior to analysis and only back-transformed to their original metrics once all analyses have been completed to assist with interpretation (Deeks, Higgins, & Altman, 2008).
Risk ratio	Ratio of the probability of the outcome of interest occurring in the intervention group as compared with the control group. The risk ratio is centered at 1.00. Therefore, a risk ratio of 1.00 indicates no difference between the intervention and control groups. A risk ratio of greater than 1.00 indicates an increased risk of the outcome occurring in the intervention group, while a value of less than 1.00 indicates a decreased risk of the outcome occurring in the intervention group (Ranganathan et al., 2015).	Risk ratios and their standard errors must be log-transformed prior to analysis and only back-transformed to their original metrics once all analyses have been completed to assist with interpretation (Deeks et al., 2008).
Risk difference	Difference in risks between the intervention and control groups in the outcome of interest.	Can be analyzed in their original metrics.

Continuous Outcomes

Continuous outcomes in suicide prevention are typically scores on a validated scale (e.g., scores on a measure of suicidal ideation). For outcomes measured on a continuous scale, common effect sizes are outlined in Table 13.8.

Table 13.8 Common effect sizes for continuous outcomes

Effect size	Interpretation	Guidance
Mean difference	The absolute difference in mean values for the outcome of interest in the intervention group as compared with the control group. A mean difference of zero means there is no difference between the two groups. If the intervention is hypothesized to lead to higher scores on the outcome of interest, than a mean difference of greater than zero would indicate the intervention was more effective than the control, while a mean difference of less than zero would indicate the intervention was less effective than the control. If the intervention is hypothesized to lead to lower scores on the outcome of interest, on the other hand, then a mean difference of less than zero would indicate the intervention was more effective than control, while a mean difference of greater than zero would indicate the intervention was less effective than the control (Faraone, 2008).	Cannot be used where studies included in the meta-analysis used different scales to measure the same outcome.
Standardized mean difference	The difference in standardized mean values for the outcome of interest in the intervention group as compared with the control group. A standardized mean difference of zero means there is no difference between the two groups. The standardized mean difference has the same interpretation as the mean difference, depending on the hypothesized direction of the treatment effect (Faraone, 2008).	Can be used where the studies included in the meta-analysis used different measures for the same outcome. Values are standardized onto the same metric so that comparison between studies is possible, irrespective of the measure used to ascertain the outcome (Deeks et al., 2008).

While converting between effect sizes for dichotomous and continuous outcomes is possible (Chinn, 2000); in practice, not all conversion formulae yield symmetric results. Additionally, converting a continuous effect size to a dichotomous effect size (and vice versa) will result in a different interpretation for the association. Therefore, the advice of a biostatistician is crucial if undertaking conversion of effect sizes.

Choosing Statistical Models

Meta-analyses in the field of self-harm and suicide prevention generally use one of two statistical methods for pooling effect sizes from the individual studies included in the analysis (Cumming, 2012).

Fixed Effect Model

A *fixed effect model* assumes that all studies included in the meta-analysis estimate the same underlying true effect size, and that any variability between studies reflects error, rather than indicating anything meaningful about differences in the effectiveness of the intervention of interest in different, potentially clinically relevant, subgroups of patients (Borenstein et al., 2009).

Implicit in the assumption of the fixed effect model is that the studies included in the meta-analysis represent the entire universe of studies that have addressed the research question; including those studies that are yet to be conducted (Hunter & Schmidt, 2000). Given that these assumptions can seldom be justified in the field of self-harm and suicide prevention, implementing a fixed effect meta-analysis will not be considered further.

Random Effects Model

A *random effects model*, in contrast, assumes that the studies included in a meta-analysis estimate slightly different effect sizes and that between-study variability in the magnitude of the effect size may be caused either by sampling error or by true differences in the effect size for different clinically relevant subgroups of patients (Borenstein et al., 2009). To account for this, the random effects model takes into account two sources of error in the calculation of the pooled effect size: *within*- and *between*-study error. Results from a random effects meta-analysis will therefore have wider confidence intervals, and are less likely to be influenced by the results of larger studies, as compared with those obtained using the fixed effect model (Borenstein et al., 2009). Therefore, results from a random effects model are typically viewed as providing a more conservative estimation of the pooled effect size. If there is no between-study variation, then a random effects model will produce the same or similar result to a fixed effect model.

The random effects model also assumes that the studies included in the meta-analysis represent only a sample of all work conducted in the area. Therefore, the random effects method is thought to be more flexible if studies have been inadvertently missed in the systematic review, or if further studies are added to the meta-analysis in the future. As a consequence, results from a random effects meta-analysis are typically viewed as possessing greater generalizability (Erez, Bloom, & Wells, 1996).

Quantifying Between-Study Heterogeneity

While some variability in effect sizes between the studies included in a pooled meta-analysis is to be expected as a consequence of combining studies of various designs conducted in various samples and settings (Higgins, Thompson, Deeks, & Altman, 2003), excessive between-study variability (termed *heterogeneity*) may lead to biased estimates of the pooled effect size. Between-study heterogeneity can reflect a number of potential causes, including:

- clinical diversity between samples, including diversity in treatment as usual;
- methodological variability in study designs; and/or
- statistical variability in the analysis of outcomes.

Assessing both the presence and extent of between-study heterogeneity therefore represents a crucial step in meta-analysis. The presence of heterogeneity is typically assessed using one of two measures: *Cochran's Q* statistic or the I^2 statistic.

Cochran's Q sums the squared deviation of each individual study's effect size from the pooled effect size. By comparing this deviation to a chi-squared distribution with k-1 degrees of freedom, Cochran's Q indicates if the overall result is affected by significant heterogeneity (Cochran, 1954). However, Cochran's Q cannot quantify the extent of this heterogeneity.

The I^2 statistic, on the other hand, indicates the percentage of variability due to between-study factors rather than error and therefore can indicate both the presence and, importantly, the extent of between-study heterogeneity (Higgins & Thompson, 2002). The I^2 statistic can take any value between 0 % and 100 %, with higher values indicative of greater heterogeneity. The Cochrane Collaboration recommends the following interpretative values for the I^2 statistic (Higgins et al., 2003):

- unimportant: 0 % to 24.9 %;
- low heterogeneity: 25.0 % to 49.9 %;
- moderate heterogeneity: 50.0 % to 74.9 %; and
- high heterogeneity: 75 % and above.

Investigating Potential Causes of Between-Study Heterogeneity

Where a meta-analysis is characterized by moderate to high between-study heterogeneity, reviewers should investigate potential causes through sensitivity analyses, subgroup analyses, or meta-regression; although it should be remembered that, ideally, reviewers should prespecify any such analyses at the outset.

It is important to remember that any factors chosen either for sensitivity, subgroup, or meta-regression analyses are unlikely to be randomly distributed between the intervention and control groups (Littell, Corcoran, & Pillai, 2008), unless of course randomization was specifically stratified for the factor(s) of interest. Therefore, these types of analyses are, by definition, observational in nature and, while they can point to potential new directions for further research (Song, Sheldon, Sutton, Abrams, & Jones, 2001), they cannot allow for causal inferences to be made (Kelley & Kelley, 2012).

Additionally, when planning analyses to investigate potential causes of between-study heterogeneity, it is important to consider whether these analyses are likely to have sufficient statistical power. For this reason it is recommended that, at a minimum, there should be at least 10 studies included in a meta-analysis for every factor investigated in these analyses (Deeks et al., 2008).

Sensitivity Analyses

Sensitivity analyses represent a simple and easily implemented approach for quantifying the effect of heterogeneity between studies on the overall (or pooled) effect size. This method relies on excluding one or more studies from the meta-analysis based on prespecified criteria, recalculating the overall (or pooled) effect size, and comparing this with the result obtained when data for all eligible studies were included (Sutton, Abrams, Jones, Sheldon, & Song, 2000).

Ideally, the choice of which study or studies to exclude from the meta-analysis is driven by a priori theoretical, methodological, and/or clinical considerations, rather than by post hoc considerations (e.g., excluding studies until the I^2 statistic is reduced to a notional level).

However, in situations where it is unclear which study or studies may be contributing to between-study heterogeneity, an algorithmic selection method has been described (Patsopoulos, Evangelou, & Ioannidis, 2008). The performance of this method in the field of self-harm and suicide prevention, where studies often vary widely in terms of clinical diversity between samples, methodological variability in study designs, and statistical variability, is, however, not understood at present. This method should be used with caution, and the guidance of a biostatistician is generally recommended.

Subgroup Analyses

Subgroup analyses involve splitting the studies included in a meta-analysis up into a smaller number of more homogeneous subgroups, either on the basis of the composition of the sample (e.g., those that investigate the effectiveness of an intervention in females vs. males), the study design (e.g., RCTs vs. observational studies), setting (e.g., hospital vs. outpatient clinic), or other factor(s) hypothesized to reflect either clinical diversity between samples, methodological variability in study designs, and/or statistical variability in the analysis of outcomes between studies. The magnitude of the pooled effect size and the degree of overlap in the pooled 95 % confidence interval is then compared between these subgroups to enable inferences to be made as to potential causes of between-study heterogeneity.

However, a primary limitation of subgroup analyses is that many relevant factors may not be measured in a dichotomous (or binary) fashion. For example, in a recent meta-analysis of 66 RCTs of interventions for the prevention of repeated self-harm in adults and young people, only 7 (10.6 %) exclusively recruited one sex (in all cases, females). The majority of studies, in contrast, recruited both females and males (Witt, Townsend, et al., 2019). Therefore, these studies could not be neatly subgrouped into those that investigated the effect of the treatment in females, and those that investigated the effect in males. While it is possible to devise a threshold and consider subgrouping all those studies in which, for example, over three quarters of the sample is male, this threshold will often be arbitrary and will lead to substantial loss in statistical power.

Meta-Regression

Meta-regression represents a statistical method of investigating whether the overall (or pooled) effect size varies between studies as a consequence of subgroup effects, but importantly, it also allows for the investigation of factor(s) measured in a continuous fashion – for example, the exact proportion of males and females recruited into the sample, or whether the apparent effectiveness of an intervention depends on suicidal ideation scores at baseline.

Specifically, meta-regression investigates where there is a statistical relationship between one or more between-study factor(s) and the pooled effect size (Thompson & Higgins, 2002) and has an interpretation similar to either traditional logistic regression, where factor(s) have been measured in a dichotomous fashion, or traditional linear regression where factor(s) have been measured in a continuous fashion.

Meta-regression can be implemented using both a fixed effect and random effects model. However, simulation studies suggest that the fixed effect model may be associated with an inflated false-positive rate, particularly in circumstances where between-study heterogeneity is high (Higgins & Thompson, 2004). For this reason, meta-regression is typically implemented using the random effects model. This is particularly so where the meta-analysis itself has been implemented using a random effects model.

Detecting Small Study Effects (Publication Bias)

Given that studies with statistically significant findings are 3 times more likely to be submitted for publication than those with nonsignificant findings (Song et al., 2009), and are between 2 and 5 times more likely to be subsequently published (Dwan et al., 2008; Hopewell et al., 2009), reviewers should always investigate the extent and impact of publication bias.

Funnel Plots

Funnel plots visually display the effect size of each study included in the meta-analysis alongside a measure of the precision of the estimate – typically the standard error of the effect size (Sterne, Egger, & Moher, 2008). Recall that where the overall (pooled) effect size is an odds or risk ratio, the measure of precision will be the standard error of the logged odds or risk ratio.

Given that the precision of an effect size increases as the sample size increases, smaller studies will tend to be scattered widely at the bottom of the funnel plot and, as the sample size of the included studies increases, there will tend to be less variability around the overall (pooled) effect size, such that the effect sizes of these studies will be symmetrically centered around the overall (pooled) effect size (Sterne et al., 2008). In the absence of significant publication bias, the funnel plot should therefore resemble the example in Figure 13.1.

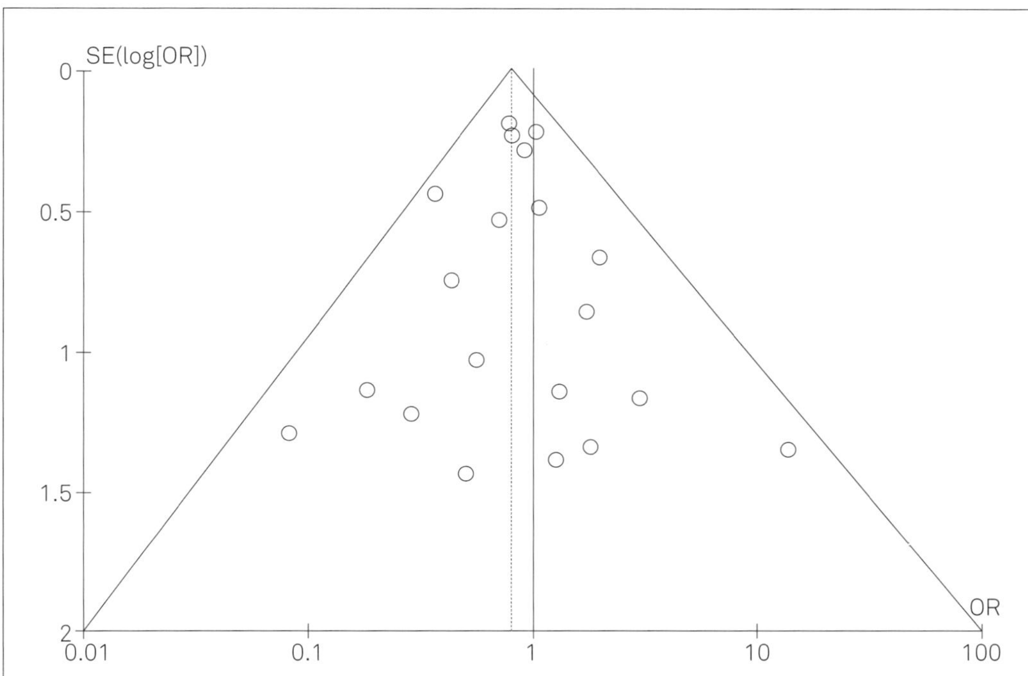

Figure 13.1 Example of a funnel plot in the absence of publication bias.

Publication bias, on the other hand, is typically inferred where asymmetry in the funnel plot is evident, particularly where individual study estimates appear to be missing from the bottom right-hand side of the plot (Sterne et al., 2008). It is important to remember, however, that factors other than publication bias can also give the appearance of funnel plot asymmetry (Hunter et al., 2014; Zwetsloot et al., 2017). These can include

- Chance effects
- True heterogeneity in the effect sizes of smaller as compared with larger studies
- Differences in methodological quality between studies
- Selective outcome reporting
- Choice of overall (pooled) effect size measure

For these reasons, funnel plot asymmetry is considered to be indicative of publication bias only (Sterne et al., 2008). Reasons for asymmetry can be particularly hard to determine where cohort and case-control studies are included in the review.

Statistical Approaches

A number of statistical approaches have also been developed to assist reviewers identify potential publication bias. These approaches all evaluate the extent to which the association between each individual study's effect size and precision is greater than may be expected by chance (Sterne et al., 2008).

While a number of these approaches can be applied to both dichotomous (binary) and continuous outcomes, choosing the correct statistical approach will depend on how the outcome has been measured. For example, the popular Egger's (Egger, Smith, Schneider, & Minder, 1997) and Begg's (Begg & Mazumdar, 1994) tests are not recommended where odds or risk ratios are used, because, in these circumstances, these tests have been found to result in a high likelihood of false-positive findings (Sterne et al., 2008). This is because the variance of these ratio-based effect sizes is mathematically related to their standard errors (Schwarzer, Antes, & Schumacher, 2002). For this reason, reviewers should obtain the advice of a biostatistician when planning which statistical approach to use to detect publication bias.

Other Specific Issues

Combining Studies of Differing Designs in a Single Meta-Analysis

While treatment effects obtained from RCTs and other nonrandomized controlled designs tend to correlate strongly, effect sizes from controlled cohort and case-control studies do tend to be larger than those obtained from RCTs (Ioannidis et al., 2001). Studies of differing designs are also often characterized by differing risks of bias.

For these reasons, pooling together effect sizes from studies of differing study designs into a single meta-analysis is problematic and also likely to lead to high levels of between-study heterogeneity. Where reviewers do include studies of differing designs in the review, it is usual to see results pooled by study design, using, for example, subgroup analyses.

Studies With Multiple Intervention Groups

Some studies in the field of self-harm and suicide prevention may compare multiple exposure or intervention groups against the same control group. Care must be taken to avoid simply entering these data into a single meta-analysis, as data from the control group will be double counted. A number of relatively simple methods are available to account for any unaddressed correlation that occurs with the inclusion of these types of studies.

First, reviewers may wish to consider whether the intervention groups are sufficiently similar in terms of therapeutic approach, dose, duration, and other relevant factors that data could be combined together (Higgins et al., 2008). It is important to note, however, that for outcomes measured on a continuous scale, appropriate formula must be used to combine data from separate groups (Higgins & Deeks, 2008).

Alternatively, depending on the nature of the research question and the way(s) in which the exposure or intervention condition has been operationalized, reviewers may choose to include data from only one intervention group (Higgins et al., 2008). Reviewers may also choose to split the shared control group up such that data from both intervention groups may be combined into a single meta-analysis without the risk of double counting data from the control group (Higgins et al., 2008). Other more sophisticated statistical methods are also available, including multilevel meta-analysis and network (or multiple treatments) meta-analysis. These are considered in further detail in the next section.

Extending the Traditional Meta-Analysis Model

Multilevel Meta-Analysis

The traditional meta-analysis model assumes each effect size included in the analysis is independent from the others (Cheung, 2019). Where multiple exposures or interventions or multiple outcomes from a single study are included in a single meta-analysis, however, data can no longer be assumed to be independent (Cheung, 2019). Reviewers commonly address potential violations of the assumption of independence by performing a series of separate meta-analyses for each exposure or intervention and outcome of interest. This approach, however, is inefficient, because only a portion of the available data is used (Van den Noortgate, López-López, Marín-Martínez, & Sánchez-Meca, 2014).

Multilevel meta-analysis, in contrast, accounts for dependencies between effect sizes due, for example, to the inclusion of multiple subgroups or outcomes from the same study, by taking the degree of dependency into account statistically. Specifically, multilevel meta-analysis calculates two sources of variance: that which occurs within studies and that which occurs between studies (Cheung, 2019). In this way, multilevel meta-analysis enables reviewers to investigate potential causes of heterogeneity not only between, but also within studies (Cheung, 2018).

However, it is rare to see multilevel meta-analyses in the field of self-harm and suicide prevention, because, at the time of writing, the model can only be implemented within the *R* statistical software environment. Reviewers interested in implementing a multilevel meta-analysis are therefore strongly encouraged to work closely with a biostatistician experienced in conducting multilevel meta-analysis.

Network (or Multiple Treatments) Meta-Analysis

Traditional meta-analyses can only estimate the relative effectiveness of two treatments (e.g., CBT vs. TAU) that have been directly compared across a number of studies. There may be times, however, where reviewers are interested in the relative effectiveness either of multiple interventions and/or interventions that have not yet been compared, head-to-head, within a single study.

Network meta-analysis allows reviewers to compare the relative effectiveness of more than two treatments within a single meta-analysis, but importantly, also enables reviewers to estimate the relative effectiveness of two interventions that have not been directly compared within a trial at present (Cipriani, Barbui, Rizzo, & Salanti, 2012). This is achieved by comparing direct effects (i.e., the effects of two or more treatments compared head-to-head within a single study) with indirect effects (i.e., the effects of multiple treatments compared with a common comparator, such as placebo or treatment as usual; Cipriani, Higgins, Geddes, & Salanti, 2013).

The guidance of a biostatistician is recommended, because network meta-analysis is characterized by a number of conceptual and technical challenges which have been discussed at length elsewhere (Cipriani et al., 2013). Importantly, however, network meta-analysis assumes that there are no important clinical, methodological, or other relevant differences between trials, other that the different treatments being compared (called the *principle of transitivity*) (Baker & Kramer, 2002). Additionally, it is important to remember that any indirect evidence is, by definition, observational in nature (Cipriani et al., 2013). Therefore, while they can point to potential new directions for further research, they cannot allow for causal inferences to be made.

However, a further challenge in the field of self-harm and suicide prevention is that, outside of pharmaceutical treatment trials, most interventions are compared with TAU. However, TAU, unlike placebo, is not a unitary construct. Instead, TAU will vary between studies conducted in different clinical centers, and particularly between studies conducted in different countries. TAU is also likely to differ between earlier and later studies, as many features of effective interventions are often integrated into TAU over time (Witt et al., 2018). Substantial variability in TAU between the studies included in a network meta-analysis may therefore bias the indirect comparisons obtained from a network meta-analysis.

Individual Participant (or Patient) Data Meta-Analysis

Thus far this chapter has only considered the use of aggregate data from each included study (i.e., where the study represents the unit of analysis). However, these analyses are unsuited to the identification of confounding unless all included studies report effect sizes adjusted for the same confounder(s) measured in the same, or similar, manner (Davey Smith, Egger, & Ebrahim, 2013).

Individual participant (or patient) data meta-analysis, in contrast, enables reviewers to:

- undertake consistent data checking and cleaning across studies,
- recalculate effect sizes consistently across studies, and
- undertake multivariate adjusted analyses to investigate the impact of one or more participant-level confounders on the effects observed.

In an individual participant data meta-analysis, reviewers obtain individual data from every individual who participated in each study included in the review (Stewart & Parmar, 1993). It is important to remember, however, that participant responses within a study are likely to be more similar to one another than those between studies. It is therefore inappropriate to analyze individual participant data as though these data were all obtained from the same study (Riley, Lambert, & Abo-Zaid, 2010).

Instead, appropriate methods must be used that account for clustering of participants within studies. In the one-step approach, reviewers analyze data from all participants in a single meta-analysis, accounting for clustering by introducing a stratification factor. Both fixed effect and random effects models are possible (Simmonds, Higgins, Stewart, Clarke, & Thompson, 2005). In the two-step approach, individual participant data are firstly analyzed to obtain study-level summary statistics. These are then synthesized across studies using the same aggregate-data meta-analysis methods previously described in the Conducting a Meta-Analysis section (Simmonds et al., 2005).

A principal advantage of individual participant data meta-analyses as compared with aggregate-data meta-analyses is that reviewers can undertake multivariate adjusted analyses to investigate the impact one or more participant confounders has on the effect observed. In the field of self-harm and suicide prevention, for example, although a number of aggregate-data meta-analyses (Bartoli et al., 2017; Witt, Potts, et al., 2019; Xu et al., 2016) and a single individual participant data meta-analysis (Wilkinson et al., 2017) have found that a single, low-dose intravenous infusion of ketamine may be associated with short-term reductions in suicidal ideation severity, only the individual participant data meta-analysis was able to investigate whether the apparent antisuicidal effect of ketamine occurred independently of its boarder effect in reducing the severity of depression symptomatology (Wilkinson et al., 2017).

However, it may not always be practical, or even feasible, to obtain individual participant data. Authors of the primary studies included in the review may no longer be traceable, may refuse permission to release raw data because of ethical and other considerations, or the data may have been destroyed or lost (Sutton, Kendrick, & Coupland, 2008). Under these circumstances, reviewers may choose to include only those studies for which individual participant data are available. Doing so, however, may introduce bias if these studies differ from those for which individual participant data cannot be obtained.

While various methods of synthesizing individual participant data, where available, and supplementing this with aggregate-level data for those studies in which individual-level data are not available have been described (Pigott, 2012), these methods have rarely been applied to the field of self-harm and suicide prevention and are therefore not considered further.

Conclusions

The intention of this chapter is to provide a general introduction to the concepts behind conducting methodologically rigorous systematic reviews and meta-analyses in the field of self-harm and suicide prevention. Reviewers interested in greater detail on specific aspects of systematic reviews and meta-analyses are referred to the following titles:

- Borenstein, M., Hedges, L.V., Higgins, J.P. T., & Rothstein, H.R. (2009). *Introduction to meta-analysis.* Chichester, UK: Wiley.
- Cooper, H., Hedges, L.V., & Valentine, J.C. (Eds.). (2019). *Handbook of research synthesis and meta-analysis* (3rd ed.) New York, NY: Russell Sage Foundation.
- Higgins, J.P. T., & Green, S. (Eds.). (2008). *Cochrane handbook for systematic reviews of interventions.* Chichester, UK: Cochrane Collaboration/Wiley.

Those desiring greater detail on more advanced topics, including multilevel meta-analysis, network meta-analysis, and individual participant data meta-analysis are referred to the following titles:

- Dias, S., Ades, A. E., Welton, N. J., Jansen, J. P., & Sutton, A. J. (2018). *Network meta-analysis for decision-making.* Oxford, UK: Wiley.
- Cheung, M. W. L. (2015). *Meta-analysis: A structural equation modeling approach.* Chichester, UK: Wiley.
- Pigott, T. (2012). *Including individual participant data in meta-analysis.* New York, NY: Springer Science + Business Media.

References

Ali Mansournia, M., Higgins, J., Sterne, J., & Hernán, M. (2017). Biases in randomized trials: A conversation between trialists and epidemiologists. *Epidemiology, 28*, 54–59. https://doi.org/10.1097/EDE.0000000000000564

Allen, I., & Olkin, I. (1999). Estimating time to conduct a meta-analysis from number of citations retrieved. *JAMA, 282*, 634–635. https://doi.org/10.1001/jama.282.7.634

Baker, S., & Kramer, B. (2002). The transitive fallacy for randomized trials: If A bests B and B bests C in separate trials, is A better than C? *BMC Medical Research Methodology, 2*, 13. https://doi.org/10.1186/1471-2288-2-13

Bar-Ilan, J. (2007). Manipulating search engine algorithms: The case of Google. *J Information Communication and Ethics in Society, 5*, 155–166. https://doi.org/10.1108/14779960710837623

Bartoli, F., Riboldi, I., Crocamo, C., Di Brita, C., Clerici, M., & Carrà, G. (2017). Ketamine as a rapid-acting agent for suicidal ideation: A meta-analysis. *Neuroscience Biobehavioral Reviews, 77*, 232–236. https://doi.org/10.1016/j.neubiorev.2017.03.010

Begg, C., & Mazumdar, M. (1994). Operating characteristic of a rank correlation test for publication bias. *Biometrics, 50*, 1088–1101. https://doi.org/10.2307/2533446

Borah, R., Brown, A., Capers, P., & Kaiser, K. (2017). Analysis of the time and work needed to conduct systematic reviews of medical interventions using data from the PROSPERO registry. *BMJ Open, 7*, e012545. https://doi.org/10.1136/bmjopen-2016-012545

Borenstein, M., Hedges, L., Higgins, J., & Rothstein, H. (2009). *Introduction to meta-analysis.* Chichester, UK: Wiley.

Bramer, W., Giustini, D., & Kramer, B. (2016). Comparing the coverage, recall, and precision of searches for 120 systematic reviews in Embase, MEDLINE, and Google Scholar: A prospective study. *Systematic Reviews, 5*, 39. https://doi.org/10.1186/s13643-016-0215-7

Bramer, W., Rethlefsen, M., Kleijnen, J., & Franco, O. (2017). Optimal database combinations for literature searches in systematic reviews: A prospective exploratory study. *Systematic Reviews, 6*, 245. https://doi.org/10.1186/s13643-017-0644-y

Buscemi, N., Hartling, L., Vandermeer, B., Tjosvold, L., & Klassen, T. (2006). Single data extraction generated more errors than double data extraction in systematic reviews. *Journal of Clinical Epidemiology, 59*, 697–703. https://doi.org/10.1016/j.jclinepi.2005.11.010

Charrois, T. (2015). Systematic reviews: What do you need to know to get started? *Canadian Journal of Hospital Pharmacology, 68*, 144–148. https://doi.org/10.4212/cjhp.v68i2.1440

Cheung, M. (2019). A guide to conducting a meta-analysis with non-independent effect sizes. *Neuropsychology Review, 29*, 387–396. https://doi.org/10.1007/s11065-019-09415-6

Cheung, M. W. (2018). Computing multivariate effect sizes and their sampling covariance matrices with structural equation modeling: Theory, examples, and computer simulations. *Frontiers in Psychology, 9*, 1387. https://doi.org/10.3389/fpsyg.2018.01387

Chinn, S. (2000). A simple method for converting an odds ratio to effect size for use in meta-analysis. *Statistics in Medicine, 19*, 3127–3131. https://doi.org/10.1002/1097-0258(20001130)19:22<3127::AID-SIM784>3.0.CO;2-M

Christensen, H., Calear, A., van Spijker, B., Gosling, J., Petrie, K., Donker, T., & Fenton, K. (2014). Psychosocial interventions for suicidal ideation, plans, and attempts: A database of randomised controlled trials. *BMC Psychiatry, 14*, 86. https://doi.org/10.1186/1471-244X-14-86

Cipriani, A., Barbui, C., Rizzo, C., & Salanti, G. (2012). What is a multiple treatments meta-analysis? *Epidemiology and Psychiatric Sciences, 21*, 151–153. https://doi.org/10.1017/S2045796011000837

Cipriani, A., & Geddes, J. (2003). Comparison of systematic and narrative reviews: The example of the atypical antipsychotics. *Epidemiologia e Psichiatria Sociale, 12*, 146–154. https://doi.org/10.1017/S1121189X00002918

Cipriani, A., Higgins, J., Geddes, J., & Salanti, G. (2013). Conceptual and technical challenges in network meta-analysis. *Annals of Internal Medicine, 159*, 130–137. https://doi.org/10.7326/0003-4819-159-2-201307160-00008

Cochran, W. (1954). The combination of estimates from different experiments. *Biometrics, 10*, 101–129. https://doi.org/10.2307/3001666

Cook, D., Mulrow, C., & Haynes, R. (1997). Systematic reviews: Synthesis of best evidence for clinical decisions. *Annals of Internal Medicine, 126*, 376–380. https://doi.org/10.7326/0003-4819-126-5-199703010-00006

Cumming, G. (2012). *Understanding the new statistics: Effect sizes, confidence intervals, and meta-analysis*. New York, NY: Taylor & Francis.

Ćurković, M. (2017). Need for controlling of the Filter Bubble Effect. *Science and Engineering Ethics, 25*, 323.

Curtin, F., Elbourne, D., & Altman, D. (2002). Meta-analysis combining parallel and cross-over trials. Part III: The issue of carry-over. *Statistics in Medicine, 21*, 2161–2173. https://doi.org/10.1002/sim.1207

Davey Smith, G., Egger, M., & Ebrahim, S. (2013). Re: Need for more individual-level meta-analyses in social epidemiology: Example of job strain and coronary heart disease. *American Journal of Epidemiology, 178*, 153–154. https://doi.org/10.1093/aje/kwt104

Deeks, J., Higgins, J., & Altman, D. (2008). Analysing data and undertaking meta-analyses. In J. Higgins & S. Green (Eds.), *Cochrane handbook for systematic reviews of interventions*. Chichester, UK: Wiley.

Donner, A., & Klar, N. (2002). Issues in the meta-analysis of cluster randomized trials. *Statistics in Medicine, 21*, 2971–2980. https://doi.org/10.1002/sim.1301

Dwan, K., Altman, D., Armaiz, J., Bloom, J., Chan, A.-W., Cronin, E., ... Williamson, P. (2008). Systematic review of the empirical evidence of study publication bias and outcome reporting bias. *PLoS One, 3*, e3081. https://doi.org/10.1371/journal.pone.0003081

Egger, M., Smith, G., Schneider, M., & Minder, C. (1997). Bias in meta-analysis detected by a simple, graphical test. *BMJ, 315*, 629–634. https://doi.org/10.1136/bmj.315.7109.629

Elbourne, D., Altman, D., Higgins, J., Curtin, F., Worthington, H., & Vail, A. (2002). Meta-analyses involving cross-over trials: Methodological issues. *International Journal of Epidemiology, 31*, 140–149. https://doi.org/10.1093/ije/31.1.140

Eldridge, S., Campbell, M., Campbell, M., Dahota, A., Giraudeau, B., Higgins, J., ... Siegfried, N. (2016). *Revised Cochrane Risk of Bias tool for randomized trials (RoB 2.0): Additional considerations for cluster-randomized trials*. Bristol, UK: Cochrane Collaboration.

Erez, A., Bloom, M., & Wells, M. (1996). Using random rather than fixed effects models in meta-analysis: Implications for situational specificity and validity generalization. *Personnel Psychology, 49*, 275–306. https://doi.org/10.1111/j.1744-6570.1996.tb01801.x

Eriksen, M., & Frandsen, T. (2018). The impact of patient, intervention, comparison, outcome (PICO) as a search strategy tool on literature search quality: A systematic review. *Journal of the Medical Library Association, 106*, 420–431. https://doi.org/10.5195/JMLA.2018.345

Faraone, S. (2008). Interpreting estimates of treatment effects: Implications for managed care. *Pharmacy and Therapeutics, 33*, 710–711.

Goodfellow, B., Kõlves, K., & De Leo, D. (2020). Contemporary classifications of suicidal behaviors: A systematic literature review. *Crisis, 41*(3), 179–186. https://doi.org/10.1027/0227-5910/a000622

Grimes, D., & Schulz, K. (2002). Cohort studies: Marching towards outcomes. *Lancet, 359*, 341–345. https://doi.org/10.1016/S0140-6736(02)07500-1

Hahn, S., Puffer, S., Torgerson, D., & Watson, J. (2005). Methodological bias in cluster randomised trials. *BMC Medical Research Methodology, 5*, 10. https://doi.org/10.1186/1471-2288-5-10

Hawton, K., Witt, K., Taylor Salisbury, T., Arensman, E., Gunnell, D., Hazell, P., ... van Heeringen, K. (2016). Psychosocial interventions for self-harm in adults. *Cochrane Database of Systematic Reviews, 5*, CD012189. https://doi.org/10.1002/14651858.CD012189

Higgins, J. (2016). *Revised Cochrane Risk of Bias tool for randomized trials (RoB 2.0): Additional considerations for cross-over trials.* Bristol, UK: Cochrane Collaboration.

Higgins, J., & Altman, D. (2008). Assessing risk of bias in included studies. In J. Higgins & S. Green (Eds.), *Cochrane handbook for systematic reviews of interventions.* Chichester, UK: Wiley.

Higgins, J., Altman, D., Gøtzsche, P., Jüni, P., Moher, D., Oxman, A., ... Sterne, J. (2011). The Cochrane Collaboration's tool for assessing risk of bias in randomised trials. *BMJ Open, 343,* d5928. https://doi.org/10.1136/bmj.d5928

Higgins, J., & Deeks, J. (2008). Selecting studies and collecting data. In J. Higgins & S. Green (Eds.), *Cochrane handbook for systematic reviews of interventions* (pp. 151–185). Chichester, UK: Wiley.

Higgins, J., Deeks, J., & Altman, D. (2008). Special topics in statistics. In J. Higgins & S. Green (Eds.), *Cochrane handbook for systematic reviews of interventions* (pp. 481–529). Chichester, UK: Wiley.

Higgins, J., & Thompson, S. (2002). Quantifying heterogeneity in meta-analysis. *Statistics in Medicine, 21,* 1539–1558. https://doi.org/10.1002/sim.1186

Higgins, J., & Thompson, S. (2004). Controlling the risk of spurious findings from meta-regression. *Statistics in Medicine, 23,* 1663–1682. https://doi.org/10.1002/sim.1752

Higgins, J., Thompson, S., Deeks, J., & Altman, D. (2003). Measuring inconsistency in meta-analyses. *BMJ, 327,* 557–563. https://doi.org/10.1136/bmj.327.7414.557

Ho, G., Liew, S., Ng, C., Shunmugam, R., & Glasziou, P. (2016). Development of a search strategy for an evidence based retrieval service. *PLoS One, 11,* e0167170. https://doi.org/10.1371/journal.pone.0167170

Hopewell, S., Loudon, K., Clarke, M., Oxman, A., & Dickersin, K. (2009). Publication bias in clincial trials due to statistical significance or direction of trial results. *Cochrane Database of Systematic Reviews, 1,* MR000006. https://doi.org/10.1002/14651858.MR000006.pub3

Hunter, J., Saratzis, A., Sutton, A., Boucher, R., Sayers, R., & Bown, M. (2014). In meta-analyses of proportion studies, funnel plots were found to be an inaccurate method of assessing publication bias. *Journal of Clinical Epidemiology, 67,* 897–903. https://doi.org/10.1016/j.jclinepi.2014.03.003

Hunter, J., & Schmidt, F. (2000). Fixed effect vs. random effects meta-analysis models: Implications for cumulative research knowledge. *International Journal of Selection and Assessment, 8,* 275–292.

Ioannidis, J., Haidich, A.B., Pappa, M., Pantazis, N., Kokori, S., Tektonidou, M., ... Lau, J. (2001). Comparison of evidence of treatment effects in randomized and nonrandomized studies. *JAMA, 286,* 821–830. https://doi.org/10.1001/jama.286.7.821

Kausar, M., Dhaka, V., & Singh, S. (2013). Web crawler: A review. *International Journal of Computer Applications, 63*(31–6).

Kelley, G., & Kelley, K. (2012). Statistical models for meta-analysis: A brief tutorial. *World Journal of Methodology, 2,* 27–32. https://doi.org/10.5662/wjm.v2.i4.27

Kwon, Y., Lemieux, M., McTavish, J., & Wathen, N. (2015). Identifying and removing duplicate records from systematic review searches. *Journal of the Medical Library Association, 103,* 184–188. https://doi.org/10.3163/1536-5050.103.4.004

Lefebvre, C., & Glanville, J. (2008). Searching for studies. In J. Higgins & S. Green (Eds.), *Cochrane handbook for systematic reviews of interventions* (pp. 95–150). Chichester, UK: Wiley.

Littell, J., Corcoran, J., & Pillai, V. (2008). *Systematic reviews and meta-analysis.* New York, NY: Oxford University Press. https://doi.org/10.1093/acprof:oso/9780195326543.001.0001

MacDonald, M., Misener, R., Weeks, L., & Helwig, M. (2016). Covidence vs. Excel for the title and abstract review stage of a systematic review. *International Journal of Evidence-Based Healthcare, 14,* 200–201.

Mateen, F., Oh, J., Tergas, A., Bhayani, N., & Kamdar, B. (2013). Titles versus titles and abstracts for initial screening of articles for systematic reviews. *Clinical Epidemiology, 5,* 89–95. https://doi.org/10.2147/CLEP.S43118

Mathes, T., Klaßen, P., & Pieper, D. (2017). Frequency of data extraction errors and methods to increase data extraction quality: A methodological review. *BMC Medical Research Methodology, 17,* 152. https://doi.org/10.1186/s12874-017-0431-4

McDonald, S., Taylor, L., & Adams, C. (1999). Searching the right database: A comparison of four databases for psychiatry journals. *Health Information and Libraries Journal, 16*(3), 151–156. https://doi.org/10.1046/j.1365-2532.1999.00222.x

Meline, T. (2006). Selecting studies for systematic review: Inclusion and exclusion criteria. *Contemporary Issues in Communication Science and Disorders, 33,* 21–27. https://doi.org/10.1044/cicsd_33_S_21

Methley, A., Campbell, S., Chew-Graham, C., McNally, R., & Cheraghi-Sohi, S. (2014). PICO, PICOS, and SPIDER: A comparison study of specificity and sensitivity in three search tools for qualitative systematic reviews. *BMC Health Services Research, 14*, 579. https://doi.org/10.1186/s12913-014-0579-0

Miettinen, O. (1976). Estimatability and estimation in case-referent studies. *American Journal of Epidemiology, 103*, 226–235. https://doi.org/10.1093/oxfordjournals.aje.a112220

Mulrow, C. (1994). Rationale for systematic reviews. *BMJ Open, 309*, 597–599.

O'Connor, D., Green, S., & Higgins, J. (2008). Defining the review question and developing criteria for including studies. In J. Higgins & S. Green (Eds.), *Cochrane handbook for systematic reviews of interventions* (pp. 81–94). Chichester, UK: Wiley. https://doi.org/10.1002/9780470712184.ch5

Page, L., Brin, S., Motwani, R., & Winograd, T. (1999). *The PageRank citation ranking: Bringing order to the web.* Retrieved from http://ilpubs.stanford.edu:8090/422/

Parsaik, A., Singh, B., Khosh-Chashm, D., & Mascarenhas, S. (2015). Efficacy of ketamine in bipolar depression: Systematic review and meta-analysis retracted. *Journal of Psychiatric Practice, 24*, 307. https://doi.org/10.1097/PRA.0000000000000106

Patsopoulos, N., Evangelou, E., & Ioannidis, J. (2008). Sensitivity of between-study heterogeneity in meta-analysis: Proposed metrics and empirical evaluation. *International Journal of Epidemiology, 37*, 1148–1157. https://doi.org/10.1093/ije/dyn065

Pigott, T. (2012). *Including individual participant data in meta-analysis.* New York, NY: Springer Science + Business Media.

Qi, X., Yang, M., Ren, W., Jia, J., Wang, J., Han, G., & Fan, D. (2013). Find duplicates among the PubMed, EMBASE, and Cochrane Library databases in systematic review. *PLoS One, 8,* e71838. https://doi.org/10.1371/journal.pone.0071838

Ranganathan, P., Aggarwal, R., & Pramesh, C. (2015). Common pitfalls in statistical analysis: Odds versus risk. *Perspectives in Clinical Research, 6*, 222–224. https://doi.org/10.4103/2229-3485.167092

Riley, R., Lambert, P., & Abo-Zaid, G. (2010). Meta-analyses of individual participant data: Rationale, conduct, and reporting. *BMJ, 340*, c221. https://doi.org/10.1136/bmj.c221

Royle, P., & Milne, R. (2003). Literature searching for randomized controlled trials used in Cochrane reviews: Rapid versus exhaustive searches. *International Journal of Technology Assessment in Health Care, 14*, 591–603. https://doi.org/10.1017/S0266462303000552

Saleh, A., Ratajeski, M., & Bertolet, M. (2014). Grey literature searching for health sciences systematic reviews: A prospective study of time spent and resources utilized. *Evidence-Based Library and Information Practice, 9*, 28–50. https://doi.org/10.18438/B8DW3K

Schwarzer, G., Antes, G., & Schumacher, M. (2002). Inflation of type I error rate in two statistical tests for the detection of publication bias in meta-analyses with binary outcomes. *Statistics in Medicine, 21*, 2465–2477. https://doi.org/10.1002/sim.1224

Sibbald, B., & Roberts, C. (1998). Understanding controlled trials: Crossover trials. *BMJ, 316*, 1719. https://doi.org/10.1136/bmj.316.7146.1719

Silverman, M., Berman, A., Sanddal, N., O'Carroll, P., & Joiner, T., Jr. (2007a). Rebuilding the Tower of Babel: A revised nomenclature for the study of suicide and suicidal behaviors: Part 1: Background, rationale, and methodology. *Suicide and Life-Threatening Behavior, 37*, 248–263. https://doi.org/10.1521/suli.2007.37.3.248

Silverman, M., Berman, A., Sanddal, N., O'Carroll, P., & Joiner, T., Jr. (2007b). Rebuilding the Tower of Babel: A revised nomenclature for the study of suicide and suicidal behaviors: Part 2: Suicide-related ideations, communications, and behaviors. *Suicide and Life-Threatening Behavior, 37*, 264–277. https://doi.org/10.1521/suli.2007.37.3.264

Simmonds, M., Higgins, J., Stewart, L. T., Tierney, J. F., Clarke, M., & Thompson, S. (2005). Meta-analysis of individual patient data from randomized trials: A review of methods used in practice. *Clinical Trials, 2*, 209–217. https://doi.org/10.1191/1740774505cn087oa

Song, F., Parekh-Bhirke, P., Hooper, L., Loke, Y., Ryder, J., Sutton, A., ... Harvey, I. (2009). Extent of publication bias in different categories of research cohorts: A meta-analysis of empirical studies. *BMC Medical Research Methodology, 9*, 79. https://doi.org/10.1186/1471-2288-9-79

Song, F., Sheldon, T., Sutton, A., Abrams, K., & Jones, D. (2001). Methods for exploring heterogeneity in meta-analysis. *Evaluation & the Health Professions, 24*, 126–151. https://doi.org/10.1177/016327870102400203

Stansfield, C., Dickson, K., & Bangpan, M. (2016). Exploring issues in the conduct of website searching and other online sources for systematic reviews: How can we be systematic? *Systematic Reviews, 5*, 191. https://doi.org/10.1186/s13643-016-0371-9

Sterne, J., Egger, M., & Moher, D. (2008). Addressing reporting biases. In J. Higgins & S. Green (Eds.), *Cochrane handbook for systematic reviews of interventions* (pp. 297–333). Chichester, UK: Wiley.

Sterne, J., Hernán, M., Reeves, B., Savović, J., Berkman, N., Viswanathan, M., ... Higgins, J. (2016). ROBINS-I: A tool for assessing risk of bias in non-randomised studies of interventions. *BMJ, 355*, i4919. https://doi.org/10.1136/bmj.i4919

Sterne, J., Savović, J., Page, M., Elbers, R., Blencowe, N., Boutron, I., ... Higgins, J. (2019). RoB 2: A revised tool for assessing risk of bias in randomised trials. *BMJ, 366*, i14898. https://doi.org/10.1136/bmj.l4898

Stewart, L., & Parmar, M. (1993). Meta-analysis of the literature or of individual patient data: Is there a difference? *Lancet, 341*, 418–422. https://doi.org/10.1016/0140-6736(93)93004-K

Sutton, A., Abrams, K., Jones, D., Sheldon, T., & Song, F. (2000). *Methods for meta-analysis in medical research.* Chichester, UK: Wiley.

Sutton, A., Kendrick, D., & Coupland, C. (2008). Meta-analysis of individual- and aggregate-level data. *Statistics in Medicine, 27*, 651–669. https://doi.org/10.1002/sim.2916

Thompson, H., Craig, P., Hilton-Boon, M., Campbell, M., & Katikireddi, S. (2018). Applying the ROBINS-I tool to natural experiments: An example from public health. *Systematic Reviews, 7*, 15.

Thompson, S., & Higgins, J. (2002). How should meta-regression analyses be undertaken and interpreted? *Statistics in Medicine, 21*, 1559–1573. https://doi.org/10.1002/sim.1187

Torgerson, D., & Torgerson, C. (2008). *Designing randomised trials in health, education and the social sciences.* Basingstoke, UK: Palgrave Macmillian. https://doi.org/10.1057/9780230583993

Twisk, J., Bosman, L., Hoekstra, T., Rijnhart, J., Welten, M., & Heymans, M. (2018). Different ways to estimate treatment effects in randomised controlled trials. *Contemporary Clinical Trials Communications, 10*, 80–85.

Van den Noortgate, W., López-López, J., Marín-Martínez, F., & Sánchez-Meca, J. (2014). Meta-analysis of multiple outcomes: A multilevel approach. *Behavior Research Methods, 47*, 1274–1294.

Wilkinson, S., Ballard, E., Bloch, M., Mathew, S., Murrough, J., Feder, A., ... Sanacora, G. (2017). The effect of a single dose of intravenous ketamine on suicidal ideation: A systematic review and individual participant data meta-analysis. *American Journal of Psychiatry, 175*, 150–158. https://doi.org/10.1176/appi.ajp.2017.17040472

Witt, K., Pache de Moraes, D., Taylor Salisbury, T., Arensman, E., Gunnell, D., Hazell, P., ... Hawton, K. (2018). Treatment as usual (TAU) as a control condition in trials of cognitive behavioural-based psychotherapy for self-harm: Impact of content and quality on outcomes in a systematic review. *Journal of Affective Disorders, 235*, 434–447. https://doi.org/10.1016/j.jad.2018.04.025

Witt, K., Potts, J., Hubers, A., Grunebaum, M., Murrough, J., Loo, C., ... Hawton, K. (2019). Ketamine for suicidal ideation in adults with psychiatric disorders: A systematic review and meta-analysis of treatment trials. *Australian & New Zealand Journal of Psychiatry, 54*, 29–45. https://doi.org/10.1177/0004867419883341

Witt, K., Townsend, E., Arensman, E., Gunnell, D., Hazell, P., Taylor Salisbury, T., ... Hawton, K. (2019). Psychosocial interventions for people who self-harm: Methodological issues involved in trials to evaluate effectiveness. *Archives of Suicide Research.* Advance online publication. https://doi.org/10.1080/13811118.2019.1592043

Xu, Y., Hackett, M., Carter, G., Loo, C., Gálvez, V., Glozier, N., ... Rodgers, A. (2016). Effects of low-dose and very low-dose ketamine among patients with major depression: A systematic review and meta-analysis. *International Journal of Neuropsychopharmacology, 19*, pyv124. https://doi.org/10.1093/ijnp/pyv124

Zelen, M. (1979). A new design for randomized clinical trials. *New England Journal of Medicine, 300*, 1242–1245. https://doi.org/10.1056/NEJM197905313002203

Zwetsloot, P.-P., Van der Naald, M., Sena, E., Howell, s. D., IntHout, J., De Groot, J., ... Wever, K. (2017). Standardized mean differences cause funnel plot distortion in publication bias assessments. *eLife, 6*, e24260.

Chapter 14
Evaluating Suicide Prevention Activities

Jane Pirkis and Keith Hawton

Summary

This chapter concerns the evaluation of suicide prevention activities. It highlights the need for rigorous evaluations in a field in which the evidence base is still emerging. It draws on the broader evaluation literature to describe different approaches to evaluation and provide advice about how evaluations might best be designed and conducted. It is peppered with examples of evaluations of suicide prevention activities from around the world.

In this chapter, we discuss the evaluation of suicide prevention activities. For the purposes of the chapter, we use the term *suicide prevention activities* to mean any specific interventions or combination of interventions designed to address the major public health problem of suicide. We begin by describing the gamut of suicide prevention activities, classifying them according to a commonly used taxonomy, and providing examples of interventions delivered in isolation and in combination. The taxonomy is important because the differences in types of suicide prevention activities have implications for how evaluations might be shaped and conducted. We follow the description of suicide prevention activities with a discussion of where the evidence is currently at with respect to what works in suicide prevention. This highlights the ongoing need for sound evaluations, and leads into the main part of the chapter which describes different approaches to evaluation and provides advice about how they might be designed and conducted. Our discussion of approaches to evaluation draws on the work of gurus in the program evaluation field such as Funnell and Rogers (2011), Owen (2006), Ovretveit (2014), and Pawson (2013). It is illustrated with examples of evaluations of suicide prevention activities that we and others have conducted.

Suicide Prevention Activities

Suicide prevention interventions are often classified using a framework developed by Silverman and colleagues in the mid-1990s (Silverman & Felner, 1995; Silverman & Maris, 1995). This framework classifies suicide prevention activities as universal, selective, or indicated depending on who they target.

Universal interventions target whole populations and focus on particular risk factors without identifying specific individuals with those risk factors. They are often designed to modify the social environment by, for example, restricting access to the means of suicide (e.g., installing barriers on bridges or cliffs where jumping suicides occur; Pirkis et al., 2013; Pirkis et al., 2015) or encouraging responsible media reporting (e.g., by disseminating guidelines for journalists to encourage them to report in a way that minimizes the likelihood of copycat acts; Pirkis, Blood, Beautrais, Burgess, & Skehan, 2006). Some are also designed to promote resilience, normalize help seeking, and/or raise awareness – for example, school-based programs (Wasserman et al., 2015) and suicide prevention media campaigns (Nicholas, Rossetto, Jorm, Pirkis, & Reavley, 2018; Pirkis et al., 2019).

Selective interventions target people in the population who are not actively suicidal, but who have recognized risk factors for suicidal thoughts and behaviors (e.g., mental health problems). Some selective interventions target these people directly (e.g., pharmacological treatments such as antidepressants and lithium; Cipriani, Geddes, Furukawa, & Barbui, 2007; Cipriani, Hawton, Stockton, & Geddes, 2013). Others aim to better equip health professionals to detect, diagnose, and manage mental health problems (e.g., education and guidelines for general practitioners; Roskar et al., 2010). Still others teach frontline workers and other professionals who come into regular contact with at-risk individuals how to identify them and refer them to appropriate services (e.g., *gatekeeper training*; Isaac et al., 2009).

Indicated interventions target individuals who are already having suicidal thoughts or engaging in suicidal behavior. These people are typically identified through screening programs or by presenting to some sort of clinical service. Examples include psychological therapies – for example, cognitive behavior therapy (CBT) and its components (Brown et al., 2005) or dialectical behavior therapy (DBT) (Priebe et al., 2012) – and/or ongoing support, such as case management (Zalsman et al., 2016) or regular communication through channels such as postcards or text messages (Hassanian-Moghaddam, Sarjami, Kolahi, & Carter, 2011; Hassanian-Moghaddam, Sarjami, Kolahi, Lewin, & Carter, 2017) for people who present to the emergency department or other health care setting having self-harmed (Hawton et al., 2016). It is worth noting here that some commentators have argued that indicated interventions constitute early intervention, rather than true prevention, because they target individuals who are already suicidal.

Often these universal, selective, and indicated interventions are not delivered in isolation but in combination. Many countries have national suicide prevention strategies, and these are usually multifaceted and call for a number of different interventions to be delivered simultaneously (Platt, Arensman, & Rezaeian, 2019). In practice, this often means that local regions within countries use what has become known as a *systems-based approach* (Baker, Nicholas, Shand, Green, & Christensen, 2018). The idea is that the whole is greater than the sum of the parts and that addressing the pernicious problem of suicide from multiple angles and in multiple ways will yield results.

A prominent example of the systems-based approach in action is the Alliance Against Depression model which was initially rolled out in Nuremberg, Germany, with four component interventions, one universal (a suicide prevention media campaign), two selective (education for general practitioners and gatekeeper training for frontline workers and other professionals) and one indicated (an *emergency card* which gives people who have made a suicide attempt ready access to professional help, as well as additional *self-help* activities). The model has since spread to numerous other regions in Europe, with an additional universal intervention included (restricting access to means) (Hegerl, Rummel-Kluge, Värnik, Arensman, & Koburger, 2013). The four-component multifaceted community-based intervention program is described in detail in Chapter 7 (Intervention Studies in Suicide Research; see also Box 7.2 in that chapter).

Need for Rigorous Evaluation of Suicide Prevention Activities

It is relatively easy to describe the kinds of interventions that are used – in isolation and in combination – in suicide prevention. It is more difficult, however, to provide a definitive picture of which ones are effective, and in what combination. Our knowledge of what works in suicide prevention is still limited because good evaluative evidence of most interventions does not yet exist. A review of the effectiveness of specific interventions by Zalsman et al. (2016) identified only a handful which were effective or showed significant promise in reducing suicide-related outcomes across the population. These were restricting access to means, school-based awareness programs, and particular psychological therapies (e.g., CBT). We know even less about interventions that are delivered in combination under a systems-based approach. The Alliance Against Depression model has been shown to be effective in reducing suicides and suicide attempts (Hegerl, Althaus, Schmidtke, & Niklewski, 2006; Hegerl et al., 2010), but it is not clear whether certain elements are necessary or sufficient to achieve this success, and caution is required in generalizing these findings to systems-based approaches that involve other combinations of interventions.

We need more – and stronger – evaluations if we are to strengthen the evidence base in suicide prevention. Our own work has demonstrated that the vast majority of studies in this field describe the problem rather than furthering knowledge about potential solutions. In a recent study, we showed that only 20 % of the suicide prevention journal articles published by Australian authors between 2010 and 2017 described intervention studies or evaluations of policies and programs, and that a far greater majority (60 %) reported on epidemiological studies (Reifels et al., 2018). This mirrored the findings from two of our previous studies; one of these also looked at Australian suicide prevention journal articles published between 1996 and 2006 (Robinson et al., 2008), and the other examined presentations at international suicide prevention conferences delivered between 2003 and 2008 (Huisman, Pirkis, & Robinson, 2010).

There is an onus on those working in suicide prevention to help to build the evidence base for suicide prevention approaches, no matter what their scale. It is just as important to evaluate complex programs that involve the delivery of a suite of interventions as it is to demonstrate the effectiveness of individual interventions delivered in isolation. Strong evaluations require careful consideration of program logic, study design, choice of outcome measures and data sources, a focus on context, and optimal use of quantitative and qualitative methods. In addition, thought needs to be given to who should conduct and participate in evaluations. These considerations are discussed in the sections below.

Program Logic

Clarifying the *program logic* of any suicide prevention activity – or describing the way in which it might be expected to achieve its desired outcomes – is a crucial step in preparing for and planning its evaluation.

The program logic is typically organized around a hierarchy of outcomes which moves from immediate outputs to short-term impacts and longer-term outcomes. The detail involved in the hierarchy of outcomes will vary, depending on the complexity of the intervention or combination of interventions being evaluated. For complex multi-intervention programs, the hierarchy of outcomes will be more complicated and may involve several streams that are aligned with the component interventions. Often these will converge toward the highest level of outcome, which is usually a reduction in suicides or suicide attempts.

Clarifying the program logic of any given suicide prevention activity has clear implications for designing and conducting an evaluation, in that it explicates the way in which the program is expected to work, thus enabling the evaluator to test whether in fact the program does work in that way. Clarifying the program logic often also has benefits for those who are designing and implementing the particular activity, because it facilitates a shared understanding of the activity, which can be communicated to others.

Box 14.1 provides an extended example of a program logic we developed for a railway suicide prevention initiative called the Community Stations Project (Ross, Reavley, Too, & Pirkis, 2018).

Box 14.1. Developing a program logic for the Community Stations Project

We developed a program logic for a railway suicide initiative called the Community Stations Project which was run at four stations in Victoria, Australia, over a 6-week period in 2016. This pilot project was instigated by Public Transport Victoria (PTV), Metro Trains Melbourne (MTT), V/Line, and the TrackSAFE Foundation, working in collaboration with local councils, and was designed to address railway suicides via two different approaches. The first involved raising community members' knowledge of and attitudes toward suicide (e.g., through special awareness-raising events), and the second involved changing the environment of the stations in a manner that might improve community members' feelings of well-being (e.g., through arts and culture initiatives and through the provision of food and beverages).

We ran a workshop with our rail stakeholders to develop the program logic. There was a clear understanding that it would be ambitious to expect a 6-week pilot project to have a demonstrable impact in terms of the ultimate outcomes of reducing suicide attempts and suicides, but there was also recognition that putting some strategies in to raise awareness of suicide among regular station users and to lift their mood might pave the way for these outcomes in the future. We helped PTV, MTT, V/Line, and TrackSAFE think through the causal pathway by which this might occur, and the result was the program logic shown in Figure 14.1.

Once the program logic for the Community Stations Project was agreed upon, we used it to guide our evaluation. We administered an anonymous survey to 1,309 station users in an effort to gauge whether they had noticed any of the activities at their particular station, and found that nearly 50 % of respondents had. We found that those who had noticed at least one activity were more likely to have positive views of the station, a better understanding of poor mental health and suicide, and a greater likelihood of assisting someone at risk. Noticing events was not associated with levels of well-being, however.

Resource and time constraints meant that our evaluation was limited in terms of its reliance on postintervention data only, its lack of a control group, and the fact that it measured relatively low-level impacts. Our use of a strong, consensus-based program logic went some way to addressing these criticisms, however. Demonstrating that certain impacts were achieved gave PTV, MTT, V/Line, and TrackSAFE confidence that they were heading in the right direction, and helped them refine their ongoing efforts. They have now developed a toolkit that can be used by railway stations wishing to take the Community Stations approach elsewhere.

Based on "Evaluation of a Novel Approach to Preventing Railway Suicides: The Community Stations Project," by A. Ross, N. Reavley, L. Too, & J. Pirkis, 2018, *Journal of Public Mental Health, 17*(2), 51–60.

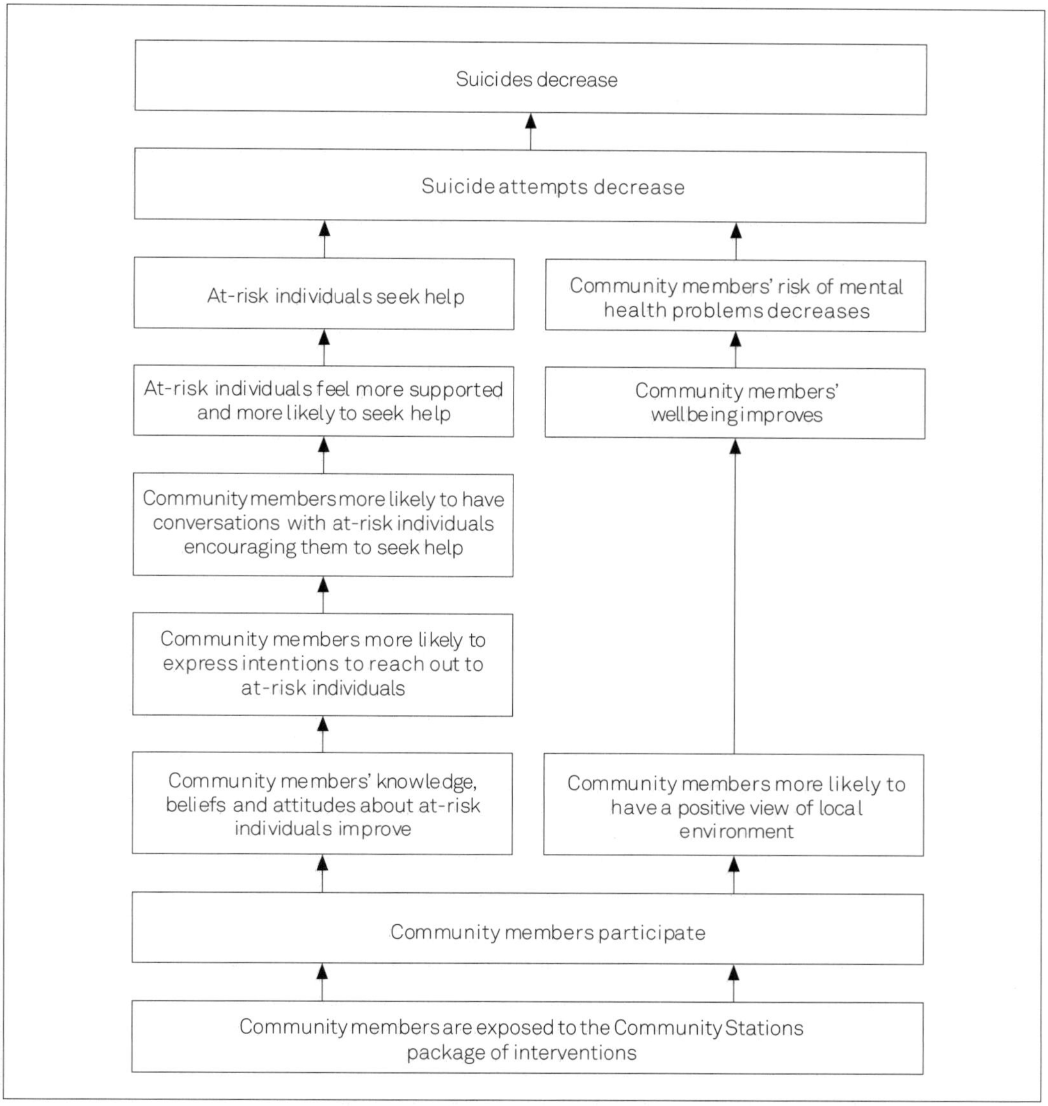

Figure 14.1 Program logic for the Community Stations Project. Reprinted with permission from "Evaluation of a Novel Approach to Preventing Railway Suicides: The Community Stations Project," by A. Ross, N. Reavley, L. Too, & J. Pirkis, 2018, *Journal of Public Mental Health, 17*(2), p.52. © Emerald Publishing Limited all rights reserved.

Study Design

Once the program logic has been clearly articulated, the next step in the evaluation is usually selecting the appropriate study design for determining the effectiveness of the given activity. In intervention research, *randomized controlled trials* (RCTs) are often regarded as the scientific *gold standard*. Participants in RCTs are randomly allocated to a group that receives the given intervention or a group that receives some sort of placebo or *control*, with randomization occurring either at the level of the individual or at the level of some sort of cluster (e.g., clinics, geographical areas). Baseline information is collected from participants in both groups before they take part (pre-), and follow-up information is collected once they have been exposed to the intervention or control condition (post-); this allows changes in the outcome of interest to be assessed. The hypothesis is usually that improvements will be observed in the intervention group but not the control group. The randomization process irons out potential between-group biases and creates a level playing field, which means that if changes are seen in the outcome of interest, then a reasonable explanation is that they were caused by the intervention. For further reading about various intervention study designs, please refer to Chapter 7 (Intervention Studies in Suicide Research).

In our own evaluation work, we have conducted a number of RCTs and cluster RCTs (cRCTs). These include an RCT of *Man Up*, a documentary on masculinity and suicide that aimed to address barriers to men's help seeking (King, Schlichthorst, Spittal, Phelps, & Pirkis, 2017) and a cRCT of locked boxes designed to reduce pesticide suicides (Pearson et al., 2017). However, we acknowledge that it is not always possible or appropriate to evaluate suicide prevention activities using RCTs. Often it is difficult to convince funders, providers, or potential recipients of an intervention that some people should wait to receive the intervention, should receive a *lesser* version of it, or should even just receive usual care or remain exposed to the status quo. In practice, when interventions are rolled out across whole health services or regions or even whole countries, it is difficult to randomly allocate the intervention to some and not others. These problems are compounded in the cases of universal interventions and complex, multi-intervention programs which typically target whole communities.

For these reasons, those in the business of evaluating suicide prevention activities often look to other study designs. None of these involve randomization, but some still have control groups and preintervention and postintervention assessments of outcomes. These include quasi-experimental or ecological designs, in which individuals, services, or regions that are allocated to receive (or not receive) the intervention are not randomly selected but instead chosen on the basis of some other criteria (see Chapter 7 for more on intervention studies and Chapter 6 for ecological studies). Often, for example, a region receiving the intervention will be matched to one that is similar in terms of its geographical and socioeconomic make-up.

Other alternatives include measuring outcomes at multiple points in time and/or making projections to determine what the trend in a given outcome might have looked like had the intervention not been introduced. We took the latter approach in our evaluation of the partial withdrawal of co-proxamol from the UK market in 2005 and its full withdrawal in 2007, examining changes in suicide rates using an interrupted time series analysis (Hawton et al., 2012). We used the same method when we evaluated the impact of legislation to reduce the pack sizes of paracetamol in the UK (Hawton et al., 2013).

On other occasions, selecting control groups or making other relevant comparisons is not possible at all. Sometimes this is because of the service-, region-, or country-wide delivery of activities and sometimes it is due to resourcing issues. In these cases, evaluations typically rely on collecting data on outcomes for the intervention group only, usually still aiming to do so pre and post the rollout of the activity, but sometimes settling for doing so post the rollout only (e.g., in circumstances where the evaluation is commissioned once the activity has been in place for some time). We collected pre and post data on suicides and police call-outs to suicide-related incidents in our evaluation of a multifaceted intervention at a known suicide hotspot in Sydney, complementing this with data from stakeholder consultations that we conducted once the intervention had been implemented (Lockley et al., 2014).

The trick for evaluators is to select the best design available in the given situation and use it to optimal effect. They must ensure that the evaluation elicits information that will allow conclusions about causality to be drawn, even if randomization is not possible, even if a control group cannot be constituted, and even if it is only possible to collect outcome data after the fact. A sound program logic is very helpful here because, as noted above, it elucidates the causal pathway by which the activity is expected to work. Seeking alternative evidence of causation is also useful (e.g., explicitly asking those who have taken part in a suicide prevention activity whether they would attribute any changes in their levels of suicidality to having participated in it).

Choice of Outcome Measures and Data Sources

The *choice of outcome measures* will be guided by the program logic or, more specifically, the hierarchy of outcomes. Evaluators should consider each output, impact, and outcome in the hierarchy, how it might best be operationalized, and which data sources lend themselves to its measurement.

Some outcome data might come from routine data collections, such as death registries (if the outcome of interest is suicides) or administrative data on hospital or emergency department admissions for self-harm (if the outcome of interest is suicide attempts). Other outcome data might be elicited directly from those who participate in the given suicide prevention activity, often via questionnaires. For example, if the outcome of interest is a reduction in suicidal thoughts or behaviors, one of a number of standardized measures might be embedded in a participant questionnaire (Batterham et al., 2015). Lower down the hierarchy of outcomes, it is likely that data on outputs and impacts will come from a range of sources, depending on their nature. Measures of engagement or satisfaction with given suicide prevention activities are common, as are measures of program fidelity and reach. Again, these can come from a variety of sources including questionnaires or interviews with those who have been exposed to or who have delivered the given activity, and other stakeholders, document reviews, audits of various kinds, fidelity checks, etc.

Often multiple data sources can be used to assess the same output, impact, or outcome. For example, the evaluation of a suicide prevention media campaign might assess its reach through social media reactions and through a population-based survey that gauges respondents' recall and recognition of campaign messages. Likewise, the evaluation of a gatekeeper training program might draw on a survey of participants and routinely collected referral data to determine whether referrals to relevant services have increased. *Triangulating* data in this way is helpful for strengthening the conclusions that can be drawn about the effectiveness of the given suicide prevention activity; the more consistently that the data from a variety of sources point in the same direction with respect to the achievement of a given outcome, the more likely it is that the result is real.

There are two key advantages to thinking about outcomes and data sources in the context of the program logic. One is that considering multiple outcomes in the context of a previously articulated causal pathway sets up the data in a way that allows a *theory of action* to be tested and, ideally, confirmed. In its simplest form, if the theory is right then the given suicide prevention activity will lead to output A, which will lead to impact B, which in turn, will lead to outcome C. This sequential thinking is helpful, particularly in cases where shifts in the highest level outcomes are difficult to demonstrate (e.g., changes in suicide rates often cannot be detected, at least in the short term, due to their low numbers); if changes in the lower and intermediate level outcomes can be demonstrated, and there is confidence in the program theory, then this is often interpreted as evidence of effectiveness of the suicide prevention activity.

The second advantage is that if the given intervention is not found to be hitting the mark in terms of achieving outcomes such as reductions in suicidal thoughts and behaviors, it is possible to explore some of the potential reasons. It might be, for example, that the intervention was not delivered in the manner it was intended to be, or that participants found it unacceptable or unsatisfactory in some way. Identifying why an activity does not work can be just as informative as determining that it does.

A Focus on Context

It is crucial to consider contextual factors when evaluating suicide prevention actitivites. Again, the program logic approach is helpful here. An exploration of the internal and external factors affecting the success of each output, impact, or outcome will help to explain why the given suicide prevention activity has been found to be effective or not. Similarly, it is worth considering the inputs and resources required to maximize the chances of achieving the given output, impact, or outcome. Often factors affecting success relate to structures and processes that act as barriers or facilitators to implementation, and the inputs and resources relate to the support given to the intervention.

It is worth returning to the discussion of study designs at this point. As noted, RCTs are often regarded as the ultimate test of whether interventions work. In fact, RCTs are usually (although not always) used to test interventions in controlled settings, before they are let loose in the real world. In addition, they typically focus on a primary outcome and pay little heed to the outputs, and to impacts that may be crucial in paving the way for that outcome. Strictly speaking, this means that RCTs usually evaluate *efficacy* rather than *effectiveness* – that is, they typically provide evidence of whether interventions work when they are delivered under ideal conditions, but frequently tell us little about how they will perform in environments where they may be affected by a range of contextual influences, some positive and some not so positive. The additional focus on structures, processes, inputs and resources is crucial, particularly if activities that have been tested by RCTs are to be adopted in real-world settings.

Much can be learned from the field of *implementation science* here. Implementation science has been defined as "the scientific study of methods to promote the systematic uptake of research findings and other evidence-based practices into routine practice, and, hence, to improve the quality and effectiveness of health services" (Eccles & Mittman, 2006, p. 1). This definition is too narrow for our purposes because much of what happens in suicide prevention occurs outside the health system. Universal interventions are typically delivered to whole communities, and although selective and indicated interventions are more likely to be offered through health services, many of these are provided outside the health system (e.g., gatekeeper training or crisis lines). Nonetheless, the principles and practices of implementation science can and should be applied in the evaluation of suicide prevention approaches. These involve a focus on how activities are implemented, whether they are delivered as intended, whether they have the desired reach, what contextual factors might promote or impede their implementation, and so on (Bauer, Damschroder, Hagedorn, Smith, & Kilbourne, 2015).

Quantitative and Qualitative Methods

Researchers evaluating suicide prevention activities often use a mix of quantitative and qualitative methods in examining whether given interventions work, and if so, how, why, in what circumstances, and for whom. Often, though not always, they rely on quantitative methods to assess outcomes, and qualitative methods to explore the contextual factors that act as barriers or facilitators to these outcomes. We took this approach when we worked with colleagues on an evaluation of a gatekeeper training program delivered to police officers (Marzano, Smith, Long, Kisby, & Hawton, 2016). We used a quantitative approach to assess outcomes, using a modified version of a standardized scale to gauge whether participants' knowledge of and attitudes toward suicide prevention improved as a result of the training, and whether their confidence in dealing with suicidal individuals increased. We also took a qualitative approach, running focus groups to explore how the police officers found the training, whether there were things about it that could have been improved, etc. (Marzano et al., 2016).

Explicitly using quantitative and qualitative methods in combination is often described as taking a *mixed methods* approach (Tariq & Woodman, 2013), and there have been calls for a greater emphasis on this approach in suicide prevention (Kral, Links, & Bergmans, 2012). In evaluation, the advantage of this approach over using either type of method on its own is that it enables the hierarchy of complex questions generated through the program logic to be answered. It also furthers *triangulation* of data by providing additional differing perspectives, sometimes on the same question. One way of looking at this, albeit a slightly blunt one, is that quantitative data offer relatively objective and systematic insights into the outcomes of the given intervention, whereas qualitative data provide more subjective interpretations of the way in which these outcomes were achieved or not achieved (Tariq & Woodman, 2013). See Chapter 10 for a discussion of mixed methods.

Involvement in Evaluation

There are two schools of thought regarding who should conduct evaluations. One is that evaluators should be external to the activity or intervention that is being evaluated, and the other is that evaluators should be internal. The arguments for external evaluators are that they are independent from the activity or intervention, and are therefore more likely to be objective, and that they have specialist evaluation training and are therefore likely to bring heightened rigor to the evaluation. The arguments for internal evaluators are that they know the activity or intervention well, understand the nuances surrounding its delivery, and may be able to conduct the evaluation relatively cheaply. In the end, decisions about who will conduct any given evaluation will inevitably be made on a case-by-case basis, and sometimes a hybrid model may be possible. Whatever the decision, attempts should be made to maximize the advantages and minimize the disadvantages (e.g., ensuring that an external evaluator is sufficiently well briefed to bring them up to speed with the activity or intervention, or ensuring that an internal evaluator has sufficient grounding in evaluation methods to adequately perform the evaluation).

Decisions about who should participate in an evaluation will also vary, depending on what is being evaluated. As a general rule, however, it is important to include the perspectives of all parties who have a stake in the activity or intervention. This will include – but not necessarily be limited to – those who fund or commission it, those who manage it, those who are directly responsible for its delivery, and those for whom it is designed. In the case of guidelines for media professionals, for example, this might translate into representatives from a government department that has funded the guidelines; the personnel who have been directly responsible for developing and rolling out the guidelines; and journalists, editors, and other media professionals who might then use the guidelines.

Conclusions

In 2005, Goldney (2005) said that we needed to get smarter about the way we evaluate suicide prevention activities. We have got smarter, and there are great examples of evaluators using ground-breaking, novel methods to test different suicide prevention activities. Some have managed to conduct well-designed RCTs of complex, systems-based approaches – for example, joining forces across multiple sites in multiple countries to evaluate a school-based suicide prevention program with a gatekeeper-training component, a component designed to raise awareness among students, and a component involving screening and referral of at-risk students (Wasserman et al., 2015). Others have mimicked randomization in clever ways, such as using propensity score matching in a large-scale, register-based evaluation of psychological therapy for people who have made a suicide attempt (Erlangsen et al., 2015). Still others have avoided randomization or pseudorandomization and instead used other best-practice evaluation methods – for example, using program logic and assessing a variety of outcomes via mixed methods in an evaluation of a program designed to increase adherence of health professionals to a national suicide prevention guideline (Hanbury, Wallace, & Clark, 2011). We need to get smarter still and make these sorts of evaluations more commonplace. That way, we will be able to consolidate and expand our existing knowledge about what works in suicide prevention, and ultimately save more lives.

References

Baker, S., Nicholas, J., Shand, F., Green, R., & Christensen, H. (2018). A comparison of multi-component systems approaches to suicide prevention. *Australasian Psychiatry, 26*(2), 128–131. https://doi.org/10.1177/1039856217743888

Batterham, P., Ftanou, M., Pirkis, J., Brewer, J., Mackinnon, A., Beautrais, A., ... Christensen, H. (2015). A systematic review and evaluation of measures for suicidal ideation and behaviors in population-based research. *Psychological Assessment, 27*, 501–512. https://doi.org/10.1037/pas0000053

Bauer, M., Damschroder, L., Hagedorn, H., Smith, J., & Kilbourne, A. (2015). An introduction to implementation science for the non-specialist. *BMC Psychology, 3*, 32. https://doi.org/10.1186/s40359-015-0089-9

Brown, G., ten Have, T., Henriques, G., Xie, S., Hollander, J., & Beck, A. (2005). Cognitive therapy for the prevention of suicide attempts: A randomized controlled trial. *Journal of the American Medical Association, 294*, 563–570. https://doi.org/10.1001/jama.294.5.563

Cipriani, A., Geddes, J., Furukawa, T., & Barbui, C. (2007). Metareview on short-term eff ectiveness and safety of antidepressants for depression: An evidence-based approach to inform clinical practice. *Canadian Journal of Psychiatry, 52*, 553–562. https://doi.org/10.1177/070674370705200903

Cipriani, A., Hawton, K., Stockton, S., & Geddes, J. (2013). Lithium in the prevention of suicide in mood disorders: Updated systematic review and meta-analysis. *BMJ, 346*, f3646. https://doi.org/10.1136/bmj.f3646

Eccles, M., & Mittman, B. (2006). Welcome to implementation science. *Implementation Science, 1*, 1. https://doi.org/10.1186/1748-5908-1-1

Erlangsen, A., Lind, B., Stuart, E., Qin, P., Stenager, E., Larsen, K., ... Nordentoft, M. (2015). Short-term and long-term effects of psychosocial therapy for people after deliberate self-harm: A register-based, nationwide multicentre study using propensity score matching. *Lancet Psychiatry, 2*(1), 49–58. https://doi.org/10.1016/S2215-0366(14)00083-2

Funnell, S., & Rogers, P. (2011). *Purposeful program theory: Effective use of theories of change and logic models.* San Francisco, CA: Jossey-Bass.

Goldney, R. (2005). Suicide prevention: A pragmatic review of recent studies. *Crisis, 26*(3), 128–140. https://doi.org/10.1027/0227-5910.26.3.128

Hanbury, A., Wallace, L., & Clark, M. (2011). Multiple outcome measures and mixed methods for evaluating the effectiveness of theory-based behaviour-change interventions: A case study targeting health professionals' adoption of a national suicide prevention guideline. *Psychology, Health and Medicine, 16*(3), 291–303. https://doi.org/10.1080/13548506.2011.554561

Hassanian-Moghaddam, H., Sarjami, S., Kolahi, A.-A., & Carter, G. (2011). Postcards in Persia: Randomised controlled trial to reduce suicidal behaviours 12 months after hospital-treated self-poisoning. *British Journal of Psychiatry, 198*, 309–316. https://doi.org/10.1192/bjp.bp.109.067199

Hassanian-Moghaddam, H., Sarjami, S., Kolahi, A., Lewin, T., & Carter, G. (2017). Postcards in Persia: A twelve to twenty-four month follow-up of a randomized controlled trial for hospital-treated deliberate self-poisoning. *Archives of Suicide Research, 21*(1), 138–154. https://doi.org/10.1080/13811118.2015.1004473

Hawton, K., Bergen, H., Simkin, S., Dodd, S., Pocock, P., Bernal, W., ... Kapur, N. (2013). Long term effect of reduced pack sizes of paracetamol on poisoning deaths and liver transplant activity in England and Wales: Interrupted time series analyses. *BMJ 346*, f403. https://doi.org/10.1136/bmj.f403

Hawton, K., Bergen, H., Simkin, S., Wells, C., Kapur, N., & Gunnell, D. (2012). Six-year follow-up of impact of co-proxamol withdrawal in England and Wales on prescribing and deaths: Time-series study. *PLOS Medicine, 9*(5), e1001213. https://doi.org/10.1371/journal.pmed.1001213

Hawton, K., Witt, K., Salisbury, T., Arensman, E., Gunnell, D., Hazell, P., ... van Heeringen, K. (2016). Psychosocial interventions following self-harm in adults: A systematic review and meta-analysis. *Lancet Psychiatry, 3*, 740–750. https://doi.org/10.1016/S2215-0366(16)30070-0

Hegerl, U., Althaus, D., Schmidtke, A., & Niklewski, G. (2006). The alliance against depression: 2-year evaluation of a community-based intervention to reduce suicidality. *Psychological Medicine, 36*, 1225–1233. https://doi.org/10.1017/S003329170600780X

Hegerl, U., Mergl, R., Havers, I., Schmidtke, A., Lehfeld, H., Niklewski, G., & Althaus, D. (2010). Sustainable effects on suicidality were found for the Nuremberg alliance against depression. *European Archives of Psychiatry and Clinical Neuroscience, 260*, 401–406. https://doi.org/10.1007/s00406-009-0088-z

Hegerl, U., Rummel-Kluge, C., Värnik, A., Arensman, E., & Koburger, N. (2013). Alliances against depression: A community based approach to target depression and to prevent suicidal behaviour. *Neuroscience and Biobehavioral Reviews, 37*(10), 2404–2409. https://doi.org/10.1016/j.neubiorev.2013.02.009

Huisman, A., Pirkis, J., & Robinson, J. (2010). Intervention studies in suicide prevention research. *Crisis, 31*(5), 281–284. https://doi.org/10.1027/0227-5910/a000049

Isaac, M., Elias, B., Katz, L., Belik, S.-L., Deane, F., Enns, M., & Sareen, J. (2009). Gatekeeper training as a preventative intervention for suicide: A systematic review. *Canadian Journal of Psychiatry, 54*, 260–268. https://doi.org/10.1177/070674370905400407

King, K., Schlichthorst, M., Spittal, M., Phelps, A., & Pirkis, J. (2017). Can a documentary increase help-seeking intentions in men? A randomised controlled trial. *Journal of Epidemiology and Community Health, 0*, 1–7. https://doi.org/10.1136/jech-2017-209502

Kral, M., Links, P., & Bergmans, Y. (2012). Suicide studies and the need for mixed methods research. *Journal of Mixed Methods Research, 6*, 3. https://doi.org/10.1177/1558689811423914

Lockley, A., Cheung, Y.-T., Cox, G., Robinson, J., Williamson, M., Harris, M., ... Pirkis, J. (2014). Preventing suicide at suicide hotspots: A case study from Australia. *Suicide and Life-Threatening Behavior, 44*, 392–407. https://doi.org/10.1111/sltb.12080

Marzano, L., Smith, M., Long, M., Kisby, C., & Hawton, K. (2016). Police and suicide prevention: Evaluation of a training program. *Crisis, 37*(3), 194–204. https://doi.org/10.1027/0227-5910/a000381

Nicholas, A., Rossetto, A., Jorm, A., Pirkis, J., & Reavley, N. (2018). Importance of messages for a suicide prevention media campaign. *Crisis, 39*(6), 438–450. https://doi.org/10.1027/0227-5910/a000517

Ovretveit, J. (2014). *Evaluating improvement and implementation for health.* Milton Keynes, UK: Open University Press.

Owen, J. (2006). *Program evaluation: Forms and approaches.* Sydney, Australia: Allen and Unwin.

Pawson, R. (2013). *The science of evaluation: A realist manifesto.* London, UK: Sage.

Pearson, M., Metcalfe, C., Jayamanne, S., Gunnell, D., Weerasinghe, M., Pieris, R., ... Konradsen, F. (2017). Effectiveness of household lockable pesticide storage to reduce pesticide self-poisoning in rural Asia: A community-based, cluster-randomised controlled trial. *Lancet, 390*(10105), 1863–1872. https://doi.org/10.1016/S0140-6736(17)31961-X

Pirkis, J., Blood, R., Beautrais, A., Burgess, P., & Skehan, J. (2006). Media guidelines on the reporting of suicide. *Crisis, 27*(2), 82–87. https://doi.org/10.1027/0227-5910.27.2.82

Pirkis, J., Rossetto, A., Nicholas, A., Ftanou, M., Robinson, J., & Reavley, N. (2019). Suicide prevention media campaigns: A systematic literature review. *Health Communication, 34*, 402–414. https://doi.org/10.1080/10410236.2017.1405484

Pirkis, J., Spittal, M., Cox, G., Robinson, J., Cheung, Y.-T., & Studdert, D. (2013). The effectiveness of structural interventions at suicide hotspots: A meta-analysis. *International Journal of Epidemiology, 42*, 541–548. https://doi.org/10.1093/ije/dyt021

Pirkis, J., Too, L.S., Spittal, M., Krysinska, K., Robinson, J., & Cheung, Y.-T. (2015). Interventions to reduce suicides at suicide hotspots: A systematic review and meta-analysis. *Lancet Psychiatry, 2*, 994–1001. https://doi.org/10.1016/S2215-0366(15)00266-7

Platt, S., Arensman, E., & Rezaeian, M. (2019). National suicide prevention strategies: Progress and challenges. *Crisis, 40*(2), 75–82. https://doi.org/10.1027/0227-5910/a000587

Priebe, S., Bhatti, N., Barnicot, K., Bremner, S., Gaglia, A., Katsakou, C., ... Zinkler, M. (2012). Effectiveness and cost-effectiveness of dialectical behaviour therapy for self-harming patients with personality disorder: A pragmatic randomised controlled trial. *Psychotherapy and Psychosomatics, 81*, 356–365. https://doi.org/10.1159/000338897

Reifels, L., Ftanou, M., Krysinska, K., Machlin, A., Robinson, J., & Pirkis, J. (2018). Research priorities in suicide prevention: Review of Australian research from 2010–2017 highlights continued need for intervention research. *International Journal of Environmental Research and Public Health, 15*, 807. https://doi.org/10.3390/ijerph15040807

Robinson, J., Pirkis, J., Krysinska, K., Niner, S., Jorm, A., Dudley, M., ... Harrigan, S. (2008). Research priorities in suicide prevention in Australia: A comparison of current research efforts and stakeholder-identified priorities. *Crisis, 29*, 180–190. https://doi.org/10.1027/0227-5910.29.4.180

Roskar, S., Podlesek, A., Zorko, M., Tavcar, R., Dernovsek, M., Groleger, U., ... Marusic, A. (2010). Effects of training program on recognition and management of depression and suicide risk evaluation for Slovenian primary-care physicians: Follow-up study. *Croatian Medical Journal, 51*(3), 237–242. https://doi.org/10.3325/cmj.2010.51.237

Ross, A., Reavley, N., Too, L., & Pirkis, J. (2018). Evaluation of a novel approach to preventing railway suicides: The Community Stations Project. *Journal of Public Mental Health, 17*(2), 51–60. https://doi.org/10.1108/JPMH-06-2017-0022

Silverman, M., & Felner, R. (1995). Suicide prevention programs: Issues of design, implementation, feasibility, and developmental appropriateness. *Suicide and Life Threatening Behavior, 25*(1), 92–104.

Silverman, M., & Maris, R. (1995). The prevention of suicidal behaviors: An overview. *Suicide and Life Threatening Behavior, 25*(1), 10–21.

Tariq, S., & Woodman, J. (2013). Using mixed methods in health research. *Journal of the Royal Society of Medicine, 0*, 1–8. https://doi.org/10.1177/2042533313479197

Wasserman, D., Hoven, C., Wasserman, C., Wall, M., Eisenberg, R., Hadlaczky, G., ... Carli, V. (2015). School-based suicide prevention programmes: The SEYLE cluster-randomised, controlled trial. *Lancet, 385*, 1536–1544. https://doi.org/10.1016/S0140-6736(14)61213-7

Zalsman, G., Hawton, K., Wasserman, D., van Heeringen, K., Arensman, E., Sarchiapone, M., ... Zohar, J. (2016). Suicide prevention strategies revisited: 10-year systematic review. *Lancet Psychiatry, 3*(7), 646–659. https://doi.org/10.1016/S2215-0366(16)30030-X

Chapter 15

Applying a Health Economics Lens to Suicide Research

David McDaid

Summary

This chapter applies a health economics lens to suicide research. Policy makers are faced with difficult choices regarding how best to make use of scarce resources to promote and improve health. Not only do they want to know what works, and in what context, but also at what cost. They may also want to know the relative cost-effectiveness of investing in different ways to prevent suicidal behavior, for instance, through alternative ways of achieving this goal or using resources, both within and beyond health care systems. The chapter begins by briefly outlining what is meant by an economic perspective on investing in suicide prevention, and then sets out some key economic questions that can be addressed in research. It illustrates how economics can be used to strengthen the case for investment in suicide prevention and considers how this evidence base may be further strengthened.

Importance of Considering the Economic Case for Action to Tackle Suicide

It may seem disquieting or even immoral to have to make an economic case for suicide prevention. The profound impacts of suicide might be thought to be enough to justify actions by policy makers to address this issue, but economic evidence can play a pivotal role in public policy making at national and local levels. Decisions on suicide prevention strategies are not made in a vacuum; all economies operate within resource constraints, in terms of budgets, available workforce, and infrastructure. These resources will be scarce relative to the expectations and needs of any population. Investing resources in interventions to tackle suicide prevention will mean that there is less money available – in the short-term, at least – for other activities such as reducing cardiovascular-related mortality or building new schools.

Choosing how to allocate resources is never easy. At the heart of all decisions on how to manage resources for health-related activities should be the desire to improve quality of life and well-being. This requires robust evidence for actions that are effective. However, in the context of ever-present budget constraints, evidence of effectiveness alone will often be insufficient for policy making; in addition to knowing what works and in what context, information about the economic costs and consequences of any suicide prevention strategy is likely to be required.

Economists nearly always takes scarcity as a *given*, and then seek to provide health and other policy makers with information to assist in the difficult task of deciding how to allocate resources to different potential uses. Economics is therefore concerned with how resources are generated and utilized, how decisions are taken about how to make use of those resources, and what criteria might be employed to inform those decisions.

In some countries, economic evidence on suicide prevention (and other health-related interventions) can be collected at a national level by public or private bodies. In England, for example, the National Institute for Health and Care Excellence (NICE) always looks at the economic case when developing guidelines on health promotion and injury prevention, including for suicide and deliberate self-harm. A lack of information on the economic benefits of investment in any health promotion or disease prevention action, including suicide prevention, may be a major barrier to investment (McDaid, Sassi, & Merkur, 2015).

How to Make the Economic Argument

So how can economic information help make the case for investing in suicide prevention? This chapter will expand on and discuss four key questions, set out in Box 15.1, where economics can play a role in increasing appropriate investment in preventing suicide and self-harm. The reader may also wish to refer to standard reference texts that set out in great detail how economic arguments can be made (Drummond, Sculpher, Claxton, Stoddart, & Torrance, 2015).

Box 15.1. Key economic questions for investment in actions to prevent suicide and self-harm

- The costs of inaction: What are the economic consequences of not taking action to prevent suicide?
- The costs of action: What would it cost to intervene through universal and targeted suicide prevention strategies?
- The cost-effectiveness of action: What is the balance between the cost of intervention and the outcomes achieved – for example, fatal and nonfatal suicidal acts averted, additional life years saved, improved mental health of families, etc.?
- Influencing the economic determinants of suicide and deliberate self-harm: What role do economic circumstances play in risk for suicide, and what can be done to address these risks in a cost-effective manner?

Measuring the Costs of Inaction

The first of these questions focuses on the economic consequences of preserving the status quo and *not* taking any additional action to prevent suicide. Understanding the magnitude and relative importance of these costs, as well as the sectors that bear them, are critical to making the economic case for any action. There will be *direct costs* to consider, typically including costs incurred by health care (or other services) associated with suicide. Within health care systems, this information may be readily available from electronic health records in some contexts, in other settings it may mean having to set up mechanisms to prospectively record health service use as part of any evaluation. There may also be longer-term costs to consider, linked to any ongoing care and support following a nonfatal self-harm event. Direct costs will also be incurred by other public bodies, such as fire, rescue, and police services or transport systems – for example, road and rail service disruption due to investigations after a suicidal event.

There will also be *indirect costs* (also known as *productivity losses*) to society due to absence from paid or voluntary work, education, or home responsibilities as a result of death and injury. There are also impacts on family members – for instance, the time they spend dealing with the consequences of any suicide event. Finally, researchers should also consider measuring what are known as the *intangible costs* (largely because they are difficult to measure) associated with suicide. Economists can use a variety of techniques to try and place a value on the loss of life over and above productivity losses – for instance, they can conduct a survey asking individuals how much they would be willing to pay to avoid death by suicide. While this may seem distasteful, economic estimates of the value of life are frequently taken into account in decisions regarding investment in other areas of injury prevention, such as assessing the costs and benefits of investing in transport safety measures. Including the intangible costs of suicide would thus level the playing field with many other public policy option appraisals.

There are many different estimates of the costs of suicide, but they are not always comparable, due to differences in which elements of cost they include. Differences in methodology can lead to greatly different estimates of cost. It is also important to be aware that much of impact of completed suicide may fall on sectors outside of the health care system, whereas for self-harm there will be much greater costs to health care systems, both for immediate treatment and longer-term mental (and perhaps physical) support. In the UK, for example, the average lifetime costs of a completed suicide were estimated to be almost US $2.4 million in 2018, but only 1% of those were due to direct costs, with 28% attributed to indirect costs and 71% to intangible costs (McDaid, 2016).

When looking at costs for nonfatal self-harm, the pattern will be different. In the US the health care costs of nonfatal self-harm events were 10-fold higher than those for completed suicide (Shepard, Gurewich, Lwin, Reed, & Silverman, 2016). This means that health system stakeholders may be more persuaded by arguments for the prevention of self-harm and suicide than for suicide alone.

Some prevention strategies – for example, measures to restrict access to means, in general, or to make bridges, in particular, safer – may not be funded by health care systems, so economic impacts beyond the health care system will resonate more with funders. For instance, when considering measures to introduce safety barriers at railway stations or to restrict access to pesticides, the transport and agricultural sectors will be particularly interested in knowing what impact this might have on train delays due to fatalities or crop yields, respectively. Understanding these impacts may strengthen the case for these non-health care sectors to fund and/or endorse measures for suicide prevention.

Capturing Resource Requirements and Costs of Actions for Suicide Prevention

When making the economic case for suicide prevention interventions, it is important to record resource use and costs associated with these interventions. Ideally this should be done prospectively as resources are used; retrospectively, estimating costs can be done, but there is more chance of estimation error.

Separating resource use from costs will also help service planners in other settings estimate how much it might cost to adapt and deliver the same strategy in their own local context. Alongside the estimation of costs, researchers may also wish to document implementation challenges that may themselves require additional resources, such as any additional actions to encourage uptake of relevant approaches. One example of this might be the need to subsidize the cost of transportation to attend any center-based psychology therapy program. It is also important to document major challenges to scaling up any intervention, such as any need for additional workforce or skills and other investment in infrastructure. The challenges and additional costs of scale-up can then be estimated.

Assessing the Cost-Effectiveness of Actions

To provide information on the cost-effectiveness of actions for suicide prevention we need to undertake an *economic evaluation*. Economic evaluations have long been used to inform health policy deliberations (Maynard & McDaid, 2003). They synthesize information on the costs of not taking action, along with the costs of any interventions and the outcomes of these interventions. This helps in determining whether it is worth investing resources in one or more suicide prevention actions compared with other possible ways that these resources could be used – that is, does preventive action achieve improved outcomes at a cost that is worth paying?

There are different ways of undertaking an economic evaluation. All approaches measure cost in the same way but differ in how they treat outcomes. It may be that a decision maker is only looking at how to spend funds to address a specific health problem, in which case they can compare changes in cost and changes in a defined relevant health outcome – for example, changes in the rate of repeated self-harm events between two or more possible interventions. This is known as *cost-effectiveness analysis* as outcomes are measured using a health topic-specific measure. However, it is much more likely that the decision maker will want to compare the value of investing in a self-harm prevention strategy versus a completely different investment in the health care system, such as helping people rehabilitate more quickly from hip replacement surgery. In these circumstances a *cost-utility analysis*, which uses a common outcome measure for all health problems will be more useful. The outcome measure for this is usually the quality-adjusted life year (QALY).

QALYs can be estimated in many ways using different instruments; the simplest approach involves asking the public to rate different health states, such as living with severe depression or suicidal thoughts, on a scale from 0 to 1, where 0 indicates the worst possible health state (usually death), and 1 indicates perfect health. For instance, if someone living with depression rated their quality of life as 0.8 and life expectancy was 5 years, this would generate 4 QALYs ($0.8 \times 5 = 4$), but immediate premature death due to suicide would mean a complete loss of the opportunity to gain any QALYs during this time period.

With both cost-effectiveness and cost-utility analysis, it should be stressed that interventions do not have to save money to be considered good investments – the question is whether the additional outcomes achieved (e.g., suicides averted) are worth the extra costs needed to achieve them. This is a value judgment which will vary between countries; in the UK, for example, a prevention or health promotion intervention is usually considered cost-effective by NICE without great debate, if it costs no more than £20,000 per QALY gained. If it costs more, further detailed deliberations looking at other factors, including immediate risk to life and implications for health inequalities in the population, will take place.

An alternative approach to economic evaluation is to undertake a *cost-benefit analysis*, where the benefits as well as the costs of interventions are valued in monetary terms. An intervention is deemed to be a good investment if the monetary values or benefits outweigh the costs associated with the intervention. Budget holders outside of the health sector are likely to prefer this cost-benefit analysis approach, as it allows for comparisons to be made between very different types of investment. For example, the case for investing in making suicide more difficult on bridges could be compared with investing more in cultural life through museums or art galleries. A variant on this approach is to perform *a return on investment analysis*; this compares the costs of an intervention against the costs that can be averted, and can include putting a monetary value on health outcomes achieved, such as improved quality of life.

How Has Economic Evidence Been Used to Make the Case for Suicide Prevention?

Despite the importance of suicide as a major contributor to the overall burden of disease and the leading cause of premature mortality in younger people, there is still relatively little evidence on the economic case for investment. Studies are of mixed quality and tend to be concentrated on actions targeted at individuals who can be identified as being at high risk or who have already presented to hospital following self-harm. It is essential to better embed economic analysis into evaluations of self-harm and suicide prevention measures. Some illustrative examples of the existing evidence base and methods used can be set out. These include retrospective analysis of restrictions on access to means, prospective economic analysis alongside trials, and modeling studies synthesizing available data on effective interventions with their costs and cost consequences. As these studies illustrate, cost-effectiveness cannot be taken for granted, and not all interventions will be a good use of limited resources.

Restricting Access to Means

Looking at examples of measures to reduce suicide risk in the community, rail-related suicidal acts are comparatively rare but have a very high fatality rate. Some city metro systems have introduced safety barriers to avoid accidental and intentional injury, and more work could be undertaken to look at the economic costs and benefits of these schemes. One example is in Hong Kong where a retrospective analysis looking at the cost per disability-adjusted life year averted has been conducted (Law & Yip, 2011). This evaluation demonstrates the importance of adopting a long time frame when looking at infrastructure investment, as well as including changes in costs that go beyond health care systems. In the analysis, the safety system was only cost-effective if the costs to the transportation network, including loss of fare revenue and additional passenger waiting time, were included.

Restricting access to pesticides is another effective way of reducing suicide risk, but there have been concerns that famers' livelihoods may be adversely affected by such restrictions. In Bangladesh, access to 21 pesticides was either restricted or completely prohibited between 1996 and 2007. When analyzing the impact of these regulatory measures, researchers looked at data not only on the impact on pesticide poisoning-related suicide rates but also on changes in agricultural crop yield (Chowdhury et al., 2018). The study found that pesticide-related deaths fell from 6.3 per 100,000 in 1996 to 2.2. per 100,000 population by 2014, while over the same period no adverse economic impact on agriculture was found; the rice crop yield had increased and was higher than that in neighboring countries. Demonstrating no adverse impacts on livelihoods more generally can also be important when seeking the support of stakeholders outside the health care sector.

Hospital-Based Interventions

Both prospective and retrospective economic evaluations have been made for interventions following hospital presenting self-harm events. In Scotland, a cost-effectiveness analysis was conducted alongside the evaluation of a volitional help sheet, a brief psychological intervention, intended to reduce the risk of future self-harm and suicide in patients admitted to hospital due to a suicide attempt (O'Connor et al., 2017). The evaluation illustrates the importance of assessing cost-effectiveness for population subgroups to determine whether narrower targeting of high-risk groups may be appropriate. In this evaluation, while there was only a modest 60 % chance of the cost per future self-harm event averted being cost-effective for all patients, for those who had a previous history of self-harm, the intervention had a very promising 90 % chance of being cost-effective.

Another example is from Switzerland where an approach for self-harm patients, involving a brief manual-based therapy and regular personalized letters over a 24-month period, was shown to be effective (Gysin-Maillart, Schwab, Soravia, Megert, & Michel, 2016). Working with a health economist, the researchers were subsequently able to make use of data already collected on intervention costs and health care service utilization to retrospectively undertake an economic evaluation (Park, Gysin-Maillart, Müller, Exadaktylos, & Michel, 2018). The intervention was found to be cost saving from the health care service perspective, because of the high costs of physical injury averted.

The importance of looking beyond a narrow health care system perspective can also be seen for interventions delivered within the health care system. This may be about capturing wider benefits of interventions rather than their costs. This can be seen in a multisite randomized controlled trial in England that evaluated the cost-effectiveness of family therapy for 832 repeat self-harmers (Tubeuf, Saloniki, & Cottrell, 2019). From a health care system perspective, the intervention was more costly than the comparator, with only a small potential improvement in QALYs gained, and would not be considered cost-effective in an English context. However, if the impacts on the quality of life of family carers were also taken into account, the intervention would then be considered cost-effective due to the additional QALYs gained by carers.

Economic Evaluations in Other Settings

It is important to look at the case for intervention in different community settings, such as school, prison, and workplaces, and including the military. Of note, the Saving and Empowering Young Lives in Europe (SEYLE), a recent multisite, multicountry, multiintervention trial of school-based suicide prevention in Europe, included a prospective economic evaluation. The SEYLE intervention arms are described in detail in Chapter 7 (Intervention Studies in Suicide Research; see Box 7.3). Cost per QALY gained due to suicide prevention was the primary outcome (Ahern et al., 2018). One of the interventions, the Youth Aware of Mental Health (YAM) program generated a cost per QALY of less than €50,000, a value that would be considered cost-effective in many European countries. A limitation of this analysis, however, was the reliance on published quality-of-life weights for adults, as the study was not able to collect quality-of-life outcomes. This is an area where more research is needed, as the impacts of suicidal ideation and behaviors on adolescents' quality of life is still not well understood.

Another example is taken from the workplace. In Australia, a return on investment analysis looked at the economic impacts of the introduction of Mates in Construction (MIC) – a multicomponent workplace suicide prevention strategy used in the building industry (Doran,

Ling, Gullestrup, Swannell, & Milner, 2016). The study indicated that suicides in this industry had fallen following the introduction of MIC. The economic value of suicides averted was then compared with the costs of implementing the program, with a positive return on investment of AU $4.6 for every AU $1 invested. The economic analysis suggested that most of the economic benefits of the program were gained by the government; analyses of this type can be used to help persuade governmental bodies to invest in suicide prevention, or provide incentives for business to invest more.

Economic Modeling Studies

Economic studies linked to trials focused on suicide or self-harm prevention as primary outcomes remain rare. However, in the absence of empirical data linked to trials, *economic modeling studies* can be used to synthesize evidence on costs and consequences of interventions, as well as make long-term projections of costs and consider the impacts of any scale up of programs (McDaid, 2014).

There are many different types of approaches to modeling. Essentially, economic models are all mathematical frameworks that look at the economic consequences of different policy and practice decisions. Typically, they will compare two or more interventions, with care pathways plotted – for instance, attaching different probabilities of having an impact on suicide rates for different prevention intervention options over different time periods. Relevant levels of cost and outcomes (such as QALYs gained) are then attached to these different pathways.

These modeling approaches are increasingly used to look at the potential cost-effectiveness of a variety of interventions in the community, as well as in specific settings. In England a return on investment analysis looked at the case for investing in improved adherence to current national guidelines that all individuals should undergo a psychosocial assessment when presenting to hospital after deliberate self-harm (McDaid, Park, & Knapp, 2017). This assessment is thought to increase the likelihood of appropriate follow-up care upon hospital discharge, but rates of psychosocial assessment vary considerably across the country. The economic model, which considered costs within the health care service, as well as for the emergency services and productivity losses and intangible costs over a 10-year time period, suggested a favorable positive return on investment of US $2.93 per $1 spent, from a narrow direct costs–only perspective, and US $39.11 when productivity and intangible costs were included. Box 15.2 provides more detail on the approach taken for this model.

Other examples of modeling studies include an analysis looking at the potential 50-year impact of implementation of a multielement suicide prevention strategy in Ontario, Canada, including an awareness campaign, increased identification of individuals at risk, training of primary care physicians, and increased treatment post-suicide attempt (Lebenbaum et al., 2019). This analysis reported a 95% likelihood cost per QALY gained of under CA $50,000, a value considered cost-effective in Canada. Costs outside the health care system, including costs to the police and for funerals, were also included in the analysis.

In the US, a modeling approach has also been used to assess the case for investing in brief psychological therapy for military personnel at high risk of suicide. This model looked at costs from the perspective of the US Department of Defense for a 2-year time period only, with the model suggesting a high probability that the intervention may actually be cost saving from a military perspective (Bernecker et al., 2020).

Box 15.2. Modeling the return on investment from better guideline adherence in England

National Institute for Health and Care Excellence (NICE) guidelines in England on management of self-harm recommend that all individuals who attend a hospital accident and emergency department for a self-harm event should receive a psychosocial assessment (NICE, 2013). Analysis suggests actual assessment rates range between 41 % and 69 % of attendees (Geulayov et al., 2016).

A return on investment model was constructed looking at risk of repeat self-harm events and completed suicides over a 10-year period for individuals who self-harmed, depending on whether they received a psychosocial assessment. Baseline impacts on future events were taken from a previous English analysis that observed a lower level of repeat events following psychosocial assessment (Kapur et al., 2013). The risk of repeat self-harm and completed suicide in each 1 year cycle of the model were taken from a meta-analysis of published epidemiological studies (Carroll, Metcalfe, & Gunnell, 2014).

The model assumed that higher rates of psychosocial assessment would lead to higher levels of use (and cost) for recommended treatment pathways following hospital discharge. Unit costs for psychosocial assessment, as well as initial costs of hospital care following self-harm, were taken from a detailed analysis of costs in one English hospital (Tsiachristas et al., 2017), as well as published national tariffs.

The analysis of costs vs. savings also includes expenditure on police and/or coroner activities, and productivity losses for individuals and their families, as well as intangible costs associated with the loss of life. Costs of coroner investigations and inquests were also included. Data from the UK Office of National Statistics were used to estimate productivity losses for the employed and economically inactive. Intangible costs associated with the loss of life (net of productivity losses) were based on the willingness to pay to avoid unexpected death in a road traffic accident as published by the UK Department of Transport (Department for Transport, 2016).

Based on "Suicide and self-harm prevention," by D. McDaid, A. Park, & M. Knapp (2017). In D. McDaid, A. Park, & M. Knapp (Eds.), *Commissioning cost-effective services for promotion of mental health and wellbeing and prevention of mental ill-health*. London. UK: Public Health England.

Influencing the Economic Determinants of Suicide and Self-Harm

Having briefly looked at approaches for the role of economic evaluation, it is also important to return to the final question in Box 15.1: setting out where economics can help in understanding and influencing some of the determinants of suicide and self-harm.

There is a long tradition in the economic literature on suicide to focus on looking at the association between macroeconomic circumstances, such as changes in unemployment rates or economic growth, or individual economic circumstances such as levels of indebtedness, and rates of suicide (McDaid & Kennelly, 2009). Although complex, it is clear that economic circumstances often play a role in suicidal risk, yet comparatively little attention has been paid by economists to assessing whether investing in economic mechanisms – for instance, support for avoiding unmanageable debt – may have a remedial impact on suicide and self-harm. In addition to focusing on conventional suicide prevention strategies, there is a need to look at the cost-effectiveness of regulatory arrangements such as bankruptcy protection or rules that prevent excess interest rates being charged on debts, as potential interventions for suicide prevention.

Another significant gap is the lack of evidence regarding interventions that address some of the underlying risks for suicide, such as investment in poverty alleviation mechanisms. While some literature on welfare reform and suicide rates is found in high-income countries (Barr, Kinderman, & Whitehead, 2015), much of this analysis looks only at associations between these factors for aggregate populations rather than causal relationships at the level of individuals. Moreover, this issue could also be explored further in low- and middle-income countries, with recent studies in Brazil and Indonesia pointing to associations between use of cash transfer programs and suicide rates (Alves, Machado, & Barreto, 2019; Christian, Hensel, & Roth, 2018).

How Can the Case Be Strengthened?

This chapter has illustrated different examples of how economic evidence has been incorporated into the evaluation of suicide and self-harm prevention. How might this evidence base be strengthened? One step would be to incorporate economic analysis more routinely into new effectiveness evaluations. This, however, would take time. One immediate possibility is to continue to retrospectively conduct economic analysis for proven effective interventions, identifying the costs of service delivery and then seeking to attach appropriate values to the benefits of those programs.

This might also be done through greater use of economic modeling. Models can be used to synthesize data from effectiveness studies where no economic analysis was undertaken, drawing on multiple sources for estimates of the costs of interventions and their impacts on costs to the health care system and other sectors. Models can also allow researchers to adapt evidence for the effectiveness and costs of suicide prevention interventions in one particular context to other contexts.

Models can also be used to deal with uncertainty regarding effectiveness and cost outcomes. In the case of the return on investment work on suicide prevention in England, a decision support tool was provided to policy makers. This allowed different scenarios to be constructed where key parameters around uptake, population targeted, costs, and effectiveness could be varied, and an updated overall return on investment generated (McDaid et al., 2017). Issues such as budgetary impact if interventions are scaled up, or their coverage is increased, can also be considered.

Adopting a Broader Cross-Sectoral Perspective to Economic Evaluation

The perspectives of economic analyses can be broadened to take account not only of impacts on health care systems, but also on wider impacts linked to participation in employment and other productive activities, as well as impacts for the transport and criminal justice sectors. Suicide prevention interventions for specific populations such as in the military (Comtois et al., 2019), workplaces (Kinchin & Doran, 2017), and schools (Ahern et al., 2018) are now being conducted. This means capturing intersectoral benefits and costs of interventions delivered outside of the health care sector (McDaid & Park, 2016), as well as documenting who is paying for the program, and the time frame for when, or if, they will get a return on their investment.

Conclusions

Shining a health economics lens on suicide research can help reinforce arguments for investment in self-harm and suicide prevention. Researchers can choose among several different ways to build economics into their evaluations, ranging from resource and costing analysis, to complex economic evaluations, including economic modeling. What is vital now is to encourage more routine collection and use of economic evidence to place suicide prevention on a level playing field with other potential options for reducing injury and improving health and well-being.

References

Ahern, S., Burke, L.-A., McElroy, B., Corcoran, P., McMahon, E.M., Keeley, H., ... Wasserman, D. (2018). A cost-effectiveness analysis of school-based suicide prevention programmes. *European Child & Adolescent Psychiatry, 27*, 1295–1304. https://doi.org/10.1007/s00787-018-1120-5

Alves, F.J.O., Machado, D.B., & Barreto, M.L. (2019). Effect of the Brazilian cash transfer programme on suicide rates: A longitudinal analysis of the Brazilian municipalities. *Social Psychiatry and Psychiatric Epidemiology, 54*, 599–606. https://doi.org/10.1007/s00127-018-1627-6

Barr, B., Kinderman, P., & Whitehead, M. (2015). Trends in mental health inequalities in England during a period of recession, austerity and welfare reform 2004 to 2013. *Social Science & Medicine, 147*, 324–331. https://doi.org/10.1016/j.socscimed.2015.11.009

Bernecker, S.L., Zuromski, K.L., Curry, J.C., Kim, J.J., Gutierrez, P.M., Joiner, T.E., ... Bryan, C.J. (2020). Economic evaluation of brief cognitive behavioral therapy vs treatment as usual for suicidal US Army Soldiers. *JAMA Psychiatry, 77*(3), 256–264. https://doi.org/10.1001/jamapsychiatry.2019.3639

Carroll, R., Metcalfe, C., & Gunnell, D. (2014). Hospital presenting self-harm and risk of fatal and non-fatal repetition: systematic review and meta-analysis. *PLoS One, 9*(2), e89944. https://doi.org/10.1371/journal.pone.0089944

Chowdhury, F.R., Dewan, G., Verma, V.R., Knipe, D.W., Isha, I.T., Faiz, M.A., ... Eddleston, M. (2018). Bans of WHO Class I Pesticides in Bangladesh-suicide prevention without hampering agricultural output. *International Journal Of Epidemiology, 47*(1), 175–184. https://doi.org/10.1093/ije/dyx157

Christian, C., Hensel, L., & Roth, C. (2018). Income Shocks and Suicides: Causal Evidence From Indonesia. *Review of Economics and Statistics, 101*(5), 905–920. https://doi.org/10.1162/rest_a_00777

Comtois, K.A., Kerbrat, A.H., DeCou, C.R., Atkins, D.C., Majeres, J.J., Baker, J.C., & Ries, R.K. (2019). Effect of augmenting standard care for military personnel with brief caring text messages for suicide prevention: A randomized clinical trial. *JAMA Psychiatry, 76*(5), 474–483. https://doi.org/10.1001/jamapsychiatry.2018.4530

Department for Transport. (2016). *Reported road casualties Great Britain: 2015 annual report. Moving britain ahead*. London, UK: Department for Transport.

Doran, C.M., Ling, R., Gullestrup, J., Swannell, S., & Milner, A. (2016). The impact of a suicide prevention strategy on reducing the economic cost of suicide in the New South Wales construction industry. *Crisis, 37*(2), 121–129. https://doi.org/10.1027/0227-5910/a000362

Drummond, M.F., Sculpher, M.J., Claxton, K., Stoddart, G.L., & Torrance, G.W. (2015). *Methods for the economic evaluation of health care programmes.* Oxford, UK: Oxford University Press.

Geulayov, G., Kapur, N., Turnbull, P., Clements, C., Waters, K., Ness, J., ... Hawton, K. (2016). Epidemiology and trends in non-fatal self-harm in three centres in England, 2000–2012: Findings from the multicentre study of self-harm in England. *BMJ Open, 6*(4), e010538. https://doi.org/10.1136/bmjopen-2015-010538

Gysin-Maillart, A., Schwab, S., Soravia, L., Megert, M., & Michel, K. (2016). A novel brief therapy for patients who attempt suicide: A 24-months follow-up randomized controlled study of the Attempted Suicide Short Intervention Program (ASSIP). *PLoS Medicine, 13*(3), e1001968. https://doi.org/10.1371/journal.pmed.1001968

Kapur, N., Steeg, S., Webb, R., Haigh, M., Bergen, H., Hawton, K., ... Cooper, J. (2013). Does clinical management improve outcomes following self-harm? Results from the multicentre study of self-harm in England. *PLoS One, 8*(8), e70434. https://doi.org/10.1371/journal.pone.0070434

Kinchin, I., & Doran, C.M. (2017). The economic cost of suicide and non-fatal suicide behavior in the Australian workforce and the potential impact of a workplace suicide prevention strategy. *International Journal of Environmental Research and Public Health, 14*(4), 347. https://doi.org/10.3390/ijerph14040347

Law, C.K., & Yip, P.S.F. (2011). An economic evaluation of setting up physical barriers in railway stations for preventing railway injury: Evidence from Hong Kong. *Journal of Epidemiology & Community Health, 65*(10), 915–920. https://doi.org/10.1136/jech.2010.115188

Lebenbaum, M., Cheng, J., de Oliveira, C., Kurdyak, P., Zaheer, J., Hancock-Howard, R., & Coyte, P.C. (2019). Evaluating the cost effectiveness of a suicide prevention campaign implemented in Ontario, Canada. *Applied Health Economics and Health Policy, 18*(2), 189–201. https://doi.org/10.1007/s40258-019-00511-5

Maynard, A., & McDaid, D. (2003). Evaluating health interventions: Exploiting the potential. *Health Policy, 63*(2), 215–226. https://doi.org/10.1016/S0168-8510(02)00068-4

McDaid, D. (2014). Economic modelling for global mental health. In G. Thornicroft & V. Patel (Eds.), *Global mental health trials* (pp. 265–286). Oxford, UK: Oxford University Press.

McDaid, D. (2016). Making an economic case for investing in suicide prevention: Quo vadis? In R.C. O'Connor & J. Pirkis (Eds.), *The international handbook of suicide prevention* (pp. 775–790). Chichester, UK: Wiley Blackwell.

McDaid, D., & Kennelly, B. (2009). The case for suicide prevention: An economic perspective. In D. Wasserman & C. Wasserman (Eds.), *The Oxford textbook of suicidology – The five continents perspective* (pp. 359–368). Oxford, UK: Oxford University Press.

McDaid, D., & Park, A.L. (2016). *Evidence on financing and budgeting mechanisms to support intersectoral actions between health, education, social welfare and labour sectors*. Copenhagen, Denmark: World Health Organization Regional Office for Europe. Available at https://www.ncbi.nlm.nih.gov/books/n/whohen48/pdf/

McDaid, D., Park, A., & Knapp, M. (2017). Suicide and self-harm prevention. In D. McDaid, A. Park, & M. Knapp (Eds.), *Commissioning cost-effective services for promotion of mental health and wellbeing and prevention of mental ill-health* (pp. 44–49). London, UK: Public Health England. Available at https://assets.publishing.service.gov.uk/government/uploads/system/uploads/attachment_data/file/640714/Commissioning_effective_mental_health_prevention_report.pdf

McDaid, D., Sassi, F., & Merkur, S. (2015). *Promoting health, preventing disease: The economic case*. Maidenhead, UK: Open University Press.

National Institute for Health and Care Excellence. (2013). *Self-harm. Quality standard (QS34)*. London, UK: Author.

O'Connor, R.C., Ferguson, E., Scott, F., Smyth, R., McDaid, D., Park, A.L., ... Armitage, C.J. (2017). A brief psychological intervention to reduce repetition of self-harm in patients admitted to hospital following a suicide attempt: A randomised controlled trial. *Lancet Psychiatry, 4*(6), 451–460. https://doi.org/10.1016/S2215-0366(17)30129-3

Park, A.L., Gysin-Maillart, A., Müller, T.J., Exadaktylos, A., & Michel, K. (2018). Cost-effectiveness of a brief structured intervention program aimed at preventing repeat suicide attempts among those who previously attempted suicide: A secondary analysis of the ASSIP randomized clinical trial. *JAMA Network Open, 1*(6), e183680. https://doi.org/10.1001/jamanetworkopen.2018.3680

Shepard, D.S., Gurewich, D., Lwin, A.K., Reed, G.A., Jr., & Silverman, M.M. (2016). Suicide and suicidal attempts in the United States: Costs and policy implications. *Suicide & Life-Threatening Behavior, 46*(3), 352–362. https://doi.org/10.1111/sltb.12225

Tsiachristas, A., McDaid, D., Casey, D., Brand, F., Leal, J., Park, A.L., ... Hawton, K. (2017). General hospital costs in England of medical and psychiatric care for patients who self-harm: a retrospective analysis. *Lancet Psychiatry, 4*(10), 759–767. https://doi.org/10.1016/S2215-0366(17)30367-X

Tubeuf, S., Saloniki, E.-C., & Cottrell, D. (2019). Parental health spillover in cost-effectiveness analysis: Evidence from self-harming adolescents in England. *Pharmacoeconomics, 37*(4), 513–530. https://doi.org/10.1007/s40273-018-0722-6

Chapter 16

Technology and the Future of Suicide Prevention

Cristian Leorin, Eloisa Stella, and Diego De Leo

Summary

New digital technologies have expanded the realm of opportunities to deliver support to those at risk of suicide. eHealth and general health apps have shown important prevention capabilities. Big data analytic methods have made possible successful applications of artificial intelligence in health care. Machine learning techniques and natural language processing methods may now offer useful interpretation of social media posts and content of talks and scripts. There is also now the capacity to use smartphone, wearable devices, and smart home technology to conduct longitudinal monitoring of putative risk factors and develop predictive algorithms for suicidal thoughts and behaviors. This chapter offers an overview of what is already available and what holds promise for the future of suicide prevention.

In recent years, the emergence of a variety of new digital technologies has expanded the realm of opportunities in the way we can create and deliver support to those who feel suicidal and/or are at risk of taking their own life. For example, although their effectiveness and safety is mostly still in question, the latest developments in *mobile health* (mHealth) technologies have introduced new, interesting monitoring, preventative, and therapeutic tools that no therapist, psychiatrist, or social worker can ever compete with: to be there at all times, especially if or when people are struggling to stay alive. These technologies are now reaching a level of sophistication that enables us to assemble and process large quantities of static and dynamic data to accurately predict a situation or a condition that endangers or safeguards personal well-being. If we compound the convenience of mobile health technologies with the ubiquity of the *internet of things* (IoT) platforms and the transformative power of *artificial intelligence* (AI), we step into scenarios in which any of us could be (and is) monitored and receive needed help, regardless of where we are, or whatever we do, at any given time.

Although on paper these innovations appear to be meaningful, several caveats still need to be addressed associated with the idea of transferring the responsibility for human care and support to a machine. This is not only a moral concern that stems from the imagery of a panopticon-type reality evoked by many of these technological solutions, it is also a very practical issue associated with the very nature of contemporary technology use and applications.

Digital Health

The broad category of *digital health* encompasses multiple technological domains, including mobile health, health information technology, telehealth (including telemedicine), and wearable medical devices. mHealth includes mobile apps, which are tools that can help individuals to promote healthy living, gain access to useful information, and in some circumstances, receive care or manage their own health.

The term *digital health* is rooted in *eHealth*, which was defined by the World Health Organization (WHO) in the context of the World Health Assembly resolution of 2005 as "the cost-effective and secure use of information communication technologies (ICT) in support of health and health-related fields, including health-care services, health surveillance, health literature, and health education, knowledge and research" (WHO, 2005). *mHealth* is a subset of eHealth and is defined as "the use of mobile wireless technologies for health"; mHealth may be part of efforts to improve access, reduce costs, reduce inefficiencies, increase quality of care, and facilitate personalized medicine for patients (WHO, 2016). More recently, the term *digital health* was redefined by the WHO (2019) as "a broad umbrella term encompassing eHealth (which includes mHealth), as well as emerging areas, such as the use of advanced computing sciences in 'big data', genomics and artificial intelligence."

Digital technologies provide concrete opportunities to tackle health care system challenges, and thereby offer the potential to enhance the coverage and quality of health care practices and services. Digital health interventions may be used, for example, to facilitate targeted communications to individuals to generate demand and broaden contact coverage. Digital health interventions may also be used by health workers to gain immediate access to clinical protocols through, for example, decision-support mechanisms or telemedicine consultations with other health professionals. The range of ways digital technologies can be used to support the needs of health care systems is wide, and these technologies continue to evolve due to the inherently dynamic nature of the field.

The enthusiasm for digital health has also driven a proliferation of short-lived implementations and an overwhelming diversity of digital tools whose impact on health care systems and people's well-being still remains unclear. This concern was highlighted most notably in the consensus statement of the WHO Bellagio eHealth Evaluation Group (2011), which opened by stating: "To improve health and reduce health inequalities, rigorous evaluation of eHealth is necessary to generate evidence and promote the appropriate integration and use of technologies." While recognizing the innovative role that digital technologies can play in strengthening a variety of health care systems, processes, and interventions, there is an equally important need to evaluate their contributing effects, to ensure that such investments do not inappropriately divert resources from alternative, nondigital, and especially, more effective approaches.

eHealth and mHealth

The 2015 global survey conducted by WHO on eHealth programs found that the most commonly reported types of programs were emergency toll-free telephone services (75%) and health call centers (72%), both accessible by mobile or fixed-line phones, which were followed by appointment reminders (69%) using mobile information communication technologies (ICT; text, voice, or multimedia). The next most common group of eHealth services include community mobilization and health promotion campaigns, access to health information and databases, mobile telehealth consultations, emergency and disaster response and management, access to patient records, and data collection for health surveys. Many of these programs were not novelties per se, but have introduced new modes of delivery of preexisting health initiatives to reach greater portions of the population (WHO, 2016). What is especially

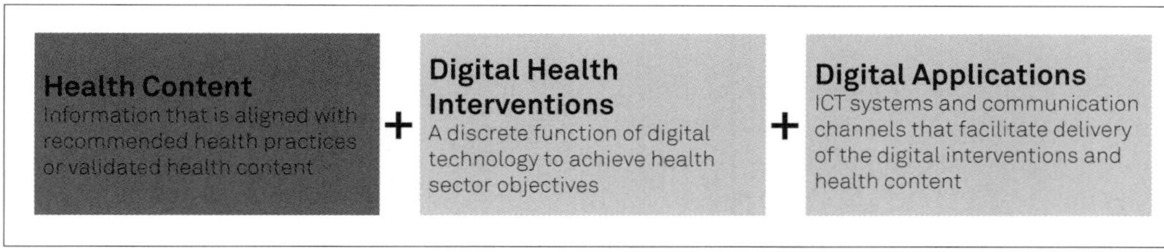

Figure 16.1 Components contributing to digital health implementations. ICT = information communication technologies. Adapted with permission from "WHO Guideline: Recommendations on Digital Interventions for Health System Strengthening." Geneva: World Health Organization, p. xiii. © 2019 by the WHO. Licence: CC BY-NC-SA 3.0 IGO

worth noting is the impact that these programs are having on developing countries, where mobile communication technologies are leapfrogging several stages of technology development, to connect remote areas of the planet without sufficient infrastructures for fixed telephone lines, computers, or traditional health care support (WHO, 2016).

Generally speaking, digital health interventions are applied within a country context and a health care system, and their implementation is made possible by a number of factors including (1) the health domain area and associated content, (2) the digital intervention or functionality provided, (3) the software and communication channels for delivering the digital health intervention, and (4) mediated by a foundational layer of the ICT and the enabling environment (see Figure 16.1).

Although digital health has the potential to help addressing problems such as distance and access, it still shares many of the underlying challenges faced by health care system interventions in general, including poor management, insufficient training, infrastructural limitations, and poor access to equipment and supplies. In other words, digital health cannot fix preexisting systemic issues, unless these are taken into account from the very early stage of development, in addition to the specific implementation requirements associated to any new technology-based tool to be introduced.

Furthermore, these components need to be made appropriate to the local context, and ensure effective implementation through reflection on the behavior and organizational changes that would also be required. Digital health interventions are intended to fit into overall digital health architecture and require an equally important level of support to ensure a cohesive approach to implementation, in which different digital interventions can leverage one another, as opposed to operating as isolated initiatives (WHO, 2019).

Digital Technology Adoption in Psychiatry and Mental Health

In recent years, the number of people who proactively sought apps to manage their personal health has massively increased. In 2017, Torous and Roberts reported more than 10,000 mental health–related smartphone apps intended to provide consumers with a convenient way to monitor their health in real time and simultaneously receive an on-the-go therapy type of support (Torous & Roberts, 2017). Among these consumers, there may well be a good percentage of people suffering from a mental condition – for example, a survey on individuals aged 45 years and younger, treated for psychiatric conditions, showed an open interest by the participants to use a mobile app to track their mental health (Torous, Friedman, & Keshavan, 2014).

In theory, mobile devices, such as smartphones and tablets, offer clinicians, researchers, and the public alike a wealth of new ways of providing and receiving clinical treatment, monitoring progress, and increasing understanding of psychiatric illnesses. However, there is not much data yet on physician and patient adoption rates, and/or how the application of this technology affects patient outcomes (Donker et al., 2013).

Mobile health apps can be either active or passive. Active apps require direct participation from the patient, whereas passive apps may access data (e.g., through smartphone functions such as GPS) without the patient or clinician even noticing. Chan et al. (2018) discussed the use of active data from mobile apps in the practice of technology-enabled psychiatry. Some examples of mobile health apps include mood trackers for patient mood self-rating (commonly with app-based prompts and rating scales), diary apps (where patients enter narrative comments on their current state), and wellness apps (where guidance on positive health behaviors that may impact psychiatric illness management are addressed and monitored). The researchers observed that users' willingness to participate in mobile research protocols (engagement) remained challenging: Although the level of engagement was high during the first 2 weeks of treatment, it fell to 44 % adherence by the fourth week (Chan, Burke Parish, Fazio & Torous, 2018).

Results from Deady et al. (2017), indicate that a range of different cognitive behavior programs produce small, but overall positive effects on symptom reduction for anxiety and depression, at both an indicated/selective and a universal prevention level. Moreover, recent studies have also shown minor but positive results in symptom reduction for eHealth interventions designed to prevent depression and anxiety, but then – again – it is still unclear whether these interventions will translate into an actual reduction of suicide attempts, depression, and anxiety in the longer term (Larsen, Nicholas, & Christensen, 2016; Deady et al., 2017).

Although the effect sizes among eHealth prevention interventions appear to be smaller than those reported for face-to-face prevention interventions (Cuijpers, Smit, & van Straten, 2007), eHealth showed potential for greater reach with fewer resources. Indeed, eHealth technologies may be able to overcome a range of financial, geographic, and time barriers that so far have prevented interventions from reaching vulnerable, underprivileged, or remote communities effectively. To this end, a systematic review and meta-analysis conducted by Deady et al. (2017) found small but positive effects of eHealth prevention interventions for anxiety and depression. However, the study also showed inadequate evidence on the medium- to long-term effect of such interventions, and importantly, on the reduction of incidence of common mental disorders.

The efficacy of general health apps as prevention tools also needs further research and understanding. For example, evidence shows that most downloaded mHealth apps are never used and that the level of patient engagement with these technologies rapidly declines over the first week of use (Owen et al., 2015). Perhaps these shortcomings may be associated with the fact that these health apps are not sufficiently user-friendly or accessible (Sarkar et al., 2016). Or perhaps they are not sufficiently relevant to the specific needs or expectations of their users. Whatever the reason behind this disappointing performance, the issue of long-term adoption is critical, especially for individuals who live with chronic or long-term psychiatric disorders that affect their lives for several months or sometimes years, if not for their entire lifetime. In other words, usability, relevance, and efficiency must be designed to work in the long run and not as quick fixes to solve temporary crises (Hategan, Giroux, & Bourgeois,

2019). Table 16.1, produced by the National Institute of Mental Health, provides a good overview of the current advantages and disadvantages of mental health apps.

Table 16.1 Advantages and disadvantages of mental health apps

Advantages	Disadvantages
Convenience MHapps may be adopted by those who have difficulty with in-person clinical appointments or avoided psychiatric care in the past. Treatment can take place anytime and anyplace. Individuals can seek treatment options without involving others.	Treatment tailoring MHapps offer the same treatment program to all users, but there is a need to understand if apps work for all individuals and for all psychiatric conditions.
Data collection Some apps can gather data without any help from the user. Receiving information from a large number of individuals at the same time can increase researchers' understanding of mental health and help them develop better interventions.	Privacy Apps manage sensitive personal data and app developers need to be able to guarantee privacy for app users.
Affordability Some apps are cost-free or cost less than usual care.	Regulation There is no industry-wide regulation to inform users if an app is proven effective; regulation of mental health technology and the data it generates needs to be developed.
Accessibility Technology can offer treatment to patients in remote areas or to individuals in times of intense need (e.g., following a natural disaster).	Effectiveness Scientific evidence that this technology works as well as the usual care is underdeveloped.
Support This technology can provide 24-hr monitoring and/or intervention support and can complement usual therapy.	Overrating There is concern that if an app promises more than it delivers, users may turn away from other more effective therapy programs.

Note. MHapps = mental health apps. Reprinted with permission from "Digital Technology Adoption in Psychiatric Care: An Overview of the Contemporary Shift from Technology to Opportunity," by A. Hategan, C. Giroux, & J.A. Bourgeois, *Journal of Technology in Behavioral Science, 4*, p. 173. © 2019 by Springer Nature Switzerland AG.

Mobile apps have significant potential to deliver high-efficacy mental health interventions. As Moock (2014) suggests, unrestricted access to adequate medical care for people with mental disorders will be one of the pressuring public mental health tasks in the near future. In addition, scarcity of human and financial resources across the public mental health sector is a powerful argument for investigating innovative alternatives for delivering services. Given the global shortage of psychiatrists and the lack of mental health care access in rural regions, mHealth technologies may represent a viable tool to bridge the mental health treatment gap and transform how treatments are delivered and accessed. This is a transformation that requires the combined mobilization of science, regulation, and design (Chandrashekar, 2018).

Artificial Intelligence, Machine Learning, and Big Data

The increasing availability of health care data and rapid development of *big data* analytic methods have made possible the recent successful applications of AI in health care. Guided by relevant clinical questions, powerful AI techniques could unlock clinically relevant information hidden in massive amounts of multidimensional data, which in turn could assist clinical decision making and intervention.

As debated in Jiang et al. (2017), the advantages of AI have been extensively discussed in the medical literature (Dilsizian & Siegel, 2014; Patel et al., 2009; Jha & Topol, 2016). AI could not only improve the efficacy and efficiency of many existing health care processes, practices, and modes of intervention, but it might also introduce new ways of conceiving how we diagnose, treat, or monitor a patient. For example, AI can use sophisticated algorithms to "learn" features from a large volume of health care data, and then use the obtained insights to assist clinical practice. It can also be equipped with learning and self-correcting abilities to improve its accuracy based on feedback. An AI system can also provide physicians with up-to-date medical information from journals, textbooks, and clinical practice reports to inform proper patient care. In addition, an AI system can help reduce diagnostic and therapeutic errors that are inevitable in clinical practice. Moreover, an AI system extracts useful information from a large patient population to assist in making real-time inferences for health risk alerts and health outcome predictions (Jiang et al., 2017).

As powerful as AI techniques can be, in the end they still have to be motivated by clinical problems and be applied to assist clinical practice. Despite the increasingly rich AI literature in health care, research has mainly concentrated on a few disease types: cancer, nervous system disease, and cardiovascular disease.

AI devices mainly fall into two major categories. The first category includes *machine learning* (ML) techniques that analyze structured data such as imaging, and genetic and electrophysiological data. In the medical applications, ML procedures attempt to cluster patients' traits or infer the probability of the disease outcomes. The second category includes *natural language processing* (NLP) methods that extract information from unstructured data such as clinical notes or medical journals, to supplement and enrich structured medical data. The NLP procedures target turning texts to machine-readable structures (Darcy, Louie, & Roberts, 2016).

In recent years, social media have shown significant value for many public health–related issues (Moorhead et al., 2013), as well as an influence on mental health and suicide-related behaviors (Luxton, June, & Fairall, 2012; Wongkoblap, Vadillo, & Curcin, 2017). The widespread popularity of social media provides unprecedented opportunities to access mental health and suicide risk data from a large-scale population. The real-time flow of information sharing on social media potentially allows early detection and intervention for at-risk users. Most previous studies have focused on analyzing the association between suicidal ideation and the linguistic features of the contents – that is, lexical analysis (Cheng, Li, Kwok, Zhu, & Yip, 2017; Zhang et al., 2014) – or posting behaviors – that is, posting frequency (Smith et al., 2017a) on social media platforms. Some recent efforts have attempted to classify tweets by levels of distress and concern (O'Dea et al., 2015; Abboute et al., 2014) or types of suicidal communication using ML or rule-based approaches. Jashinsky et al. (2014) tracked suicide risk factors from Twitter using keywords-based approaches. The comparison with traditional ML algorithms showed the superiority of deep learning–based approaches and indicated the potential to use this approach for automated stressor recognition in social media (Du et al., 2018).

Moreover, a lot of data for the NLP methods include social media and smart devices; platforms such as Twitter, Facebook, and Instagram offer important information about mental health and even risk of suicide (Oexle, Niederkrotenthaler, & De Leo, 2019). Both the patterns of use and the nature of content posted on Instagram have been correlated with mood in nonclinical samples offering real-time data that may inform risk. In Du et al. (2018), the authors suggested that mentions of stressors are often embedded in narratives such as clinical text or social media posts, and thus need to be recognized first for further investigation. Fortunately, the advances in ML and NLP provide great opportunities to access mental health issues from large-scale narrative data.

Digital Technology and Suicide Prevention

Rather than a mere psychiatric problem, suicide and suicidal behavior should more globally be considered as a major public health commitment (WHO, 2014). While frequently associated with several different psychiatric conditions (particularly depressive disorders, bipolar disorders, psychotic disorders, neurocognitive disorders, and certain personality disorders), suicide risk is also increased in several systemic medical illnesses (e.g., multiple sclerosis, Huntington's disease, seizure disorder, renal failure, and HIV/AIDS) and numerous psychosocial conditions (e.g., unemployment, separation, losses, abandonment, forced migration, etc.; De Leo & Arnautovska, 2016).

As described in Oexle et al. (2019), there is now the capacity to use smartphone, wearable computing, and smart home technology to conduct intensive longitudinal assessments monitoring putative risk factors with minimal participant burden and modern computational techniques to develop predictive algorithms for suicidal thoughts and behaviors (De Leo et al., 2016; Oexle et al., 2019). Current research and theory on short-term risk processes for suicidal thoughts and behaviors, combined with the emergent capabilities of new technologies, suggest that this is an important research agenda for the future (Allen, Nelson, Brent, & Auerbach, 2019). Big data and ML certainly hold promise for suicide prevention (Braithwaite, Giraud-Carrier, West, Barnes, & Hanson, 2016). If based on good-quality data, the availability of algorithms would permit reliable assessments also for personnel not particularly specialized in suicide risk evaluation, such as first aid and emergency ward professionals, who are used to working under strong pressures (Barak-Corren et al., 2017). Wearable technologies have become quite popular for checking a number of physical functions, such as heart and blood pressure, sleep patterns, number of steps, and calories spent in sport activities. Reliable indications are soon to be expected on levels of anxiety and depression; the same could happen for suicide ideation (Oexle et al., 2019).

Wearable devices and smartphones could be the monitors for *experienced sampling methodology* (ESM). This innovative approach may allow for timely assessments of suicide ideation, as well as its potential correlates and predictors (Oexle et al., 2019; Perry, Werner-Seidler, Calear, & Christensen, 2016). In ESM investigations, suicidal thoughts and other related factors (e.g., mood swings) are briefly assessed multiple times a day using wearable devices and smartphones. This seems to increase the chance for someone to report precisely their experiences with suicide ideation, without significantly impacting on their risk of suicide (Law et al., 2015; Torous et al., 2015).

Until now, ESM has only offered insights into the prediction of suicide ideation and not behavior; bigger sample sizes and longitudinal observations might eventually confirm the potential of ESM for generating the knowledge needed for effective suicide prevention (Oexle et al., 2019).

There are many reasons that technology looks appealing these days:

1. As rates of suicide continue to represent a major public health problem, there is urgent need for innovative approaches to better understand, predict, and care for those at high risk of suicide. Numerous mobile and sensor technology solutions have already been proposed, are in development, or are available today.
2. With worldwide shortages of mental health clinicians and services, there is now widespread interest and excitement in using digital technologies and AI software to help understand, predict, and prevent suicide (Torous, Luo, & Chan, 2018).

mResearch could allow the creation of detailed data collections, including information about their dynamic relationships (Torous et al., 2014). Similarly to algorithms dedicated to temporal dynamics risk assessment (Selby, Yen, & Spirito, 2013), algorithms may be created specifically for the variable or the psychological construct that needs to be studied. In this way, they could enable us to make stronger assumptions on causal inferences between the different variables, compared with those resulting from cross-sectional or longitudinal studies. It appears that online and mobile psychosocial interventions developed specifically for the management of suicide ideation have greater impact on the reduction of suicide and attempted suicide, compared with interventions that target indirect symptoms associated with suicidal behavior, such as anxiety, depression, or hopelessness (Witt et al., 2017).

As Christensen has recently argued (2018), one good reason to invest in technology for suicide prevention is that it can reach more people, like no other service or professional can. In her view, it is not just a matter of insufficient infrastructures, it is also because about 60 % of individuals with suicidal thoughts do not seek professional help (Christensen, 2018). Technology could fill this gap. It is not a matter of substituting professional face-to-face services with technological interventions, rather it is an opportunity to harness the power that mainstream technologies are providing today (through apps, social media, websites, and other digital outlets) to provide a few crucial functions that no one can do at the moment: namely, help those at risk to find the services they need and assist health professionals to monitor patients and deliver help to them as required. Christensen also suggests that by investing in better data, we could also obtain information about suicide rates, risk factors, treatments, and outcomes that would enable us to better identify those at risk, deliver interventions that are more relevant and efficient, and help communities tailor their suicide prevention strategies.

Moreover, among young people aged 15–29 years, suicide is the second leading cause of death globally (WHO, 2014); this is a demographic that is juxtaposed with the highest segment of the US population to own smartphones and use mobile apps (National Institute of Health, 2018). This convergence of demographic and social trends suggests that increasing efforts for understanding and predicting suicide using new digital technologies could not only make a great deal of sense but could also lead to an unprecedented positive impact among this cohort of people.

Although these approaches have enormous potential to create new knowledge, the current empirical literature is limited. Moreover, all of this kind of technology may provide one point of access that might facilitate both early identification and intervention implementation and thus represent a key area for future suicide prevention research (Allen, Nelson, Brent, & Auerbach, 2019). However, passive monitoring of risk for suicidal thoughts and behaviors raises complex ethical issues that will need to be resolved before large-scale clinical applications become operative.

Based on considerations expressed by Vahabzadeh, Sahin, and Kalali (2016), digital technology could theoretically help clinicians to identify and quantify objective predictors in clinical assessment of suicide risk. This would include information on:

1. the singular impact of each suicide risk factor versus combined interaction of various suicide risk factors;
2. the individualized suicide risk profile of a given person; and
3. the immediate risk for a person at any given time, with consideration given to newly acquired information regarding nuances of suicidality (Vahabzadeh et al., 2016).

Another possible step in predicting suicide is the ability to analyze large amount of data and generate clinical insights with tools such as AI, ML, and statistical modeling. Such predictive analytical models can be used to identify both long-term and short-term risk, each of which requires different approaches. Focusing first on long-term risk prediction for populations, better forecasting of risk could lead to better allocation of resources, targeted prevention strategies, and improved clinical decision support (Iniesta, Stahl, & McGuffin, 2016).

New statistical methods are being developed to improve the use of existing data and make more accurate risk predictions. These more recent statistical methods include ML-based tools, such as support vector machines, deep neural nets, random forests, and many others. Many current efforts also center around clustering individuals into novel subtypes that may offer a more accurate assessment of risk. For example, instead of using a few variables currently utilized in clinical risk assessments such as access to weapons, history of prior suicide attempts, etc., researchers are now looking at hundreds of predictors to generate a more personalized risk profile (Christensen, Batterham, & O'Dea, 2014).

Due to their lack of rigid modeling assumptions, modern ML methods have a general advantage over classical statistical methods in their being able to adaptively identify complex relationships between large variable sets and suicide risk (Thompson, Gershonm, O'Hara, Bernert, & Depp, 2014). However, prospective comparisons of ML tools to predict short-term suicide risk have not yet been conducted, despite their tremendous potential. This is in part due to the fact that the short-term risk factors derived from social media and smartphone are still not well-characterized or validated. Crucially, even the best computational methods for risk assessment will only ever be as good as the risk factor data provided to them. Thus, improvements in smartphone and sensor data quality (i.e., the way such data are collected, processed, and stored) and interoperability are critical for realizing the full potential of new ML methods operating with these data (Torous et al., 2018).

Researchers from the World Well-Being Project (WWBP) analyzed social media with an AI algorithm to pick out linguistic cues that might predict depression (Eichstaedt et al., 2018). It turns out that those suffering from depression express themselves on social media in ways that those dealing with other chronic conditions do not, such as mentions of loneliness and using words such as *feelings*, *I*, and *me*. The team's findings were published in the journal *Proceedings of the National Academy of Sciences*: After analyzing half a million Facebook posts from people who consented to provide their Facebook status updates and medical records, researchers were able to identify depression-associated language markers. What they found was that linguistic markers could predict depression up to 3 months before the person received a formal diagnosis (Wongkoblap et al., 2017). Other researchers use technology to explore the way facial expressions, enunciation of words, and tone and language could indicate suicide risk (Fromkin, Rodman, & Hyams, 2018).

Only a few automated approaches have been proposed to extract psychiatric stressors from Twitter, mainly due to (1) the lack of annotated corpora that are time-consuming and costly to build and (2) the inherent linguistic difficulties that stressors present beyond well-defined clinical concepts such as diseases. Nevertheless, the results collected so far indicate the potential to use deep learning–based methods for automated stressor recognition in social media (Du et al., 2018).

Other studies have focused on social media monitoring powered by ML technologies to detect persons at risk for suicide based on their social media posting behavior. And yet the accuracy of suicide risk detection through these technologies remains uncertain for a number of reasons connected to the very complexity of social media *culture* (e.g., the pervasive use of pseudonyms rather than actual identities in social media contexts) and the complexity associated with putting together and processing massive amounts of data about the potential population at risk, which would also involve the combination of qualitative and quantitative methods to deliver relevant interventions to the right people at the right time (Notredame et al., 2018).

mHealth solutions can be especially advantageous for suicide prevention purposes: They can improve access and availability of sources of support in very cost-effective, convenient, and discreet ways. More importantly, mobile apps could do something that no therapist or physician can do at the moment: be there on a 24-hr-a-day basis to provide support in time of need. Given that suicide ideation and suicide risk tend to change rapidly for individuals at risk of suicide, access to a technology that provides the right intervention at the right time in the right way may literally save lives (Larsen et al., 2016). However, current wisdom based on evidence-based reviews says that the majority of commercially available apps are not appropriate for clinical care and may even embed potentially harmful content. In a survey conducted by Larsen et al. (2016), 123 mHealth apps specifically designed to prevent suicide were identified, downloaded, and reviewed to verify their content and efficacy. According to this study, none of these apps provided comprehensive evidence-based support, and in some of them, potentially harmful content, such as listing access to lethal means or encouraging risky behavior in a crisis, was also identified. In light of this evidence, the authors encourage professionals to recommend caution to their patients, especially with regard to potentially harmful information that can be presented as helpful.

However, other researchers have demonstrated the positive impact of some apps on suicide ideation (Firth et al., 2017). Although many of the apps are not yet available to the public, or still require large-scale assessment before being ready for mainstream clinical care, they nevertheless demonstrate the potential of mHealth technologies to improve treatment outcomes. Hopefully, as this field of research progresses rapidly, new and effective mental health apps may become available (Torous et al., 2018).

The gap between what is theoretically possible and what is clinically effective has been observed by Franco-Martín et al. (2018) in their systematic review of a variety of suicide prevention technologies (Web-based, mobile, and social media). In light of their research, the authors argue that, in spite of the wealth of solutions currently available, much remains to be done in this field and that needs to be created as a collective and collaborative effort among technologists, health professionals, patients, and family members to develop a new generation of reliable, relevant, and safe digital technologies able to save lives.

Risks and Barriers

The potential of a closed-loop system using mobile technology to collect real-time data on dynamic risk factors is impressive, and the prospect of using AI to prevent suicide "just in time" is exciting. However, there are several key barriers that should also be considered. For example, ethics, real-world implementation, and legal liability are complex issues that cannot be overlooked. From an ethical standpoint, the amount of personal data that today's smartphone sensors are able to gather, and the implications of using algorithms that predict false-positive suicide risk or, conversely, false-negative risk, raise a number of human rights questions related to informed consent, basic privacy protection, and autonomy. A number of these issues have been raised at the launch of the Samaritans' Radar app for Twitter in 2014, and they emerged again with Cambridge Analytica's misuse of Facebook data (Ahmed, Bath, & Demartini, 2017). Further ethical issues are associated with real-world implementation of suicide prevention algorithms and apps outside of the research environment, in relation to unforeseen costs, data stewardship and control, and clinical systems integration (Tucker, Tackett, Glickman, & Reger, 2019). A list of different barriers and shortcomings are summarized in Table 16.2.

Table 16.2 Barriers and shortcomings in current state of the art of suicide prevention technologies

Barrier	Description
Scientific evidence	There is limited scientific evidence that clearly demonstrates the cost-efficacy of mHealth technology focused on suicide prevention (Melia et al. 2018). While apps may appear to be appealing and user-friendly, limited data are currently available to demonstrate their effectiveness. Most apps do not have peer-reviewed research to support their clinical claims, and it is unlikely that every mHealth app will go through a rigorous, scientific trial to test its effectiveness.
Ethical issues	The amount of personal data gathered by today's smartphone sensors is problematic at best, and the implications of algorithms predicting a false positive or false negative suicide risk raise fundamental questions related to informed consent, basic privacy protections, and autonomy.
Legislation issues	Lack or limited governmental funding, as well as lack or limited legislation or regulation at the institutional level may hinder the development of these technologies as well as their large-scale implementations (WHO, 2016).
Operational issues	Real-world implementation raises issues of suicide prevention algorithms and apps outside of the research environment – for example, unknown or unforeseen costs, data stewardships and control, and clinical systems integration.
Medical legal issues	Medical legal issues around technology-driven suicide prevention interventions are mostly unclear.
Security and privacy	Regulations on security, privacy, and mobile communications vary across regions. Spam advertising, security, and privacy regulations may interfere with the ability to deliver and achieve the sustainable levels of efficacy or scalability of mHealth programs (WHO, 2016).
Literacy, language, and disability	Important challenges still threaten the potential of eHealth strategies to improve people's health on a large scale and reduce health disparities. Although Internet and other digital media usage is growing rapidly, many people lack effective access, due to barriers related to literacy, language, disability, or income (Czyz et al., 2013).
Web-based suicide interventions	Web-based suicide interventions appear to be effective if they specifically target suicide content, as opposed to the associated symptoms of depression through cognitive behavior therapy (Christensen et al., 2014)

Possible Benefits

Possible benefits for the use of the technology, from clinicians' and patients' perspectives, are presented in Table 16.3.

Table 16.3 Benefits for the use of suicide prevention technology from clinicians' and patients' perspectives

Benefits for clinicians	Benefits for people at risk of suicide
Enable the collection of a great quantity of specific data to be used to customize interventions (Khan & Costanza, 2018).	Help overcome help-seeking barriers by reducing stigma and embarrassment, and social and geographical isolation (Melia et al., 2018).
Increase patients' own reflexivity, support their empowerment, and improve their involvement in the self-care process (Marzano et al., 2015).	Provide support to store data issued from *safety planning* interventions, tailored to personal needs and resources to empower patients to seek help during suicidal crises (Khan & Costanza, 2018).
Support, complement, and deliver personalized psychological interventions in a way that is more specific to one's needs, desires, expectations, and values – right time, right place, right way (Melia et al., 2018).	Provide support for *safety planning* interventions capable of identifying and managing vulnerabilities and delivering personalized resources during a suicidal crisis (Jobes et al., 2019).
Facilitate or increase access to and provision of health services in areas where there is little infrastructure or traditional health services, but where mobile communications technology infrastructure has been prioritized (WHO, 2016).	As part of the *caring contacts*, strategies post-ED help maintain and/or reinforce patients' supporting network from both a medical and personal standpoint. Provide support to guarantee a contact-person within patients' network of contacts in case of emergency (Betz et al., 2016).
The possibility of tracking mental health in a specific period of time or for many years (Aung, Matthews, & Choudhury, 2017).	Usefulness as a tool to monitor physical, psychological, and behavioral symptoms (Aung, Matthews, & Choudhury, 2017).

Note. ED = emergency department.

Technology should be envisioned as a tool that fits into what Larsen et al. (2016) identified as the basic ingredients for suicide prevention: a complex system approach that incorporates public health strategies, screening at-risk individuals, targeted interventions, and follow-up for suicide survivors and those bereaved by suicide. Moreover, the increasing ubiquity of sensor-enabled smartphones and the use of online social media platforms offer the potential for passive, background data collection, and automatic detection of suicidality and its associated risk factors (Larsen et al., 2016).

Ultimately, technologies are means to an end: they cannot substitute for clinical evaluation and human presence to support a suicidal individual, but they can be perceived and utilized as complementary tools to other interventions (Khan & Costanza, 2018).

Self-Care Strategies That May Save Lives

How Do They Survive?

Although technology does hold enormous potential in terms of detecting and preventing suicidal ideation, it is still difficult to provide relevant and meaningful assistance to those individuals who need help. However, many individuals already use online technologies to seek information and support. For example, one study that conducted an online survey of individuals with schizophrenia noted that some patients are using their smartphones to play music to block auditory hallucinations (Gay, Torous, Joseph, Pandya, & Duxkworth, 2016; Torous, 2018).

Contemporary online human connections have become a primary source of understanding and coping with the world we live in and the struggles we endure, both as individuals and as a society. How and why these conversations take place represents an important area of research because it expands our current understanding about emerging opportunities for suicide prevention associated with current technology usage. These are opportunities that may shed new light into not only how and when individuals are at risk of taking their own life, but also – and especially – how they manage to stay alive. In other words, their online behavior provides precious clues regarding the self-care practices that enable them to resist their suicide thoughts even when they are at their absolute wit's end.

Searching for Clues in a Connected World

The rise of social media platforms has prompted the emergence of countless public, private, and hidden peer support groups initiated by and for individuals experiencing a variety of health conditions and life challenges. The Internet is also riddled with articles, personal stories, and self-help resources (from poetry to blogs and videoblogs, etc.) written by individuals living with one or more mental health conditions or who have survived suicide attempts (Ali, Farrer, Gulliver, & Griffiths, 2015; Naslund, Aschbrenner, Marsch, & Bartels, 2016; Newhouse, Atherton, & Ziebland, 2018; Sangeorzan, Andriopoulou, & Livanou, 2019; Ziebland & Wyke, 2012).

In many ways, this is the Internet at its best: a huge sharing machine that enables people to reach out to one another for reassurance, deeper mutual understanding, and support. In these informal peer support settings, relationships between individuals tend to nurture a sense of belonging, friendship, and mutual and individual self-empowerment, as well as a greater sense of self-worth and self-efficacy (Naslund, Grande, Aschbrenner, & Elwyn, 2014; Ziebland & Wyke, 2012). As Ziebland and Wyke have observed (2012), the opportunity to access these environments with anonymity is an additional plus that enables people to share their most intimate life experiences or raise embarrassing questions that many would find hard to discuss face to face. For example, in a study conducted by Naslund et al. (2014), the authors describe the growing phenomenon of individuals with severe mental illness uploading videos and posting and responding to comments on YouTube, as a form of naturally occurring peer support. This is a mental illness recovery strategy that enables individuals to overcome a number of significant challenges and reclaim agency and control for themselves and others: They minimize their sense of isolation; they seek hope and support through mutual interactions with people who may be experiencing similar struggles; they also share everyday coping strategies that they have found useful and meaningful; they access additional experiential information on the use of medication and mental health care services; and they learn new self-care strategies to improve their quality of life while feeling empowered to pursue personal life goals.

Careful Whisper of Autonomous Sensory Meridian Response Community

One of the most interesting examples of an online peer support subculture, particularly sensitive to mental health issues and challenges, is represented by the *autonomous sensory meridian response* (ASMR) community. This is an underground community that, although it has been silently but steadily thriving on YouTube since 2007, has recently become a pop culture phenomenon, praised and co-opted by a number of Hollywood celebrities, mass media communicators, musicians, and corporate sponsors (Keiles, 2019).

According to the Wikipedia official page to which most ASMRrists or creators refer, "autonomous sensory meridian response (ASMR) ... is an experience characterized by a static-like or tingling sensation on the skin that typically begins on the scalp and moves down the back of the neck and upper spine. It has been compared with auditory-tactile synesthesia and may overlap with frisson" (Autonomous Sensory Meridian Response, n. d.). These triggering stimuli are often visual or auditory, as they are social, almost intimate, in nature (e.g., hearing whispering, or watching someone brush their hair), and they are designed to elicit a calm and positive emotional state. ASMR videos are produced by individuals who called themselves *ASMR creators* or *ASMR artists* who may be followed by from a few hundred followers to the over 7 million subscribers registered to the top ASMR creator. More specifically, their videos can range from purely auditory triggers such as the sound of rain, or fingers scratching or tapping a surface, to full video productions in which the authors engage in a variety of role plays. The term *brain tingles* is also commonly used to describe these sensations (Lochte, Guillory, Richard, & Kelley, 2018).

What is especially interesting is that, according to ASMR creators and their followers, the relaxing tingling sensations generated by the trigger techniques reproduced in their videos help alleviate stress anxiety, chronic pain, insomnia, depression, and suicide ideation (Gallagher, 2018; Smith, Fredborg, & Kornelsen, 2017b). In fact, two peer-reviewed research studies of ASMR published in 2015 and in 2017 reported that viewers of ASMR videos felt the strongest tingles in response to whispering and personal attention and that they watched the videos to help them to relax (98 %), fall asleep (82 %), and deal with stress (70 %), with 80 % reporting a positive effect on their mood (Barratt, Spence, & Davis, 2017; Barratt & Davis, 2015). Barratt and Davis (2015) have also suggested that ASMR provides a temporary uplifting effect on mood for those suffering from depression, while individuals with symptoms of chronic pain experience a significant reduction in their discomfort for several hours following an ASMR session.

According to a study conducted by Lochte et al. (2018) of 10 ASMR-sensitive subjects, the exposure to ASMR *tingling sensations* activated brain regions associated with self-awareness, social cognition, and social and affiliative behaviors including grooming. In other words, the attention-receiving or observation-granting behaviors featured in many ASMR videos have similar effects to being cared for by, or looking after, someone. More recently, Ahuja and Ahuja (2019) have argued that the benefits of ASMR videos could be comparable to an improvement in well-being associated with a placebo effect.

Another valuable aspect to consider is that, by their own admission, several ASMR creators have themselves suffered (or still suffer) from depression, anxiety, or other mental conditions, and have decided to produce their own ASMR videos after benefitting themselves from this type of modern-day peer support. Moreover, a number of these YouTubers have specifically produced videos aimed at helping viewers who are experiencing suicide ideation. For example, in his channel, the ASMR YouTuber Ephemeral Rift (aka Paul) features several videos specifically addressing people at risk of suicide. In these videos, he shares his own experiences with suicidal thoughts and encourages his viewers to resist the impulse to take their own life (see example in Box 16.1).

Box 16.1. Ephemeral Rift – Paul

In the video "Late Night ASMR 2 – Suicidal Thoughts & Depression" published February 13, 2016 (watched by 709,000 people at the time of writing this chapter, https://www.youtube.com/watch?v=SdtfOVYFS04), Ephemeral Rift (Paul) puts in the video description:

> I hope you are doing well. Welcome to another, somewhat impromptu, Late Night ASMR video dedicated to those who are dealing with suicidal thoughts and depression. I ramble about a few things both related and unrelated to these video topics, while sharing some of my own personal experiences and advice on how I survived coping with these issues. Always seek the help of a professional if you feel the thoughts or urges are too strong. Remember: You're not alone. Keep battling. It *can* get better. And in time, you *can* heal and reach a better place on your own path in life. All my best, Paul. (Ephemeral Rift, 2016)

The following are a couple of comments left by viewers who appear to have been positively impacted by this experience:

> I don't know if you look at your comments or not, Paul. I just wanted to say thank you. I have watched this video every time I feel sad or mildly depressed. It has always cheered me up over the years and will forever. You are a true inspiration and I'm really glad you kept at it when you started at a few thousand subscribers. I hope you made this your job because I know you wanted that a while back and never gave up. You are truly a wonderful man. Thank you Paul.
>
> Almost 3 years later and my go-to video when I'm depressed. You're the best with your dry humor and sounds. Very soothing and comforting.

In another role play video entitled "ASMR Supportive Friend for Dealing with Suicidal Thoughts, Bullying, Depression, Anxiety" (https://www.youtube.com/watch?v=9DvlWjy5-Pc), Ephemeral Rift shares his own personal experience with these issues and how he managed to deal with them over the years. Notably, in each description box of these videos, the author encourages viewers who feel suicidal to call for help:

> First off, if you are having suicidal thoughts right now, please call someone, whether it's family, friend, 9-1-1, your physician, check yourself into an emergency room or the National Suicide Prevention Lifeline/Hotline. (Ephemeral Rift, 2012)

Two Specialized Platforms That Encourage Resist and Stay

Another area of research worth exploring is represented by Web platforms produced by and for people with mental health issues or at risk of suicide. For the purpose of this discussion, we provide two examples: *The Mighty* and *Live Through This*.

The Mighty (https://themighty.com) is a digital health community created to empower and connect over 2 million registered users facing health challenges and disabilities. The platform functions as a specialized social network that collects and shares personal stories posted by thousands of individuals across the world, which are viewed and shared more than 90 million times a month. The Mighty followers engage in peer support interactions in one or more of the over 700 forums dedicated to a variety of health conditions and disabilities, which may vary from general topics such as #mentalhealth (which currently has 3 million registered followers), #AutismSpectrumDisorder (with almost 200,000 followers), #RareDisease (with over 100,000 followers), or more specific health conditions or disabilities such as #Agoraphobia (with 2,000 followers) and #LimbAmputation (with 229 followers). Since its foundation in 2014, The Mighty has invested considerable effort in providing a safe and inspiring space of discussion for individuals with mental health issues, by providing a valuable collection of personal stories and blog posts written by and for people with a variety of mental conditions and challenges. The tagline associated with their mental health forums conveys two of the main reasons so many people find refuge in these online environments: "Our community talks about mental health with compassion and without judgment." Thanks to this level of care and specialization, the platform currently counts on hundreds of thousands of users registered in their mental health forums: about 600,000 in the #anxiety forum, 568,000 individuals for #depression, 232,000 for #bipolardisorder, and 17,600 for #suicide.

Platforms such as these can prove to be very valuable for research purposes, not only because they provide a more granular perspective into the everyday struggles and coping strategies of a variety of individuals who may be at risk of suicide due to their health or disability challenges, but also because they offer the opportunity to gain additional understanding of why a growing number of individuals prefer to share their struggles with a world of strangers rather than with somebody who has been trained to help them. For both registered contributors and followers, The Mighty community offers a precious meeting space where they can find each other and share the kind of support they may not be able to receive elsewhere. For example, a recent posting appeared in the forum #checkinwithme featured a video about the importance of taking "high-functioning anxiety seriously" (https://themighty.com/video/why-we-need-to-take-high-functioning-anxiety-seriously/). In the video a woman debunks a few myths about people living with anxiety and describes how her invisible illness prevents her from asking for help in time of need, even when she feels suicidal.

Live Through This (https://livethroughthis.org) is an online collection of stories and interviews of suicide attempt survivors. Established in 2010, by photographer, writer, and suicide attempt survivor and activist Dese'Rae L. Stage, the website claims to be the largest catalogue of suicide attempt survivor narratives in existence, featuring almost 200 portraits and interviews of individuals from across the US. Their main mission is to improve public attitudes about suicide and reduce prejudice and discrimination against attempt survivors by promoting their voices and perspectives on the circumstances that led them to attempt to take their own life.

By featuring a variety of stories about people who are of very different ages and have very different personal, cultural, and social backgrounds, the platform conveys a key message to its readers: Suicide does not discriminate and can affect everybody. To this end, the platform provides an internal search engine that enables one to filter through the collection of narratives available by a number of meaningful variables – for example, age at the time of interview and age at the time of attempt, ethnicity, sex and gender identity, faith and religion, treatments and support received, etc.

The platform is also intended to provide comfort to those experiencing suicidality as well as insight into a better understanding of suicidality in general. Its content is available to be used as a teaching tool for anybody interested in promoting suicide prevention. According toDese'Rae Stage, one of the main problems that contributes to a culture of stigma and inadequate support for those who may have suicidal thoughts is that media coverage and public attention usually focus on those who have died from suicide, and very rarely on those "who lived to tell the tale." From her perspective, these narratives provide an in-depth perspective on not only how people got to the point of wanting to end their life but also (and especially) how they managed to survive their suicidal tendencies. Their main message is of hope, and empowerment is mainly directed to those who are experiencing similar challenges: "You can live through this." Box 16.2 provides an excerpt from one of the stories featured in the platform.

Box 16.2. *Live through this* – The story of Linda Gray Sexton

Linda Gray Sexton is a writer and suicide attempt survivor who was interviewed for *Live Through This* in 2017.

In her story, she explains how the relationship with her mother, poet and Pulitzer Prize winner Anne Sexton, who suffered from mental illness and attempted suicide several times, led her to self-harm behavior, depression, and ultimately a suicide attempt.

In her story, followed by a written and a video interview, she also discusses how getting to know others who have experienced similar circumstances has made a difference in her life (https://livethroughthis.org/linda-gray-sexton/):

> Those of us who are sitting here having survived, becoming intact, and going on to lead really fulfilled lives can say, "Hey, it doesn't have to be this way. It doesn't have to end this way. I know because I was there once and now I'm here. I can tell you that it doesn't have to be that way." That's substantially different than a doctor saying, "Lots of people get through this. You can too." When you hear somebody else who was on the other side of the fence saying, "Yes, you can make it," I found those kinds of stories and talking to people who had been in the same boat to be compelling and convincing. (Gray Sexton, 2017)

Every story featured in the website is told in the first person and is accompanied by an interview which is mostly intended to further explore issues related to past and current personal struggles and challenges to stay alive. To this end, many interviews start from the question, "Is suicide still an option for you?" While a number of the interviewed survivors have replied that they believe they have finally overcome their suicidal thoughts, according to Ms. Stage the majority of those she interviewed so far keep the option open, acknowledging that the fear of wanting to die never really goes away:

> I won't say it's never an option because I'm scared. What if I backslide? What if I get depressed again? I know that that's a route. Once you've examined that route, once you've driven down it —even if you took a detour at the end — that road is always there. You have to be ever vigilant that you're not going to turn your blinker on and make that left hand turn. That's what I think about that. (Gray Sexton, 2017)

From the "Live Through This" (livethroughthis.org/linda-gray-sexton/) website, part of the Live Through this Project, Linda Gray Sexton, is the author of *Half in Love: Surviving the Legacy of Suicide*, lindagraysexton.com. Used by permission of Brandt & Hochman Literary Agents, Inc.

The Dark Side of Online Peer Support

Although the experiences presented here confirm the potential benefits of online peer support, we cannot deny that, in the era of fake news, social media bots, and online mobbing, the Internet is also an unregulated place that can be extremely dangerous, especially for those who are psychologically vulnerable or undergoing mental challenges. For example, many of the websites and social media groups dedicated to mental health are often responsible for sharing or promoting information that may be inaccurate, biased, misleading, or distorted, and which as such may lead to extreme decisions (Leydon et al., 2000; Winterbottom, Becker, Conner, &Mooney, 2008). Exposure to conflicting information from people with different experiences may create unrealistic expectations and be the cause of more confusion, anxiety, false hope, despair, fear, guilt, anger, or inadequacy. By engaging in the wrong conversations, many people may even end up questioning their own perspective or developing an additional layer of shame or stigma (Hinton, Kurinczuk, & Ziebland, 2010).

Even the idea of overcoming social isolation at least partially, through online support has its own caveats. Overreliance on online peer support may be interpreted by some people to mean that they can open up or be understood only by those who experience similar conditions in specific social settings, thus limiting the boundaries of their social world. Overreliance on the Internet in a time of need can also prevent people from benefiting from face-to-face social contacts in their own communities, thus paradoxically enhancing their social isolation (Hinton, Kurinczuk, & Ziebland, 2010) – not to mention that those who post their own stories online are at risk of an array of shaming behaviors from other users, including the risk of being publicly criticized, ridiculed, or even just corrected regarding facts. In contrast, if no one comments on a heartfelt posting, the author may feel even more isolated and ignored, thus exacerbating feelings of social rejection, inadequacy, or shame.

Finally, hearing about other people's experiences may reinforce unhealthy behaviors: In today's online worlds, individuals at risk of suicide can easily find forums or comments that offer advice (and possibly encouragement) about how to end their life (Ziebland & Wyke, 2012).

Participatory Research and Study Design

A deep appreciation of how technology is currently supporting individuals at risk of suicide may provide a privileged inside perspective into the self-care strategies they may adopt to endure their life-threatening challenges. This knowledge could be used to conceive new preventive or therapeutic solutions that stem out of everyday practices, as well as the values and expectations of those who get to use such technologies. Although several studies have provided ample evidence on the opportunities and threats of the modern, hyperconnected world, too little is known still about the impact on people's health outcomes of having access to other people's experiences on a 24/7 basis. More specifically, there are a number of questions pertaining to the use of the Internet by people who are at risk of suicide that are still unanswered. For example, how do they find each other online? To what extent does the health and digital literacy of these individuals shape their experience of seeking, using, and exchanging support? What are the immediate and long-term impacts of their coping and self-care strategies? Do these change over time, or are they contingent on specific circumstances, contexts, states of mind, time of day, etc.? How can we measure their impact or translate such strategies into evidence-based digital support for suicide risk prevention? In other words, how can we integrate our current evidence-based knowledge about suicide prevention and technology design with the everyday practices of those we are seeking to reach, support, and treat?

Engaging With a New Category of Experts

A participatory approach to developing new services, products, and intervention is one of the most powerful modern tools at our disposal to capture, integrate, and align input and expectations of the very *users* we wish to engage with and support. In fact, *codesign* – or as is also known, *participatory design* – goes beyond merely asking users what they want or need. At the more general level, codesign can be broadly described as a collective creative approach that attempts to actively involve all stakeholders, including users (along with health care providers, engineers, policy makers, etc.), to understand and translate their contextual everyday practices, needs, and values into design solutions or interventions that are more relevant, and therefore more likely to achieve a greater overall reach and impact (Schuler & Namioka, 1993).

Codesign processes are characterized by an active collaboration between researchers, designers, developers, and users at all levels (i.e., not only end-users per se, but also, e.g., physicians or other health or social care providers who use or have access to the proposed technology from their own professional purposes) who meet at the same creative table as *experts of their experiences* to contribute to a work of collective knowledge, idea generation, and concept development (Sanders, 2002; Sleeswijk Visser, Stappers, Van der Lugt, & Sanders, 2005). In contrast to the more traditional user-engagement approach, where users are involved to express what they want from a given intervention, product, or service, or where they are observed while they use such interventions or services, codesign presupposes a more horizontal relationship among all the stakeholders involved in the creative process. This is to facilitate a more organic exploration and articulation of each respective needs, expectations, and priorities, leading to the development of a solution that reflects shared perspectives (Sanders, 2002; Schuler & Namioka, 1993).

Codesign aims to achieve a better and more effective design based on a richer, deeper understanding of what all users and experts know, feel, and even dream. The mutual learning process nurtured by codesign experiential and action-based methods and tools generates fresh new knowledge stemming from a deeper understanding of the contemporary lived experience of those involved in the process, the variety of problems that need to be solved, and the dynamics, constraints, and opportunities that inform how they can be addressed (Kleinsmann & Valkenburg, 2008).

For example, when it comes to technology design, the appreciation of diversity and individuality plays a much larger role than the traditional biomedical approach to mental health usually affords. Individuals at risk of suicide do vary according to a virtually infinite number of variables that range from their personal and social background and current circumstances, to their mental health status, to the level of their awareness regarding the challenges that have led them to suicidal thoughts or ideation, etc. But even more importantly, each individual is different as they lead very different lives and have very specific and personal values, expectations, and life priorities that shape their current worldviews and lifestyle, the level of family and community support they receive, and so on.

In other words, what works for one person might not work for another individual who is experiencing similar challenges. This is an aspect that becomes especially clear when *potential users* are invited to join the design table: From the very first conversation, it becomes evident that not only are both the dynamics and impact of the life-threatening challenges very contextual and personal, but there is also a significant variation in the way each individual may seek support to cope with such issues, even when they belong to an apparently homogenous social or health-related group (e.g., ASMR or The Might followers and contributors). For this reason, the more diverse the group of users involved in the codesign process, the better the chances of developing technologies that can realistically improve their everyday life. In fact, one-size-fits-all solutions that attempt to solve too many problems for too many people are both misguided and unrealistic. The goal is not to create average products for average individuals, but to pave the way for a new generation of technologies that provide personalized and relevant solutions that originate out of the expressed needs and desires of those who will make use of them.

Another crucial aspect to consider is that not everybody is keen on, or interested in, improving or changing their lifestyle or behavior by adopting a new technology – even if or when such technology is designed to save their life. The resistance to the uptake of new eHealth technologies is an issue that affects virtually all health conditions and patients, for a variety of complex reasons that have recently been explored by Zhao, Ni, & Zhou (2018). In this regard, it is always pivotal to consider that some people may be variably resistant to using or adopting a new technology or have an ambivalent relationship with the technologies they use. This is especially relevant if users are older or vulnerable individuals whose abilities to access or use digital technologies are variable.

Finally, not everybody is ready to be involved as an expert and codesigner, to be creative, and to behave accordingly. Even the capacity to share one's knowledge and experience with others is not a given. Many people, especially if they live with a stigmatized health or social condition, need to feel safe and at ease to open up with others about the challenges they face in their everyday life. This is another crucial issue that invokes caution and careful vetting at the time of recruiting possible codesign participants. In Box 16.3, we provide a brief review of three codesign projects that are relevant to this discussion.

Box 16.3. Examples of codesign projects

Hetrick et al. (2018) report a codesign experience of a mobile phone app that facilitates self-monitoring and management of mood symptoms in young people with major depression, suicidal ideation, and self-harm. More specifically, a human-centered codesign *design studio* methodology was adopted where a total of eight young people aged 18 to 25 years designed the features of the new app, first individually and then as a group in codesign workshops. Clinicians were also involved throughout the process via focus groups. The resulting app incorporated a number of specific requirements by the young users involved in the project, including a mood monitoring feature with innovative design aspects that allowed customization, as well as brief personalized interventions designed to support young people in the intervals between face-to-face appointments with clinicians. In contrast, clinicians involved in the codesign process expressed concerns in managing expectations associated with providing timely support in case the app indicated high levels of distress and suicidal ideation of their patients. Such notifications would require significant additional clinical resourcing that needed to be taken into account when implementing such a solution.

Tighe, Shand, Ridani, Mackinnon, De La Mata, and Christensen (2017) have also worked with a population of young adults, aged 18 to 35 years, to codesign the delivery of an acceptance-based therapeutic intervention aimed at preventing suicide among Australian indigenous youths living in remote communities. The project consisted of an RCT pilot study conducted with 61 participants, which aimed to evaluate the effectiveness of a new self-help mobile app (ibobbly) targeting suicidal ideation, depression, psychological distress, and impulsivity. Although the study found that the app reduced depression symptoms and psychological distress in the target population, it did not lead to significant changes in suicidality or impulsivity. The project also indicated that an eHealth app developed in partnership with Indigenous communities had the potential of being more widely accepted and promoted by the target community and to improve mental health symptoms among its members.

Gordon, Henderson, Holmes, Wolters, & Bennett (2016) established a longitudinal participatory design group that developed specifications for a suite of eHealth applications to improve the quality of perinatal mental health care. Over the 24 months of the study, the group – which consisted of low-income women with a history of antenatal depression, their prenatal providers, mental health specialists, an app developer, and researchers – developed three new apps to support high-risk women after discharge from hospital, a screening tool for depression, and a patient decision aid for supporting treatment choice. The first app (MyGamePlan) was designed for patients discharged from an inpatient hospitalization for suicide risk. It included a set of functionalities to support the transition following hospitalization including (1) scheduling and reminder features for follow-up, (2) standard safety plan support, and (3) connections to local resources which take advantage of geo-location capabilities of the mobile device. Overall, the project confirmed that a multistakeholder participatory design approach can be effective to develop patient-centered, eHealth solutions for vulnerable populations that face multiple social, health and economic challenges.

Conclusions

There are a few things to note in the dynamics of those who look for help in the connected world. An evident aspect is that they access a wealth of online resources that are available on a 24/7 basis, regardless of the time of day or night, or the places from which they are produced or retrieved. In the Web-based world, suicidal individuals have the opportunity to feel less alone and share their challenges with like-minded people, who know first-hand what it means to be at the end of one's rope. What is remarkable in this case is that the people who receive support from others are often the very same people who also transform their own experience of suffering into support material for others: ASMR followers become ASMR creators; individuals who ask for help in comments often reciprocate by offering support to other people they encounter elsewhere online; people who share their stories of suicide and resilience may have been inspired by others who opened up about their own experiences of struggle and survival; and so on.

Behind these everyday coping and survival practices is the very mechanism that grounds most peer support communities: What makes them powerful is not merely getting the support one needs, but it is especially the sense of mutual engagement and empowerment that such sharing implies. By joining these communities, they stop focusing solely on their own challenges, to become themselves active agents of support and change invested in their own well-being and that of others they may encounter in these environments. The common thread for all these relationships is that when people are in pain, they do not merely seek support, they also seek meaningful interaction and dignity to remind themselves that they too can live through their own challenges and stay. They also look for some kind of control over what they are experiencing, which is why they may be more prone to seek support in environments where they feel themselves to be active subjects of their own domain, rather than passive objects in need of external help.

Further, codesign techniques have the potential to become even more sophisticated and powerful for developing intelligent interactive health communication programs when they are associated with AI tools and methodologies. However, before this potential can be fully realized, new and more granular data collection mechanisms are needed to develop more refined ML models and enable suicide markers to be tested in validation studies. This will need to be conducted with the complex ethical landscape of technological innovation in mind, to encourage users to engage with and trust these novel applications.

Ultimately, it is expected that a new wave of technologies, driven by peer support interactions and enhanced by artificially intelligent models, will enable health care providers to reach those experiencing suicide ideation in real time (whenever it is needed, wanted, and expected), and customized in a variety of ways that are appropriate or relevant to those specific individuals in contexts that are highly specific to personal needs, values, and expectations. This will occur bypassing the fear of stigma and social disconnection, while ensuring that people feel safe, supported, and in control.

References

Abboute, A., Boudjeriou, Y., Entringer, G., Azé, J., Bringay, S., & Poncelet, P. (2014). Mining Twitter for suicide prevention. In E. Métais, M. Roche, & M. Teisseire (Eds.), *Natural language processing and information systems. 19th International Conference of Application of Natural Language to Data Bases/Information Systems*. Basel, Switzerland: Springer, pp. 250–253. https://doi.org/10.1007/978-3-319-07983-7_36

Ahmed, W., Bath, P.A., & Demartini, G. (2017). Using Twitter as a data source: An overview of ethical, legal, and methodological challenges. In R. Iphofen & K. Woodfield (Eds.), *The ethics of online research* (pp. 79–107). Bingley, UK: Emerald.

Ahuja, A., & Ahuja, N.K. (2019). Clinical role-play in autonomous sensory meridian response (ASMR) videos: Performance and placebo in the digital era. *JAMA*, *321*(14), 336–1337. https://doi.org/10.1001/jama.2019.2302

Ali, K., Farrer, L., Gulliver, A., & Griffiths, K.M. (2015). Online peer-to-peer support for young people with mental health problems: a systematic review. *JMIR Mental Health, 2*, e19. https://doi.org/10.2196/mental.4418

Allen, N.B., Nelson, B.W., Brent, D., & Auerbach, R.P. (2019). Short-term prediction of suicidal thoughts and behaviors in adolescents: Can recent developments in technology and computational science provide a breakthrough? *Journal of Affective Disorders, 250*, 163–169. https://doi.org/10.1016/j.jad.2019.03.044

Aung, M.H., Matthews, M., & Choudhury, T. (2017). Sensing behavioral symptoms of mental health and delivering personalized interventions using mobile technologies. *Depression and Anxiety, 34*, 603–609. https://doi.org/10.1002/da.22646

Autonomous Sensory Meridian Response. (n.d.). In *Wikipedia*. Retrieved from https://en.wikipedia.org/wiki/Autonomous_sensory_meridian_response

Barak-Corren, Y., Castro, V.M., Javitt, S., Hoffnagle, A.G., Dai, Y., Perlis, H.R., ... Reis, B.Y. (2017). Predicting suicidal behavior & from longitudinal electronic health records. *American Journal of Psychiatry, 174*, 154–162. https://doi.org/10.1176/appi.ajp.2016.16010077

Barratt, E.L., & Davis, N.J. (2015). Autonomous sensory meridian response (ASMR): A flow-like mental state. *Peer Journal, 3*, e851. https://doi.org/10.7717/peerj.851

Barratt, E.L., Spence, C., & Davis, N.J. (2017). Sensory determinants of the autonomous sensory meridian response (ASMR): understanding the triggers. *Peer Journal, 5*, e3846. https://doi.org/10.7717/peerj.3846

Bellagio eHealth Evaluation Group. (2011). E-Health evaluation evidence. *Consensus Statement of the WHO Global eHealth evaluation meeting*, Bellagio, Italy, September 9th.

Betz, M.E., Wintersteen, M., Boudreaux, E.D., Brown, G., Capoccia, L., Currier, G., ... Harkavy-Friedman, J. (2016). Reducing suicide risk: Challenges and opportunities in the Emergency Department. *Annals of Emergency Medicine, 68*, 758–765. https://doi.org/10.1016/j.annemergmed.2016.05.030

Braithwaite, S.R., Giraud-Carrier, C., West, J., Barnes, M.D., & Hanson, C.L. (2016). Validating machine learning algorithms for Twitter data against established measures of suicidality. *JMIR Mental Health, 3*(2), e21. https://doi.org/10.2196/mental.4822

Chan, S.R., Burke Parish, M., Fazio, S., & Torous, J. (2018). Data collection from novel sources. In P. Yellowlees & J.M. Shore (Eds.), *Telepsychiatry and health technologies: A guide for mental health professionals* (pp. 183–226). Arlington, VA: American Psychiatric Association Publishing.

Chandrashekar, P. (2018). Do mental health mobile apps work? Evidence and recommendations for designing high-efficacy mental health mobile apps. *MHealth, 4*, 3. https://doi.org/10.21037/mhealth.2018.03.02

Cheng, Q., Li, T.M.H., Kwok, C.-L., Zhu, T., & Yip, P.S.F. (2017). Assessing suicide risk and emotional distress in Chinese social media: A text mining and machine learning study. *Journal of Medical Internet Research, 19*, e243. https://doi.org/10.2196/jmir.7276

Christensen, H. (2018). Three actions to reduce suicide deaths and attempts. *Australasian Psychiatry, 26*, 125–127. https://doi.org/10.1177/1039856218762641

Christensen, H., Batterham, P.J., & O'Dea, B. (2014). E-health interventions for suicide prevention. *International Journal of Environmental Research and Public Health, 11*(8), 193–212. https://doi.org/10.3390/ijerph110808193

Cuijpers, P., Smit, F., & van Straten, A. (2007). Psychological treatments of subthreshold depression: a meta-analytic review. *Acta Psychiatrica Scandinavica, 115*, 434–441. https://doi.org/10.1111/j.1600-0447.2007.00998.x

Czyz, E.K., Horwitz, A.G., Eisenberg, D., Kramer, A., & King, C.A. (2013). Self-reported barriers to professional help seeking among college students at elevated risk for suicide. *Journal of American College Health, 61*, 398–406. https://doi.org/10.1080/07448481.2013.820731

Darcy, A.M., Louie, A.K., & Roberts, L.W. (2016). Machine learning and the profession of medicine. *JAMA, 315*(6), 551–552. https://doi.org/10.1001/jama.2015.18421

Deady, M., Choi, I., Calvo, R.A., Glozier, N., Christensen, H., & Harvey, S.B. (2017). eHealth interventions for the prevention of depression and anxiety in the general population: A systematic review and meta-analysis. *BMC Psychiatry, 17*(1), 310. https://doi.org/10.1186/s12888-017-1473-1

De Leo, D., & Arnautovska, U. (2016). Prevention and treatment of suicidality in older adults. In R. C. O'Connor & J. Pirkis, *The international handbook of suicide revention* (pp. 323–345). Chichester, UK: Wiley.

Dilsizian, S.E., & Siegel, E.L. (2014). Artificial intelligence in medicine and cardiac imaging: harnessing big data and advanced computing to provide personalized medical diagnosis and treatment. *Current Cardiology Reports, 16*, 441. https://doi.org/10.1007/s11886-013-0441-8

Donker, T., Petrie, K., Proudfoot, J., Clarke, J., Birch, M., & Christensen, H. (2013). Smartphones for smarter delivery of mental health programs: A systematic review. *Journal of Medical Internet Research, 15*(11), e247. https://doi.org/10.2196/jmir.2791

Du, J., Zhang, Y., Luo, J., Jia, X., Wei, Q., Tao, C., &Xu, H. (2018). Extracting psychiatric stressors for suicide from social media using deep learning. *BMC Medically Informed Decision Making, 18*(Suppl 2), 43. https://doi.org/10.1186/s12911-018-0632-8

Eichstaedt, J.C., Smith, R.J., Merchant, R.M., Ungar, L.H., Crutchley, P., Preotiuc-Pietro, D., ... Schwartz, H.A. (2018). Facebook language predicts depression in medical records. *Proceedings of the National Academy of Sciences, 115*, 11203–11208. https://doi.org/10.1073/pnas.1802331115

Ephemeral Rift. (2012, October 24). *ASMR supportive friend for dealing with suicidal thoughts, bullying, depression, anxiety* [Video]. YouTube. https://www.youtube.com/watch?v=9DvIWjy5-Pc

Ephemeral Rift. (2016, February 13). *Late Night ASMR 2 – suicidal thoughts & depression* [Video]. YouTube. https://www.youtube.com/watch?v=SdtfOVYFS04

Firth, J., Torous, J., Nicholas, J., Carney, R., Pratap, A., Rosenbaum, S., & Sarris, J. (2017). The efficacy of smartphone-based mental health interventions for depressive symptoms: A meta-analysis of randomized controlled trials. *World Psychiatry, 16*(3), 287–298. https://doi.org/10.1002/wps.20472

Franco-Martín, M.A., Munoz-Sanchez, J.L., Sainz-de Abajo, B., Castillo-Sanchez, G., Hamrioui, S., & de la Torre-Diez, I. (2018). A systematic literature review of technologies for suicidal behavior prevention. *Journal of Medical Systems, 42*(4), 71. https://doi.org/10.1007/s10916-018-0926-5

Fromkin, V., Rodman, R., & Hyams, N. (2018). *An introduction to language*. Boston, MA: Cengage Learning.

Gallagher, R. (2018). 'ASMR' autobiographies and the (life-) writing of digital subjectivity. *Convergence, 25*, 260–277.

Gay, K., Torous, J., Joseph, A., Pandya, A., & Duxkworth, K. (2016). Digital technology use among individuals with schizophrenia: Results of an online survey. *JMIR Mental Health, 3*(2), e15. https://doi.org/10.2196/mental.5379

Gordon, M., Henderson, R., Holmes, J. H., Wolters, M. K., Bennett, I. M., & the SPIRIT Group. (2016). Participatory design of ehealth solutions for women from vulnerable populations with perinatal depression. *Journal of the American Medical Informatics Association, 23*(1), 105–109. https://doi.org/10.1093/jamia/ocv109

Gray Sexton, L. (2017, November 6). *I survived a suicide attempt*. https://livethroughthis.org/linda-gray-sexton/

Hategan, A., Giroux, C. & Bourgeois, J.A. (2019). Digital technology adoption in psychiatric care: An overview of the contemporary shift from technology to opportunity. *Journal of Technology in Behavioral Science, 4*, 171–177. https://doi.org/10.1007/s41347-019-00086-x

Hetrick, S.E., Robinson, J., Burge, E., Blandon, R., Mobilio, B., Rice, S.M., ... Davey, C.G. (2018). Youth codesign of a mobile phone app to facilitate self-monitoring and management of mood symptoms in young people with major depression, suicidal ideation, and self-harm. *JMIR Mental Health, 5*(1), e9. https://doi.org/10.2196/preprints.9041

Hinton, L., Kurinczuk, J.J., & Ziebland, S. (2010). Infertility; Isolation and the Internet: A qualitative interview study. *Patient Education and Counseling, 81*(3), 436–441. https://doi.org/10.1016/j.pec.2010.09.023

Iniesta, R., Stahl, D., & McGuffin, P. (2016). Machine learning, statistical learning and the future of biological research in psychiatry. *Psychological Medicine, 46*(12), 2455–2465. https://doi.org/10.1017/S0033291716001367

Jiang, F., Jiang, Y., Zhi, H., Dong, Y., Li, H., Ma, S., ... Wang, Y. (2017). Artificial intelligence in healthcare: Past, present and future. *Stroke And Vascular Neurology, 2*(4), 230–243. https://doi.org/10.1136/svn-2017-000101

Jashinsky, J., Burton, S.H., Hanson, C.L., West, J., Giraud-Carrier, C., Barnes, M.D., & Argyle, T. (2014). Tracking suicide risk factors through Twitter in the US. *Crisis, 35*(1), 51–59. https://doi.org/10.1027/0227-5910/a000234

Jha, S., & Topol, E.J. (2016). Adapting to artificial intelligence: Radiologists and pathologists as information specialists. *JAMA, 316*, 2353–2354. https://doi.org/10.1001/jama.2016.17438

Jobes, D.A., Haddock, L.A., & Olivares, M.R. (2019). Military and veteran suicide prevention. In E.C. Ritchie & M.D. Llorente (Eds.). *Veteran psychiatry in the US* (pp. 51–71). Heidelberg, Germany: Springer International Publishing. https://doi.org/10.1007/978-3-030-05384-0_5

Keiles, J.L. (2019, April 4). How A.S.M.R. became a sensation. *New York Time Magazine*. Retrieved from https://www.nytimes.com/2019/04/04/magazine/how-asmr-videos-became-a-sensation-youtube.html

Khan, R., & Costanza, A. (2018). m-Health approaches in suicide prevention at the emergency department: Some theoretical and practical considerations. *International Journal of Emergency Mental Health and Human Resilience, 20*(2), 1–8. https://doi.org/10.4172/1522-4821.1000401

Kleinsmann, M., & Valkenburg, R. (2008). Barriers and enablers for creating shared understanding in co-design projects. *Design Studies, 316*(4), 369–386. https://doi.org/10.1016/j.destud.2008.03.003

Larsen, M.E., Nicholas, J., & Christensen, H. (2016). A systematic assessment of smartphone tools for suicide prevention. *PLoS One, 11*(4), e0152285. https://doi.org/10.1371/journal.pone.0152285

Law, M.K., Furr, R.M., Arnold, E.M., Mneimne, M., Jacquett, C., Fleeson, C., & Fleeson, M. (2015). Does assessing suicidality frequently and repeatedly cause harm? A randomized control study. *Psychological Assessment, 27*, 1171–1181. https://doi.org/10.1037/pas0000118

Leydon, G.M., Moynihan, C., Boulton, M., Mossman, J., Boudioni, M., & McPherson, K. (2000). Cancer patients' information needs and information seeking behaviour: in-depth interview study. *BMJ, 320*, 909–913. https://doi.org/10.1136/bmj.320.7239.909

Lochte, B.C., Guillory, S.A., Richard, C.A.H., & Kelley, W.M. (2018). An fMRI investigation of the neural correlates underlying the autonomous sensory meridian response (ASMR). *BioImpacts, 8*(4), 295. https://doi.org/10.15171/bi.2018.32

Luxton, D.D., June, J.D., & Fairall, J.M. (2012). Social media and suicide: a public health perspective. *American Journal of Public Health Association, 102*, S195–S200. https://doi.org/10.2105/AJPH.2011.300608

Marzano, L., Bardill, A., Fields, B., Herd, K., Veale, D., Grey, N., & Moran, P. (2015). The application of "mHealth" to mental health: Opportunities and challenges. *Lancet Psychiatry, 2*, 942–948. https://doi.org/10.1016/S2215-0366(15)00268-0

Melia, R., Francis, K., Duggan, J., Bogue, J., O'Sullivan, M., Chambers, D., & Young, K. (2018). Mobile health technology interventions for suicide prevention: protocol for a systematic review and meta-analysis. *JMIR Research Protocols, 7*(1), e28. https://doi.org/10.2196/resprot.8635

Moock, J. (2014). Support from the Internet for individuals with mental disorders: Advantages and disadvantages of e-mental health service delivery. *Frontiers in Public Health, 2*, 65. https://doi.org/10.3389/fpubh.2014.00065

Moorhead, S.A., Hazlett, D.E., Harrison, L., Carroll, J.K., Irwin, A., & Hoving, C. (2013). A new dimension of health care: Systematic review of the uses, benefits, and limitations of social media for health communication. *Journal of Medical Internet Research, 15*, 1–16. https://doi.org/10.2196/jmir.1933

Naslund, J.A., Aschbrenner, K.A., Marsch, L.A., & Bartels, S.J. (2016). The future of mental health care: Peer-to-peer support and social media. *Epidemiology and Psychiatric Sciences, 25*(2), 113–122. https://doi.org/10.1017/S2045796015001067

Naslund, J.A., Grande, S.W., Aschbrenner, K.A., & Elwyn, G. (2014). Naturally occurring peer support through social media: The experiences of individuals with severe mental illness using YouTube. *PLOS One, 9*(10), e110171. https://doi.org/10.1371/journal.pone.0110171

National Institute of Mental Health. (2018). *Technology and the future of mental health treatment*. Retrieved from https://www.nimh.nih.gov/health/topics/technology-and-the-future-of-mental-health-treatment/index.shtml

Newhouse, N., Atherton, H., & Ziebland, S. (2018). Pain and the Internet: Transforming the experience? In E. J. Gonzalez-Polledo & J. Tarr, *Painscapes* (pp. 129–155). London, UK: Macmillan Publishers.

Notredame, C.-E., Grandgenevre, P., Pauwels, N., Morgieve, M., Wathelet, M., Vaiva, G., & Seguin, M. (2018). Leveraging the web and social media to promote access to care among suicidal individuals. *Frontiers in Psychology, 9*, 1338. https://doi.org/10.3389/fpsyg.2018.01338

O'Dea, B., Wan, S., Batterham, P.J., Calear, A.L., Paris, C., & Christensen, H. (2015). Detecting suicidality on Twitter. *Internet Interventions, 2*, 183–188. https://doi.org/10.1016/j.invent.2015.03.005

Oexle, N., Niederkrotenthaler, T., & De Leo, D. (2019). Emerging trends in suicide prevention research. *Current Opinion in Psychiatry, 32*, 336–341. https://doi.org/10.1097/YCO.0000000000000507

Owen, J.E., Jaworski, B.K., Kuhn, E., Makin-Byrd, K.N., Ramsey, K.M., & Hoffman, J.E. (2015). mHealth in the wild: Using novel data to examine the reach, use, and impact of PTSD coach. *JMIR Mental Health, 2*(1), e7. https://doi.org/10.2196/mental.3935

Patel, V.L., Shortliffe, E.H., Stefanelli, M., Szolovits, P., Berthold, M.R., Bellazzi, R., & Abu-Hanna, A. (2009). The coming of age of artificial intelligence in medicine. *Artificial Intelligence in Medicine, 46*, 5–17. https://doi.org/10.1016/j.artmed.2008.07.017

Perry, Y., Werner-Seidler, A., Calear, A.L., & Christensen, H. (2016). Web-based and mobile suicide prevention interventions for young people: A systematic review. *Journal of Canadian Academy of Child and Adolescence Psychiatry, 25*(2), 73–79.

Sanders, E.B.N. (2002). From user-centred to participatory design approaches. In J. Frascara (Ed.), *Design and the social sciences: Making connections* (pp. 1–8). London, UK: Taylor & Francis.

Sangeorzan, I., Andriopoulou, P., & Livanou, M. (2019). Exploring the experiences of people vlogging about severe mental illness on YouTube: An interpretative phenomenological analysis. *Journal of Affective Disorders, 246*, 422–428. https://doi.org/10.1016/j.jad.2018.12.119

Sarkar, U., Gourley, G.I., Lyles, C.R., Tieu, L., Clarity, C., Newmark, L., ... Bates, D.W. (2016). Usability of commercially available mobile applications for diverse patients. *Journal of General Internal Medicine, 31*(12), 1417–1426. https://doi.org/10.1007/s11606-016-3771-6

Schuler, D., & Namioka, A. (1993). *Participatory design: Principles and practices*. Hillsdale, NJ: Lawrence Erlbaum.

Selby, E. A., Yen, S., & Spirito, A. (2013). Time varying prediction of thoughts of death and suicidal ideation in adolescents: Weekly rating over 6-month follow-up. *Journal of Clinical Child and Adolescent Psychology, 42*(4), 481–495. https://doi.org/10.1080/15374416.2012.736356

Sleeswijk Visser, F., Stappers, P. J., Van der Lugt, R., & Sanders, E. B. N. (2005). Context mapping: Experiences from practice. *CoDesign, 1*, 119–149. https://doi.org/10.1080/15710880500135987

Smith, R. J., Crutchley, P., Schwartz, H. A., Ungar, L., Shofer, F., Padrez, K. A., & Merchant, R. M. (2017a). Variations in Facebook posting patterns across validated patient health conditions: A prospective cohort study. *Journal of Medical Internet Research, 19*, 1–11. https://doi.org/10.2196/jmir.6486

Smith, S. D., Fredborg, K. B., & Kornelsen, J. (2017b). An examination of the default mode network in individuals with autonomous sensory meridian response (ASMR). *Social Neuroscience, 12*, 361–365. https://doi.org/10.1080/17470919.2016.1188851

Thompson, W. K., Gershonm, A., O'Hara, R., Bernert, R. A., & Depp, C. A. (2014). The prediction of study-emergent suicidal ideation in bipolar disorder: A pilot study using ecological momentary assessment data. *Bipolar Disorders, 16*, 669–677. https://doi.org/10.1111/bdi.12218

Tighe, J., Shand, F., Ridani, R., Mackinnon, A., De La Mata, N., & Christensen, H. (2017). Ibobbly mobile health intervention for suicide prevention in Australian Indigenous youth: a pilot randomised controlled trial. *BMJ Open, 7*(1), e013518. https://doi.org/10.1136/bmjopen-2016-013518

Torous, J. B. (2018). Focusing on the future of mobile mental health and smartphone interventions. *Psychiatric Services, 69*(9), 945. https://doi.org/10.1176/appi.ps.201800308

Torous, J., Friedman, R., & Keshavan, M. (2014). Smartphone ownership and interest in mobile applications to monitor symptoms of mental health conditions." *JMIR Mental Health, 2*(1), e2. https://doi.org/10.2196/mhealth.2994

Torous, J., Luo, J., & Chan, S. R. (2018). Mental health apps: What to tell patients. *Current Psychiatry, 17*(3), 21.

Torous, J., & Roberts, L. W. (2017). Needed innovation in digital health and smartphone applications for mental health: Transparency and trust. *JAMA Psychiatry, 74*(5), 437–438. https://doi.org/10.1001/jamapsychiatry.2017.0262

Torous, J., Staples, P., Shanahan, M., Lin, C., Peck, P., Keshavan, M., & Onnelam, J. P. (2015). Utilizing a personal smartphone custom app to assess the Patient Health Questionnaire-9 (PHQ-9) depressive symptoms in patients with major depressive disorder. *JMIR Mental Health, 2*, e8. https://doi.org/10.2196/mental.3889

Tucker, R. P., Tackett, M. J., Glickman, D., & Reger, M. A. (2019). Ethical and practical considerations in the use of a predictive model to trigger suicide prevention interventions in healthcare settings. *Suicide & Life-Threatening Behavior, 49*, 382–392. https://doi.org/10.1111/sltb.12431

Vahabzadeh, A., Sahin, N., & Kalali, A. (2016). Digital suicide prevention: Can technology become a game-changer? *Innovations in Clinical Neurosciences, 13*(5–6), 16–20.

Winterbottom, A., Becker, H., Conner, M., & Mooney, A. (2008). Does narrative information bias individual's decision making? A systematic review. *Social Science & Medicine, 67*(12), 2079–2088. https://doi.org/10.1016/j.socscimed.2008.09.037

Witt, K., Spittal, M. J., Carter, G., Pirkis, J., Hetrick, S., Currier, D., ... Milner, A. (2017). Effectiveness of online and mobile telephone applications ('apps') for the self-management of suicidal ideation and self-harm: A systematic review and meta-analysis. *BMC Psychiatry, 17*(1), 297. https://doi.org/10.1186/s12888-017-1458-0

Wongkoblap, A., Vadillo, M. A., & Curcin, V. (2017). Researching mental health disorders in the era of social media: Systematic review. *Journal of Medical Internet Research, 19*(6), e228. https://doi.org/10.2196/jmir.7215

World Health Organization. (2005). *Resolution WHA58. 28. eHealth* (pp. 16–25). Geneva, Switzerland: Fifty-eighth World Health Assembly.

World Health Organization. (2014). *Preventing suicide: A global imperative.* Geneva, Switzerland: Author.

World Health Organization. (2015). *Atlas of eHealth country profiles: the use of eHealth in support of universal health coverage: Based on the findings of the third global survey on eHealth.* Geneva, Switzerland: Author.

World Health Organization. (2016). *Global diffusion of eHealth: making universal health coverage achievable: report of the third global survey on eHealth* (No. 9789241511780). Geneva, Switzerland: Author.

World Health Organization. (2019). *WHO guideline: Recommendations on digital interventions for health system strengthening.* Geneva, Switzerland: Author. Retrieved from https://www.who.int/reproductivehealth/publications/digital-interventions-health-system-strengthening/en/

Zhang, L., Huang, X., Liu, T., Chen, Z., Zhu, T., & Li, A. (2014). *Using linguistic features to estimate suicide probability of Chinese microblog users.* International conference on human centered computing, November 2014, ArXiv. https://doi.org/10.1007/978-3-319-15554-8_45

Zhao, Y., Ni, Q., & Zhou, R. (2018). What factors influence the mobile health service adoption? A meta-analysis and the moderating role of age. *International Journal of Information Management, 1*(43), 342–350. https://doi.org/10.1016/j.ijinfomgt.2017.08.006

Ziebland, S., & Wyke, S. (2012). Health and illness in a connected world: How might sharing experiences on the Internet affect people's health? *Milbank Quarterly, 90*, 219–249. https://doi.org/10.1111/j.1468-0009.2012.00662.x

Contributors

Editors

Kairi Kõlves is a principal research fellow/associate professor at the Australian Institute for Suicide Research and Prevention (AISRAP), and codirector of the WHO Collaborating Centre for Research and Training in Suicide Prevention, School of Applied Psychology, Griffith University, Brisbane, Australia. She is also course convenor of master courses in suicidology at Griffith University. With a background in sociology, epidemiology, and public health, she has been working in suicide research and prevention since 1998. Prior to joining the AISRAP team in 2008, she worked at the Estonian-Swedish Mental Health and Suicidology Institute (ERSI), Tallinn, Estonia. Dr. Kõlves has been involved in several Australian, Estonian, and international projects and is a member of different advisory committees and professional organizations. In 2010 she was the recipient of the Australian LiFE Award in the Emerging Researcher category. In 2017 she received the Health Pro Vice Chancellor's Research Excellence Award (Mid-Career Researcher) from Griffith University, Australia.

Merike Sisask is professor of social health care at Tallinn University, School of Governance, Law and Society (SOGOLAS), and board member of the Estonian-Swedish Mental Health and Suicidology Institute (ERSI), Tallinn, Estonia. Her educational background is in law (Dipl iur in 1991, University of Tartu, Estonia), psychological counseling (in 2003, Private School of Psychology in Tallin, Estonia), public health (MSc in 2005, University of Tartu, Institute of Public Health), and sociology (PhD in 2011, Tallinn University, Institute of International and Social Studies). Her main research interest is the public health view on suicidality, mental health and well-being, and suicide prevention over the lifespan. She has been involved in several international and Estonian research and development projects on suicide prevention and more widely on mental health protection and promotion (e.g., WHO SUPRE-MISS, EAAD, OSPI-Europe, SEYLE, WE-STAY, MHP-Hands, Joint action MH-WB). She is a member of several international and national organizations, networks, and committees (e.g., International Association for Suicide Prevention, International Academy of Suicide Research).

Peeter Värnik is board member of the Estonian-Swedish Mental Health and Suicidology Institute (ERSI), Tallinn, Estonia. His educational background is in management and international economics (1994, TalTech University, School of Economics and Business Administration, Tallinn), finance and management (1990, Pacific Lutheran University, Seattle–Tacoma, USA), banking and financial management (1992, Stockholm University, Sweden), and demography (PhD in 2015, Tallinn University, Estonian Institute for Population Studies). He has been the leader of numerous companies and worked as the advisor to the Minister of Economic Affairs of Estonia between 2001 and 2002. He has a broad interest in mortality, particularly suicide and external causes, and its relationship to the development of societies. He has investigated death registration quality issues. At ERSI he has taken part in many internationally acclaimed projects such as EAAD, SEYLE, and their follow-ups. Dr. Värnik was an expert reviewer for the WHO's first world suicide report *Preventing Suicide: A Global Imperative*.

Airi Värnik is a professor of mental health at the School of Natural Sciences and Health at Tallinn University in Estonia and visiting professor of psychiatry at the Faculty of Social Sciences and Education at the University of Tartu in Estonia. She was visiting professor in suicidology at Karolinska Institute in Stockholm, Sweden, between 2003 and 2010. She is the founder of the Estonian-Swedish Mental Health and Suicidology Institute (ERSI) in Tallinn, Estonia, as well as a board member and principal investigator. She graduated from the Medical Department at the University of Tartu as a psychiatrist and obtained PhD degrees in psychiatry from the Bekhterev Psycho-Neurological Institute in St. Petersburg, Russia, and the Karolinska Institute in Solna, Sweden. She is a member of the International Academy of Suicide Research and has been an expert and principal investigator in several European projects on suicide research and prevention. She is editorial board member and reviewer of scientific journals and member of advisory committees. In 2005 she was awarded the First Class Order of the Estonian Red Cross.

Diego De Leo is emeritus professor of psychiatry at Griffith University in Brisbane, Australia, where he directed the Australian Institute for Suicide Research and Prevention (AISRAP) and the WHO Collaborating Centre for Research, Methods Development and Training in Suicide Prevention. Prof. De Leo is Past President of the International Association for Suicide Prevention (IASP) and Cofounder and Past President of the International Academy for Suicide Research (IASR). He cofounded the journal *Archives of Suicide Research*, is editor emeritus of the journal *Crisis*, and was the initiator of the World Suicide Prevention Day in 2003. Presently, he is President of the NGO De Leo Fund, Vice President of the Italian Psychogeriatric Association, Head of the Slovene Centre for Suicide Research, and Director of the Department of Psychology at the University of Primorska, Slovenia. Being the winner of several international awards, Prof. De Leo was honored with the title of Officer of the Order of Australia for his activities in suicide prevention in 2013.

Authors

Karl Andriessen is a NHMRC ECF research fellow in the Centre for Mental Health, School of Population and Global Health, The University of Melbourne, Australia. He is also a conjoint senior lecturer in the School of Psychiatry at the University of New South Wales in Sydney, and a research fellow in the Faculty of Psychology and Educational Sciences at the University of Leuven, Belgium. Recipient of the Farberow Postvention Award of the International Association for Suicide Prevention, his main research focuses on suicide bereavement and ethics in suicide research. He has published widely on suicide prevention and postvention, including Postvention in Action: The International Handbook of Suicide Bereavement Support (Hogrefe Publishing, 2017).

Ella Arensman is a research professor with the School of Public Health, University College Cork, Ireland, and chief scientist with the National Suicide Research Foundation (NSRF) in Ireland. She is Vice President of the European Alliance Against Depression, and Past President of the International Association for Suicide Prevention (IASP). She is a visiting professor with the Australian Institute for Suicide Research and Prevention, Griffith University, Brisbane, and an expert advisor for WHO. She has been involved in research into and prevention of suicide, self-harm and related mental health, and social issues for more than 30 years. Prof. Arensman leads a multidisciplinary research team.

Eleanor Bailey is a provisional psychologist and a doctoral candidate at Swinburne University of Technology in Melbourne, and a research assistant at Orygen, the National Centre of Excellence in Youth Mental Health, Melbourne, Australia.

Georgia Dempster is a senior ethics advisor and a PhD candidate in the Melbourne School of Population and Global Health at The University of Melbourne, Australia. Her work involves advising public health researchers on issues associated with human research ethics.

Ciro De Vincenzo is a PhD student in social sciences at the Philosophy, Sociology, Education and Applied Psychology Department of the University of Padova, Italy. He has a BA and MA in clinical psychology. He carries out studies related to the social memory and collective mourning of the deaths of cross border migrants in the Mediterranean Sea, in the Channel of Sicily.

Annette Erlangsen is Program Head and Associate Professor at the Danish Research Institute for Suicide Prevention, Copenhagen. She is an honorary associate professor at the Centre for Mental Health Research, Australian National University, and an adjunct associate professor at the Department of Mental Health, Johns Hopkins Bloomberg School of Public Health, Baltimore, MA. Dr. Erlangsen has worked with suicide prevention and register-based research since 2000. Her areas of interest are profiling of risk groups, assessment of interventions, and linkage of individual-level databases. Her work has been published in *Science, JAMA, The Lancet*, and other scientific journals.

Benjamin Goodfellow is a psychiatrist who works in various international settings and is an advocate for community centered mental health care. He has taken part in several research projects such as the WHO – Mental Health in the General Population Study. He is now a practicing psychiatrist in New Caledonia where he implemented the WHO/START study on suicidal behaviors deepening his knowledge of cultural influences on mental health care. He received his PhD from the Australian Institute of Suicide Research and Prevention (AISRAP) at Griffith University, Brisbane. His dissertation focused on the definitions of suicidal behaviors.

Keith Hawton is a professor of psychiatry and Director of the Centre for Suicide Research at Oxford University, UK. He is a consultant psychiatrist with the Oxford Health NHS Foundation Trust, UK. His research group has been conducting investigations concerning the causes, treatment, prevention, and outcome of suicidal behavior for over 40 years. He has published nearly 600 research papers and 15 books and has received numerous awards: Stengel Research Award from the International Association for Suicide Prevention (IASP), Dublin Career Research Award from the American Association of Suicidology (AAS), Research Award of the American Foundation for Suicide Prevention (AFSP), and the Morselli Medal from the International Academy for Suicide Research (IASR).

Ulrich Hegerl holds the Johann Christian Senckenberg Distinguished Professorship at Goethe University in Frankfurt, Germany, since 2019. He was the Chair and Medical Director of the Department of Psychiatry and Psychotherapy at Leipzig University, Germany, between 2006 and 2019, and Full Professor of Psychiatry in the Department of Psychiatry and Psychotherapy at Ludwig Maximilian University in Munich, Germany, between 1998–2006. He is a member of the Scientific Advisory Council of the German Medical Association, President of the German Depression Foundation, and President of the European Alliance Against Depression (EAAD). He has coordinated several EU-funded research networks and has published over 500 articles in peer-reviewed journals.

Karolina Krysinska is a research fellow at Orygen, The National Centre of Excellence in Youth Mental Health, and at the Centre for Mental Health, Melbourne School of Population and Global Health, The University of Melbourne, Australia. She is an experienced research psychologist, whose main interest is suicide research, prevention, and postvention. She is coeditor of Postvention in Action: The International Handbook of Suicide Bereavement Support (Hogrefe Publishing, 2017).

Cristian Leorin is an adjunct professor at the University of Padua and at the University of Modena-Reggio Emilia, Italy, where he holds courses on assistive technology and speech-language pathology as well as on augmentative and alternative communication. He assists the European Commission as an external expert in the evaluation of research projects focused on e-Health technologies for disability and the aging population. He collaborates with NGOs and public health institutions in the codesign of services for individuals with chronic and degenerative conditions and disabilities. He is the President of Novilunio, a non-profit association dedicated to improving the quality of life and social inclusion of people with dementia and their families, in Padua, Italy.

David McDaid is an associate professor in health policy and health economics at the Care Policy and Evaluation Centre of the Department of Health Policy at the London School of Economics and Political Science, UK. The primary focus of his work is on using economic arguments to support investment in mental health promotion as well as in the prevention of self-harm, suicide, and mental illness within and beyond the health sector. He has written extensively on these issues and advised many national governments and international agencies, including the WHO and the OECD.

Ellenor Mittendorfer-Rutz is a professor at the Karolinska Institute in Stockholm, Sweden, where she is also Acting Head of the Department of Clinical Neuroscience. She holds a guest professorship at the Medical University in Vienna, Austria. She is a board member of several international medical journals and research consortia. Her work responds to the complexity of research in suicidology and insurance medicine by conducting interdisciplinary and translational research, which spans from etiologic and prognostic to prevention and treatment research. Due to the rising number of refugees to Sweden and other European countries, her research has a specific focus on transcultural aspects.

Jane Pirkis is a professor and the Director of the Centre for Mental Health at the University of Melbourne, Australia. She is Vice President of the International Association for Suicide Prevention and Editor-in-Chief of the journal *Crisis*. She has worked in the suicide prevention field for nearly 25 years and is particularly well known for her work on suicide and the media. She has been the recipient of a number of awards, including the Suicide Prevention Australia's Lifetime Research Award (2010) and IASP's Erwin Stengel Research Award (2019).

Ping Qin is a professor at the National Centre for Suicide Research and Prevention, University of Oslo, Norway, and head of the research group for register-based studies on suicide and self-harm. She is also a distinguished visiting professor at Shandong University, PR China, and current Vice President of the International Association for Suicide Prevention. Prof. Qin has been studying suicidal behavior for more than 20 years with particular interest in contextual effect of socioeconomic disadvantages, physical and psychiatric illnesses, life stresses, clinical treatment, as well as bio-genetic vulnerabilities.

Jo Robinson is an associate professor at Orygen, The National Centre of Excellence in Youth Mental Health in Melbourne, Australia, where she leads the suicide prevention research unit. She has worked in the field for over 20 years focusing on suicide prevention among young people and, in particular, testing novel interventions, including online and social media-based interventions.

Ian Rockett is a professor emeritus of epidemiology at West Virginia University and adjunct professor of psychiatry at the University of Rochester Medical Center, NY. He is a fellow of the American College of Epidemiology. Dr. Rockett's research focuses on the interconnected areas of suicide data validity and substance abuse. He led the development and application of two novel concepts, death from drug self-intoxication (DDSI), and an enhanced category of self-injury mortality (SIM) that transcends known suicides. Prior research includes a population-based hospital emergency department study of unmet substance abuse treatment need and international studies on injury mortality and suicide data quality.

Victoria Ross is a senior research fellow at the Australian Institute for Suicide Research and Prevention (AISRAP), Griffith University, Brisbane, Australia. She has research expertise across the areas of workplace suicide prevention, suicide prevention in schools, suicide bereavement and postvention support, preventing suicide at hot spots, and suicide prevention program evaluation. She provides expert advice to suicide prevention advisory committees at regional, state, and national levels. Her research interests span all aspects of evidence-based suicide prevention, policy, and practice.

Morton M. Silverman was the Senior Science Advisor to the American Suicide Prevention Resource Center (SPRC) between 2004 and 2017, and the Editor-in-Chief of the journal *Suicide and Life-Threatening Behavior* between 1996 and 2009. He is an assistant adjunct professor of psychiatry at the Medical College of Wisconsin, Milwaukee, WI. Dr. Silverman is a distinguished life fellow of the American Psychiatric Association (APA) and member of the International Association for Suicide Research (IASR). He is the coauthor or author of over 60 peer-reviewed publications and over 40 book chapters, and coauthor of *The Comprehensive Textbook of Suicidology* (2000) and *Adolescent Suicide: Assessment and Intervention* (2006).

Matthew Spittal is an associate professor and fellow of the Australian Research Council Future at the University of Melbourne, Australia. He is a biostatistician by training. His research crosses several areas of public health and health services research. He studies the epidemiology of suicide and self-harm as well as the role of individual practitioner performance on patient safety and quality of care. He has published a number of meta-analyses and has undertaken methodological research to better estimate pooled estimates for rare outcomes like suicide.

Eloisa Stella is an applied anthropologist, an independent expert of the European Commission, and the cofounder of Novilunio, a non-profit organization dedicated to improving both the social inclusion and quality of life of people with dementia and their families, in Padua, Italy. At Novilunio, she coordinates a wide range of online activities, including a post-diagnostic psychosocial program, a network of peer-to-peer support groups, and monthly webinars with experts. Her areas of research include the anthropology of mental and social health as well as the intersection between aging and digital technology codesign.

Lynn Tang is an assistant professor in the Department of Sociology and Social Policy at Lingnan University, Hong Kong SAR. Her core research areas include mental health, social inequalities, and related policies. She completed her PhD at the University of Warwick, UK. She has worked at the Centre of Excellence for Interdisciplinary Mental Health at the University of Birmingham, UK, and at Hong Kong Jockey Club Centre for Suicide Research and Prevention at the University of Hong Kong. Her book *Recovery, Mental Health and Inequality* (2017) was the finalist for the book prize of the Foundation for the Sociology of Health and Illness.

Ines Testoni is a professor at the University of Padova, Italy, and a research fellow at the University of

Haifa, Israel. She leads a master course in death studies and the end of life, and has been recognized among the 100 most important female scientists in Italy for her studies on death, end-of-life, palliative care, and suicide. She is the author of about 100 journal articles and about 20 books, is a member of the bilateral table MIUR – Ministry of Health for the teaching of palliative care in degree courses in psychology, and scientific director of an Erasmus Plus project on death education for palliative psychology.

Elice Tucholski is a highly respected legal professional with over 20 years of experience. She is currently working toward the completion of her Bachelor's thesis in psychology at Griffith University, Brisbane, Australia. Her research interest within the forensic and clinical disciplines of psychology include psychological autopsy, death investigations, decision-making, reconstructed memories, malingering, and jealousy.

David Watling is a research assistant with the Australian Institute for Suicide Research and Prevention (AISRAP) at Griffith University, Brisbane, Australia. He completed his undergraduate and honors degree in the School of Applied Psychology at Griffith University in 2015 and has worked as a research assistant across multiple projects since this time. David has experience in a range of research designs, including surveys, experiments, observational designs, and reviews. He is currently undertaking his PhD at Griffith University exploring executive functioning in late adolescence and young adulthood.

Katrina Witt is a National Health and Medical Research Council Emerging Leader in self-harm and suicide prevention at the Centre for Youth Mental Health at The University of Melbourne, Australia. She is also a senior editor for the Suicide and Self-Harm Satellite and the Children and Young Person Satellite of the Cochrane Common Mental Disorders Group (CCMD). Her work focuses on effective interventions for self-harm and suicide, and dynamic health systems modeling. She has published Cochrane and non-Cochrane meta-analyses. She has numerous accolades, including the 2019 Andrej Marušič Early Career Award from the International Association for Suicide Prevention (IASP).

Paul S. F. Yip is the founding director of the Hong Kong Jockey Club Centre for Suicide Research and Prevention, and professor in the Department of Social Work and Social Administration at the University of Hong Kong. He was the Vice President of the International Association of Suicide Prevention (IASP) between 2009 and 2013. In 2011, he was the recipient of IASP's Stengel Research Award for his contribution to suicide research and prevention. In 2017, he received the Medal of Honor from the Hong Kong SAR Government. His current interests include the adoption of a public health approach in suicide prevention and the evaluation of evidence-based suicide prevention programs.

Adriano Zamperini is Professor of Psychology of Violence and Psychology of Social Discomfort at the Philosophy, Sociology, Education and Applied Psychology Department of the University of Padova, Italy, where he is also the Director of the Center of Research and Services for Migration and Intercultural Studies (CIRSIM). He leads a master course called Urban Manager for Security, Safety, and Violence Management and is the founder of the Italian Society of Psychosocial Sciences for Peace (SISPa). His research focuses on health and psychosocial distress, social memories and collective mourning, urban security and safety, and the psychology of violence.

Subject Index

Peer Commentaries

Suicide prevention globally has never had a higher profile and research into suicide has never been more important. This excellent multiauthor book is unique because it brings together the latest thinking about how we might best investigate the causes of suicide and ultimately reduce its devastating toll. In addition to providing practical how-to advice on observational, interventional, and systematic review methodologies, the book also covers areas that are sometimes neglected, such as qualitative and mixed methods, health economics, and the evaluation of prevention strategies at scale. It also includes a very important discussion of the ethical aspects of suicide research. This book will be of great use to all researchers who work in the field of suicidal behavior, but it will be invaluable to early-career researchers. I wish there had been something like it when I started out!

Nav Kapur, MBChB, MMedSc, MD, FRCPsych, Professor of Psychiatry and Population Health, University of Manchester, UK

This book is a tree of knowledge! Beginning from the roots of suicide research, it branches into nomenclature, epidemiology, ethics, and methods of research, and then culminates in the new leaves of digital technology. The book distills the essentials of suicide research methods and describes them with clarity for all current and future suicide researchers.

Lakshmi Vijayakumar, PhD, FRCP (Edin), FRCPsych (Hon), Founder of SNEHA Suicide Prevention Centre, India; Head of the Department of Psychiatry, Voluntary Health Services, Chennai, India; Honorary Associate Professor, University of Melbourne, Australia

Advancing Suicide Research is the research methods course I never had, written by many of the world's leading suicide researchers and preserved in print for generations of suicide researchers to come. Ambitious and encyclopedic, this volume serves as a foundational document for the broad range of research efforts that will inform actions yet needed to significantly reduce the burden of suicide across the globe.

Lanny Berman, PhD, Past-President of the International Association for Suicide Prevention; Past-President of the American Association of Suicidology